STUART ENGLAND 1603–1714

The formation of   state

Barry Coward

 LONGMAN

Contents

Contents

Contents

Editorial introduction

This aim of this book is to give you as clear a picture as possible of the events and developments in the period you are studying. You may well be using this book to prepare for an examination and the book has several special features, listed below, to help you in this. Most of all, we hope it will help you to develop a critical awareness about, and a continuing interest in, the past.

FOCUS: Each chapter has a main focus, listed in the contents. These are the main issues and 'concepts', like cause and consequence, the evaluation of evidence, the role of the individual, key themes, historical controversies or interpretations and so on. All of these are important in studying and understanding history. Identifying a focus does not mean that the chapter only looks at the past in one way; rather that you are encouraged to find out about topics from a different slant.

TIME CHARTS: Most chapters begin with a time chart. It helps you follow the chronology. Some time charts develop a basic point which is not in the main text. You should also find that the charts provide you with a handy reference point.

KEY TERMS: There are some words or phrases which it is important to know in order to understand a wider topic. These have been highlighted in the text so that you can easily look up what they mean. Sometimes quite simple ideas appear in unfamiliar form or in jargon. Decoding these should help you to make sense of the wider ideas to which the terms relate. Towards the end of the book you will find a separate index of the key terms.

PROFILES: There is not space in a book like this to provide full biographies of the people you will meet. The profiles give you the information you need to understand why an individual is important and what his or her main achievements were. Like the time charts, you might want to use these for reference. As with 'key terms', there is a separate index of people who are the subject of profiles.

TASKS: Nearly all the chapters end with some suggestions for follow-up work and further study. These include:

- guidance on how, and why, to take notes
- suggestions for class discussion and debate

- help on how to use historical evidence of different types
- tips on answering source questions
- hints on planning and writing essays
- specimen examination questions so that you can prepare for assessment.

FURTHER READING: You will find that you need more help on certain topics than can be provided in a book like this. The further reading guides you to some more detailed or specialist texts. The reading is listed with the most immediately obvious supporting texts placed first, followed by others – some of which may be considerably more detailed – and ending with articles and other shorter pieces, where these are appropriate.

MAIN INDEX: Many individuals, issues and themes are mentioned in more than one chapter. The index is designed to help you find what you are looking for quickly and easily by showing you how to collect together information which is spread about. Get practice in using an index; it will save you a lot of time.

The historian's job is to recreate the past. On one level, this is obviously an impossible task. There is far too much of it to put into one book while at the same time much of the information we need has been long since lost. Most of it can never be recovered. It is because there is so much of it that the historian has to impose his or her priorities by selecting. It is because so much more has been lost that he or she has to try to fill in the gaps and supply answers which other people can challenge. The processes of **Selection** and **Interpretation** are the key tasks of the historian and they help to make the subject endlessly fascinating. Every time a historian makes a decision about what to put in and what to leave out that decision implies a judgement which others might challenge. Historians try to get as close to the truth as they can, in the knowledge that others may disagree with what they say. Don't be surprised, then, to find a number of personal views or 'interpretations'. Some of these will make comparisons between the present and the period you are studying. These personal views have not been included in order to persuade you to agree with them. We aim to make you *think* about what you are reading and not always to accept everything at face value. If this book helps you to tell the difference between fact and opinion while keeping up your interest in the past, it will have served its purpose.

Christopher Culpin
Eric Evans
Series Editors

Part One   Introduction:
Early Stuart
England

1 How was England governed in 1603?

England was governed by a 'personal monarchy'

'Personal monarchy' is a term historians use to indicate that the central feature of English government in the seventeenth century was the immense personal political power held by the king or queen. This is, of course, in complete contrast to the situation in Britain today, when the monarch, Queen Elizabeth II, has very little political power. At the beginning of the seventeenth century English government had little in common with the government of modern Britain; it had more continuities with the Middle Ages, which most historians are agreed came to an end round about 1500.

At the end of Elizabeth I's reign in 1603, as in the Middle Ages, English monarchs still ruled as well as reigned. They were not just constitutional figureheads. They were able to make major government decisions without first having to consult a cabinet and then having to get the agreement of a majority in parliament, as do modern prime ministers. As you will see, the propaganda image of supreme monarchical power portrayed in paintings like Rubens' superb ceiling panel in the Banqueting Hall in Whitehall (see Figure 1.1) did not fully reflect reality. The early Stuarts were as anxious as governments before and since to portray their regime in the best possible light and to hide its weaknesses. Yet the painting does capture the personal nature of royal government in the early seventeenth century. The personal nature of government was reflected not only in visual images like this but also in the widespread belief in the **Divine Right of Kings**.

KEY TERM:

Divine Right of Kings

This is the belief that monarchs receive their powers from God and that anyone who questions or resists royal power is guilty of sin against God. Biblical texts were commonly used to prove that this was the case. For example, Proverbs Chapter 8 verse 15 ('By me kings reign, and princes decree justice') and Romans Chapter 13 verse 1 ('Let every soul be subject unto the highest powers, for there is no power but of God: the powers that be are ordained of God').

Here is an example of the Divine Right of Kings idea:

'Almighty God hath created and appointed all things in heaven, earth and water in a most excellent and perfect order. In heaven he hath appointed distinct orders and states of archangels and angels. In the earth he has assigned Kings, princes, with other governors under them, all in good and necessary order ... Let us mark well and remember that the high power and authority of Kings, with their making of laws,

Figure 1.1 *'The Reign of Solomon: the Golden Age of James I' by Paul Rubens, c.1635*

KEY TERM:

Patriarchalism

This is the belief that fathers, like kings, hold political power given them by God. **Patriarchalism** therefore requires unquestioning obedience at all levels of society: of wives to husbands, children to parents, tenants to landlords and apprentices and servants to employers. Unquestioning obedience to monarchs is well in line with this.

judgements and officers are the ordinances not of man but of God ... We may not resist, nor in any wise hurt, an anointed King which is God's lieutenant, vice-regent and highest minister in that country where he is King.'

The Book of Homilies (1547) [This was regularly read in churches in the seventeenth century.]

What makes it easier to understand why arguments like this were accepted is that they fitted comfortably into other contemporary theories of obligation. Of these the most influential was **patriarchalism**.

KEY TERM:

The royal prerogative

The royal prerogative is the phrase used to describe the powers possessed by the crown.

There were also persuasive legal and practical justifications for concentrating power largely in the hands of one person. At the start of the seventeenth century it was generally accepted that **the royal prerogative** should include wide powers enabling the crown to conduct war and diplomacy, to act as an impartial arbitrator in disputes between subjects, and to cope with the consequences of rapidly rising population and rocketing inflation – like frequent riots, a rising crime rate and the danger of a popular rebellion by the desperate 'many-headed monster' of the poor.

General acceptance of a large degree of personal control by the crown was helped also by considerations of geography and history. The size of England, in which no region was more than three or four days' horseback ride from London, did not provide the kind of barrier to royal rule that existed in European countries like France, which was many times bigger than England. Moreover, also unlike France, England had been united under one monarch for centuries, so that by 1603 many of the medieval independent jurisdictions (like the secular powers of prince-bishops) had already been subordinated to the crown. As in modern times, regional loyalties were strong in seventeenth-century England; but not as strong as in seventeenth-century France, where provinces like Brittany and Languedoc had developed separate representative assemblies or estates and where there were different legal traditions (customary law and Roman law) and even different languages. In contrast, in England in 1603 Cornish was the sole surviving regional language and the country had a common system of law and justice, as well as a uniform system of government.

In post-Reformation England, too, the crown controlled the main means of spreading information, *via* the pulpit, the press and schools and universities. As a result, by the start of the seventeenth century the crown had wide personal powers. Although monarchs often sought advice from members of their privy council, either formally or more often informally, these were advisers who were appointed by and who owed their positions solely to the crown. Consequently, monarchs were not bound to follow the advice they received. They could obstruct parliamentary legislation by veto or by dissolving parliament. They had the power to exempt individuals from the law, and, above all, they made all the key decisions of government, since they (in reality) were 'the government'. One of the best examples of this is the way in which for much of the seventeenth century English foreign policy was essentially the foreign policy of the monarch for the time being. England kept out of the Thirty Years' War before 1625, despite parliamentary pressure to the contrary, because James I determined that this should be the case; while Charles II made an international treaty between England and France in 1670, the full details of which were known only by himself and a small handful of his advisers.

Was England in 1603 an 'absolute' monarchy?

Acts of parliament and **royal proclamations**

Acts of parliament or parliamentary statutes are laws enacted by both houses of parliament which have received the royal assent. **Royal proclamations** are issued solely by the crown.

England was governed by a personal monarchy in the early seventeenth century, but this was not the same thing as an absolute monarchy. 'Absolutism' is a word which is often used by historians to mean that monarchs had unlimited powers to make laws and raise taxes without getting the consent of representative assemblies like parliaments. English monarchs did not exercise absolute power in this sense. They had both theoretical and practical limitations on their exercise of power.

One principal effect of the break with Rome in the 1530s had been to confirm that the superior legislative authority in England was the king-in-parliament and to establish that **Acts of parliament** were far more powerful than **royal proclamations**. Moreover, very few people claimed that English monarchs had absolute power. The first part of James I's speech to parliament in March 1610 might seem to disprove this point (see below). But note the second part of the speech, in which he explained that there was a great difference between these *theoretical* royal powers and those that kings held *in reality*. This view was widely held and was popularised in the most influential book on political ideas in the later sixteenth and early seventeenth centuries: Sir John Fortescue's *De Laudibus Legum Angliae [In Praise of the Laws of England]* which was written in the late fifteenth century, published in 1537, and then often reprinted. The central idea of this book was that English government was a 'mixed monarchy', in which the king's personal powers should be exercised within the law and with the consent of his greater subjects – especially the nobility and gentry, the great landowners of the country.

'The state of monarchy is the supremest thing on earth; for kings are not only God's lieutenants upon earth and sit upon God's throne, but even by God himself they are called gods ... Kings are justly called gods for that they exercise a manner or resemblance of divine power upon earth.'

But he went on to say that the king is bound 'by a double oath to the observation of the fundamental laws of the kingdom: tacitly, as by being a king, and so bound to protect as well the people as the laws of his kingdom; and expressly by his oath at his coronation ... A king governing in a settled kingdom leaves to be a king, and degenerates into a tyrant, as soon as he leaves off to rule according to his laws...'

James I's speech to Parliament, 21 March 1610 quoted in J. Kenyon (ed.), *The Stuart Constitution: Documents and Commentary* (1986).

In normal circumstances by the beginning of the seventeenth century Fortescue's theory of a 'mixed monarchy' matched reality. English monarchs did not have the financial, military or bureaucratic machinery to exercise unlimited personal and absolute power. As will be seen, the crown could not afford to maintain a standing army or police force that are key elements in modern strong nation-states. In time of war or threats of invasion the English crown had to rely on the poorly organised local **militia**.

Moreover, the administrative bureaucracy employed by the crown in the early seventeenth century put serious limitations on what governments could do. The crown did have a developed administrative machinery through which it could issue orders and letters *via* the office of the crown's secretaries, the Lord Privy Seal and the Lord Chamberlain. It also used established financial departments, notably the Exchequer, the Court of Wards and the Duchy of Lancaster. It can be misleading to describe this bureaucracy as a 'civil service' in the early seventeenth century, since, unlike the modern civil service, there were no clear divisions between politicians and administrators; administrative and financial departments had overlapping functions; official salaries were very low; and, above all, it was miniscule in scale, consisting of only about 1,000 officials.

Parliaments

These circumstances ensured that royal government would only be successful when monarchs ruled with the consent and cooperation of their most powerful subjects. This was achieved in part by calling parliaments.

The history of parliaments in the later sixteenth and early seventeenth centuries has recently been rescued by **revisionist** historians like G. R. Elton and C. Russell from many misleading assumptions based on the undoubted fact that parliament's constitutional status was enhanced from the 1530s onwards.

As a result of parliament's role in carrying out the Reformation in the reigns of Henry VIII, Edward VI and Elizabeth I, not only was the superiority of statutes passed by king-in-parliament over royal proclamations established, but so too was its role in deciding matters relating to the Church. Moreover, parliament's right to levy taxation was also confirmed and parliament became accepted by many as a part of the 'ancient constitution' that was vital to securing statutory sanction for dealing with local concerns.

As revisionist historians have shown, it is misleading to go further than this – as did J. E. Neale in his books on Elizabethan parliaments, published in the 1950s, and whose views were followed by most historians until the mid 1970s – and argue that there took place a 'Rise of Parliament'. By this Neale meant that the later sixteenth century witnessed a marked growth in the authority of parliament and especially that of the House of Commons. He also believed that many Elizabethan MPs were so anxious to extend the power of parliament that they carried on a campaign of constitutional aggression, resulting in constant conflicts between crown and parliaments during the reign of Elizabeth I. Neale's idea of a late sixteenth-century 'Rise of Parliament' was supported by the influential views of an American historian, Wallace Notestein, who in 1924 had seemingly established that the early Stuart House of Commons was seeking (in his words) 'to win the initiative' in the making of government policy from the crown.

However, as a result of work done since the mid 1970s, few historians would now accept this Neale–Notestein interpretation of the parliamentary history of the later sixteenth and early seventeenth centuries. The House of Lords was as important as the House of Commons in this period, and few (if any) MPs seem to have been intent on increasing parliament's power and engaging in constitutional conflicts with the crown. A better way of approaching the parliamentary history of the period is to see parliaments not as battlegrounds between crown and MPs but as 'points of contact' (in G. R. Elton's words) where the crown could keep in touch with powerful opinion in the country.

The royal court

Parliaments met infrequently during the later sixteenth and early seventeenth centuries and therefore had a limited role in maintaining cooperation between the crown and its greater subjects. There were only 13 sessions of parliament in Elizabeth I's 45-year reign, and parliaments only met during nine of the 37 years between 1603 and 1640, with especially long gaps between parliamentary sessions from 1614 to 1621 and 1629 to 1640. It would be wrong to deduce from this that parliaments were totally unimportant in the governmental structure of the country at the beginning of the seventeenth century. As was noted in the last section, parliaments did have important – if limited – constitutional functions.

There is little doubt that the political importance of the royal court has not been given due recognition. It was more important than parliaments as a 'point of contact' between the crown and the most influential political opinion in the country, because it was a place where different factions could meet regularly and where conflicting views could be expressed yet be contained by the crown and prevented from getting out of hand.

KEY TERM:

Patronage

Patronage literally means
favours given by patrons to
their clients. Favours could be
in the form of cash, lands and
offices or, more generally,
support – for example, in times
of trouble.

KEY TERMS:

Justices of the Peace (JPs)

JPs were the officials who, as
members of the commissions
of the peace, bore the brunt of
English local government.
During the later sixteenth and
early seventeenth centuries an
enormous expansion in the
administrative and judicial
duties of Justices of the Peace
took place. JPs were the key
officials responsible for
maintaining local law and
order and for exercising
criminal jurisdiction (which
they did singly or in groups at
petty sessions) and for more
important criminal matters (at
county quarter sessions which
were held four times at year at
the major towns and cities in
the counties). In addition, JPs
were made the agents for the
execution of much of the
legislation concerning poor
relief, vagrancy,
apprenticeship and other
social legislation passed by
parliament in this period.
Surprisingly, despite this
increasingly heavy workload
and the fact that JPs were
unpaid, a place on the
commission of the peace was
highly prized and the numbers
of JPs appointed in all counties
rose dramatically in the later
sixteenth and early
seventeenth centuries.

Assize judges

These were judges appointed
by the crown to visit counties
periodically to hear legal cases.

Factional court politics were an essential feature of the working of government at the start of the seventeenth century.

What also made the royal court a (perhaps *the* most) vital part of the governmental structure of the country was that it was a source of **patronage**, which was used to retain the support of the nobility and greater gentry. 'For a king not to be bountiful were a fault', wrote Sir Robert Cecil, James I's principal minister at the start of his reign. The truth of this is illustrated by the serious political tensions between the crown and its greater subjects that occurred when patronage was not distributed widely during the last part of Elizabeth I's reign and at the beginning of the reign of Charles I. The court and royal patronage were valuable means of preventing this from happening.

Tension between the crown and the nobility and greater gentry, however, was not the normal state of affairs in early modern England. Some historians have wrongly depicted English history since the fifteenth century as a constant war between the crown and its 'overmighty subjects'. In this period, there were few reasons why wealthy landowners should want to challenge the power of the crown or why the crown should want to weaken the power of the nobility and gentry. On the contrary, both needed each other. The landed classes needed royal patronage and the support of the crown in order to maintain their own influence in the localities. They also valued the existing system of extremely low taxation, as well as sharing the crown's fears of insurrection from below. The crown, for its part, needed the landed classes to govern the localities, and it issued a stream of proclamations in the later sixteenth and early seventeenth centuries ordering the gentry to leave London and return to their estates, to ensure good government.

Local government

For the vast majority of ordinary people in this period 'government' meant not monarchs, parliaments or the royal court, but local government. The government officials they came into contact with on a day-to-day basis were **Justices of the Peace (JPs)** and an army of lesser local government officers in towns and villages.

The structure of local government in this period reflected the interdependence of crown and landowning classes. Although the crown used **assize judges** and bishops as means of communicating with and gathering information about the provinces, the main agents of royal government in the localities were wealthy local landed men.

By the beginning of the seventeenth century the sheriff was no longer

Lord lieutenants and **deputy lieutenants**

These officials were appointed regularly from the mid sixteenth century onwards in single counties or groups of counties. Their principal duty was to organise the local militias (see page 6).

Hundreds

Hundreds were the administrative subdivisions of counties.

Yeomen

Yeomen was a term used at this time to describe wealthy working farmers below the rank of gentleman. They were fairly well-to-do, large-scale farmers. Whether they were owner-occupiers or tenants of others was relatively unimportant. The main feature they had in common was moderate wealth.

the major local official that he once had been. During much of the Middle Ages sheriffs had been the main administrative and judicial officers of the crown in the localities. By the end of the sixteenth century the authority of sheriffs had diminished greatly, except at times of parliamentary elections, when sheriffs presided over the county courts where MPs for the counties (knights of the shire) were chosen. By this time the main officials of English local government were **lord lieutenants**, **deputy lieutenants** and JPs.

During the later sixteenth and early seventeenth centuries most lord lieutenants were wealthy noblemen and most deputy lieutenants were members of the landed elites in the areas under their control. Moreover, although the crown chose JPs its choice was also largely confined to the most wealthy and influential landed families in each county.

Office-holding in the localities was not confined to the wealthy. Lower down the social scale, as at the top, local government reflected the structure of local society. In towns and villages there was an army of local government officials, from high and petty constables in the **hundreds** to churchwardens, overseers of the poor and surveyors of roads in parishes. These, like the grand juries that made reports to the county quarter sessions, were made up of a fairly wide section of the population, including **yeomen** farmers.

Others well below the rank of yeoman farmer were also employed as petty local government officials. In a book published in 1583, describing England in his day, Sir Thomas Smith included a category of people poorer than the nobility, gentry and yeomen, which he called 'the fourth sort of men who do not rule'. This is often quoted in attempts to prove that the vast majority of people in England were excluded from government at this time. Yet Smith's description in fact supports a very different conclusion, since he pointed out that many men who were poorer than yeomen – like small farmers, labourers and tradesmen – often held offices in local government.

> 'For in cities and corporate townes for default of yeomen, they are faine to make their enquests [i.e. all kinds of legal and judicial investigations] of such manners of people. And in villages they be commonly made churchwardens, alecunners [i.e. aleconners, inspectors of the quality of ale and ale-measures], and manie times constables.'
>
> Sir Thomas Smith, *De Republica Anglorum*, 1583.

In the London parish of Cornhill in the 1640s one in every 16 inhabitants was an office-holder, reflecting the extensive participation of English people in government in early Stuart England. Nothing could more clearly demonstrate that many English people had a vested interest in the government of their country in this period.

Threats to stability

The interlocking interests of the crown and many of its subjects formed the basis of a fairly stable system of government at the beginning of the seventeenth century. But it was a system that was threatened by serious structural problems that made the task of governing the country increasingly difficult.

Of these problems three were potentially very serious indeed.

1 The British Problem

The first was a new problem. Unlike Elizabeth I, her successor was not only ruler of the multiple kingdoms of England, Wales and Ireland but of Scotland as well, ruling England as James I and Scotland as James VI. For centuries previously Scotland and England had been independent countries with their own governments, and with long histories of mutual hostility. The only thing that changed in 1603 was that the accession of James VI and I brought his British kingdoms under one monarch.

There were potential opportunities in this new situation. The running sore of border hostilities in northern England between England and Scotland was healed, and there was a chance of using Scottish troops and settlers in the long-running campaign to bring Ireland under English domination. However, the problems of ruling multiple kingdoms far outweighed these opportunities. This is demonstrated by the protests and rebellions faced by the Spanish monarchy in the later sixteenth and early seventeenth centuries, when it attempted to impose unified rule on its multiple kingdoms and provinces in Portugal, Catalonia, the Netherlands and the Italian peninsula. It was possible that the British monarchy might face similar problems. Although by 1603 Wales was firmly under English control, the new British king's three other kingdoms were divided by different economic, social, political and legal traditions. Union under a single monarch was bound to raise mutual racial antagonisms, as well as national fears that the interests of one country would be subordinated to those of one of the others.

Above all, there were major religious differences between Catholic

Ireland, half-reformed Protestant England and Lowland Scotland, where there had been a far-reaching Protestant Reformation. The result was that James I inherited a lethal cocktail of mutual national antagonisms, different historical traditions and religious diversity that threatened to breed national suspicions and fears that might seriously disrupt British political stability.

The other two major governmental problems facing James I in 1603 were not new, but were bequeathed to him by his predecessor. It is highly likely that Elizabeth's achievements in the fields of finance and religion have been vastly overrated.

2 The Financial Problem

James I inherited a government with an unreformed, ramshackle financial system. While the crown's expenditure rose as a consequence of inflation that had been under way since the early sixteenth century, its income declined.

The crown had four major sources of income:

- crown estates
- customs dues
- feudal incidents, notably **wardships**
- parliamentary **subsidies**.

During the later sixteenth and early seventeenth centuries the crown's receipts from each of these fell as a result of:

- massive sales of crown properties
- **customs farming**
- opposition to wardships
- collection of parliamentary subsidies that bore little relation to the true wealth of taxpayers.

KEY TERMS:

Wardships and **subsidies**

Wardship was the right of the crown over any estates that had once been held by feudal military service. If these estates were inherited by anyone who was not yet an adult, the crown had the right to hold them until the heir came of age and also to arrange the heir's marriage.
Subsidies were direct taxes levied by parliament on people's income and wealth.

Customs farming

This is what we would now call privatising the customs service, since the right to collect import and export duties was sold to private syndicates of merchants for fixed sums of money.

Elizabeth's principal response to this situation had been to cut royal expenditure, ignoring the important problem of the crown's declining income. The result was that in wartime the crown's desperate shortage of money drove it to resort to emergency measures, like raising cash by forced loans, that were not approved by parliament. Not surprisingly, such measures aroused an outcry because they were interpreted as designs to change 'the ancient constitution'. It is likely that the fear of royal absolutist threats to parliamentary liberties that appeared at the end of Elizabeth's reign and at the start of James's reign grew directly out of the weak financial situation bequeathed by the Tudors to the early Stuarts.

3 The Religious Problem

Elizabeth bequeathed James an equally difficult religious legacy. It is true that Elizabeth succeeded in preventing England from being torn apart by a war of religion between Catholics and Protestants, as happened in France. The religious 'settlement' made in 1559 was moderate enough not to force English Catholics into open rebellion to it. But, unlike the vast majority of her Protestant subjects, Elizabeth believed that the 'settlement' was literally a final settlement of the Church and she blocked all attempts to bring about religious reform, as well as refusing to recognise that there were major differences among Protestants about the future of the Church (see chapter 4). This was a situation fraught with political peril. If the national Church could not contain different points of view among Protestants, then it was possible that the ecclesiastical debate would spill over into the political arena, raising fears that the future of Protestantism was as insecure as some believed was the future of parliaments.

Was England becoming ungovernable in 1603?

After considering structural problems like these it is tempting to think that it was. This is a view, however, which assumes that these were problems that could not be overcome and that they made the collapse of the monarchy in the 1640s inevitable. 'Inevitable' is a word that historians ought to use infrequently, if at all. The contrasting achievements of James I and Charles I in handling these problems (see chapters 5 and 6) suggest that the key problem of government at the start of the seventeenth century was none of the above – the British Problem, the Financial Problem or the Religious Problem – but the Personality Problem, the perennial one inherent in a system of personal monarchy.

In such a system, political stability was threatened if there was no clear successor (as in the 1590s), if the monarch was a minor (as in the reign of Edward VI in the mid sixteenth century) or if the monarch lacked the political good sense to rule with the cooperation of the bulk of his or her powerful subjects (as did Henry VI in the mid fifteenth century).

As regards the succession and the perils of minority rule, there is a very marked contrast between the Tudor and Stuart periods. In the reigns of all the Tudor monarchs there was an ever-present danger of a disputed succession and civil war when the monarch died. After 1603 the succession to the throne was not in doubt for about a century, nor was there a royal minority: both James I and Charles I were adult kings with legitimate male heirs. In both these respects, then, 1603 brought *improved* chances of political stability.

Therefore, part of the explanation for the crisis faced by the early Stuart monarchy in 1640 must be sought in the personalities of James I and Charles I. Charles I, unlike his father, followed policies that so offended many of his leading subjects that they were eventually driven to oppose him in 1640. This, however, was not an 'inevitable' outcome. The Elizabethan legacy of government to the early Stuarts was not an easy one, but it did not ensure that Britain was put on a high road to civil war.

Tasks

1 Make a list of all the differences you can think of between the way Britain was governed in the seventeenth century and the way it is governed now. You will find most of the information you need in this chapter. You could make a chart like this:

	Similarities	Differences
The monarchy and its power		
Armed forces		
The civil service		
Taxation and finance		
Parliament		
Government of Scotland and Ireland		
Local government		

2 Working in groups, consider whether you agree with the final judgement in this chapter that, on balance, the government of the country was fairly stable.

As you work consider the following questions:

■ Why might the fact that James VI and I was ruler of multiple kingdoms cause political trouble?

■ What were the dangers to political stability of the country's unreformed financial system?

■ Why was the fact that people had different religious views of political importance?

13

■ Why was the character and ability of the monarch so important at this time?

■ What might have persuaded people to support, not rebel against, the system of government that existed in the early seventeenth century?

Further reading

M. Hawkins, 'Government: its role and aims' in C. Russell (ed.), *The Origins of the Civil War*, Problems in Focus (Macmillan, 1973).

G. C. F. Forster, 'The English local community and local government' in A. G. R. Smith (ed.), *The Reign of James VI and I*, Problems in Focus (Macmillan, 1973).

For the revisionist view of parliaments see:

C. Russell, 'Perspectives in parliamentary history', *History*, vol. 61 (1976).

G. R. Elton, 'Parliament under the Tudors: its functions and fortunes', *Historical Journal*, vol. 22 (1979).

C. Russell, 'The nature of parliaments in early Stuart England' in H. Tomlinson (ed.), *Before the English Civil War* (*Macmillan*, 1983).

The important political role of the early Stuart court is dealt with in the articles by N. Cuddy and K. Sharpe in D. Starkey (ed.), *The English Court from the Wars of the Roses to the Civil War* (Addison Wesley Longman, 1987).

2 How advanced was the English economy in 1603?

Was it like a Third World economy today?

The short answer to this question *seems* to be 'yes'. Three features of the English economy at the beginning of the seventeenth century are very similar to those found in some backward, underdeveloped economies in parts of Africa and Asia at the present day:

1 The economy of England in 1603 was overwhelmingly agrarian and pre-mechanised. The vast majority of people were engaged in some capacity in the production of food or industrial raw materials like wool and leather.

2 Like fragile economies nowadays in parts of Africa, Asia or Latin America, the economy of England at the start of the seventeenth century was highly vulnerable to national disasters, like droughts, excessive rainfall or outbreaks of epidemics, including plague. The pamphlet in Figure 2.1 commemorates one of many attacks of plague (in 1625) that hit the country in this period.

3 It was characterised by the kind of permanent underemployment that can be seen in some modern backward economies. 'The obvious source of it', writes Donald Coleman in the best discussion of this aspect of the seventeenth-century English economy, 'was the seasonality of work in backward agriculture, the inability of this form of productive activity to produce constant or continuous employment.' As will be seen, the underemployment of the rural labour force was, to an extent, compensated for by part-time employment in the domestic cloth industry – the importance of which is explained on pages 22–4. But this kind of employment, too, was irregular and subject to disruptions caused by fluctuations in demand and the spasmodic supply of raw materials.

In all these respects the pre-industrial economy of seventeenth-century England was very different from that of some modern industrialised nations. The comparatively backward nature of the early modern English economy is reflected in statistics of high infant mortality, low average expectation of life at birth (the upper 30s) and a relatively youthful

Figure 2.1 '*The Fearefull Summer' – a pamphlet by John Taylor, published in 1636*

population (nearly 40 per cent of people were under 15 years of age). All these are strikingly different from those in the United Kingdom today, when infant mortality is very low, the average expectation of life at birth is 78 years for women and 72 years for men, and the proportion of the population under 15 years old is only 24 per cent.

It would be misleading, though, to exaggerate both the similarity of the seventeenth-century English economy to modern underdeveloped economies and its backward nature. Three features of England in 1603 are strikingly *different* from modern backward economies:

KEY TERMS:

Dependency burden

This is the jargon phrase for the proportion of the population who are too young or too old to work at full productive capacity and who therefore need supporting by those who are in employment.

Nuclear family

A **nuclear family** is relatively small, consisting only of parents, unmarried children and living-in servants. Couples did not get married until they were able to set up their own independent households.

Extended family

An **extended family** is often very large, consisting of parents, grandparents, married children and, sometimes, aunts and uncles as well.

Subsistence economies

Subsistence economies are those in which the main economic activities are the production of food and goods solely for those that produce them and not for the market.

1 It had a lower '**dependency burden**'. Although, as has just been noted, its population structure was different from that of modern industrialised nations, early modern England had slightly higher expectation of life at birth figures and a slightly less youthful population than many Third World countries in Africa and Asia after the end of the Second World War. This meant that it had a higher percentage of the population who were capable of working at full productive capacity than have some modern underdeveloped countries.

2 It had few of the large, extended families that are typical of some Third World societies. There is now a mass of evidence to show that the typical family in early modern England was a **nuclear** one. What is the economic significance of this? It is that, whereas an **extended family** is likely to consume most of the food and goods it produces, a nuclear family is more likely to produce a surplus for the market over and above its immediate needs. This is one of the reasons why much commercial manufacturing, as well as farming, in seventeenth-century England was based on the nuclear family unit.

3 These two features contributed towards a third aspect of the English economy in 1603 that sets it apart from some modern Third World countries, which are primarily **subsistence economies**. In contrast, the economy of England by the beginning of the seventeenth century was commercialised and geared to the demands of not only local but, in some cases, national and international markets. This was not new. In the thirteenth century, as in the seventeenth, there was much subsistence agriculture by 'peasant' farmers producing food only for their own needs. But in both periods there was a significant commercial farming sector that sought, with some success, to increase the production of food demanded by rising populations. In the thirteenth century both lay and monastic estate-owners strove to increase agricultural productivity and to maximise their profits, taking advantage of soaring food and wool prices.

In the early seventeenth century similar enterprising attitudes are to be seen. Read the following two extracts from the farming books of a Berkshire farmer, Robert Loder, in the reign of James I. Do you agree that they are good evidence to support that statement?

Obviously the first thing you must do before you can answer that question is to understand what Loder is saying! Because of the strangeness of Loder's language no one will find these extracts as easy to read as a modern document. But if you read them two or three times you will be able to see the points that Loder is making.

The first extract was written in 1611, when Loder was deciding whether to grow wheat or barley in future. [Quarters, bushels and pecks were measures of weight and a shilling was a silver coin worth 5p in modern money.] Why does Loder conclude that what had happened in 1611 means that it would be a good idea to sow more wheat and less barley in future?

> **a** *'Memorandum that the wheat lands being 36 acres bore me 20 quarters, 7 bushels and 1 peck; and the 75 acres of barley lands 46 quarters, 2 bushels and 2 pecks . . ., so that the barley lands did not bear so much upon a land one with another as the wheat by about 6 quarters, and yet the wheat was worth 30 shillings the quarter; and the barley by 23 shillings the quarter . . . wherefore here is to [be] seen great reason for sowing more wheat and less barley.'*
>
> **b** *'This was the greatest rot year that hath been known in many years before . . . for the seething of their [i.e. his sheep] livers they broke all to pieces, which were so in the last of November and beginning of December, and these had in their bellies water in jelly places [and] great galls . . .*
>
> *'Memorandum ever herafter that I sell away my sheep afore winter if I know them to be rotten.'*
>
> Taken from 'The Farming Book of Robert Loder' quoted in J. Cooper and J. Thirsk (eds), *Seventeenth-Century Economic Documents* (1972).

Loder wrote the second extract in 1613, after a difficult year when he had lost many sheep from a disease known as liver-fluke. Put into your own words Loder's reasons for deciding in future to sell some of his sheep before winter.

Now, what words come to mind to describe Loder's economic attitudes?

Not all farmers (or merchants and manufacturers) in early modern England were driven by this spirit of enterprise and desire to maximise profits. Others were characterised either by conservatism or by a concern primarily for subsistence. But there is little doubt that there were people willing to take advantage of, and to adapt to, the new economic conditions, and that the English economy in 1603 was one that was capable of responding to market forces.

Market forces: price inflation and population growth

At the beginning of the seventeenth century England was affected by market forces that were influenced by two major developments: a long-term rise in both population and prices that had been under way since the early sixteenth century. From that point, following an equally long period of price stability and falling population since the early fourteenth century, both prices and population levels began to rise throughout western Europe, including England. They continued to do so until about the middle of the seventeenth century.

The price revolution

The history of price trends is complicated in that the speed of inflation from the early sixteenth century was not constant. In England it was most rapid in the first and last decades of the sixteenth century and again in the 1620s and 1640s. Nor did the prices of all commodities move at the same rate. Before 1650 grain prices rose more rapidly than livestock prices; while prices of wool and manufactured goods rose even less steeply. But the overall price trends are clear: between the early 1500s and about 1650 there was an average fivefold price rise, while food prices rose by about seven times. Although the scale of this inflation was small in comparison with twentieth-century examples, it was serious for those who had to buy grain or bread. Sandwiched as it was between two long periods of price stability, it does deserve to be called a price revolution.

Although it was once the subject of a fierce historical debate, there is now fairly general agreement among historians that, although monetary factors like **debasement of the coinage** were not unimportant in explaining inflation in the short term, the main reason for the long-term price revolution was the demand created by a rising population.

KEY TERM:

Debasement of the coinage
This is the practice of melting silver coins and then using the metal to make more coins of greater face value. Henry VIII, for example, did this on an extensive scale to finance wars against France and Scotland in the 1540s.

Population expansion

Until recently there was less agreement about the reasons for the population expansion that occurred at the same time. This uncertainty has to some extent been removed by the conclusions of the Cambridge Group for the History of Population and Social Structure that were published in 1981. These have not only brought greater statistical definition to the chronology and scale of population growth in England and Wales; they have also thrown light on the complicated problem of why this growth occurred after a long period of population decline in the fourteenth and fifteenth centuries, both before and after the massive mortality caused by the Black Death (the epidemic of bubonic plague that occurred in

1522–3: 2.3 millions
1541:   2.774 millions
1601:   4.110 millions
1656:   5.281 millions

Figure 2.2 *Population figures supplied by the Cambridge Group for the History of Population and Social Structure, 1522–1656*

1348–9). Figure 2.2 shows the rapid rise in the population of England and Wales in the sixteenth and early seventeenth centuries.

Why did the population of England grow in the later sixteenth and early seventeenth centuries?

One possible explanation for this long-term rise is that outbreaks of plague and other epidemic diseases occurred less frequently during the sixteenth and seventeenth centuries than in the later Middle Ages and that mortality rates consequently declined. To a certain extent this explanation has been found to be valid. From the beginning of the sixteenth century outbreaks of plague that affected the whole country (as happened in 1348–9) were rare, causing mortality to decline slightly.

Yet 'slightly' is the key word. Until the 1660s towns were still frequently afflicted with plague epidemics that brought very high mortality (the Great Plague that hit London in 1665 was the last, see chapter 26). Moreover, outbreaks of other contagious diseases – like influenza, smallpox and typhus – still occurred in towns and countryside throughout the sixteenth and seventeenth centuries. In addition, at times when harvests failed in successive years (as they did periodically in early modern England), mortality rose as diseases hit an undernourished population or (less frequently) as people died of starvation.

For these and other reasons it may be that the *key* explanations for the new population trends in the sixteenth and early seventeenth centuries lie in changes in fertility, not mortality, patterns. What has reinforced this conclusion is the discovery of the remarkable ability of populations to recover quickly after quite severe mortality crises. In many such crises, short periods of abnormally high burial rates resulting from a plague epidemic or severe harvest failure are followed in parish registers by abnormally high baptismal figures until the normal population level was reached.

Therefore, it may be that changes in fertility patterns were more crucial than changes in the impact of plague and other diseases in bringing about longer-term population changes. In an age when illegitimacy rates were very low (as they were at the beginning of the seventeenth century) the key factors governing changes in the birth rate were the average age at first marriage.and the percentage of people who never married. One of the most significant discoveries of the Cambridge Group is that generally in the later sixteenth and early seventeenth centuries there occurred a slight drop both in the average age at first marriage and in the percentage of people who never married.

At first sight both figures do not seem very significant. Indeed their most striking aspect is the late age at which people married in this period and the large numbers of people that never married at all, compared with modern times. In all the parishes looked at by the Cambridge Group for the sixteenth and seventeenth centuries the average age at which men and women first married was quite late (the mid–late 20s) and nuptiality rates (percentage of those who marry) were comparatively low. In the parish of Ealing (now part of west London) in 1599, 25 per cent of the women between 40 and 70 were unmarried.

Yet the Cambridge Group's figures suggest that in the later sixteenth and early seventeenth centuries people married earlier and more people got married than in the period after 1650. In an age when it is likely that contraceptive techniques, when used at all, were very primitive, and when illegitimacy rates were very low, then even a slight increase in the number who married, combined with a slightly earlier age at first marriage for women, could affect the birth rate significantly. That it did so in the later sixteenth and early seventeenth centuries is confirmed by the Group's figures for gross population reproduction rates, which rose rapidly especially in the last decades of the sixteenth century.

In what ways did the English economy respond to these market forces?

'Our multitudes, like too much blood in the body, do infect our country with plague and poverty. Our land hath brought forth but it hath not milk sufficient in the breast thereof to nourish all those children which it hath brought forth.'

Robert Gray in 1609.

Contemporaries were well aware that they were living in an age when the population was growing fairly rapidly and some were frightened that it might lead to overpopulation and greater poverty. Whether or not contemporary pessimists like Robert Gray (see the quote above) were correct in their gloomy analyses of the impact of a rapidly growing population on resources is the subject of a historical controversy that will be discussed in chapter 8. What is more certain is that at the beginning of the seventeenth century all the major sectors of the English economy were undergoing changes as people attempted to adapt to the new circumstances of rising prices and growing demand.

Agriculture

Changes in agricultural practice are the least noticeable but the most important of all. They are not obvious because they took place in a slow, undramatic fashion and because agrarian history is concerned with mundane matters like crop rotations, drainage and manure. With the exception of enclosures, they are not calculated to grab the attentions of historians, unlike more exciting topics, such as voyages of overseas exploration, trading ventures and the foundation of new colonies. But, given the need to increase the production of food and of industrial raw materials like leather and wool, they are more important than any other economic changes that were under way at the start of the seventeenth century.

Three major ways of increasing agricultural production were attempted in the later sixteenth and early seventeenth centuries:

1 The area under cultivation was extended by deforestation, transforming woodland into farmland; by drainage of waterlogged land, most famously in the Fens of eastern England; and by taking into cultivation marginal land (like the Cumbrian moorlands) that had not been farmed since similar conditions of rising population in the thirteenth century.

2 Attempts were made to increase output from the land already under cultivation by:

- **enclosure**
- **'up and down husbandry'**
- attempts to increase the size of the sheep population, primarily to supply animal manure. The principle technique employed to do this was called **'floating the water meadows'**.

3 The size of farms was increased by amalgamating smaller farms (called 'engrossing'), so facilitating the introduction of new farming methods.

Manufacturing

At the beginning of the seventeenth century there is similar evidence of enterprise and innovation in industry. However, 'industry' can be a misleading word to use, since it tends to conjure up images of factories and production in towns. These are far removed from the reality of what happened in early modern England. The vast majority of manufacturing in England at the start of the seventeenth century was done in people's homes and in a rural setting, often as part-time occupations, combined

KEY TERMS:

Enclosure

Enclosure was the systematic fencing of large open fields, in some of which individual holdings were held in scattered strips. The enclosed land was divided into smaller fields that were then allocated to the existing farmers, allowing more effective use of the land at no social cost. Sometimes, however, the land was enclosed in order to change the use of the land from arable to pasture farming. In these cases, there was social distress as many small arable farms were replaced by large cattle or sheep farms, resulting in some farmers being forced off the land.

'Up and down husbandry'

This was a term used at the time for a rotation system in which arable farming was periodically alternated with pastoral farming, thus ensuring that the soil's fertility was maintained by the manure of the animals kept on it.

'Floating the water meadows'

This was a fairly complex procedure, which involved building sluices to flood meadow land with a few centimetres of water to protect it against spring frosts. This promoted the early growth of grass and facilitated a longer lambing season.

The domestic or putting out system

This describes the main way in which industry was organised at this time. Goods were produced in people's homes, often by part-time workers who were mainly farmers. The organisation was usually directed by a merchant entrepreneur, who distributed raw materials to the part-time workers, collected the finished products from them and then sold them.

New Draperies

These were dyed in bright colours and were lighter than the heavy broadcloths traditionally produced in England, which were exported undyed.

with farming. This is often called (rightly and aptly) the **domestic system of production (or putting out system)**.

On the face of it this might seem to be (compared with the modern 'progressive' factory system) an unsophisticated and primitive form of production that was not conducive to innovation and change. It is true that it did have economic disadvantages, including large costs in distributing and collecting materials, the possibilities of pilfering and the difficulty of maintaining uniform standards of quality in the finished products. But it did have the prime advantage of providing a means of tapping the pool of underemployed labour that was available in early modern England. It was also a flexible system that did not tie up capital in plant and factories, but which enabled entrepreneurs to respond to sudden increases in demand by investing short-term capital in raw materials and rural labour costs and then by withdrawing capital and laying off labour when demand slackened.

The outstanding example of the flexibility and economic sophistication of the domestic system is the production of woollen cloth. By the early seventeenth century this was the country's major industry, centred on the West Country and East Anglia. Here wealthy clothiers put out wool to be spun and woven in the homes of part-time workers (who were usually also farmers). The cloth was then sold, much of it in London, from where it was exported to Europe. Some clothiers began to experiment with newer types of woollen cloth called **New Draperies**, using techniques brought to England by Dutch Protestant refugees.

Overseas trade

The enterprise of merchants in the later sixteenth and early seventeenth centuries needs little emphasis. The records of great London mercantile corporations, like the Company of Merchant Adventurers, reveal a high level of commercialisation, especially in the well-established trade in woollen cloth to northern Europe. The enterprise of English merchants in the same period in developing new trade routes has had an even higher profile. Elizabethan and early Stuart merchants not only began to trade again with southern Europe, the Mediterranean and the Baltic, but also began to open up new trade routes to the Far East (the East India Company was founded in 1600) and to search for colonies across the Atlantic (the first permanent English colony there was established at Jamestown in Virginia in 1607).

Threats to economic stability

There is, then, ample evidence of enterprise in the economic life of England at the beginning of the seventeenth century. However, three weaknesses in the country's economic structure can be seen that threatened England's stability as seriously as did the political and religious problems that were identified at the end of the last chapter.

1 There were severe limitations on the ability of English farmers to increase the output of food either by extending the area under cultivation or by increasing the fertility of the soil. Deforestation was expensive, and drainage of waterlogged land was not only costly but was limited by technical problems and by local opposition. Moreover, cultivation of marginal, infertile moorland was also a very risky economic venture and subject to diminishing returns.

Efforts to increase the productivity of established farms were also limited by the inability to maintain and increase the fertility of the soil. The only means available to do this were by leaving land fallow periodically, or by spreading on it animal manure which, in the days before the invention of chemicals in the later nineteenth century, was the main source of fertilisers. Unfortunately, the supply of animal manure was limited by the inability to increase substantially the animal population. Techniques designed to do this – like up and down husbandry and floating of water meadows – were expensive and, in any case, by themselves they did not provide a major way of increasing the animal population. What was needed were new supplies of winter fodder to supplement stored natural grasses (hay). In the more advanced Low Countries (modern Belgium and Holland) farmers were beginning to use fodder crops like turnips and artificial grasses, including clover. But in England at the beginning of the seventeenth century these were not yet used on a large scale. Farmers were still forced to leave land fallow to allow the soil to recoup its fertility naturally. The first weakness of the English economy at this period can be expressed as a fairly basic equation:
the lack of fodder crops + a small animal population + a shortage of fertilisers = the limited ability to increase agricultural productivity.

2 The second major weakness of the English economy at the start of the seventeenth century was its dangerous dependence on woollen cloth. It was not the only commodity that was produced in England, which is a point that Joan Thirsk has made often, when writing about thriving domestic manufactures as diverse as button-making and woad production. But woollen cloth was by far and away the most important manufacture produced in England for national and international markets in this period. Its dominance, therefore, meant that the English manufacturing economy was very vulnerable to changes in demand in European markets.

3 This overdependence on one manufactured product is linked closely with a third economic weakness that was very obvious in the early seventeenth century: overseas trade (despite a half-century of attempts at diversification) was still largely focused on one trade route as well as one commodity, the export of woollen cloth via London to north Europe. English trade was thus very vulnerable to changes that affected this trade route. The dangerous 'all your eggs in one basket' nature of that situation needs no further emphasis.

How fragile was the English economy at this time?

As will be seen in chapter 8, this is a highly contentious question, to which there can be no one 'correct' answer. What is certain is that the weaknesses noted above ensured that the English economy in the later sixteenth and early seventeenth centuries was afflicted by a series of serious economic crises. It was an economy that was periodically hit by harvest failures. It was also an economy that was equally vulnerable to trade crises.

However, there is a danger of exaggerating the fragility of the economy as well as the political system of England at the beginning of the seventeenth century. Much of the evidence for qualifying overly-gloomy assessments of the economy will be seen in chapter 8. It is sufficient to note here that against the weaknesses that threatened the English economy at the start of the Stuart period must be set the fact that it was an economy that was at least commercialised and advanced enough to stave off the worst effects of famine and starvation that afflicted poorer and more backward countries in continental Europe, as well as Ireland and Scotland, in this period.

Task: note-taking

All historians need to become skilful at making notes. You **must** always make notes on what you read because your notes will help you:

- understand what you read *as you go along*, and
- remember what you have read *later on* (especially when you come to write an essay or to revise for an examination).

Notes on B. Coward, Stuart England (1997) chapter 2:
How advanced was the English economy in 1603?

A   The 17thc. econ. and modern underdeveloped econs.

1   Similarities
(a) agrarian and pre-mechanised
(b) easily upset by natural disasters, e.g. plagues/famine/harvest failure
(c) permanent underemployed labour force
(d) high infant mortality & low expectation of life at birth = youthful pop.

2   Differences
(a) smaller % of pop. dependent on others [Why do econ. historians use jargon?
     'Dependency burden'. Ugh!]
(b) nuclear X extended families > prod. for market not for themselves
(c) commercial X subsistence econs. (See Loder for e.g. of commercial attitudes)

B   Factors > econ. change

1   The Price Revn, esp. food prices.
2 possible causes (monetary, e.g. debasement, & pop. outstripping resources)
[Coward opts for 2nd explanation. Is he right? Why not both?]

2   Pop. expansion   Doubled 1520s > 1750s (See p. 20 for stats)
Was it caused by falling mortality e.g. fewer plagues or rising fertility (people marrying earlier)?
[NB rising pop. not in doubt but how can historians know the causes? Is there enough evidence
e.g. parish registers?]

C   Responses of econ. to price and pop. rises
1   Inc. in agric. productivity by
(a) bringing more land into cultivation e.g. drainage
(b) inc. output of same piece of land by
         (i)   enclosure – more efficient than med. open fields
         (ii) up & down husbandry
         (iii) floating the water meadows (b & c used to increase animal pop. > inc. fertility of soil)
(c) inc. size of farms – more efficient.

2   Industry (or is manufacturing better word because domestic system not factories common?)
Main change in cloth ind. Switch to New Draperies.

3   Trade
Opening new trade routes: S. Europe and Medit./Baltic/Far East/New World.

D   Main limits to econ. progress

1   Agric. (expense/diminishing returns/lack of fodder > few animal > lack of fertilisers > infertile soil

2 & 3   Manufacturing and trade: overdependence on woollen cloth > N. Europe.
Hence vulnerable to trade crises.

E   How serious were these problems?
Controversial.
[NB See chapter 8 for this]

There is no standard way of note-taking. The main rule you should bear in mind is that since the notes are only for your own use they should be in a form that will help you. However, the most useful notes are those that:

- have a clear heading, telling you what book or article you made the notes on

- are summaries of what you have read, *i.e.* they are always much shorter than the originals

- record mainly the key points of what you have read. They should not be cluttered with a lot of details. They should enable you to make sense of the topic quickly.

- are written largely in your own words. Doing this will force you to think about and understand what you are reading. Making notes in your own words is much better than photocopying pages and highlighting certain passages. This is easier but it does not encourage you to think.

Try to follow this advice by making notes on this chapter. Use a form (flow chart, spider diagram etc.) that suits you.

The one that suits me is shown in the box opposite.

[NB I use some abbreviations, but only for words that occur frequently, like economic (econ.), social (soc.) or agriculture (agric.). I have discovered that when I invent abbreviations for words I use less frequently – like 'dom. sys.' for 'domestic system' – I sometimes forget what that stands for when I come to use the notes much later on!

Note also that I have included comments, noting my own thoughts on what I have read. I have put these in square brackets [ ] to distinguish them from the other notes. Doing this encourages me to read critically and not accept everything I read as 'true'. It also makes note-taking more interesting and less of a mechanical exercise.]

Further reading

The best introductory textbook on the seventeenth-century economy is D. C. Coleman, *The Economy of England 1450–1750* (Oxford University Press, 1977).

There are good pamphlets on population, prices and various aspects of the economy in the Macmillan Studies in Economic and Social History series:

R. B. Outhwaite, *Inflation in Tudor and Early Stuart England* (1982)

R. A. Houston, *The Population History of Britain and Ireland 1500–1750* (1991)

R. Davis, *English Overseas Trade 1500–1700* (1973)

D. C. Coleman, *Industry in Tudor and Stuart England* (1975)

J. Chartres, *Internal Trade in England 1500–1700* (1977)

J. Thirsk, *England's Agricultural Regions and Agrarian History 1500–1750* (1987).

3 How was English society organised in 1603?

How different was it from modern British society?

Until fairly recently it was commonly assumed that the social structure of early modern England had more in common with present-day Third World peasant societies than with Britain in modern times. Unlike modern British society the social structure of early modern England was thought to have been dominated by five main features:

▓ An hierarchical pyramid of landed social groups, among which wealth was distributed very unequally.

▓ Extended families of grandparents, parents, married children and other relatives, living in large households.

▓ An immobile population, consisting mainly of people who married, lived and died in the towns and villages in which they had been born.

▓ Much stronger kinship ties than nowadays.

▓ Weaker loyalties to country or nation than to counties or the localities in which people lived.

Each of these assumptions has been questioned to a greater or lesser degree as a result of discoveries made by social historians of this period.

Was England a landed, hierarchical society?

Of all the above five assumptions, the first needs qualifying least of all. Contemporary analyses of English society – like Sir Thomas Smith's *De Republica Anglorum* (1583) or Thomas Wilson's *The State of England, AD 1600* – describe a society made up predominantly of people who gained their living off or from the land. They classify people of their own day in a hierarchy of four landed social groups: **gentlemen,** yeomen (see key term, page 9), **husbandmen, cottagers and labourers**.

This contemporary classification of society into four landed social groups was not an idealised or unreal one. It is what one might expect given the overwhelming predominance of agriculture in the economy of early seventeenth-century England, seen in the last chapter. Moreover, if one were able to go back in time to the household of a landed gentleman of this period – like that of the Stanleys, earls of Derby in Lancashire – one would quickly find much to confirm the picture of England as a predominantly hierarchical landed society, one bound together by ties of patronage and clientage.

The earls of Derby owned vast estates in Lancashire and Cheshire and from their mansions at Knowsley and Lathom, near Liverpool, they exercised enormous social and political influence in north-west England. The survival of the Derby household books from the end of the sixteenth century enables one to see the importance of those at the top of the landed social pyramid and their relations with those below them. In 1587 the household of Henry, the fourth Earl of Derby, consisted of well over a hundred people. It is clear that it was not simply a domestic establishment, but was also (using a phrase Mark Girouard has coined to describe similar establishments) 'a power house'. Like a mini royal court the Derby household was a source of patronage and favour. At least 26 gentlemen or their sons from wealthy gentry families in Lancashire and Cheshire served there. The earl's council arbitrated in local disputes, and from his household the Earl distributed to his clients land, annuities and the benefit of his influence at court.

This 'good lordship' embraced his tenants also. It was not a one-sided relationship because the Earl's favour had to be bought by service and obedience to him. One impressive demonstration of this occurred in 1597 when the Earl of Derby returned home from London. He was met by huge numbers of local gentlemen, tenants and retainers, who turned out to welcome their lord home. That occasion is a snapshot of the hierarchical nature of English landed society at the end of the sixteenth century.

Yet it is a picture that, though important, is incomplete. Contemporaries never satisfactorily solved the problem of incorporating into their classification of society newer non-landed social groups. As a result of the economic changes seen in the last chapter, such people, especially merchants and professional people, were growing in numbers. So too were craftsmen and smaller-scale tradesmen, as well as apprentices and labourers working in manufacturing trades. It is possible to exaggerate the social gulf between such people and those working on or getting their incomes from the land. Merchants were often sons of landowners, or used their wealth to become landowners. The sons of yeomen farmers were often apprenticed to craftsmen and merchants; farmers were often also part-time woollen cloth weavers, metalworkers, and so on. But this should not obscure the fact that non-landed groups were becoming increasingly important in English society in the early seventeenth century, a process that is an important qualification to the broad generalisation that this was primarily a landed society.

Was England a country of extended families who lived in large households?

The picture of England as a country largely of extended families and large households can be dismissed with much less qualification. Of course, such families and households existed in early modern England (one, the Derby household, has just been mentioned), but they were mainly to be found among the tiny elite of wealthy, landowning gentlemen. Elsewhere, the normal family was a nuclear one, consisting only of husband, wife, young children and servants. It has been estimated that the average household at this time was made up of 4.75 people. While recognising that averages like this always conceal variations, small households were undoubtedly the norm in England in the sixteenth and seventeenth centuries.

One of the principal reasons for this is that (as was seen on page 21) the average age at which people married in this period was comparatively late (in their mid to late 20s). People did not marry until they were able to set up a household independent of their parents. Until then, many adolescents and young adults lived away from home working as apprentices or as **'servants in husbandry'**. Again, the exceptions are to be found largely among the children of the wealthy, whose marriages were sometimes (although not always) arranged by their parents for economic reasons.

KEY TERM:

'Servants in husbandry'

These were mainly young people, employed on annual contracts, moving from farm to farm, employed in tasks that suited their abilities (menial tasks – like picking stones from fields – when young; to more demanding jobs – like ploughing – when older).

Was England an immobile society?

This question, too, can be answered with a clear, negative answer. One of the great achievements of English social historians during the last 20 years has been to explode as a myth the idea that England before the Industrial Revolution was a country of insular communities from which people rarely moved. It is now certain that it was far more common for men and women in the early seventeenth century (and for a long time before and after) to move from the town or village where they were born, than it was to stay at home.

Comparisons of baptismal, marriage and burial information from registers in the same parish show that individuals recorded as being baptised in the parish, rarely married or died there. More dramatically, studies of individual communities – like David Hey's book about the Shropshire village of Myddle – reveal migrants flocking there, as they did to other forest or pastoral regions like the Northamptonshire Forest, Sussex Weald or the moorland areas of Cumbria. Many of these were **subsistence migrants**, who often travelled long distances. Between 1580 and 1640 poor migrants poured into three Kentish towns from all parts of Britain. Some

KEY TERMS:

Subsistence and betterment migrants

Subsistence migrants were those who were *compelled* to tramp the roads to look for work; while **betterment migrants** *chose* to move to work, for example, as apprentices or 'servants in husbandry' (see page 30).

KEY TERMS:

Charivari or skimmingtons

These were communal demonstrations by neighbours outside the homes of anyone thought to have broken orthodox values, *e.g.* scolding wives or adulterers. Henpecked husbands were frequently condemned for allowing women to upset the 'natural' order of female obedience to men. It was also assumed that such men were cuckolds [*i.e.* husbands who allowed their wives to be unfaithful to them]. Often the victims would be merely intimidated by abuse, mocking laughter, the playing of loud music or banging pots and pans outside their homes and, as in Figures 3.1 and 3.2, paraded in humiliating circumstances (*e.g.* sitting backwards on a mule). But sometimes they were attacked and beaten up, or ducked in the local pond.

Rogation week

This is part of the Christian calendar in the week preceding Ascension Day after Easter, *i.e.* the day commemorating Christ's ascension to heaven.

went further afield to Ireland and (later from the 1620s onwards) to American colonies like Virginia. Other **betterment migrants** often moved much shorter distances.

From this it can be seen that the reasons why migration was so common are to be found in other characteristics of early modern English society, notably the instability of the agrarian economy, which failed to provide constant employment opportunities, and the pattern of contemporary marriage and family customs (outlined above).

Was England a society bound together by strong kinship ties?

Relationships between kin outside the nuclear family were much weaker in this period than might be thought by those who persist in comparing early modern England with Third World countries today. Ever since the early Middle Ages kinship ties in England had been weak, and by the early seventeenth century they were as weak as in some modern communities.

Like most historical generalisations this one needs to be qualified. For people like landowners and merchants, kinship ties were more important than for others because they determined the inheritance of land and property. But most people seem to have had a much closer relationship with neighbours than with distant kin, as might be expected in a country of small, nuclear households and a highly geographically-mobile population. In such circumstances in times of trouble, most people looked not to their kin but to their neighbours and the local community for help. The most obvious illustration of this is the development of official poor relief schemes, based on parishes. But the evidence of diaries, like that of the mid-seventeenth-century Essex clergyman, Ralph Josselin, reveals other, less systematic, means of support for the poor and needy provided by voluntary charity by those able to afford it.

Other evidence also supports this picture of communities bound together by ties of neighbourliness rather than of kin. Local customs and festivities provide important illustrations of the strength of communal ties at this time. Sometimes, like **charivari or skimmingtons**, they were used to enforce orthodox values.

Other, less menacing, examples of communal solidarity were traditional festivities that marked the church and seasonal calendars, like annual **Rogation week** processions by the whole community around the parish boundary, or harvest suppers and sheep-shearing feasts. Interestingly (and slightly surprisingly), similar strong communal ties have been found

Figure 3.1 *'A riding out' of a victim*

Figure 3.2 *Punishments for henpecked husbands: a beating and sitting backwards on a mule*

in towns at this time. This is true even of London parishes (including a suburban parish like Southwark).

Were loyalties to localities stronger than those to country?

There are dangers in taking this emphasis on the strength of local ties too far. In books and articles published in the 1960s Alan Everitt demonstrated the importance of 'the county community' in people's lives at this time. Subsequent research by younger historians provided support for this view, showing that it was fairly common for people to use the word 'country' to describe their own locality and not England. They demonstrated too that meetings of the county quarter sessions and assizes were important centres of political and social life, and not only for the landed elites. Yeomen, husbandmen, cottagers and labourers can be found among those appointed to grand juries and among witnesses before the quarter sessions and assizes. It is, though, possible to exaggerate the importance of localism in early modern England. Was Everitt right to conclude that England was 'a union of partially independent county states, each with its own ethos and loyalty'? This takes the emphasis on local loyalties too far. The major reason for taking this view was explained in chapter 1. England had long been a unified state with a common governmental and legal system, and its relatively small size made it even more unlikely that local particularism would have been as well developed as in larger countries like France. Moreover, as we have seen in this chapter, people of all social groups commonly moved about the country, making it unlikely that local identities prevented the development of a sense of being English.

What is most likely is that most people felt themselves to be members of *several* overlapping 'communities': family, kin, patrons, neighbours, county and country. Their preoccupations with each probably shifted from time to time. What happened in their localities was very important to them, but they were not insulated from events taking place elsewhere.

How stable was the social structure of England?

This is as debatable and uncertain as the question of how fragile was the English economy in the early seventeenth century, that was raised at the end of the last chapter. Both will be considered in chapter 8. What needs to be noted here is that (as with other aspects of the country at the beginning of the seventeenth century) it is possible to pick out features of English society that might have posed a threat to social stability.

The growing polarisation of wealth in English landed society – gentlemen and large yeomen farmers getting richer and husbandmen, cottagers and labourers getting poorer – produced growing poverty that occasionally exploded into popular riots against, for example, merchants transporting grain from famine-stricken areas. A geographically-mobile population and the flood of migrants into the suburbs of London must have undermined some of the social control exercised by landed and urban elites. Certainly fear of 'masterless' men was widespread among the propertied classes in this period, complementing their fear of rebellion by what some called 'the many-headed monster' of the poor. This anxiety was also heightened by the growing importance of non-landed elites, that were seen as being potentially subversive of the traditional landed social order.

What is less certain is whether these ever became more than *potential* threats to social stability. The evidence for believing that they did not become *actual* threats to stability is examined in chapter 8. England in the early seventeenth century was not free of social tensions, but food riots never escalated into popular rebellions. In this respect, as in its lack of subsistence crises in which many people died of starvation, England's experience was already different from many parts of continental Europe.

Task: historical debate

This chapter gives you examples of how historians' ideas on early seventeenth-century English society have changed. Look carefully at the evidence in this chapter and see if you can work out why historians have different ideas about the same period, or the same themes, in history. As you read, it is worth keeping the following ideas in mind:

- looking at new research – new document studies
- looking at information already known in new ways
- historians asking different kinds of questions from one another
- historians using new techniques: for example, using computers to analyse huge amounts of data.

Further reading

B. Coward, *Social Change and Continuity in Early Modern England 1550–1750,* Seminar Studies in History (Addison Wesley Longman, 1988).

K. Wrightson, *English Society 1580–1680* (Hutchinson, 1982).

J. A. Sharpe, *Early Modern England: a Social History 1550–1760* (Arnold, 1987).

A good way of understanding the organisation of English society at this time is by reading a study of one community, for example:

D. Hey, *An English Rural Community: Myddle under the Tudors and Stuarts* (Leicester University Press, 1974)

M. Spufford, *Contrasting Communities: English Villagers in the Sixteenth and Seventeenth Centuries* (Cambridge University Press, 1979)

or of an individual:

A. Macfarlane, *The Family Life of Ralph Josselin* (Cambridge University Press, 1970).

If you want to follow up the debate about the relative importance of national and local allegiances, start with:

C. Holmes, 'The community in Stuart historiography', *Journal of British Studies*, vol. 37, 1980.

4 What were the major religious divisions in England in 1603?

Read carefully the following extracts from contemporary sources. They have been chosen to indicate some of the major religious divisions in early Stuart England that are discussed in this chapter.

Source 1

'In some parts where I have travelled, where great and spacious wastes, mountains and heaths are ... many ... cottages are set up, the people given to little or no kind of labour, living very hardly with oaten bread, sour whey, and goats' milk, dwelling far from any church or chapel, and are as ignorant of God or of any civil course of life as the very savages amongst the infidels.'

(From John Norden's *The Surveyor's Dialogue*, 1607 quoted in K. Thomas, *Religion and the Decline of Magic* (1971).)

Source 2

Deposition in 1601 against a Wisbech tailor, who was charged with blasphemy after he had heard a sermon by his vicar on the text: 'Thou art Peter and upon this rock I will build my church'.

'He in an alehouse taking a full pot in his hand in jesting manner pronounced these words: "Upon this rock I will build my faith". And there being in the company one whose name was Peter he applied the matter unto him, saying, "Thou art Peter", and then, taking the pot he said, "But upon this rock I will build my church".'

(Quoted in K. Thomas, *Religion and the Decline of Magic*.)

Source 3

From the diary of a Puritan, Lady Margaret Hoby of Hackness in Yorkshire, Friday 21 December 1599.

'After privat praier I ded a litle, and so went to church: after the sermon I praied, then dined, and in the after none, was busy tell 5 a clock: then I returned to private praier and examenation: after supped, then hard publick praers and, after that, praied privatly, havinge reed a Chapter of the bible, and so went to bed.'

(Quoted in J. T. Cliffe, *The Yorkshire Gentry from the Reformation to the Civil War* (1969).)

Source 4

From the autobiography of Richard Baxter, telling of his youth in his Puritan family household in a Shropshire village, c.1620.

'In the village where I lived the reader read the Common Prayer briefly, and the rest of the day [Sunday] even till dark night almost, except eating-time, was spent in dancing under a maypole and a great tree not far from my father's door, where all the town did meet together. And though one of my father's tenants was the piper, he could not restrain him nor break the sport. So that we could not read the Scripture in our family without the great disturbance of the tabor and pipe and noise in the street. Many times my mind was inclined to be among them, and sometimes I broke loose from my conscience and joined with them; and the more I did it the more I was inclined to it. But when I heard them call my father Puritan it did much to cure me and alienate me from them; for I considered that my father's exercise of reading the Scripture was better than theirs, and would surely be better thought on by all men at the last.'

(Quoted in N. H. Keble (ed.), *The Autobiography of Richard Baxter* (1974).)

Source 5

What Susan Kent, a young woman from Wylie in Wiltshire, was alleged to have said about her local rector, John Lee, who had recently arrived in the parish in 1619. The following is part of the case against her and her father in the bishop's court in 1624:

'When once he ... takes the green book [i.e. the catechism, see page 43] in hand we shall have such a deal of bibble babble that I am weary to hear it, and I can then sit down in my seat and take a nap ... We had a good parson here before but now we have a puritan ... A plague or a pox in him that ever he did come hither, and I would we had kept our old parson for he did never dislike with [games and dances] ... These proud puritans are up at the top now but I hope they will have a time to come as fast down as ever they come up.'

(Quoted in M. Ingram, *Church Courts, Sex and Marriage in England 1570–1640* (1987).)

Source 6

Extract from an Act of 1606 'for the better discovering and repressing of Popish recusants'.

Forasmuch as it is found by daily experience that many of His Majesty's subjects that adhere in their hearts to the popish religion, by the infection drawn from thence, and by the wicked and devilish counsel of Jesuits [see key term, page 39], seminaries and other like persons dangerous to the Church and state, are so far perverted in the point of their loyalties and due allegiance unto the king's Majesty and the Crown of England, as they are ready to entertain and execute any treasonable conspiracies and practices, as evidently appears by that more than barbarous and horrible attempt to have blown up with gunpowder the king, queen, princes, Lords and Commons in the Houses of Parliament assembled ... and where[as] divers persons popishly affected do nevertheless, the better to cover and hide their false hearts, and with the more safety to attend the opportunity to execute their mischievous designs, repair sometimes to church to escape the penalties of the laws in that behalf provided ... be it enacted. [There then follow new penalties against Catholic recusants, see page 38.]

(Quoted in J. P. Kenyon (ed.), *The Stuart Constitution: Documents and Commentary* (1986).)

In order to understand the main religious divisions in early Stuart England it is necessary to go back into the sixteenth century and look at the impact of the Reformation in England – that is, the break away from the Catholic Church that was begun by Henry VIII in the 1530s and that became permanent after the accession of Elizabeth I in 1558. Only by doing this will you be able to see that in early Stuart England:

- there was only one national Protestant Church to which everyone was forced to belong
- the monarch was not only head of the State but also head of the Church
- the Church and its officials, including archbishops and bishops, were firmly under the control of the crown
- religious divisions were of major political importance.

The Elizabethan 'religious settlement'

In 1559 Elizabeth I and her advisers had steered through parliament the Act of Uniformity and the Act of Supremacy. These, together with the 39 Articles of Faith that were drawn up in 1563 by **Convocation**, have often been called 'the Elizabethan religious settlement'. The Acts of Uniformity and Supremacy decreed that England should be officially a Protestant country with a national Church with the monarch, not the Pope, as its head (its 'Supreme Governor'). The services which were to be followed in every parish church were to be Protestant in form as set out in the Book of Common Prayer, which was largely that devised by Protestant reformers in the reign of Edward VI in 1552. It was also to be a truly *national* Church in that everyone was legally forced to attend it and **recusants** were liable to be fined, imprisoned and (in cases of persistent refusal) executed.

But was it really a religious settlement?

As will be seen, very few people, apart from Queen Elizabeth I, considered that the Church that was established in 1559 was finally 'settled' and should not be changed in any way. Not all people in England by any means were willing to accept that what parliament had decided in 1559 was a religious settlement. There was a big difference between what crown and parliament said should be the case and the actual situation in the hearts and minds of the people. The new Protestant Church had to contend with the survival of Catholicism and the existence of those who were either indifferent or antagonistic to Christianity of whatever colour.

The survival of Catholicism

The story of English Catholicism in the later sixteenth and early seventeenth centuries is not the straightforward one of gradual, inevitable decline that Protestant-dominated history would have us believe. Traditionally, the victory of Protestantism in England has been depicted as inevitable because the nation was ready to reject a Catholic Church which was riddled with corruption. Anti-clericalism was rife and, so the argument goes, the English enthusiastically embraced the new Protestant Church that was erected by crown and parliament. In the books of A. G. Dickens and others the official Reformation of the statute book was followed by a quick, popular Reformation of the hearts and minds of the people.

In recent years, however, a group of historians – notably J. J. Scarisbrick, C. Haigh and E. Duffy – have successfully challenged this traditional picture by showing that there is much evidence of spiritual vigour in the pre-Reformation English Church and of widespread popular attachment to it. The implication for the history of the Church in the later sixteenth and early seventeenth centuries of this important historical reinterpretation is to suggest that the progress of the *actual* Reformation at the grass roots in English parishes, as opposed to the *official* Reformation of Westminster and the statute book, was bound to have been very slow.

This seems to have been the case, especially since Elizabeth I in the first part of her reign followed a 'soft' policy towards Catholics. The queen was determined not to push the many Catholics among her subjects into opposition to her by a systematic campaign of persecution. In one important sense, her policy was successful: unlike contemporary France, there were no prolonged wars of religion in England in the years immediately after the Reformation. As will be seen, Protestantism did spread among the English during the later sixteenth century. Yet Catholicism survived fairly strongly in the years after the Elizabethan 'religious settlement', nurtured by the large reservoir of support for the traditional Church in English parishes and helped by the lack of a strong official campaign of persecution against it in the early years of Elizabeth's reign.

After about 1568, Elizabeth's attitude to Catholicism hardened as relations between Protestant England and Catholic Spain worsened, culminating in a prolonged Anglo–Spanish war in the 1580s and 1590s. It now became much harder for Catholicism to survive. Yet embattled Catholics were helped to sustain their faith by the efforts of missionary English Catholic priests, trained at continental colleges or seminaries, including those run by the **Jesuits**. The alliance of Catholic gentry, Jesuits and seminary priests was as vital in keeping Catholicism alive as was the alliance of magistrates and church ministers in popularising the new Protestant faith (see below).

As a result, Catholicism survived in England by the end of the sixteenth

KEY TERM:

Jesuits

Members of the Society of Jesus, a Catholic religious order founded in 1540 by Ignatius Loyola, to combat the threat throughout Europe of the Reformation to Catholicism by promoting a Counter-Reformation.

century. In some places, especially in Lancashire and areas that ministers of the national Church began to call 'the dark corners of the land', it continued to retain a strong, popular hold. Of course, historians need to guard against assuming that what happened in Lancashire was typical of the situation everywhere in England. They also need to be wary of accepting totally the pessimistic picture painted by some Protestant ministers of 'dark corners' of England untouched by the new faith. But it would be equally misleading to exaggerate the rapidity and extent of Catholicism's decline during the later sixteenth century.

Religious indifference and scepticism

The new Church also faced opposition from another direction. As at other times, at the beginning of the seventeenth century there were people in England who were at best indifferent to and at worst sceptical of Christianity. As with Catholicism, historians in the past have given different estimates of the numbers who came into this category. What is certain is that religious indifference and scepticism existed. Church ministers continually bemoaned the lack of attention paid to their sermons by their congregations. Typical of these is the complaint made by a Lancashire preacher, about his congregation.

> 'Some sleep from the beginning to the end [of sermons] as if they come for no other purpose but to sleep, as if the Sabbath were made only to recover the sleep they have lost in the week.'
>
> The sermon of John Angier, a Lancashire preacher, in the 1580s.

The records of the church courts are peppered with cases of people brought before the courts for making blasphemous statements, like that of the Wisbech tailor in source 2 on page 35.

Nor can the circumstantial evidence of parish churches that were not large enough to seat all the members of the community be ignored. In some areas (like those mentioned by John Norden in source 1) where parishes were large and communities very scattered, people lived miles away from a church or church minister. In these areas it is not hard to imagine that the influence of the Church was slight.

Alongside this, too, needs to be set the findings of the research of historians, notably K. Thomas and A. Macfarlane, who have confirmed the prevalence of the belief in magic and witchcraft in early seventeenth-century English society.

Moreover, an influential study of a village in Essex – Terling – has demonstrated the way in which during the later sixteenth and early seventeenth centuries a major division emerged between the ruling elite of the village and the rest. Increasingly in Terling the minor gentry, wealthy yeomen farmers and craftsmen who held the principal local government offices in the village avidly set about promoting the national Church; while the poorer and illiterate villagers seem to have drifted into ungodliness, certainly in the eyes of their 'betters'.

As when evaluating contemporary attachment to Catholicism, historians need to guard against accepting at face value contemporary accounts of propertied officials who were frightened by the prospects of a Church being overrun by a godless multitude. As will be seen, there is little evidence to substantiate such fears. Moreover, studies of some other areas do not reveal the godly-elite *versus* godless-poor divide seen in Terling. In this period in the Wiltshire villages studied by M. Ingram the vast majority of people conformed to the national Church and both zealous commitment to Protestantism and rejection of the Church were rare.

Yet it is important not to ignore altogether religious indifference and scepticism. Indeed one of the most important discoveries of recent research is the existence of religious indifference primarily among young people. What makes this idea especially convincing is the fact that, as was seen in chapter 3, most adolescents in early modern England spent as much as ten years from their early teens onwards living away from their parents, unmarried and working as domestic or farm servants. It is likely that this situation contributed towards what M. Ingram calls 'an adolescent culture associated with servants, one of the features of which was some measure of irresponsibility'. You will probably not need convincing of the attractions that drew many young people away from the Church in the early seventeenth century, especially since it was a Church that turned its disapproval against popular amusements like dancing, as well as alehouses. This comment in a contemporary book has a timeless ring about it:

> 'The Youth said to the church minister: "That place [the church] is more fitte for suche olde fatherly men as you are than for such young men as I am ... Cannot I finde Christe as well in a tavern as a temple?"'
>
> Christopher Fetherston, *Dialogue Against Light, Lewd and Lascivious Dancing* (1582).

When, then, did England become a Protestant nation?

Despite these challenges, the Protestant national Church established in 1559 made huge advances by the end of Elizabeth I's reign. It ought to be no surprise, given the divisions among historians about the extent both of Catholicism and religious indifference in post-Reformation England, that there is no agreement either about the speed or the scale of the spread of Protestantism in the later sixteenth and early seventeenth centuries. Consequently, the question 'Was England a Protestant nation by 1603?' is a very difficult one to answer with any certainty. Yet, leaving aside qualifications that have been made in the last two sections, the most likely answer is 'yes: England was broadly a Protestant nation by 1603'.

What are the reasons for coming to this conclusion? The first is the strength and vitality of the prolonged campaign undertaken to convert the English to the new faith in the later sixteenth and early seventeenth centuries. One important element in the campaign was an effort to destroy much that remained of the old Church that could be seen both inside churches and outside them in the everyday life of towns and villages. From the mid sixteenth century onwards, church ministers and churchwardens began to destroy altars, rood screens (which divided the chancel at the east end of churches from the nave, the central body of the church – see Figure 4.1) and all carved, sculpted and painted images of saints and the Virgin Mary.

At the same time, medieval wall paintings were whitewashed over. This is called iconoclasm, a word that triggers vivid pictures of mindless and violent mobs smashing statues and stained-glass windows. This rarely happened in the later sixteenth and early seventeenth centuries. On the contrary, the work of destruction was legalised by royal proclamations and was carried out in an orderly fashion by local church officials in an attempt to make church interiors much plainer. Catholic imagery was stripped away and the only decorations that were allowed were painted texts, usually the Ten Commandments and the Lord's Prayer, and the royal coat of arms.

Gradually, many of the traditional festivals that were associated with the old Church – like mystery plays, Corpus Christi processions and saints' day holidays – were abolished and attempts made to replace them with Protestant festivals. National and local fast days were held, devoted to fasting, sermons and prayer. Slowly a Protestant calendar of holidays developed, celebrating key Protestant events, like the accession of Elizabeth I in 1558, the defeat of the Spanish Armada in 1588 and the

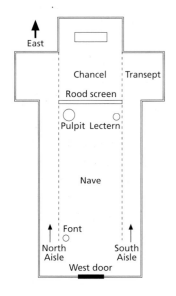

Figure 4.1 *Plan of a church interior*

KEY TERMS:

Gunpowder Plot

On 5 November 1605 Guy Fawkes was discovered in the cellars beneath the Houses of Parliament guarding barrels of gunpowder. He confessed under torture that he was part of a Catholic conspiracy to blow up the building at the state opening of parliament. He and his fellow conspirators were hung, drawn and quartered. There has been a major debate among historians about whether or not the Plot was masterminded by Robert Cecil, the king's minister, in order to use it as a pretext for the introduction of harsh anti-Catholic measures. There is not much conclusive evidence for this and the Plot seems to have been the work of a few Catholics from minor English gentry families, disappointed that James's accession had not brought relief from persecution of their faith. Fawkes seems to have been a minor figure in the conspiracy. Doubts there may be about the origins of the Plot, but there are none about its effects. It became a central part of a tradition of anti-Catholicism in England that continued for centuries.

Catechisms

These were printed versions of a teaching aid that was widely and more commonly used to spread the Protestant message by word of mouth. Using a series of set questions and answers, **catechisms** were used by church ministers to try to instil into their congregations the key elements of the Protestant faith.

Lay improprations

These were the right to appoint ministers to churches on estates that had once belonged to the Church and that had often passed into lay hands at the Dissolution.

discovery of the **Gunpowder Plot** in 1605. None of these attempts were, of course, totally successful – for example, in Catholic Lancashire some church interiors remained unchanged from pre-Reformation days; and elsewhere traditional festivals, like May Days, survived – but slowly the traditional forms of worship and celebration were altered in a Protestant direction.

The main device in this campaign of protestantisation was the use of the spoken and written word. In this regard the new Protestant Church was at a distinct disadvantage compared with Catholicism, which relied on visual aids – like mystery plays, paintings, sculptures and processions. These had for centuries proved highly effective among an illiterate population. To overcome this disadvantage ministers and officials of the new Church attempted to exploit the press, flooding the market in the later sixteenth and early seventeenth centuries with cheap popular ballads and tracts, which were priced at one or two pennies and which carried simplified versions of the Protestant message. T. Watt estimates that between 600,000 and 4 million ballads had been sold by the end of the sixteenth century. Alongside these, over 1 million **catechisms** were published.

The main propaganda device of the new Church, however, was preaching. The pulpit, not the altar (which was replaced by a communion table), was given pride of place in post-Reformation churches. But as every student who has sat in lectures knows, this form of teaching is not always effective. To be effective, sermons, like lectures, have to be well informed and to be delivered in a clear and attractive manner. This quality can, in part, be acquired by training. Accordingly, the universities were encouraged to turn out graduates who could preach and, under some fairly vigorous direction by bishops and with the support of Protestant landowners who owned **lay improprations**, these were increasingly employed by the Church. As a result, the educational level of the clergy rose rapidly until by the 1620s it was very rare for a church minister not to be a graduate. It needs to be pointed out that attainment of a university degree did not automatically guarantee that graduates would be effective preachers and pastors. Moreover, the rank-and-file clergy continued to be badly paid, especially in those cases where the most valuable source of their income, **tithes**, were creamed off by landowners who had rights of impropriation. Yet by the early seventeenth century the Church was recruiting clergy who were much better educated and more fitted for the task of trying to establish Protestantism in England than the clergy it had employed in 1559.

Their success rate was patchy. In counties like Kent, Essex and Suffolk, that were nearest to the reforming influences of the continent, or areas like the Chilterns and upper Thames valley, where there was a long tradition of religious dissent, progress was fairly rapid. Elsewhere Protestant preachers found fertile ground for their message in areas like Manchester and south-east Lancashire, where Protestant ideas had been brought by commercial contacts, or where the sons of local gentry were fired with enthusiasm for the new faith that they had acquired at university. Indeed the areas where Protestantism spread fastest were often those where there existed an effective partnership between a local magistrate who was an enthusiastic Protestant and a church minister who was well educated and was a good preacher and pastor. The alliance of magistrate and minister was fundamental in bringing about the spread of Protestantism in England.

As a result Catholicism retreated, so that by the first decades of the seventeenth century the numbers of committed Catholics could be counted in hundreds of thousands rather than millions. The old faith gradually became confined to the households of Catholic nobles and gentry, and popular attachment to it slowly withered away. The advance of Protestantism can be measured by the:

- appearance of Protestant preambles in wills
- regularity with which the Book of Common Prayer was used in church services
- refurbishing of church interiors along Protestant lines
- important role that the church courts played in the life of the community
- evidence of regular attendance at communion. In Wiltshire the records of the church courts convey 'the distinct impression that regular attendance at church, and certainly annual participation in the communion, were far more widely accepted by the 1620s and 1630s than they had been in the middle years of Elizabeth's reign'.

In three Cambridgeshire villages in the later sixteenth and early seventeenth centuries 'even the humblest members, the very poor, and the women, and those living in physical isolation, thought deeply on religious matters and were often profoundly influenced by them'. Most surprisingly of all, since the teeming suburbs of London do not seem likely areas for the spread of Protestantism, between 80 per cent and 90 per cent of all adults in Southwark received annual communions during the last years of Elizabeth's reign and that of James I. There seems little doubt that the reformed Church was becoming firmly embedded in the centre of life in most English towns and villages during the early years of the seventeenth century.

Puritans and Anti-Calvinists

Although by 1603 the reformed Protestant Church had made a great deal of progress in becoming accepted as a truly national Church in England, there were few people at the beginning of the seventeenth century who believed (as had Elizabeth I) that the Church was fully reformed. Few believed that it should remain exactly as it had been established in 1559. There was a general desire for further reform of the Church in order to support the preaching campaign in the 'dark corners of the land', where the traditional religion still survived, and to educate the ignorant about Christ and the Church. This commitment to continuing evangelisation was one of the key elements that gave the national Church its strength and unity in the early seventeenth century. But there was far from total agreement within the Church on what other changes were necessary. As K. Fincham has recently put it: 'almost everyone in early Stuart England desired religious unity, but on whose terms?'

Two of the most vocal calls for reform of very different types came from 'Puritans' and 'Anti-Calvinists'.

Puritans

This term has been used in so many misleading ways in the past that it is essential at the outset to stress what Puritans were *not*. Puritans were *not* a group different from 'Anglicans'. Puritans were *not* drawn exclusively from one social group – 'the middling sort' or any other group. Puritans did *not* have a distinctive radical, social or political philosophy.

KEY TERMS:

Religious Independents

Religious Independents wanted to establish congregations that were to some extent independent of the national Church. Some, but not all, wanted to be completely separate from the national Church and would have been happy if there were no national Church.

Religious Presbyterians

Religious Presbyterians wanted to retain a national Church but one based on a Presbyterian structure, with bishops replaced by elders and a hierarchy of local classes and national synods. (See also key term, page 133.)

The opposite beliefs were all widely held by historians in the 1950s and 1960s, when it was assumed that Puritans mounted a campaign against the 'Anglican' structure of the Church. Some historians (like C. Hill) also depicted Puritans as people with revolutionary political and social aspirations, who attempted to subvert the traditional political and social order as well. Many historians believed that in the later sixteenth and early seventeenth centuries there took place 'a Rise of Puritanism' against the monarchy and state Church that climaxed in the Civil War of the 1640s and the establishment of an English republic in 1649.

Important research since the early 1970s by, among others, P. Collinson and N. Tyacke has demolished this idea of 'a Rise of Puritanism', including the 'Anglican versus Puritan' model. What has been most influential in doing this is the discovery that Puritans were members of the national Church at the start of the seventeenth century, as were the vast majority of Protestants. At this time there were very few **religious Independents** or **religious Presbyterians**. This being the case, 'Anglican' is an irrelevant, superfluous word when writing about the period before 1640, and this is the last time it will appear in these pages on that period. Puritans were part of the establishment within the Church, not revolutionaries seeking to subvert it from outside.

Yet Puritans were an identifiable group within the Church. Their principal distinctive characteristic was that they were more keen than other Protestants to bring about 'further reformation' of the Church. What did they mean by 'further reformation' (a term they themselves frequently used)?

What were the aims of the Puritans? These can be usefully (if artificially) divided into two parts:

KEY TERMS:

Liturgy

Liturgy is the form in which church services are conducted.

Vestments

Vestments were the robes – often long, richly embroidered cloaks – worn by church ministers when conducting church services.

1 The first was to bring about 'further reformation' of the **liturgy** and ceremonies practised in the national Church. For Puritans the Church was, as they often said, only 'halfly-reformed', by which they meant that it still contained Catholic practices that to them were odious and repugnant. Church ministers still wore **vestments** like those of Catholic priests. This and Catholic practices like bowing at the name of Jesus, the use of the ring in the marriage ceremony and making the sign of the cross when children were baptised were all allowed by the Book of Common Prayer. To Puritans they were symptoms of the fact that the campaign of iconoclasm and destruction of the remnants of Catholicism within the English Church had not proceeded far enough.

KEY TERMS:

Sabbatarianism

Sabbatarianism is the word often used to describe the practice of preventing people from working or playing on Sunday (the Sabbath), so that the day could be spent solely on religious activities.

Churchales

Churchales were festivities, including dancing and sports like bowling, held in churchyards – the seventeenth-century equivalent of church fetes.

2 But Puritans also wanted another kind of 'further reformation', not simply one of destruction but of construction. They wanted an inner spiritual reformation of the lives of every man, woman and child in the country. This is what they meant when they called for 'a reformation of manners', to be undertaken by the Protestant alliance of magistrate and minister. The campaign for 'a reformation of manners' was designed to eliminate sins from people's lives by enforcing adherence to strict personal moral codes of behaviour. **Sabbatarianism** was also an essential feature of Puritan beliefs. Drunkenness and adultery were put high on the Puritans' target list of sins to be wiped out. Hence, Puritans spearheaded a campaign against alehouses, which were seen not only as the main cause of drunkenness but also the origin of personal debauchery and crime. Some popular sports and pastimes too were seen by Puritans as sources of sinful behaviour. For example, **churchales** were condemned for allegedly leading to disorder, drunkenness and illegitimacy. Dancing was especially singled out for encouraging sinful behaviour. As they dance, according to a late sixteenth-century Puritan tract, 'maydens and matrones are groped and handled with unchast handes and kissed and dishonestly embraced'. Another made the connection between dancing and illicit sex even more explicitly. Girls who dance, it was said, 'do return home to their friends sometimes with more than they carried forth'.

For Puritans their pursuit of 'a reformation of manners' was, if anything, even more important than their concern to root out remaining 'popish superstition' in the Church. What drove them on was not a kill-joy spirit, which seems to have been absent from seventeenth-century Puritanism, but a conviction that the continuation of God's support for their cause depended on their living pure lives. What they read in the Bible convinced them of this, especially the Old Testament story of the success of the Israelites in escaping from Egyptian bondage and then eventually inheriting the Promised Land of Jerusalem. As English Puritans often pointed out, the Israelite success was only achieved after they had won God's blessing by first purging themselves of sin. For them, they believed, like the Israelites, moral reformation was essential to their – and the nation's – future prosperity.

Not surprisingly, given these beliefs, what distinguished Puritans from other Protestants was the godliness of their lifestyles. Significantly, the word they used to describe themselves was 'the godly' ('Puritan' was a term that their critics used to describe them). The godly spent a lot of time examining their lives in order both to convince themselves that they were one of the Elect (those chosen by God to go to heaven) and to try to discover God's will. Family prayers were held many times each day in Puritan households. They not only listened avidly to church sermons but often also took notes to use afterwards at **exercises**. If they were not satisfied with the preaching of their own local church minister, they would travel ('gadding' was the word they used) to other parishes to hear sermons.

By their great zeal for 'further reformation' and 'a reformation of manners' and by their personal godliness, Puritans were different and felt themselves to be different from other members of the Church. Like the young Richard Baxter in his father's house in Eaton Constantine in Shropshire in the 1620s (Source 4, page 36), Puritans felt that they were an embattled minority cut off from their neighbours by the intensity of their commitment to the cause of maintaining and reforming Protestantism. Susan Kent's comments (Source 5) reflect the resentment this sometimes caused among their neighbours. As will be seen, Puritans had much in common with other Protestants. Yet they were not like other Protestants in all respects. They were an identifiable group, 'the hotter type of Protestants', or a 'militant tendency within the Church' as they have been aptly described by P. Collinson.

Anti-Calvinists

Puritans were visible within the Church from at least the 1570s. By the 1590s and early 1600s another 'tendency' within the Church had formed, that is people with an alternative vision of what the Church should become. Again it is difficult to give them a label. Sometimes such people have been called 'Arminians' after a Dutchman, Jacob Arminius, who in the second decade of the seventeenth century published similar theological views to theirs. Other historians have called them 'Laudians' after William Laud, who became Archbishop of Canterbury in 1633. But neither of these words are exactly appropriate to describe the situation at the beginning of the seventeenth century, since this reforming tendency predated both Arminius and Laud. Hence the term 'Anti-Calvinists' is preferred here and will be used to describe this group within the Church before it became associated with William Laud in the reign of Charles I. Only then (see chapter 7) will the term 'Laudian' be used.

What were the aims of the Anti-Calvinists? What principally differentiated them from Puritans is that they did not want to push the Church any further in an anti-Catholic direction. On the contrary, they wanted some return to the theology and liturgy of the pre-Reformation Church. In the last years of Elizabeth I's reign, a small group of conservative theologians began to voice criticisms of the Calvinist doctrine of **predestination** that had gained much ground in the post-Reformation English Church. They began to claim that salvation was open to all people and was not predetermined by God. Salvation, they argued, could be gained by what people did during their lives. 'Good works' would be rewarded by salvation. This is known as the theology of free will and was an explicit challenge to the doctrine of predestination, that was much more popular among English Protestants at this time. Moreover, Anti-Calvinists extended their criticisms to other aspects of the reformed Church, like sermons and preaching. They maintained that the sacraments (notably the celebration of communion) and other ceremonies were more important parts of the church service than sermons.

In 1603 these Anti-Calvinist criticisms were as yet largely confined to a few intellectuals within the universities and a tiny group of theologians. Puritanism was far more pervasive and influential in England at large at the beginning of the seventeenth century. Both Anti-Calvinism and Puritanism, however, were symptomatic of the divisions within the Church when James VI ascended the throne of England as James I.

KEY TERM:

Predestination/ predestinarianism

This is the belief that people's fate after death, whether they are chosen as one of the Elect in heaven or condemned to eternal damnation, is decided by God before they are born and regardless of any good works they might do during their lives.

KEY TERM:

Hindsight

Hindsight is the historian's knowledge of what happened later. In this case, what happened later was that religious divisions helped to bring about the Civil War (see chapter 9).

How serious were these religious divisions in 1603?

These divisions and tensions within the Church are crucial to a full understanding of the political history of the reign of James I and Charles I and to the development of the crisis that culminated in the outbreak of the English Civil War in 1642. But it is important that historians should not allow **hindsight** to influence their analysis of the situation 40 years earlier at the start of the seventeenth century. At that time the issues that divided Protestants were much less important than those that they had in common.

What were the main issues that united most Protestants in 1603?

1 The first is a zeal for spreading Protestantism by an enthusiastic campaign of evangelism (preaching of the Gospel). As will be seen, this was a zeal that was not monopolised by Puritans but was shared by James I and many of his bishops.

2 The second is a commitment to the theology of predestination. A few Anti-Calvinists were beginning to question that commitment, but in 1603, outside a small circle of conservative clerics, there is no evidence of hostility to it.

3 The third is a widespread Protestant enthusiasm for a sermon-centred church service, supplemented by a programme of catechising and Bible-reading.

4 Alongside these positive beliefs, Protestants were bound together by a powerful negative force, a deep loathing of Catholicism.

The fear of popery

The intensity of the fear of popery felt by many English people in the early seventeenth century can be difficult to understand, because it appears to have been an 'irrational' fear. As has been seen, popular support for Catholicism was dwindling; there were relatively few committed Catholics in England; and those that there were seemed, unlike their Elizabethan predecessors, to have abandoned political activism and to have reconciled themselves merely to practising their faith within the confines of the households of a handful of wealthy Catholic landowners. What is even more surprising is that Protestant gentry seem to have lived quite happily alongside *individual* Catholic gentry. Why, then, did they fear and loathe Catholics *in general*?

Figure 4.2 *Woodcut from Foxe's* Acts and Monuments

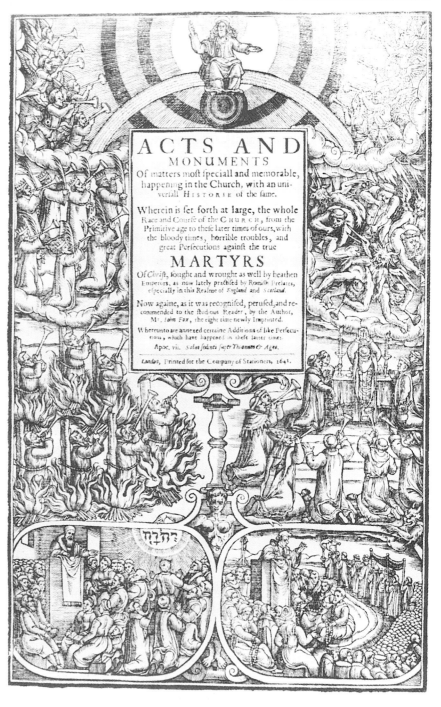

KEY TERM:

Millenarianism

This is the term used to describe the belief in the coming of the Millennium, *i.e.* the 1,000-years reign on Earth of Jesus Christ, which it was stated in the Bible would take place before the final Day of Judgement. It was believed that the Millennium would be inaugurated by the defeat of the forces of Antichrist in a final battle of a long-running war between the forces of Christ and Antichrist. Central to millenarian beliefs was the idea that the world had always been and would be (until the beginning of the Millennium) involved in such a struggle. Most Protestants in the late sixteenth and early seventeenth centuries assumed that in their day the forces of Antichrist were Catholicism; that the defeat of Antichrist and the establishment of the Millennium would take place in the very near future; and that (some English Protestants believed) the English had been chosen by God as the Elect Nation to spearhead (in alliance with continental Protestantism) the war against popery and Antichrist.

The first reason is the widespread acceptance by Protestants of **millenarianism**. What helped this belief to gain ground was its popularisation in John Foxe's best-selling book, *Acts and Monuments* (see Figure 4.2), better known by its popular title *The Book of Martyrs*, which was first published in 1565 and subsequently re-issued in many editions. The most well-known part of the book is Foxe's lurid descriptions of the deaths of Protestant 'martyrs' in the reign of Mary Tudor. Yet this was merely one episode in Foxe's millenarian history of the world, that made a powerful contribution to the escalating fear of popery in seventeenth-century England.

What also made anti-Catholicism such a potent force by the start of the early seventeenth century is that popery had not only become firmly identified with Antichrist but also with absolutism. It was widely assumed that Catholicism was the principal prop of the tyrannical rule of absolutist regimes in France and Spain. Given these assumptions, what was happening seemed to confirm that there was a popish plot from abroad aimed at the Protestant Church and State. Catholic resistance to Protestant English colonisation in Ireland supplemented the powerful anti-Catholic image that emerged during the Elizabethan war against Spain. This was stamped on the collective Protestant consciousness of the English by events like the Spanish Armadas of the 1580s and 1590s and the Gunpowder Plot in 1605, that gave credence to the growing English fear and loathing of Catholicism.

Conclusion

Broadly speaking, although in 1603 religious tensions and divisions bubbled beneath the surface in England – like the political, social and economic problems that have been identified in the previous three chapters – their seriousness should not be exaggerated. Protestantism was now firmly established in England and the national Church was strong and united enough to embrace differing points of view. Preventing the divisions from getting out of hand called for political skill on the part of the monarch. But the collapse of the national Church that occurred in the 1640s could not possibly have been foreseen in 1603.

Task

Work out answers to the following questions. Write a paragraph on each question.

a Why might the phrase 'the religious settlement of 1559' give a misleading impression of the religious situation at the start of the seventeenth century?

b What arguments can you think of to support the belief that
  i Catholicism
  ii religious indifference
  survived in England in 1603?

c **i** What were the main methods used by the new Protestant national Church in England to try to gain support among the people?

ii How effective do you think these methods were? What were their main strengths and weaknesses?

Further reading

The best general book on the religious situation in England in this period:

S. Doran and C. Durston, *Princes, Pastors and People: the Church and Religion in England 1529–1689* (Routledge, 1991).

There are also good Longman Seminar Studies in History books:

A. Foster, *The Church of England 1570–1640* (1994)

A. Dures, *English Catholicism 1558–1642* (1983)

R. J. Acheson, *Radical Puritans in England 1550–1660* (1990).

K. Fincham (ed.), *The Early Stuart Church*, Problems in Focus series, (Macmillan, 1993) – the introduction is an excellent survey.

The most accessible of P. Collinson's major works is the Historical Association pamphlet, *Elizabethan Puritanism* (1983).

N. Tyacke, 'Puritans, Arminians and Counter-Reformation' in C. Russell (ed.), *The Origins of the English Civil War*, Problems in Focus series, (Macmillan, 1973) sets out briefly the argument he develops fully in his *Anti-Calvinists: The Rise of English Arminianism, c. 1590–1640* (Oxford University Press, 1987).

Books on magic and witchcraft in this period:

K. Thomas, *Religion and the Decline of Magic: Studies in Popular Beliefs in the Sixteenth and Seventeenth Centuries in England* (Penguin, 1971)

A. Macfarlane, *Witchcraft in Tudor and Stuart England* (Routledge, 1971).

Dip into these books and you will find them easy to read.

The detailed books referred to in the text are:

K. Wrightson and D. Levine, *Poverty and Piety in an English Village: Terling 1525–1700* (Academic Press, 1979)

M. Ingram, *Church Courts, Sex and Marriage in England 1570–1642* (Cambridge University Press, 1982), chapter 3

T. Watt, *Cheap Print and Popular Piety 1560–1640* (Cambridge University Press, 1991).

Part Two   **Stuart England and the formation of the British State**

5 Was James I 'the wisest fool in Christendom'?

England and the British context

In 1603 a Scottish king, James VI, became James I of England. However, until 1707 (apart from during the Cromwellian Protectorate in the 1650s) the union of England and Scotland was only a regal one – that is, they only shared the same monarch. Before 1707, therefore, it is misleading to use the term 'Stuart Britain'. It will not be used in this book.

Yet, this is not a reason why anyone studying the history of England in the seventeenth century should ignore the history of the rest of the British Isles. What happened in Scotland, Ireland, England and Wales affected events in Britain as a whole. In this and the following chapters you will be encouraged to take full account of the *British* context and not to focus only on English history.

Time chart

1603: Elizabeth I dies and is succeeded by James VI of Scotland, who becomes James I of England

1604: Hampton Court ecclesiastical conference meets; Anglo-Spanish Treaty of London ends the long war between the two countries. Between now and 1607 the king's proposal to unite England and Scotland causes a parliamentary outcry in England

1605: Gunpowder Plot (see chapter 4) is discovered

1606: The judges in the Bate Case approve the crown's right to collect impositions (see page 58)

1608: A new Book of Rates is issued and collection of impositions begins
The plantation [colonisation] of Ulster is started

1609: The 12-year truce between Spain and the United Provinces is signed

1610: MPs clash with the king over impositions
The Great Contract (radical proposal to reform public finances by granting the crown a permanent revenue from land taxes in return for the abolition of feudal dues) collapses

1611: Baronetcies are created to be sold for £11,095 each

1612: Prince Henry, elder son of James I, dies

1613: Princess Elizabeth, the king's daughter, marries Elector Palatine Frederick

1614: More clashes over impositions bring about end of a brief parliament; hence its nickname, 'the Addled Parliament'

1616: James I's favourite, Robert Carr, Earl of Somerset, and his wife are convicted of the murder of Sir Thomas Overbury

1618: Lord Treasurer Suffolk sacked after being found guilty of financial corruption
Bohemia is invaded by the army of the Holy Roman Emperor (the beginning of the Thirty Years' War)
The General Assembly of the Scottish Kirk accepts the Five Articles of Perth

1619: Elector Palatine Frederick crowned King of Bohemia

1620: Elector Palatine Frederick suffers a crushing defeat at the Battle of the White Mountain, near Prague

1621: Parliament meets for the first time since 1614 and James I bans parliamentary discussions of foreign policy
Lord Chancellor Francis Bacon impeached by parliament for taking bribes

1624: James's last parliament meets. After approving impositions and opposing demands for war, it impeaches Lord Treasurer Cranfield
Anglo-French treaty is signed, providing for the marriage of Prince Charles and Henrietta Maria, the French king's daughter

1625: James I dies and his son becomes Charles I

The historical reputation of James I

King Henry IV of France allegedly called his fellow monarch, James I, 'the wisest fool in Christendom'. There is no evidence that he ever did so, yet the label has stuck. From the seventeenth century until recently the historical reputation of James I has been very low. The popular image of the king is of a learned, scholarly man but one whose political judgements were invariably inept and whose public inadequacies were matched by a repellent private personality. In many older history books the first Stuart monarch of Britain is portrayed as a king totally unfitted to cope with many of the problems identified in the first chapters of this book. As a result, it is alleged, parliamentary opposition to the Stuart monarchy was so great that by his death in 1625 the country was already on the high road to civil war.

More recently, some historians have begun to question this critical view. A Scottish historian, Jenny Wormald, has wondered whether James VI, who had a successful record as king of Scotland since he came of age in 1585, could possibly have been the inept James I of England after 1603! These doubts have been confirmed by the discovery that one of the main historical sources for older, unfavourable views of King James – Anthony Weldon's *The Court and Character of King James I* – was written in the 1640s by a man who had two reasons for not writing objectively about the king. The first is that Weldon hated Scotland and all things Scottish. This is clearly illustrated in one of Weldon's earlier books, which he wrote after going with James on a state visit to Scotland in 1617.

> Scotland is 'too good for those that possess it, and too bad for others to be at the charge to conquer it. The aire might be wholesome but for the stinking people that inhabit it … There is a great store of fowl too, as foul houses, foul sheets, foul dishes and pots, foul trenchers and napkins …'
>
> A. Weldon, *A Perfect Description of the People and Country of Scotland* (1617, quoted in *History*, vol. 68, 1983).

The second reason for doubting Weldon's objectivity is that, after James read his comments on his native country, he sacked him from his minor court office. Weldon now had no reason not to use his venomous pen against James as well as the king's fellow countrymen. His book *The Court and Character of King James I* is the result (see source D on page 64). It is clearly not a good source on which to base assessments of James's character and his performance as king.

In this chapter we will be re-assessing James's record as the first Stuart king of Britain between 1603 and 1625. After looking at aspects of James's character and actions that damaged the monarchy, we will examine more successful parts of James's record that have not always been given as much prominence. The chapter will end with a fairly favourable assessment of King James, the validity of which you can consider yourself when evaluating some of the sources on pages 63–7.

The case against James I

Not all the evidence that portrays James in a poor light can be dismissed quite so conclusively as Weldon's hostile comments. The ways in which James failed to calm the disquiet some people in England already felt at the activities of the crown can be summarised under five headings:

- The poor image he projected
- James's financial extravagance
- James's abortive scheme to unite England and Scotland
- James's efforts to raise money by means not approved by parliament
- James's foreign policy.

The poor image he projected as king

James hardly appeared to be 'God's lieutenant on earth', which he was generally considered to be. It was not just that he had peculiar personal habits, like addressing his ministers and courtiers as 'my little beagle' and 'my litle wiffe-waffe' (Robert Cecil, Earl of Salisbury) and 'my little fat pork' (George Keith, the earl marshal of Scotland) – but his well-known fear of assassination was not becoming in an age when military prowess was still valued in monarchs. He also seemed uncouth, typified by scandalous reports of drunkenness at court (see source E on pages 64–5) and his displays of public affection for male favourites like Robert Carr and George Villiers. ('Christ had his John and I have my George', he once commented.) All this contributed to the **Jacobean** court's corrupt and decadent reputation.

KEY TERM:

Jacobean

Jacobean is the common adjective used for 'James's'. It derives from the Latin for James, which is *Jacobus*.

Gentlemen brought up on classical literature which dwelt on the contrasting theme of the immorality of 'the court' and the purity of 'the country' were horrified at a series of sex and financial scandals at the Jacobean court. These included the Overbury murder, for which the Earl of Somerset (Robert Carr) and his wife were found guilty, a sex case involving Sir Thomas Lake, James's secretary of state, and charges of embezzlement against Lord Treasurer Suffolk. There is no denying that James's political standing was weakened as a result.

James's financial extravagance

In many respects James also deserves his reputation for being unduly extravagant. Salisbury, his chief minister, told him frankly that his extravagance was a major cause of royal indebtedness: 'It is not possible for the king of England ... to be rich or safe, but by frugality.' That James ignored his advice is well documented in James's lavish grants of cash, office and lands.

What were the political consequences? One is that James's English subjects felt aggrieved because he seemed to be giving too much favour to his Scottish friends. Another is that James's extravagance caused MPs to wonder whether they should vote parliamentary subsidies to be wasted in this way (see source I on page 66). An even more damaging consequence was that James's extravagance contributed to the failure of attempts made in his reign (principally by Salisbury and later by Cranfield) to undertake fundamental reform of the royal administration and finances. An extravagant king who presided over a court in which financial corruption was rife was not the ideal leader of a successful reform programme.

Abortive scheme to unite England and Scotland

This was one of James's most cherished plans at the start of his English reign. In parliamentary sessions between 1604 and 1607 he pursued it energetically, hoping that eventually his two kingdoms would enter 'a perfect union', including a common parliament, government and laws. After centuries of hostility, including bitterly-fought wars and Scottish friendship with France (the Auld Alliance), such hopes were too optimistic. The sneering comments of English MPs at Scottish political barbarism and economic backwardness (see source H on page 66) show that Weldon's racist attitudes towards the Scots were not unique.

Even so, something more serious lay behind the virulence of English opposition to the union than empty-headed racist emotion. A clue to what this was is to be found in the ruling of the senior judges to whom James appealed for support in April 1604. They refused by joining 'with the opinion of three parts of the House [of Commons] that the first hour the Parliament gives the King the name of Great Britany there followeth necessarily ... an utter extinction of all the laws now in force'. In other words, the union scheme was seen in England as a radical threat to English laws and the constitution and encouraged fears of creeping royal absolutism.

Efforts to raise money by means not approved by parliament

In 1604 a group of MPs drafted a document, 'The Form of Apology and Satisfaction'. It was never presented to the king but it reflects the belief of some that parliamentary liberties were being eroded (see source G on page 65). It was not only the union scheme that caused those fears to continue. Far more important were James's efforts to raise money without calling on parliament. 'The sale of honours' (baronetcies after 1611 and peerages from 1615) was seen as devaluing the existing peerage. Sales of **monopolies**, too, were opposed as keenly as they had been in Elizabeth's last parliaments.

Yet much more politically damaging was James's practice from 1608 of levying **impositions**. This only served to confirm people's fears that the English crown was intent on undermining the powers of parliament in ways similar to those being adopted by European monarchs. That

KEY TERMS:

Monopolies

Monopolies at this time, as now, were grants giving individuals or companies the sole right to make and sell a particular commodity (*e.g.* playing cards and soap), to trade to a particular region (*e.g.* the East India Company) or in a particular commodity (*e.g.* 'sweet' wines), or to carry out specified administrative functions (like the licensing of alehouses). The main differences between then and now are that monopolies were granted solely by royal prerogative and sometimes they were issued purely to increase royal revenue, disregarding other considerations.

Impositions

Impositions were customs duties on imported goods that had not been approved by parliament. What made impositions a major political issue is that in a test case in 1606 (the Bate Case), Chief Baron Fleming had ruled that impositions were lawful since the crown had an 'absolute' prerogative which was not guided by rules which direct only at the common law.

impositions raised constitutional opposition to the crown can be seen in speeches in the parliaments of 1610 and 1614 (see source J on page 66). It is also reflected in the recent discovery that a book called *Motives to Induce Annual Parliaments* was circulating among the parliamentary classes between 1614 and 1621. Its title is a useful reminder not to accept the view that ideological opposition to the early Stuarts was something that emerged for the first time in the reign of Charles I.

James's foreign policy

This is a conclusion that is confirmed by the reactions of some to James's foreign policy. Not everyone found James's international diplomacy distasteful. Indeed the ending of England's long war with Spain by the Treaty of London in 1604 and James's role in arbitrating in European disputes seems to have been broadly welcomed. So too, initially, was James's strategy of non-commitment to any power bloc in Europe, whether Habsburg or French, Catholic or Protestant. James saw himself as a *rex pacificus* [a peacemaker king], maintaining diplomatic contacts with both power blocs by dynastic marriages. His hope was to balance the marriage of his daughter Elizabeth to a prominent German Protestant prince, the Elector Palatine Frederick, by securing the marriage of his son Charles and the Infanta, the daughter of the king of Spain (the so-called Spanish Match). Until 1618 there is little evidence that this foreign policy caused much disquiet.

The outbreak of the Thirty Years' War in Europe in 1618, however, transformed this situation, especially when James's son-in-law was defeated at the Battle of the White Mountain in 1620, expelled from the throne of Bohemia to which he had been elected by the Protestant rebels of the Emperor, and then hounded from his homeland, the Palatinate, by Catholic troops. In a country in which fear of popery was strong (see chapter 4), many found incomprehensible James's continued negotiations for the Spanish Match. In James's last parliaments demands that the king use force to support the Protestant cause in Europe (see source K on pages 66–7) were made by the king's councillors as well as MPs. In the 1621 parliament James's critics included George Abbot (the Archbishop of Canterbury) and the Earl of Pembroke. In the 1624 parliament even his son, Charles, and his favourite, Buckingham, joined the pro-war lobby. Charles and Buckingham had been converted to war against Spain by the humiliation they had suffered in the previous summer in Madrid, when they tried personally to conclude the Spanish Match. In these circumstances opposition to James's foreign policy can hardly be seen as evidence of a gulf between 'court' and 'country'. Yet it was fuelled (in the minds of many MPs if not of Charles and Buckingham) by ideological fears about the future of Protestantism.

The case for James I

From the evidence considered above, it might be concluded that James was a disastrous monarch who raised opposition to the crown to such a pitch that the country was on 'the high road to civil war' by 1625. Certainly it would be unwise to portray James I as an unqualified success as a monarch. But there are many successful aspects of James's kingship that more than counterbalance his failures. He dealt successfully with the three major problems of government identified in chapter 1.

1 James and the British Problem

One of James's greatest qualities was his ability to recognise what was politically possible and what was not. In the face of the opposition to his beloved scheme to unite England and Scotland he dropped it, yet continued gradually and much less publicly to bring about as much Anglo-Scottish uniformity as was possible. The pacification of the once-unruly border region between the two countries allowed a large measure of cooperation between the two governments. Even though James only revisited his native country once after 1603, he kept in touch with opinion north of the border by employing agents, like the Earl of Dunbar, who shuttled to and fro between the two kingdoms.

The most remarkable consequence of this political astuteness was James's achievement in persuading the Presbyterian Scottish Kirk to accept bishops. Slowly from 1607 bishops were re-introduced in Scotland and gradually given more power until in 1612 full episcopal authority was recognised by the General Assembly of the Scottish Kirk. Perhaps emboldened by this startling success, James attempted to go further and faster in bringing the Scottish Kirk in line with the English Church. In 1618 the General Assembly accepted the so-called Five Articles of Perth, which allowed church practices, like private baptism, that had been abolished in Scotland. In the face of the resulting outcry at what was seen as a move towards popery, James characteristically accepted that he could go no further for the time being.

He showed a similar mixture of visionary British imperialism and realism in his other kingdom, Ireland. The sweeping – if brutal – plan devised in 1608 to clear Ulster of Irish landowners and tenants and to settle English and Scottish colonists there ran into problems, when not enough non-Irish settlers could be found. Typically, the Jacobean government back-pedalled, amended the regulations to allow both grants of land in Ulster to Irish landowners and leases to Irish tenants. The compromise worked (at least for the time being) in making the Irish 'plantation' the most successful colonisation scheme in the early seventeenth century.

2 James and the Religious Problem

James's ecclesiastical policies exhibited the same politically-astute mixture of idealism and realism. His ideal was to preside over a uniform Church which was to be brought about by compromise and persuasion, and not by force. Only twice, briefly, did he depart from this role. The first was in 1604–5, when the religious 'settlement' worked out at an ecclesiastical conference at Hampton Court appeared to be threatened by some godly ministers and laymen whose anxiety to proceed with the reforms at Hampton Court James interpreted as disobedience. The second was in the early 1620s, when his peaceful foreign policy came under attack from godly Protestants who were anxious to see England enter a war against Catholicism in Europe. James instinctively (and temporarily) veered towards the more conservative, anti-Calvinist (see chapter 4) faction within the Church who were supportive of his foreign policy.

But these brief episodes were not typical of his ecclesiastical policy. More typical was his role at the Hampton Court Conference, where he acted as an arbitrator between different factions within the Church. Unlike Elizabeth, who had consistently refused to amend 'the religious settlement' of 1559, James encouraged bishops to promote preaching and ecclesiastical exercises (see key term, page 47) and to stop laymen (as well as bishops) plundering the Church's wealth. His appointment of George Abbot in place of Bancroft as archbishop of Canterbury in 1611 symbolised his commitment to 'further reformation' in the Church. But he was not the patron of one ecclesiastical faction. Those with anti-Calvinist views were also promoted in the Jacobean Church. Under James the Church remained broad enough to encompass without much friction the religious divisions that were identified in chapter 4.

3 James and the Financial Problem

Rather surprisingly, given the damaging consequences of James's financial extravagance, it is possible to conclude that James's handling of the country's financial problems was not totally inept. In two ways he coped with them with some astuteness.

1 The first is less important because it was an eventual failure. Yet the Great Contract of 1610 was a genuine attempt to tackle the root cause of the financial problem: the refusal of those with wealth to pay taxes that bore some realistic relation to their true incomes. What was offered as an inducement to them in 1610 to do this was the abolition of their feudal payments to the crown. That they failed to accept the deal is only due in part to lack of confidence in James's financial commonsense. What also lay behind their reluctance was their conservatism that it took

two major wars (the Civil War and the wars against France after 1689) to break down.

2 The second is more important because it was successful. James's foreign policy was a recognition of the financial limitations of the early Stuart monarchy. The war against Spain in the 1580s and 1590s had shown how war abroad, embarked on by a country that had a financial system incapable of raising enough money to pay for it, was a recipe for the outbreak of political tensions at home. James's persistent refusal to enter such a war did not allow that to happen.

There is one other important defence of James's extravagance. Monarchs in this period needed the cooperation of their leading subjects and the distribution of royal patronage (see key term, page 8) was one major way of securing it. This is what the Earl of Salisbury meant when he said that 'for a king not to bountiful were a fault'. James may have been unduly extravagant in distributing patronage, but the damaging political consequences of this were offset by the political support James gained from grateful recipients of his bounty. By distributing royal patronage widely, James was more successful in this than either his immediate predecessor and successor. Elizabeth I had distributed few royal favours. Charles I, as will be seen, was to distribute them to a very small circle of favourites (principally the Duke of Buckingham). In both cases, the result was to cause disaffection.

For these reasons James hardly deserves the black 'wisest fool in Christendom' reputation he has often been given. In the last resort the key to his qualified success lay in Scotland, since it was his experiences as king of Scotland that taught him the art of political compromise and flexibility. Above all, it was from the Scottish court that he learned the importance of maintaining a court that was open and that was as representative of as wide a variety of opinion in the country as possible. Under James the court continued to be an important 'point of contact' between the king and his principal subjects. As a result, before 1625 political tensions between the court and country never escalated into the kind of serious crises that erupted shortly after the accession of his son.

Task: interpretation of sources

One of the major problems facing all historians (including you!) when trying to make a balanced judgement about James I is that much of the source material that is available gives an unfavourable view of him. It may be, of course, that this view is correct. But before accepting it, you need to consider carefully the evidence (the secondary and primary sources) on which it is based. Read the following sources and answer the questions about them.

Secondary sources: three judgements on James I by historians

Source A

'The more self-respecting of the Lords preferred the retirement of their mansions ... to Court masques, in which ladies were too drunk to perform their parts, divorce cases and adulteries favoured by their sovereign, and the whisper, scarcely hushed, of scandals yet more vile ... English politics were more a matter of personal relations than they have been before and since ... At this epoch the royal government ... was a chaos of personal intrigue. The change from a wise Queen to a foolish King removed all the good, and brought out all the bad which this most elastic type of polity rendered possible.'

G. M. Trevelyan, *England under the Stuarts* (1904).

Source B

'As a hated Scot, James was suspect to the English from the beginning, and his ungainly presence, mumbling speech and dirty ways did not inspire respect. Reports of his blatantly homosexual attachments and his alcoholic excesses were diligently spread back to a horrified countryside ... it was reported that when hunting the king did not dismount in order to relieve himself, and so habitually ended the day in a filthy and stinking condition. In the light of these stories it was clear that the sanctity of monarchy itself would soon be called into question.'

L. Stone, *The Causes of the English Revolution 1529–1642* (1972).

Source C

'James's faults were only too apparent, but they should not be allowed to conceal his considerable achievements. He kept his country at peace for more than 20 years, he prevented religious divisions from tearing Church and state apart, and despite rhetorical flourishes about the unlimited nature of divinely-appointed kings he held the monarchy to the course prescribed by common law.'

R. Lockyer, *The Early Stuarts: a Political History of England 1604–1642* (1989).

Figure 5.1 *James I*

Questions on sources A, B and C:

1 Do sources A and B agree on what were James's defects as a king?

2 Is the view of James in source C totally different from those in sources A and B?

You should especially consider the following questions:

3 Is it possible that sources A and B are influenced by the knowledge that the English Revolution occurred in the 1640s and 1650s?

4 Is source C necessarily the best judgement on James I because it is the most recent of the three?

Primary sources: three contemporary views of James's character and court

Source D

Anthony Weldon's description of James I in his book *The Court and Character of James I*, which was published in the 1640s. [Some information about Weldon that you need to know in order to evaluate this source was given on page 56.]

'He was naturally of timorous [i.e. timid] disposition, which was the reason of his quilted doublet; his eyes large, ever rolling after any stranger that came into his presence, insomuch that many for shame have left the room ... His beard was very thin, his tongue too large for his mouth, which ... made him drink very uncomely, as if eating his drink, which came out of his cup each side of his mouth ... His walk was ever circular, his fingers in that walk fiddling with that codpiece; he was very temperate [i.e. moderate and self-restrained] in his exercise and in his diet, and not intemperate in his drinking ... he would not change his clothes until worn out to very rags.'

Source E

Sir John Harington's account of a masque at the court of James I, given to celebrate the visit of his brother-in-law, Christian IV of Denmark, in 1606. [Harington was a poet and a wit, who had served at Elizabeth I's court. At the start of James's English reign his application for royal patronage was turned down by the king. Christian IV of Denmark was described by M. Lee, *Great Britain's Solomon: James VI and I in his Three Kingdoms* (1990), as 'notoriously the greatest royal alcoholic in Europe'.]

'One day, a great feast was held, and, after dinner, the representation of Solomon his Temple and the coming of the Queen of Sheba was made, or (as I may better say) was meant to have been made ... The entertainment went forward and most of the presenters went backward or did fall down ... Hope did essay [try] to speak but wine rendered her endeavours so feeble that she withdrew ... Charity ... returned to Hope and Faith who were both sick and spewing in the lower hall ... Now did Peace make her entry and

strive to get foremoste to the king; but I grieve to tell how much great wrath she did discover unto her attendants; and, much contrary to her semblance, most rudely made war with her olive branch and laid on the pates [heads] of those who did oppose her coming, bringing to my remembrance what passed of this sort in our Queens days.'

Source F

[John Chamberlain was a relatively unimportant courtier but a major letter-writer. His massive correspondence is an important primary source for what happened in England at this time. This letter was written at a time when James I was reported to be ill.]

'I am glad to see the world so tenderly affected towards him, for I assure you all men apprehend what a loss we should have if God should take him from us, and do earnestly enquire, and in general heartily wish and pray for his welfare.'

Questions on sources D, E and F:

5 What are the main criticisms of James's character made in sources D and E?

6 On what aspect of James's habits do sources D and E disagree?

7 Use the information given about Weldon and Harington, the authors of sources D and E. How reliable and useful are their judgements on James I likely to be?

8 Can you think of any reasons why the author of source F might have been unduly favourable to the king?

9 In the light of the evidence in this chapter, how should we react to the disapproving views of James and his court in sources D and E?

Primary sources: James I and parliaments

Source G

An extract from *The Form of Apology and Satisfaction*, 1604. [This was drawn up by some MPs in James's first parliament in 1604, but was never presented to the king.]

'The prerogatives of princes may easily and daily grow; the privileges of the subject are for the most part at an everlasting stand ... they may be by good providence and care preserved, but being once lost are not recovered but with much disquiet.'

(Quoted in J. R. Tanner (ed.), *Constitutional Documents in the Reign of James I* (1960).)

Source H

An extract from a parliamentary debate in February 1607 on the king's proposal to unite England and Scotland. [Nicholas Fuller MP explained his opposition by comparing England and Scotland to two fields ('pastures').]

'One man is owner of two pastures, with one hedge to divide them; the one pasture bare, the other fertile and good: a wise owner will not pull down the hedge quite, but make gated, and let them in and out ... If he do, the cattle will rush in multitudes, and much against their will return.'

(From *Commons Journal*, vol. 1.)

Sources I and J

Two extracts from a parliamentary debate in 1610 in which two MPs explain their opposition to granting the king more money.

[Here Thomas Wentworth (like Fuller in source G) uses a metaphor to explain his point, comparing giving the king money to pouring water into a tank that has many outlets.]

'For ... to what purpose is it [i.e. to grant the king large sums of money] for as to draw a silver stream out of the country into the royal cistern, if it shall daily run out thence by private cocks.'

[Here James Whitelocke explains why he opposes impositions ('this power of imposing') – see the key term on page 58.]

'If this power of imposing were quietly settled in our kings, considering what is the greatest use they make of assembling parliaments, which is the supply of money, I do not see any likelihood to hope for often meetings in that kind because they would provide themselves by that other means.'

(Quoted in S. R. Gardiner (ed.), *Parliamentary Debates in 1600*, Camden Society, 1st series, vol. 81, 1862.)

Source K

An extract from a Commons' petition, 3 December 1621, calling for James to take England into the war in Europe in support of his son-in-law Elector Palatine Frederick against the Catholic Habsburgs.

'Princes of different religion ... have taken [the] opportunity to advance their own ends, tending to the subversion of religion and disadvantage of your affairs and estates of your children; by reason whereof your ill-affected subjects at home, the popish recusants, have taken too much encouragement ... We foresee and fear there will necessarily follow very dangerous effects both to Church and state. For
I The popish religion is incompatible with ours in respect of their positions.
II It draweth with it an unavoidable dependency on foreign princes.
III It openeth too wide a gap for popularity to any who shall draw too great a party.

IV It hath a restless spirit, and will strive by these gradations: if it once but get a connivancy, it will press for a toleration; if that should be obtained, they must have an equality; from thence they will aspire to superiority, and will never rest till they get a subversion of the true religion. The remedies against these growing evils, which in all humility we offer unto you most excellent Majesty, are these:
... That seeing this inevitable necessity is fallen upon your Majesty which no wisdom or providence of a peaceable and pious king can avoid, your Majesty would not omit this just occasion speedily and effectually to take the sword into your hand ...'

(Quoted in J. P. Kenyon (ed.), *The Stuart Constitution: Documents and Commentary* (1986).)

Questions on sources G to K:

10 Read each source and then explain what is the main concern that is expressed in each of them about the king and his policies.

11 In the light of evidence in this chapter:
   a Why do you think that the authors of source G wrote this document?
   b How typical of opinion among English MPs were the views in source H?
   c How justified were the criticisms of the king in source I?
   d How serious were the effects of the views expressed in source J in their impact on relations between James I and MPs?
   e What were the main reasons for the hatred of Catholicism expressed in source K? Why did James resist the warlike demands expressed in this source?

12 Finally, here is a question that gives you an opportunity to come to an overall judgement on James's record as king:
   'James I was a more successful king than he has often been said to have been.' Do you agree? (Use the sources A–K together with other information of your own in your answer.)

Further reading

In addition to the relevant section in B. Coward *The Stuart Age: A History of England 1603–1714* (Addison Wesley Longman, 2nd edn, 1994) – pages 117–158 – and D. Hirst, *Authority and Conflict: England 1603–58* (Arnold, 1985) – pages 96–137 – the best sources on James are:

C. Durston, *James I* (Lancaster pamphlet, 1993)

S. Houston, *James I*, Seminar Studies in History (Addison Wesley Longman, 2nd edn, 1995)

J. Wormald, 'James VI and I: two kings or one?', *History*, vol. 68 (1983)

The following are more detailed sources:

R. Lockyer, *The Early Stuarts: a Political History of England 1603–42* (Addison Wesley Longman, 1989), chapters 7 and 8

P. Croft, 'Annual parliament and the Long Parliament', *Bulletin of the Institute of Historical Research*, vol. 59 (1986)

K. Fincham and P. Lake, 'The ecclesiastical policies of James I and Charles I' in K. Fincham (ed.), *The Early Stuart Church*, Problems in Focus series (Macmillan, 1993).

6 Why was the Petition of Right passed in 1628?

Petition of Right, 1628

The 1628 **Petition of Right** made three demands:
- The king should never again levy taxes without parliament's approval.
- No one should be imprisoned without either cause being given or being brought to trial.
- Soldiers and sailors should not be billeted in private houses by martial law.

What makes this a very intriguing historical question is that, as was seen in chapter 5, at the time of James I's death in March 1625 the political system worked reasonably well. The king had not lost the confidence of the majority of the political nation. Channels of communication between the court and the country were open, facilitating understanding between the king, courtiers and the leading nobility and gentry in the country. Yet within weeks of the accession of Charles I relations between the court and the country, king and parliamentarians, were characterised by growing and extreme mutual mistrust. Within three years the political system came close to a state of collapse, and in June 1628 both houses of parliament agreed on a **Petition of Right** to be presented to the king.

Explanations for the deterioration of relations

This chapter is focused on causation. Why did relations between the crown and those represented in parliament deteriorate so rapidly and seriously in the late 1620s, after the accession of Charles I?

Two types of explanation have been put forward recently.

1 The first might be called a 'functional or short-term explanation'. This has been put forward by historians who have successfully demolished the belief that there were 'long-term' forces at work in the early seventeenth century, that were once thought to have made the growth of opposition to the crown inevitable. [If you need reminding of this point, re-read the sections on 'Parliaments' in chapter 1 (pages 6–7) and 'Puritans' in chapter 4 (pages 45–7).] These historians focus instead on a 'short-term' explanation. They argue that the major cause of the political crisis of the late 1620s was the impact on an unreformed English administrative and financial system of the wars which Charles I embarked on in the later 1620s.

As the experience of Elizabeth's wars against Spain in the 1580s and 1590s had shown, this system could not cope with the pressures of war. This, it is argued, is reflected in the failure of those represented in parliament to appreciate the huge amounts of money that were needed to fight a war. Members of Parliament were consequently unwilling to vote sufficient wartime taxes. This forced the crown to devise extra-parliamentary taxation. The consequent 'functional' crisis was accelerated by Charles's lack of political ability and the ineptitude of his favourite, Buckingham, as a war leader. On this view, the main reason for growing opposition to Charles I in the late 1620s was localist resentment at the demands being made by the crown to pay for war.

2 The second type of explanation, which is followed here, might be called an 'ideological explanation'. This does not exclude the fact that the wars of the late 1620s generated much mistrust of Charles I and his regime in the country. The causes of the Petition of Right, like explanations of all historical events, are not to be found solely in one factor or set of factors. The Petition of Right was brought about by a combination of causes. However, the main argument of this chapter is that these included not only localist resentment at high wartime taxation and royal mismanagement of the war, but also constitutional and religious principles, based on concern for the future of parliaments and Protestantism in England.

An area of agreement: the Charles I factor

Despite these differences about what caused the political crisis of the later 1620s, most historians are agreed that some of the responsibility lies with Charles I. No one attempting to explain the political crisis of the late 1620s should ignore the importance of the character of the new king. In an age of personal monarchy (see chapter 1) it was inevitable that the personality of the monarch would have a decisive influence on political developments. There is no doubt that Charles I was a very different man and monarch from his father. Most historians agree that Charles suffers badly when comparisons are made between them. While the reputation of James I as a monarch has risen in recent years, that of Charles I has rightly plummeted. He was one of the least capable monarchs to have sat on the English throne.

His political ineptitude derived from three major ways in which Charles was a very different man from his father.

1 The first is his personality. Charles was a shy, private and taciturn man, who liked order and decorum in all aspects of his life. One damaging consequence of this was that frequently his actions and policies

Figure 6.1 *Charles I*

KEY TERM:

Caroline

Caroline is the common adjective used for 'Charles'. It comes from the Latin for Charles, which is *Carolus*.

went unexplained and so were often misunderstood. Another was that he saw no need to indulge in the messy business of political negotiation. This meant that he never developed his father's political astuteness in hammering out compromise solutions to tricky problems. Instead Charles's authoritarian temperament caused him to react to criticism, not with disarming compromises, but with a stubborn determination to push ahead regardless, interpreting moderate criticism as radical subversion. On occasions, as will be seen, this rigid attitude caused him to deal harshly with his opponents and sometimes even to adopt illegal methods. This, of course, inflamed, rather than defused, tense situations.

2 Unlike his father, Charles presided over a dignified and decorous court, that was in tune with his love of order in all things. This meant that, from one point of view, the **Caroline** court was a more attractive place than the disorderly court presided over by James I. Moreover, it gained a sparkling reputation as a centre of artistic patronage. But the privacy of Charles's court made it increasingly difficult for anyone other than his intimate advisers to gain access to the king.

> '*The King observes a rule of great decorum. The nobles do not enter his apartments in confusion as heretofore, but each rank has its appointed place ... The King has also drawn up rules for himself, dividing the day from his early rising ... it is said that he will set apart a day for private audience, and he does not wish anyone to be introduced to him unless sent for.*'
>
> The Venetian ambassador's report, 1625 quoted in J. Richards, '"His nowe Majestie" and The English monarchy, the Kingship of Charles I before 1640', *Past and Present*, no. 113 (1986).

KEY TERM:

Point of contact

This is a term historians use about both the royal court and parliaments, in order to emphasise the importance that both had as places where the monarch could meet his or her leading subjects and so maintain the cooperation between them that was necessary for political stability (see pages 7–8).

The Venetian ambassador's comment at the very beginning of Charles's reign does not describe a court that was an effective **point of contact** between the king and his major subjects. Charles compounded this political error by allowing his favourite, **George Villiers**, to dominate the control of royal patronage (though not royal decision-making, as is sometimes supposed), so that the king's favour was not distributed widely but was channelled to Buckingham's family and friends. Not only was a vital means of communication between court and country closed, but natural allies of the court, like Thomas Wentworth, a Yorkshire gentleman (see his profile in chapter 7), were forced to pursue their local interests not at court but in parliament.

3 Within months of his accession, Charles demonstrated that he was likely to be much less successful than his father in handling the

PROFILE: *George Villiers, Duke of Buckingham*

Buckingham (1592–1628) was only the second son of a minor Leicestershire gentleman but gained rapid promotion at court as a young man in his twenties because James I liked him. He also secured the backing of a powerful group at court (including the Archbishop of Canterbury, George Abbot). Villiers became a favourite of Prince Charles as well as James I and was Charles's closest confidant in the early years of the new reign. He was given command of the war effort against France and Spain. He became the focus of parliamentary opposition to the court in the mid 1620s and was only saved from impeachment by Charles's dissolution of parliament. On 23 August 1628 he was assassinated in Portsmouth by John Felton, who had been sacked from his army post.

There are two major historical problems about Buckingham's career:

▨ How competent an administrator was he? He has been rescued from the charge of complete incompetence by the discovery of his achievements as a naval administrator as Lord Admiral. But it is doubtful whether he can totally escape the blame for the war disasters at Cadiz and La Rochelle.

▨ How much influence did he have in the making of royal policies? It is impossible to be certain because there are no formal records of debates that preceded governmental decisions. His closeness to the king gave him ample opportunity to influence decisions, but it would be unwise to underestimate the personal influence of Charles I himself. He was never Buckingham's puppet.

major problems facing the early Stuart monarchy: the British Problem, the Religious Problem and the Financial Problem, identified at the end of chapter 1.

Charles I and the British Problem

His approach to this problem is well illustrated by his rash announcement in November 1625 that he was going to revoke [*i.e.* to cancel and recover for the crown] all crown grants of royal and kirk land in Scotland which had been made since 1540. This, hardly surprisingly, brought the Scottish landed classes to the point of rebellion. Charles responded typically by refusing to back down. The result was that not only was his policy a total failure, but the hostility of Scottish landowners to the crown rumbled on, with serious consequences when Charles turned his attention to Scotland again in the 1630s (see chapter 7).

Charles I and the Religious Problem

Equally ominous for the future were the early signs of Charles's religious views. From the beginning of his reign his attraction to anti-Calvinist divines was marked, probably because their stress on ceremonialism and 'the beauty of holiness' appealed to Charles's obsession with orderliness. The damaging consequences of this were not immediately apparent, but Charles's commitment to one ecclesiastical faction was eventually to prevent him from playing his father's role of a peacemaker-arbitrator in the English Church. Religion was to become a more seriously divisive political issue in English politics than it had been during the reign of James I.

Charles I and the Financial Problem

Finally, Charles's decision to enter major wars – first against Spain in 1625 and then against France in 1627 – meant that the crown's financial problems were bound to become more serious. As in the 1590s, so in the late 1620s it became obvious that the existing revenue system was not geared to satisfying the demands of wartime finance. This made it necessary to resort to emergency fiscal expedients that risked fuelling political fears about arbitrary government that had been awakened in the 1590s and kept alive by James's reliance on impositions during his reign.

For all these reasons, Charles's character and his political ineptitude were clearly causes of the political crisis of June 1628. What is less certain is how serious were the consequences of Charles's unsuitability as king. In the following brief sections it will be argued that they were more serious than they are often said to have been by those who ignore the way the king's policies raised constitutional and religious opposition to the court.

By splitting the period from Charles's accession (March 1625) to the passage of the Petition of Right (June 1628) into three chronological phases, it becomes possible to see how mistrust of Charles quickly became less characterised by narrow localism than by a deep, ideological commitment to parliament and the Protestant Church.

Ideological opposition to the war with Spain, 1625–6

Time chart

1625: January An army of 12,000 soldiers, led by a German mercenary, Count Mansfeld, on its way to fight in the Palatinate is reduced by starvation and disease to only 3,000 men

March Charles I is crowned king of Britain

May Charles I marries Henrietta Maria

June Charles I's first parliament meets. Asked for money to fight the Spanish, it only grants two subsidies and customs dues (tonnage and poundage) for one year (instead of for the king's life, as was customary)

July Richard Montague, an anti-Calvinist divine, appointed as royal chaplain

August Parliament meets in Oxford because of an outbreak of plague in London. MPs criticise Buckingham, causing the king to dissolve parliament

September Buckingham's expeditionary force to Cadiz is a dismal failure

1626: February Ecclesiastical conference at York House. Charles's second parliament meets and impeaches Buckingham

May Charles dissolves parliament to save Buckingham from impeachment

As can be seen from this time chart, the most notable feature of this period is the failure of Charles's first two parliaments to grant realistic wartime finance. Instead, MPs mounted a fierce campaign against Buckingham's conduct of the war. Why were parliamentarians so unenthusiastic for Charles's war against Spain when many of them had been pressing for war since 1621 and when many had joined with Charles and Buckingham in a pro-war alliance as late as 1624? Was this caused, as is sometimes alleged, merely by locally-minded MPs who were blinded to the realities of the cost of warfare and who were concerned to protect local pockets?

There were more serious reasons than that for MPs to be unenthusiastic for Charles's war. First, it was not the war that they had been promised by Charles and Buckingham in 1624 after the pair had returned from Madrid – that is, a war attacking the Spanish *at sea*. Instead Charles now seemed intent on fighting a *land* war in Europe.

Second, as a result of the Anglo-French marriage alliance made in 1624,

Huguenots

Huguenots were French Protestants, who had been given limited freedom of worship by the Edict of Nantes (1598). In 1685 Louis XIV revoked [*i.e.* cancelled] the Edict.

Impeachment

Impeachment was a judicial procedure used by the House of Commons against an individual and the charges were then tried by the House of Lords. Before the impeachment of Bacon (1621), Cranfield (1624) and Buckingham (1626), this procedure had not been used since the fourteenth century. It continued to be used by parliament throughout the seventeenth century against unpopular king's ministers (notably Strafford in 1640–41 and Clarendon in 1667, see pages 118 and 240).

'New counsels'

'New counsels' was the phrase used frequently by Dudley Carleton and the king's other close advisers in the mid 1620s to describe those who were urging Charles I to rule without parliaments.

Charles began to suspend the recusancy laws against Catholics in England and to lend ships to the French king to use against his rebellious Protestant subjects, the **Huguenots**. To MPs this did not fit in with their idea of a war that would be a godly crusade against the Catholic Antichrist. Charles's excuses were reasonable: his diplomatic options were limited by the terms of the French alliance. Yet he failed to explain that to prominent parliamentarians. Consequently, to many MPs the war they were being asked to finance was the 'wrong' war.

Nearly as damning in their eyes, it was a war that quickly went wrong. To the disaster of Count Mansfeld's expedition to the Palatinate was added Buckingham's humiliating expedition to Cadiz in September 1625, when more English soldiers and sailors died from the effects of poor food and cheap Spanish wine than enemy action. Not surprisingly, in the 1626 parliament MPs were more concerned to push through the **impeachment** of Buckingham than to vote money to be squandered in this way.

Buckingham's abuse of power was the main focus of MPs' disenchantment by June 1626. But already there were signs that behind it lay religious and constitutional concerns. In February 1626, at the York House Conference (a debate between representatives of all factions within the Church), to the dismay of Calvinist leaders like Archbishop Abbot, Buckingham and Charles demonstrated their partisan ecclesiastical position by supporting the beliefs of an anti-Calvinist divine, Richard Montague, who was appointed one of the king's chaplains.

Not only did this seem an alarming drift towards Catholicism at court, but some of Charles's actions appeared to suggest that he was also considering adopting absolutist policies. He took steps to prevent the re-election of MPs who had criticised royal policies in the 1625 parliament. Even more worrying for parliamentarians were the speeches of Charles's secretary of state, Dudley Carleton, in the 1626 parliament that threatened that, unless MPs became more cooperative, the king would turn to **'new counsels'**.

'In all Christian kingdoms you know that parliaments were in use anciently, by which their monarchs were governed in a most flourishing manner, until the monarchs began to know their own strength, and, seeing the turbulent spirit of their parliaments, at length they little by little began to stand upon their prerogatives, and at last overthrew the parliaments throughout Christendom, except here only with us.'

Dudley Carleton's speech in parliament, 12 May 1626 in J. P. Kenyon (ed.), *The Stuart Constitution: Documents and Commentary* (1986).

The threat to do away with English parliaments if MPs continued to oppose the king could hardly have been made more explicit.

Rule without parliaments, June 1626–March 1628

The principal effect of the period of non-parliamentary rule after June 1626 was to confirm the constitutional and religious fears that had surfaced during the parliaments of 1625 and 1626.

Time chart

1626: September The Privy Council decides to raise a forced loan, equivalent to five parliamentary subsidies. Lord Chief Justice Carew is dismissed for refusing to endorse the legality of the forced loan

1627: October England is now at war with France as well as Spain
Buckingham's expedition to the Isle of Ré, off La Rochelle, suffers an humiliating defeat
Archbishop Abbot is suspended for refusing to license a sermon defending the forced loan
November Five loan refusers ('the Five Knights') are imprisoned without trial

As war with France as well as Spain loomed and then became a reality, Charles's need for money became more desperate. Hence his decision to collect a **forced loan**. At least 70 per cent of the forced loan was paid. This success, however, should not obscure the widespread opposition both to the loan and to the use of martial law to enforce householders (largely in the southern counties of England) to feed soldiers and seamen bound for the wars. Loan refusers included many peers and their case, based on a principled commitment to parliamentary government, was put in contemporary pamphlets.

KEY TERM:

Forced loan

Forced loans to the government were periodically demanded from wealthy individuals by monarchs in the sixteenth and early seventeenth centuries. The forced loan that Charles I and the Privy Council decided to collect in September 1626 was different in that *all* people who normally paid parliamentary taxes were to contribute loans and the total sum to be collected was the equivalent of five parliamentary subsidies. The forced loan of 1626–7, therefore, was clearly an attempt to collect parliamentary taxation without parliament's approval.

> '*If this cause be not withstood, but take effect, we shalbe ourselves the instruments of our owne slavery and of the losse of the priviledge which we have hitherto enjoyed, that our goods cannot be taken from us without consent of Parliaments.*'
>
> A pamphlet called *To All English freeholders from a Well-Wisher of Theirs*, January 1627.

Ominously for Charles, some MPs also linked the threat of royal absolutism to Catholicism at court. Charles's suspension from office of Archbishop Abbot for refusing to license a sermon in defence of forced loans by an anti-Calvinist divine, Robert Sibthorpe, gave credence to what was to become one of the most powerful political slogans of the seventeenth century: the belief that Popery and Absolutism went together.

Parliament and the Petition of Right

It is not necessary to go into the complicated parliamentary politics of the first session of Charles's third parliament that culminated in the passage of the Petition of Right. Parliament met in March and Charles accepted the Petition in June 1628. The important points to stress are that the Petition was the culmination of many causes:

- mistrust of Charles's intention in the wars against Spain and France
- Buckingham's mishandling of the war
- the blocked channels of communication between court and country
- the development among some MPs of principles of commitment to parliaments and the rule of law.

What finally triggered the decision to draw up the Petition of Right was news that broke early in 1628 providing confirmation that Charles was endangering the rule of law. It became known that in the aftermath of the Case of the Five Knights (five loan refusers) Charles had illegally altered the ruling that had been made in that case.

What Attorney-General Robert Heath did (on Charles's orders) after the Case of the Five Knights

In November 1627 the judges of the Court of King's Bench ruled that in the *particular* case of these five loan refusers the king was right in not bringing them to trial, and the five men remained in prison.

After that ruling was made, however, Attorney-General Heath altered the legal record to show that the English monarchy had a *general* right to imprison people without trial. This had not been the intention of the King's Bench judges.

To many MPs what was at issue in 1628 was (as one of them, Benjamin Rudyerd, said) 'the crisis of parliaments'. Another, Dudley Digges, said: 'We are now upon this question whether the King may be above the law or the law above the king. It is our unhappiness but it is put upon us.'

These words of people at the time ought to warn students who want to understand why the Petition of Right was passed not to ignore the *ideological* beliefs of those who voted for it.

Tasks

Here are two extracts from prominent historians of the 1620s. Read them and then try to answer the questions that follow.

'If the Parliaments of the 1620s were not the scene of a power struggle between "government" and "opposition", if they were not polarised by ideological disputes ... why did they generate so much ill-will? There appear to be three important answers to this question. The first, and fundamental, reason is what Professor Aylmer has called the "functional breakdown" of English administration: the straining of the links between central and local government, which meant that the King was constantly unable to collect an adequate revenue. He was therefore forced to resort to methods of revenue collection which only increased the collectors' unpopularity. The second was the complex and rapid manoeuvring of the Duke of Buckingham ... The third reason, bred from the other two, is the pressure of war on the English local administration. Because the wars of the 1620s were so unsuccessful, it is too readily forgotten that they were seriously intended, and prepared for on such a scale as to create a severe administrative burden. It was this burden of war, imposed on an administration already in a state of functional breakdown by a Duke of Buckingham whose purposes, and even whose enemy, appeared unidentifiable, that brought relations between central and local government, and hence between Kings and Parliament, to the point of collapse. The crisis of 1626–8, like the crisis of 1640, was the result of England's administrative inability to fight a war.'

C. Russell, *Parliaments and English Politics 1621–9* (1979).

'The extent of this [ideological division] has been underplayed in some of the recent accounts of the period. In particular the marked stress on the need for consensus and harmony ... has been taken to imply an absence of division or concern with matters of principle. To judge by the loan this would be a mistake. It forced into the open a distinction between what Dr Sommerville [J. Sommerville, Politics and Ideology in England 1603–40, 1986] has identified as two separate and conflicting themes within the political thought of the early seventeenth century. One emphasised the absolute and unlimited extent of royal power, while the other stressed that this was bounded by common law and the law of nature. These themes were normally able to coexist because of the general desire for unity and the readiness of contemporaries to paper over their differences. However, when a crisis arose which touched on basic liberties, then inevitably the conflicts were brought to the surface; and in the circumstances of the loan they were exacerbated because they came to be identified with differing views of the nature of true religion.'

R. Cust, *The Forced Loan and English Politics 1626–8* (1987).

1 What are the main differences between Russell and Cust on the question of what caused the political troubles of the 1620s?

2 What are the main reasons put forward by **a** Russell and **b** Cust to explain the troubles?

3 Based on your knowledge of events in the 1620s which explanation of the political difficulties do you agree with?

4 Is it possible to construct an explanation for the crisis of 1626–8 that combines both Russell's and Cust's views?

Further reading

B. Coward, *The Stuart Age: A History of England 1603–1714* (Addison Wesley Longman, 2nd edn, 1994) pages 158–65, D. Hirst, *Authority and Conflict: England 1603–58* pages 136–59 (Arnold, 1985) and B. Quintrell, *Charles I 1629–40*, Seminar Studies in History (Addison Wesley Longman, 1993) have more detailed accounts of this period.

The leading exponent of the 'functional' explanation described in this chapter is: C. Russell, *Parliaments and English Politics 1621–9* (Oxford University Press, 1979). For a summary of some criticisms of it see the introduction to R. Cust and A. Hughes (eds), *Conflict in Early Stuart England* (Addison Wesley Longman, 1978).

C. Carlton, *Charles I* (Routledge, 1995) and P. Gregg, *King Charles I* (Dent, 1981) are readable biographies.

The details of Charles I's chicanery in the Case of the Five Knights can be found in: J. Guy, 'The origins of the Petition of Right reconsidered', *Historical Journal*, vol. 25 (1982).

The best detailed books on this period are: R. Cust, *The Forced Loan and English Politics, 1626–8* (Oxford University Press, 1987) L. Reeve, *Charles I and the Road to Personal Rule* (Cambridge University Press, 1989).

7 How serious was opposition to Charles I during the Personal Rule, 1629–40?

Time chart

1628: August Buckingham assassinated
December Appointment of Wentworth as president of the Council of the North

1629: 2 March Speaker of the Commons prevented from dissolving parliament until three resolutions are passed, condemning as traitors
- those who have promoted popery and Arminianism
- those who have advised the king to levy extra-parliamentary taxes
- merchants who have voluntarily paid customs dues

April War between England and France ended (Treaty of Suza)

1630: August Exchequer judges support the king's rights to levy knighthood fines
November Peace is made between England and Spain (Treaty of Madrid)

1631: January Books of Orders issued

1632: January Wentworth appointed lord deputy of Ireland

1633: June Charles crowned in Scotland and announces that a new prayer book is to be introduced there

1634: October Ship-money writs sent to maritime counties

1635: June Ship-money extended to inland counties
Medieval forest courts are revived

1636: March William Juxon, Bishop of London, appointed Lord Treasurer

1637: July Riots in St Giles Church, Edinburgh, against the prayer book

1638: February Scottish National Assembly issues a National Covenant abolishing the new prayer book
November Scottish National Assembly abolishes bishops, sparking war with England (First Bishops' War)

1639: June First Bishops' War ends with Truce of Berwick

September Wentworth returns from Ireland and advises recall of parliament

1640: January Wentworth created Earl of Strafford

April Short Parliament meets for a few weeks

August Second Bishops' War begins and Scots take Newcastle

October Second Bishops' War ends (Treaty of Ripon)

November First meeting of the Long Parliament

Between 1629 and 1640 Charles I ruled without calling parliaments. Hence these years are often known as 'the Personal Rule'. The history of the Personal Rule is the subject of much controversy among historians: some portraying it as a period when the opposition to the court, seen during the Petition of Right crisis, not only continued but grew in intensity; others claiming that it was a period that saw the transformation from crisis to political stability and harmony.

It is essential that you make up your own mind about this controversy and that you come to your own view about the period. The task at the end of this chapter will encourage you to do that. But first, you need to consider the nature of the primary and secondary sources for the Personal Rule and the problems that they pose all historians of this period. Here are some questions (in italics) that you should try to answer.

The problem of the primary sources

1 Since no parliaments met between 1629 and 1640, unlike the 1620s, historians of the Personal Rule are deprived of parliamentary records as evidence of contemporary political opinion.

How might this influence historians' views of the period?

How likely is it that lack of parliamentary records might give an illusion of political harmony?

2 Despite the lack of parliamentary proceedings, there are sources that can be used to assess political opinion in the 1630s. However, one problem these sources pose is a common one found by historians in all periods: the sources provide conflicting evidence, as do the following two examples:

KEY TERM:

Ship-money

Ship-money was a rate (*i.e.* the total sum of money to be raised was fixed in advance), *not* an old-style parliamentary tax, in which only the sums to be paid by individual taxpayers were fixed. It had been levied traditionally only on specified maritime counties or towns in emergencies to pay for naval defence. But in 1634 ship-money was levied on all maritime counties; and from 1635 five successive annual ship-money writs were issued to all counties of England and Wales. The amounts demanded were much higher than those collected by traditional parliamentary taxes.

a John Burghe's view of the political situation in England in 1637. [Burghe wrote this in October 1637 in one of his weekly letters to Viscount Scudamore, the English ambassador in Paris. He refers to **ship-money** which was a principal means Charles I used extensively in the 1630s to raise money.]

*'All things are at this instant here in that calmness that there is very little matter of novelty to write, for there appears no change or alteration either in court affairs, for all business goes undisturbedly in the strong current of the present time to which all men for the most part submit, and that effects this quietness. And although payments here are great (considering the people have not heretofore been accustomed unto them) yet they only breathe out a little discontented humour and lay down their purses, for I think that great tax of the **ship-money** is so well digested ... I suppose it will become perpetual; for indeed if men would consider the great levies of monies in foreign parts for the service of the state, these impositions would appear but little burdens.'*

(Quoted in K. Sharpe (ed.), 'The personal rule of Charles I', in H. Tomlinson (ed.), *Before the English Civil War* (1983).)

b Notes from the private papers of a Kent gentleman, Sir Roger Twysden. [These notes, made a few months earlier than the date of Burghe's letter, show a different attitude to ship-money. They record the reactions of some of Twysden's gentry friends to the news brought them by Sir Richard Weston at the assizes at Maidstone in February 1637 that Charles I had secured a declaration from leading judges that ship-money was legal.]

'When he came to speak of ship-money, the audience which had before hearkened but with ordinary attention did then ... listen with great diligence, and after the declaration [of the judges approving of ship-money] made I did ... see a kind of dejection in their very looks ... Many were persuaded this way would not last to raise money by. They did observe that ... the introducing of a new way had no greater enemy than the many inconveniences that might arise by putting it in execution. That this was full of many such, by giving the High Sheriff [whose job it was to collect ship-money] an unlimited power, from whom there was no appeal but the council board [i.e. the Privy Council], so full of trouble.'

(Quoted in K. Fincham (ed.), 'The judges' decision on ship-money in February 1637: the reaction of Kent', *Bulletin of the Institute of Historical Research*, vol. 67, 1984.)

How should historians deal with conflicting evidence like this?

What should historians take into account when considering to what extent individual expressions of political opinion are typical of generally-held views?

3 Another common problem posed by historical sources is the uncertainty about whether the reasons given by people for their actions are their real ones. The 1630s is no exception.

It was very common in the 1630s to object to ship-money on the grounds that, since there were no rules about how it was to be assessed and collected, the amounts individuals had to pay had been worked out unfairly. They did not object to ship-money on grounds of principle.

> When parliament met in 1640 MPs like Sir John Culpepper, MP for Kent and one of Charles I's principal advisers at the start of the Civil War in 1642, put other reasons why they objected to ship-money. This is part of Culpepper's speech on 9 November 1640.
>
> *'The next grievance is the ship-money: this cries aloud, I may say, I hope without offence; this strikes the first-born of every family, I mean our inheritance: if the laws give the king power in any danger of the kingdom, whereof he is judge, to impose what and when he pleases, we owe all that is left to the goodness of the king, not to the law.'*
>
> (J. Rushworth, *Historical Collections*, vol. 4.)

What considerations might lead you to accept or to doubt that contemporary explanations were genuine?

4 Another question historians often have to ask is whether people's actions are a good guide to their attitudes and motives. One example of this problem from the 1630s is the fact that between 1634 and 1638 over 90 per cent of ship-money was paid.

Are historians justified in using this fact as evidence that few people opposed the ship-money rate on grounds of principle?

5 Historians also use autobiographies and memoirs as source material. One such source from this period is Sir Edward Hyde's *The History of the Rebellion*. Like Culpepper, Hyde, after opposing the king in 1640–41, became one of Charles I's chief ministers during the Civil War. He also served both the king and then his son in exile in the late 1640s and 1650s. He became the Earl of Clarendon and Charles II's chief minister at the Restoration until he fell from power in 1667. He ended his life as an exile again on the continent, where he completed writing his memoirs.

An extract from *The History of the Rebellion* in which Hyde describes his assessment of what happened after the fierce political conflicts of the later 1620s.

'There quickly followed so excellent a composure throughout the whole kingdom that the like peace and plenty and universal tranquillity for ten years was never enjoyed by any nation.'

How much weight should be placed on accounts of the period written long after the event?

6 Historians of the 1630s might suffer from a lack of written sources. They have, though, a plentiful supply of visual sources, largely because Charles I was a major patron of architects and painters. He amassed a huge collection of paintings, some of which were dispersed during and after the Civil War. One that was not is the magnificent painting by Rubens, which Charles I commissioned in the mid 1630s for the ceiling of the newly-built Banqueting Hall in Whitehall. Part of it – 'The Reign of Solomon: the Golden Age of James I' – is reproduced on page 3. Its title tells us that the central figure is James I depicted as Solomon. He was an Old Testament king of Israel, who is so famous for making wise decisions in disputes between his subjects that we still praise people for having 'the judgement of Solomon'. The figure to the king's left (above the soldier holding a torch) with a helmet and shield is Minerva, the Roman goddess of war. The figures to the king's right are goddesses of peace and plenty. Beneath them is Mercury, the messenger of the gods.

Study the painting and ask yourself how useful to the historian of politics and religion in the 1630s are paintings like this one by Rubens.

Answer the following questions:

1 From your reading of chapter 5 do you think that James I would have approved of being portrayed as Solomon?

2 Why might Rubens have painted James/Solomon pointing to the goddesses on his right?

3 What is the view of monarchy that Rubens is trying to get across?

4 Is it reasonable to assume that the painting represents Charles I's view of monarchy as well?

The problem of the secondary sources

The main problem here is the great diversity of historical interpretations of the Personal Rule. Here are three examples:

The first is by an historian who believes that the failure of the Personal Rule was inevitable long before the disastrous outcome of Charles's policies in Scotland at the end of the decade.

> 'During the decade before the crash in 1640, a series of developments took place which may be regarded as precipitants of crisis, for they brought the collapse of governmental institutions from the realm of possibility to that of probability. The main emphasis must be placed upon the folly and intransigence of the government, its blind refusal to respond constructively to criticism, and its obstinate departure upon a collision course. Most contemporaries would have agreed that the opposition leaders had gone too far in 1629 in refusing the crown its traditional right to levy customs and in holding down the Speaker while they forced through some extravagantly worded resolutions of defiance. The Duke of Buckingham, whom many had come to view as the source of all evil in the nation, was now dead, and many hoped for reconciliation and a healing of the wounds. But the ruthless and uncompromising nature of the royal policies after 1629 steadily drove more and more of the silent majority into the arms of the opposition.'
>
> L. Stone, *The Causes of the English Revolution* (1972).

The second is by an historian who also portrays the Personal Rule as one in which mistrust of the court in the country (or at least in the part of it he studied, Essex) was strong.

KEY TERM:

Forest fines

These were levied by revived royal forest courts, which had not sat since the Middle Ages. The traditional royal forest boundaries were restored and all those who held property within them were found guilty of trespassing on the royal forests.

> 'The coincidence of severe economic depression with the suspension of Parliament made the taxpayers of Essex doubly resentful of royal exactions, and doubly suspicious of fiscal innovations [like knighthood fines – see page 89] ... But all these grievances were minor compared to the great fiscal schemes of the 1630s, **Forest Fines** and Ship-Money ... The combination of arbitrary taxation with ecclesiastical innovations magnified popular hostility to both, since tyranny and popery were so intimately connected in the minds of English Protestants ...'
>
> W. Hunt, *The Puritan Moment: the Coming of Revolution in an English County* (1983).

The third is a more recent interpretation of the Personal Rule as one characterised by reforming vigour and considerable success. This view has much in common with Hyde's assessment of the 1630s (quoted on page 83) as days of peace, relative prosperity and political stability, which was only brought to an end by the collapse of English rule in Scotland after 1638.

> 'After the unruly scene of 1629, the early 1630s were marked by calm and quiet at Court and throughout the country ... Peace brought the expansion of trade and the benefits of neutrality in a Europe at war ... The calm and peace continued. The ordinary budget was better balanced. Ship-money was generally paid despite the difficulties. Undoubtedly there were tensions and grievances: Charles's religious policy, framed to unite the realm in a common liturgy, divided the Church and alienated some of the gentry. But these tensions and grievances neither stymied government nor threatened revolt ... [In explaining the crisis of 1640] we come back to the Bishops' Wars [with Scotland in the later 1630s]. War undoubtedly provided the opportunity for the expression of discontents. But more significantly ... it created problems and grievances not in evidence before.'
>
> K. Sharp, 'The personal rule of Charles I' in H. Tomlinson (ed.), *Before the English Civil War* (1983).

Sharpe's view has by no means gained general acceptance; but neither has anyone else's. This means that you have an opportunity to form your own conclusions about the Personal Rule. Before attempting to do that, read the rest of this chapter which sets out an answer to one of the key historical questions about this period.

Cooperation with the crown

Given the problems posed by the available sources, there can be no 'correct' answer to the question at the head of this chapter. Therefore the argument that is presented here – that beneath the surface calm reflected by many of the historical sources there was growing opposition to the crown's policies during the Personal Rule – should not be treated as a definitive one. You should read it critically.

This argument will emphasise the main reasons why mistrust of the king and the court grew during the Personal Rule. Before looking at these, though, it is important to mention two reasons why the intensity and the scale of this mistrust should not be exaggerated.

1 The first is that the high level of opposition to the crown seen at the time of the passage of the Petition of Right in 1628 was not maintained for long. It did continue for a few more months, largely because Charles failed to convince many that his acceptance of the Petition was genuine. Despite the Petition, he continued to collect tonnage and poundage that had not been approved by parliament. He still also promoted anti-Calvinist divines who had approved the collection of forced loans. This caused the extraordinary events in the Commons on 2 March 1629, when three resolutions were passed that were highly critical of the king (see time chart on page 79).

However, that was the high water mark of opposition. After the dissolution of parliament in 1629 much happened to cause it to diminish. Not only were some conservative MPs horrified by the radical tactics used against the Speaker of the Commons on 2 March 1629, but Buckingham's assassination in August 1628 had removed a major cause of resentment of the court. During the next few months, too, another vital element that had produced the political tension of the later 1620s disappeared, when peace was made with France and Spain. Moreover, after the severe economic depression caused by harvest failures and plague outbreaks between 1629 and 1631, the country entered a period of relative prosperity and good harvests.

2 The second point that is sometimes ignored about this period is that there was much that the crown and its most powerful subjects had in common. In the first chapter of this book it was stressed that it is misleading to depict the course of English history since the Middle Ages as a constant struggle between the crown and its 'overmighty subjects' (see page 8). This remained true in the seventeenth century. Consequently, it is not surprising to find many of those who had been critical of the crown in the later 1620s rebuilding their links with the court very soon after the passage of the Petition of Right. A prominent example of someone who did so is **Thomas Wentworth**.

Wentworth's promotion to royal office in 1628 has sometimes been portrayed as an unprincipled act on his part. But no one at the time condemned it. Many men who had supported the Petition of Right followed Wentworth in returning to the normal path of cooperation with the crown in the early 1630s, most of them working assiduously as deputy lieutenants or JPs in their local communities.

The **Books of Orders** are the best example of this kind of cooperation in the 1630s. The idea for this reform of local government came from a privy councillor, the Earl of Manchester, and a Northamptonshire JP, his brother Lord Montague. There is no evidence that any JPs considered the

KEY TERM:

Books of Orders

The **Books of Orders** were printed books of instructions sent by the Privy Council to local magistrates. Like earlier ones, the Books of Orders of January 1631 were intended to deal with an economic crisis. But what was new about them was that (a) they gave comprehensive instructions about all areas of local government from poor relief to the maintenance of roads, and (b) they established administrative procedures for local authorities to send regular reports of their work to the Privy Council *even after the crisis was over*.

PROFILE: *Thomas Wentworth*

Wentworth was a wealthy Yorkshire gentleman. In the later 1620s he was a critic of the management of England's war in Europe and was out of favour with Buckingham (partly because his chief competitor for power in his native Yorkshire, Sir John Saville, was Buckingham's client). In May 1627 he was imprisoned for six weeks for refusing to pay the Forced Loan. Yet in 1628 he accepted appointment as president of the Council of the North, and from 1632 onwards he was the king's main official in the government of Ireland. In 1640 he was created Earl of Strafford. In the first session of the Long Parliament he was one of the prime targets of the parliamentary opposition to the king. He was executed in May 1641.

Books of Orders an undue interference by central government in local affairs. The Books reflected the shared aspirations of Charles I, his ministers and magistrates in towns and the countryside for good, effective local government.

Reasons why opposition to the crown grew

To carry much further this emphasis on the reforming vigour of Caroline government and cooperation between the crown and local governing elites would be to exaggerate the extent of political harmony during the Personal Rule and the government's success. There are two general reasons for taking this view.

1 Many of the long-term reforming plans discussed by Charles I and his councillors to bring order and uniformity in Church and state were pushed aside by urgent, short-term matters. Two of Charles's ministers, Wentworth and Laud, wrote to each other about their desire for **'thorough'**, but the Caroline government did not have a large enough bureaucracy to put these ambitious plans into effect.

KEY TERM:

'Thorough'

What Wentworth and Laud meant by this was fair and just paternalistic government, with corruption rooted out. Such hopes were too idealistic, given the day-to-day pressures of government at this time.

2 The second general reason for coming to a critical view of the government's success during the Personal Rule is that Charles I made most of the key decisions of government himself. 'The Personal Rule' is an apt label for this period. In the 1630s no minister had the influence on the king that Buckingham had wielded in the previous decade. William Laud (see profile on page 91) had a key role only in executing Charles's ecclesiastical policies. The man who might perhaps have had the strength of character to impose his views on the king, Thomas Wentworth, spent the 1630s away from the king, governing the North and Ireland.

Charles's character, therefore, greatly influenced the nature of the Personal Rule. One reflection of this is that the royal court became even more isolated from mainstream political opinion in the country than in the later 1620s. Gentry were ordered to return to their localities and Star Chamber proceedings were begun against those who refused to do so. Charles's court was no longer a 'point of contact' between the crown and many of his greater subjects. Worst still, to some the court seemed to be the centre of a popish plot, centred on Charles's wife, Henrietta Maria.

Charles I, Henrietta Maria and Popish Plot

The marriage of Charles and Henrietta Maria had been arranged by the Anglo-French Treaty of 1624. He was 24 and she was 15. The first four years of their marriage were stormy. On one occasion, in 1626, after a particularly violent argument, she threatened to return home to France. The change that took place in their relationship after Buckingham's death in 1628 was dramatic. There is no reason to doubt the truth of Henrietta Maria's later comment on her life in the 1630s: 'I was the happiest and most fortunate of queens, for not only had I every pleasure the heart could desire, I had a husband who adored me.' They remained in love until the end of their lives.

However, the public consequences of this private bliss were disastrous. It contributed to a growing suspicion that those responsible for the Popish Plot were not only to be found abroad as they had been earlier (see chapter 4), but were now also inside the English government. From outside the closed court what seemed to be happening was that the king was being dominated by a woman associated with the pro-Catholic clauses of the 1624 marriage treaty and who established Catholic chapels and a house of Capuchin monks in London. The vacuum at court caused by the exclusion of the king's 'natural' advisers seemed to be being filled by Catholics. This fear was confirmed by the break-up of the queen's alliance with Protestant courtiers, including future parliamentarians in the Civil War, like the earls of Northumberland and Holland, who had wanted a French alliance. From 1637 her association with a pro-Spanish faction at court was well known, as was the welcome given there to the papal agents, Gregorio Panzani and George Con.

Charles I and the Financial, Religious and British Problems

Charles's handling of the three major problems of government with which the early Stuarts had to contend also caused many of his subjects to view his government with increasing mistrust.

Financial policies

This mistrust is least obvious with regard to Charles's attempts to cope with the crown's long-standing financial problems. This is so because, judged by the amounts of money they raised, his financial expedients were fairly successful.

During the Personal Rule:

- revenue from non-parliamentary customs duties, impositions and monopolies rose from £273,000 to £425,000; £174, 284 was collected by **distraint of knighthood** from over 9,000 men.
- forest fines brought in new income
- over £800,000 of the £1,000,000 demanded in ship-money between 1634 and 1640 was paid; non-payment did not become a serious problem until 1639–40.

During the Personal Rule the king's annual income rose from £600,000 to nearly £900,000 per annum. However, the relative success of these measures in financial terms was achieved at a great political cost. The evidence for this statement is unfortunately not conclusive. Yet it is reasonable to assume that the constitutional disquiet at impositions voiced earlier in the century (see chapter 5) did not evaporate in the 1630s. Nor does it seem likely that sales of monopolies would have been any more acceptable than they had been earlier, especially when Charles blatantly sold them for financial and not commercial reasons. This became apparent in 1635, when Charles licensed a group of interloping merchants led by Sir William Courteen to trade within the area of the East India Company's monopoly.

What is more certain is that forest fines and ship-money caused much opposition among wealthy and powerful people. Some were fined huge sums in the forest courts (the Earl of Salisbury was fined £20,000 for his estates within the Rockingham Forest, for example). Even though the fines were sometimes reduced, they were a great grievance.

The clearest evidence that such grievances were caused partly by constitutional fears relates to ship-money. It is significant that many of those who had refused to pay forced loans in the 1620s on constitutional grounds also objected to ship-money. Moreover, in the Ship-Money Case of 1637–8 even some of the judges showed that they doubted the legality of the levy, doubts shared by at least some Kentish gentlemen (see the extract from Sir Roger Twysden's notebook on page 81). The most convincing evidence of the depth of opposition to ship-money is in the petitions to and speeches in the parliaments of 1640 (see Sir John Culpepper's speech on page 82). Surely these reflected sentiments that it had not been possible to voice earlier?

The Ship-Money Case

In November 1637 John Hampden was brought before the Court of Exchequer and in June 1638 was found guilty of non-payment of ship-money. Five of the twelve judges, however, refused to support this verdict.

Ecclesiastical policies: Laudianism

The biggest cause of opposition to Charles I during the Personal Rule was his attempt to impose religious uniformity on all his British kingdoms. As was seen in chapter 6, Charles was greatly attracted to what has been until now referred to in this book as 'anti-Calvinism' (see chapter 4). By the time of the Personal Rule the most important anti-Calvinist was **William Laud**, who was appointed Archbishop of Canterbury in 1633. Hence Laudianism is the term that will be used here for Charles's ecclesiastical policies.

Despite some recent attempts to argue otherwise (see the books and articles by Sharpe, Bernard and White in the reading list on page 93), Laudianism aroused violent hatred in England. Lord Brooke, a prominent Puritan, called Laudians *'excrementa mundi'* – 'the refuse of the world'. Harbottle Grimston, an MP in the Long Parliament, described Laud as 'the Sty of all the Pestilential filth, that hath infested the State and government of this Commonwealth'.

How can one account for these extreme reactions? The answer lies in another common contemporary description of Laudians as 'innovators'. The Laudians were felt to be making revolutionary changes in the Church and government for the following reasons:

■ Unlike James, Charles promoted and patronised them to the exclusion of all other factions within the Church.

PROFILE: *William Laud*

Laud (1573–1645) was the son of a Reading clothier. His career demonstrates that it was possible in this period for intelligent boys of fairly lowly origins to go to university and to rise to eminence in the Church. He became Archbishop of Canterbury in 1633. As with Buckingham, the extent to which Laud influenced Charles I is an open question. It is at least possible that the king would have adopted 'Laudian' policies without Laud. Nevertheless, Laud was widely seen as the architect of the king's ecclesiastical policies. He became, as a result, probably the most hated archbishop in English history. His arrest and impeachment in November 1640 by the Long Parliament is therefore not surprising. Unlike Wentworth, though, he did not pose a direct threat to the lives of the king's opponents. Although he was imprisoned in 1640, he was not executed until much later, in 1645.

- Since they preferred the doctrine of free will (*i.e.* that God's salvation was open to all and could be won by good works on earth) they represented a challenge to the predominance of the Calvinist theology of predestination (see key term on page 48) within the Church.

- Laudians shifted the emphasis of church services away from preaching and sermons towards the sacraments and ceremony. Laudians wanted ministers to wear elaborate vestments and images and stained-glass windows to be restored to churches.

- Laudians insisted that altars be re-sited in a central place in churches: at the east end, not in the nave. This often necessitated rearranging family pews, which caused great offence.

- Laudians wanted the clergy to play a much greater role in lay affairs (William Juxon, Bishop of London, the Lord Treasurer from 1635, was the first cleric to hold a major secular post since the Reformation). Laud also gave church courts the power to interfere in secular affairs.

For many, what these changes amounted to was an attempt to reverse the Reformation and to threaten the social and political power of the nobility and gentry.

British policies

Charles's aim, like his father's, was to bring England, Scotland and Ireland into greater uniformity. Unlike James, though, Charles pursued his aim without much political subtlety. In Scotland the result was armed resistance, the so-called Bishops' Wars. These forced Charles to recall parliament twice in 1640, providing a platform for his English critics. The consequences of Charles's British policies were disastrous in two other major respects.

1 The first is that Charles's policies united all the main sections of opinion in Ireland and Scotland against him. In Ireland, Wentworth's strong-arm methods brought together against him both Catholic **'Old English'** and Protestant **'New English'**. Similarly in Scotland, Charles's attempt to impose Laudianism there, by ordering the use of the new Prayer Book, united against him radical Presbyterians and moderates in an alliance of **Covenanters**.

2 The second disastrous consequence of Charles's policies in Scotland and Ireland was to strengthen the opposition he faced in England. Wentworth's policies in Ireland were seen in England as a foretaste of what might happen to them. Wentworth's large army in Ireland, too, provided a chilling threat of royal power that might be used against them rather the Irish. These were among the main reasons why, when the Long Parliament met in November 1640, the immediate priority of many MPs was to get rid of Wentworth (see pages 118–119).

Similarly, events in Scotland strengthened the determination of some in England to oppose Charles. What happened later (see page 133) showed that there was much on which English Protestants and Scottish Presbyterians disagreed. But by the later 1630s these differences were masked by a common hatred of Laudianism. This drove some of Charles's English opponents, including Lord Saye and Sele and John Pym, to begin secret, treasonable negotiations with Scottish Covenanters who shared their godly commitment.

Conclusion

All this supports the case for seeing the situation that faced Charles I at the end of the Personal Rule as a British crisis. This raises the intriguing question of whether there would have been a crisis in England without the impact of events in Ireland and Scotland. There is no doubt that events in all three kingdoms were interlinked in bringing about the collapse of the Personal Rule. But it is worth considering whether what Charles had done during the 1630s in England alone ensured that, whenever a parliament did eventually meet again, he would face a crisis that would be at least as serious as that which he had faced at the time of the Petition of Right.

Tasks

1 Write an essay on the following question:

What were the causes of the opposition faced by Charles I in 1640?

After reading this chapter, you will appreciate that this is an essay that is not as straightforward as it seems. Among the questions you will need to bear in mind are:

▨ Are the causes to be found mainly in relatively recent events in the later 1630s, or are they to be found mainly in what had happened much earlier?

▨ What is the relative importance of royal ecclesiastical and financial policies in bringing about opposition to the crown?

▨ Are the principal causes to be found in the interconnection of events in Britain or was this primarily an English crisis?

2 As a way of clarifying your ideas about this, before you write your essay, you might take part in a class debate on the last of these questions: was the crisis of 1640 essentially a British crisis? Divide into two groups:

Group A should develop the case that there would have been no crisis in England without the contribution of what happened in Scotland and Ireland.

Group B should develop the opposite case: that the main causes of the crisis of 1640 are to be found solely in England.

Further reading

B. Coward, *The Stuart Age: A History of England 1603–1714* (Addison Wesley Longman, 2nd edn, 1994) pages 165–82, D. Hirst, *Authority and Conflict: England 1603–58* pages 160–87 (Arnold, 1985) and B. Quintrell, *Charles I 1629–40*, Seminar Studies in History (Addison Wesley Longman, 1993), pages 45–91 – all develop further the themes of this chapter.

The main proponent of the opposite view of the Personal Rule to the one taken in this chapter is K. Sharpe. The most accessible of his interpretation is 'The personal rule of Charles I' in H. Tomlinson, (ed.), *Before the English Civil War* (Macmillan, 1983). The full version of it is in his book *The Personal Rule of Charles I* (Yale University Press, 1992).

G. Bernard, 'The Church of England c. 1529–1642', *History*, vol. 75 (1990) and P. White, 'The rise of Arminianism reconsidered', *Past and Present*, no. 101 (1983) [and in his book *Predestination, Policy and Polemic* (Cambridge University Press, 1982)] follow Sharpe in arguing that Charles's ecclesiastical policies were not new or controversial. Their target is N. Tyacke, 'Puritans, Arminians and counter-revolution' in C. Russell, (ed.), *The Origins of the English Civil War* (Macmillan, 1973) [and his book *Anti-Calvinists: the Rise of English Arminianism c. 1590–1640*, Seminar Studies in History (Addison Wesley Longman, 1994)] and A. Foster, 'Church policies in the 1630s' in R. Cust and A. Hughes (eds), *Conflict in Early Stuart England* (Addison Wesley Longman, 1989).

If you want to find out more about Scotland and Ireland, have a look at:
K. Brown, *Kingdom or Province? Scotland and the Regnal Union 1603–1715* (Macmillan, 1993)

T. Moody, F. Martin and F. Byrne (eds), *A New History of Ireland III: Early Modern Ireland 1534–1691* (Oxford University Press, 1976), pages 243–69.

For the interconnection between events in the British Isles, see: B. Bradshaw and J. Morrill (eds), *The British Problem, c. 1534–1707*, Problems in Focus (Macmillan, 1996).

8 The social and economic consequences of the Price Revolution

The last three chapters have been concerned with estimating why and how seriously the political stability of England was threatened during the first 40 years of the seventeenth century. This chapter assesses the impact of economic and social changes on the country in the same period. Was the political breakdown that had occurred by 1640 accompanied by serious social and economic strains and stresses?

The first part of this chapter examines the views of historians who argue that a major consequence of over a century of price inflation and population growth since the early sixteenth century was escalating poverty and social discontent in the England of James I and Charles I. The second part takes issue with this 'pessimistic' assessment, showing how it is possible to come to a more 'optimistic' conclusion about the prosperity and social stability of early Stuart England.

The pessimistic argument: a Malthusian crisis

The basic assumptions of the pessimistic argument are those developed by a late eighteenth-century clergyman, Thomas Malthus. He argued that at any time, if the population expands at such a rate that existing resources prove inadequate to support it, the growth in population will eventually be checked by outbreaks of famine and disease. Some historians believe that late sixteenth-century and early seventeenth-century England saw such a Malthusian crisis.

As was noted in chapter 2, the population of England and Wales had been rising since the early sixteenth century. Moreover, the period from the 1580s to the 1640s was punctuated by outbreaks of famine (notably in 1586–8, 1596–8, 1622–3 and 1647–9) and plague epidemics (especially in 1603 and 1625). It *could* be that this is evidence of over-population, of the inability of the English to produce enough food to feed themselves adequately by the early seventeenth century. Some local studies, like that by V. Skipp of the Forest of Arden in central England, have concluded that there took place 'a mild Malthusian check' in the second decade of the seventeenth century. P. Bowden goes even further, writing that the 1620s, 1630s and 1640s 'witnessed extreme hardship in England, and were probably the most terrible years through which the country has ever passed'.

Rising food prices and harvest failures

What *seems* to support this picture is the way that food prices throughout this period rose much more steeply than the prices of manufactured goods. This could have been caused by the demand for food outstripping supply. Just how seriously and frequently the harvest failed in early modern England has been demonstrated statistically by W. G. Hoskins (and by C. J. Harrison). Hoskins classified all English harvests between 1480 and 1759 on a six-point scale ('abundant', 'good', 'average', 'deficient', 'bad' and 'dearth') and concluded that 25 per cent of harvests in the period were 'deficient' and over 16 per cent were 'bad'. What made matters worse in the later sixteenth and early seventeenth centuries is that bad harvests were bunched together (the worst examples being between 1594 and 1597 and between 1646 and 1650). In these circumstances food (especially bread) prices soared, bringing nearer the threat of famine and death from starvation.

An industrial and commercial crisis

KEY TERM:

The pessimists have also found confirmation of their views in the history of the manufacture of woollen cloth, which was England's major commercial industry in the later sixteenth and early seventeenth centuries (see chapter 2). In 1550–51 the first of a cycle of major crises hit the industry. During the first decade of the seventeenth century the industry appears to have been fairly prosperous, probably because the ending of the war with Spain in 1604 and the truce in the revolt of the Netherlands in 1609 made it easier for English merchants to sell their cloth in northern Europe.

KEY TERM:

Cockayne Project

This was a scheme proposed to James I by a London merchant, Alderman William Cockayne, to ban the export of all unfinished woollen cloth by the Company of Merchant Adventurers and to establish a new monopolistic company that would finish and dye the cloth in England before it was exported. It was a disaster because the new company lacked the old company's commercial contacts in Europe. Nor did it have the technological know-how to dye cloth at a consistently high and uniform standard. Sales of cloth in Europe fell and in 1617 the Cockayne Project was abandoned.

But this was a temporary respite from the cycle of crises that continued in 1614–16, 1621–3 and 1640–42. The immediate causes of each crisis varied. The first was brought about by the unwise intervention of James I in the cloth trade in the **Cockayne Project**.

The immediate causes of the severe trade depression of the early 1620s were the Thirty Years' War, which disrupted the north European markets for English cloth, and currency debasement (see key term, page 19) carried out by some princes of north German and east European states, which raised the prices of imported goods, including English cloth. Yet all of these crises were symptomatic of more fundamental long-term

KEY TERM:

Tobacco

Tobacco was new to Europeans and met with some resistance when it was first brought to England. James I wrote a book called *A Counterblast Against Tobacco*, pointing out its dangers to health. Others condemned it for its association with radical groups, in much the same way that cannabis and some other drugs cause hostile reactions today. It was not until the later seventeenth century (see chapter 26) that this resistance was fully overcome and sales of tobacco in England (and Europe) rose rapidly.

problems facing the English woollen cloth industry. These included the development of foreign competition largely from the Dutch, together with a change in fashion throughout Europe that demanded lighter, more highly-coloured cloths than the traditional heavy English broadcloth.

The long-term decline of England's woollen cloth industry and trade to northern Europe in the century after 1550, the pessimists would argue, was not compensated for by the development of alternative overseas trading patterns. Sales of new varieties of lighter, coloured cloths – the New Draperies – did not make up for the decline in the export of broad-cloths. Nor were new trade routes to the Baltic, Mediterranean and Far East totally successful. English merchants faced damaging competition from the Dutch. This is illustrated by the early history of the English East India Company (founded in 1600), which was out-traded and out-fought by merchants of the Dutch East India Company in the battle for the valuable trade in pepper and spices in the Indonesian islands. In 1623 many English merchants were killed in a battle with the Dutch at Amboyna in the East Indies. Nor were the early efforts to found colonies in the Americas trouble-free. For example, the Virginia Company, founded in 1607 to run the first permanent English colony in America at Jamestown in Virginia, collapsed in 1624, suffering from a serious labour shortage in the colony and the troubles affecting its main cash crop, **tobacco**.

Social polarisation

What makes the overall situation even worse, argue the pessimists, is that efforts to cope with the growing demand for food from a rising population involved a high social cost. As was seen in chapter 2, one means of raising agricultural productivity was by increasing the average size of farms. Where this happened small farmers were squeezed out, especially in **'fielden'** or **'champion'** regions. The numbers of landless labourers also increased. In a situation of rising population the standards of living of labourers who were, it is argued, largely reliant on wages for their incomes, were bound to suffer. As the labour supply rose, **real wages** fell dramatically. Though money wages rose (between 1500 and 1640 typical daily wage rates of agricultural labourers rose from 4 pence [2p] to 1 shilling [5p] and those of building craftsmen from 6 pence [2½ p] to 1 shilling and 5 pence [7p]), they did not keep pace with inflation. Consequently in the second decade of the seventeenth century the real daily wage rates of farm labourers were 44 per cent and those of building craftsmen were 39 per cent of the level they had been in the later fifteenth century.

KEY TERMS:

'Fielden' or 'champion'

These were the terms used by contemporaries to describe communities whose economies were largely arable (*i.e.* producing grain and other field crops) and which developed close-knit social organisations, closely controlled by magistrates and the Church.

Real wages

Real wages are what can be bought with money wages.

According to this pessimistic interpretation of the period, then, the Price Revolution and population expansion brought a massive increase in poverty. It also widened the gap between the wealth of the rich and the poor. The rental incomes of large landowners rose rapidly as demands for tenancies boomed and large farmers profited from rising food prices. The result (in the words of K. Wrightson) was 'social polarisation' – that is, growing inequality in the distribution of wealth. This, it is assumed, was the source of mounting tensions within early seventeenth-century English society, illustrated by a rising crime rate, particularly crimes against property, and a rash of popular riots and disturbances, particularly directed against high food prices, grain shortages and agricultural enclosures.

The optimistic argument: was there a Malthusian crisis?

It is possible, however, to argue for a more optimistic view of the economic and social situation in early Stuart England by countering each of the arguments found in the last section.

What crisis?

First, there are reasons to doubt whether the Malthusian model fits early Stuart England. D. M. Palliser has argued convincingly that, looked at in a long perspective, the rise in population in the sixteenth and early seventeenth centuries was not excessively rapid or large. Recent estimates of the size of the English population in the thirteenth century suggest that it was higher than in the early seventeenth century. If this is so, then it follows that the population pressure on economic resources in the later period was less severe than is often assumed.

KEY TERM:

Subsistence crisis

This is the term historians use to describe situations in which large numbers of people died of starvation.

This, together with the success (albeit limited) that farmers had in increasing agricultural productivity by the means looked at in chapter 2, accounts for one of the most significant and well-supported features of the economy and society of early Stuart England. This is the fact that – in contrast to other countries at this time, including France, Scotland and Ireland – England saw no widespread **subsistence crises**. It is now certain that the examples of famine in early seventeenth-century England, in 1622–3 and 1647–9, were few and far between and that they largely occurred in poorer parts of the country, like Lancashire and Northumberland, or regions like Cumbria where marginal land had been taken into cultivation. The mid 1590s is the last time in English history when there was a major subsistence crisis that affected the *whole* country.

Manufacturing and commercial expansion

Secondly, in concentrating on the manufacture of woollen cloth, many historians have missed the proliferation of the manufacture of many other goods, apart from 'the New Draperies', in England at this time. One of J. Thirsk's many important contributions to the economic history of this period has been to bring to light a myriad of other industries in Elizabethan–early Stuart England, producing goods like buttons, nails, axes, stockings, shoes, saddles and countless other consumer products. Like woollen cloth these were all produced by the domestic system, but have been neglected because they were largely bought and used in England and therefore are not recorded in overseas customs accounts.

It is likely, too, that the above gloomy, cloth-centred picture of late Elizabethan and early Stuart overseas trade misrepresents the true state of affairs. The crisis in the affairs of the Company of Merchant Adventurers brought about by the Cockayne Project and the relative failure of the new trades to Virginia in tobacco (and also to the Caribbean in sugar) cannot be swept under the carpet. But they ought not to mask the profits that were made by merchants of the London Levant Company in trades like the import of fine Italian silks and Greek currants and the export of New Drapery cloths. Despite their problems in the eastern trades, merchants of the English East India Company also prospered, judging by their rise to prominence in the government of early Stuart London.

A more important but underemphasised, successful aspect of England's commerce at this time is internal trade, which has only recently been the subject of serious historical investigation. What has emerged, through the barrier of sparse sources, is a picture of busy markets in cities and towns, served by countless drovers, packhorse men, pedlars and ships plying round the English coast, unimpeded by internal tolls.

Social polarisation?

Moreover, the concentration on inland, rather than overseas, trade points to another major reason for doubting overly-pessimistic assessments of the economy and society of early Stuart England. This is the existence of a domestic market for overseas goods like currants and luxury cloths and for home-produced items like nails and buttons. The chance survival of the probate inventory of James Backhouse, a shopkeeper in Kirkby Lonsdale who died in 1578, indicates the range of goods that were available in this tiny village in Westmorland.

According to historian T. S. Willan, James Backhouse's shop sold

'almost every conceivable type of cloth in a wide range of colours: kersey, friezado, bays, mockado, borato, camlet, bustian, fustian, rash, buckram, sarsenet, cambric, lawn, linen, canvas and sackcloth. There were hose and nethersocks, gloves, hats of felt and of silk, taffeta and camlet, pins and needles, points and laces, laces of all types, "Skotishe bobin syllke", "Spaynish sylke", "London sylk", "Bridgis sylke", French garters and Coventry thread. In addition Backhouse stocked a complete range of groceries; all the dried fruits, the sugar and the spices were there. So, too, was the stationery "department" with its paper and books. The latter included primers, ABCs, grammars, psalms and catechisms, and Aesop, Terence and Virgil.'

T. S. Willan, *The Inland Trade: Studies in English Internal Trade in the 16th and 17th Centuries* (1976).

This should be a reminder to historians not to underestimate the diffusion of wealth in late sixteenth-century and early seventeenth-century England on which shops like that of James Backhouse depended.

There are other grounds for doubting whether 'social polarisation' had proceeded as far as some pessimistic historians have suggested. This is not to deny that poverty was widespread in early seventeenth-century England, or that the Price Revolution favoured some social groups at the expense of others. What seems likely, though, is that some contemporaries and historians have exaggerated the scale of poverty in this period and minimised the effects of means by which some people were cushioned from the worst effects of inflation. Contemporary attempts to calculate the scale of poverty may reflect a novel awareness of the problems posed by it rather than an increase in its scale. Poverty was probably not as widespread or rising as rapidly as some have maintained.

KEY TERM:

'Forest-pasture' regions

This is a term used to distinguish areas from 'fielden' or 'champion' districts (see page 96). In 'forest-pasture' regions economies were largely pastoral (dairying, cattle-rearing etc.) and communities more scattered in small hamlets than in 'champion' regions.

Not all small-scale farmers suffered a drastic drop in their standards of living in the later sixteenth and early seventeenth centuries. This is especially true of those living in **'forest-pasture' regions**. Moreover, these were the areas where small-scale farmers were able to supplement their incomes by taking on part-time employment, making cloth, stockings, wooden implements and so on. Social continuity, not change, is typical of many 'forest-pasture' regions like forest communities in the Forest of Arden or the New Forest, and pastoral areas like the 'cheese' country of Wiltshire, the south Lancashire Pennines and south Yorkshire moors, where there was a thriving 'dual economy' of farming and textile manufacturing or metal crafts.

Similarly, the picture of a universal decline in living standards of labourers in early Stuart England is too simplistic. So-called 'servants in husbandry' (see key term on page 30) had more secure lives than lifetime labourers who were hired on a daily basis and whose real wages fell. Yet many daily-wage labourers could cushion themselves from falls in wage rates by living and eating in the houses of their employers, by growing food on allotments, by supplementing their incomes by the wages paid to their wives and children (child labour long predated child employment in mines and factories of industrial Britain), and by part-time employment in rural industries.

Conclusion

When Britain was undergoing an often-painful transformation to industrialisation in the later eighteenth and early nineteenth centuries, Romantic poets like Oliver Goldsmith painted a picture in verse of a pre-industrial rural idyll.

> *'A time there was 'ere England's griefs began [i.e. industrialisation]*
> *When every rood of ground maintained its man.*
> *For them light labour gave its fruitful store,*
> *Just gave what life required and gave no more.'*
>
> Part of Oliver Goldsmith's poem 'The Deserted Village' (1770).

Historians need to guard against that kind of distortion. Life for many in early Stuart England was often a grim struggle for survival. Yet what this chapter has suggested is that some historians have followed some contemporaries in exaggerating the amount of poverty and social discontent that existed.

Task

'Why were there no popular rebellions in early Stuart England?'

A useful way of bringing together a lot of the economic and social themes that have been mentioned in chapters 2 and 3 and in this chapter is by considering this fascinating historical question. You could do this by writing an essay *or* by means of a class discussion on this question.

It is particularly fascinating because many people at the time believed that popular rebellions would happen one day. Given the great differences in the distribution of wealth at this time, many landed gentry feared that 'the many-headed monster' of the poor would inevitably soon rise against them in large-scale rebellions, as was happening in other parts of Europe at this time.

> *'There were few if any years, in the first half of the century at least, when there was not a popular rising somewhere in the French countryside. In towns, major violence was liable to occur at almost any time.'*
>
> D. Pennington, *Europe in the Seventeenth Century* (1989).

These were rebellions on a large scale and involving much violence. For example, the rising of the Nu-Pieds in Normandy in 1639, a great anti-tax peasant rebellion, produced an army said to have been 20,000 strong.

Why, then, did the fears of the propertied not come true; why did early Stuart England not see rebellions on the French scale?

Some of the features of the country mentioned already in this book should help you answer this question and some hints will follow shortly. First, there is a possible reason that has not been mentioned yet. This stems from the fact that riots (not rebellions) were common in early modern England. People frequently rioted when, for example, fields were enclosed or when grain was taken from their villages by merchants in times of scarcity to sell elsewhere. But such riots were small in scale and (surprisingly) the demands of the rioters were not radical but moderate. Food rioters, for example, rarely looted grain stores but instead often demanded that the laws against exporting grain and restricting the prices of grain in times of dearth should be put into effect.

In order to explain this, the historian E. P. Thompson has invented the phrase 'the moral economy of the English crowd' to describe the motivation of the rioters. He argues that rioters shared with people in authority a belief that there was a 'just' price for food and that there were customary regulations preventing merchants from taking and selling grain elsewhere in times of harvest failure. Studies of riots in early Stuart England support his picture of people rioting in order to ensure that regulations and the law were upheld; they did not want to rebel against the existing social and political order.

You should discuss whether beliefs in 'the moral economy' explain the absence of rebellions in early seventeenth-century England.

Here are some other questions (arising from features of early Stuart England that have already been described in this book) that might suggest to you some other explanations why people did not rebel in early Stuart England:

In what ways might the belief in the Divine Right of Kings (see chapter 1) have been a check on rebellion?

Is it likely that migration (which was common at this time – see chapter 3) would have acted as a kind of safety valve to defuse social tensions?

Would neighbourhood festivities and customs (see chapter 3) have been effective in maintaining communal solidarity? Note that some annual celebrations included 'role-reversal' (for example, when servants acted as masters for a day). Might these have strengthened the traditional social order for the rest of the year?

How convincing (and relevant to this question) do you find the arguments put in this chapter that wealth was not distributed as unequally as was once thought?

Why might it be important to note the fact that one reason for the crown's weak financial situation is that taxation was very low in early Stuart England compared with European countries like France?

You should also think about the effectiveness of the country's complex welfare system (including private charity and compulsory parochial poor rates and indoor and outdoor poor relief, that were enforced by parliamentary statute and royal order – see, for example, the Books of Orders in chapter 7). Did these help to provide a cushion against the worst effects of poverty and so to contain social tensions?

Further reading

B. Coward, *Social Change and Continuity in Early Modern England 1550–1750*, Seminar Studies in History (Addison Wesley Longman, 1988) and the economic and social history textbooks by D. C. Coleman and D. M. Palliser, listed at the end of chapter 2, are useful general books.

The most extreme version of the optimistic argument is D. M. Palliser, 'Tawney's century: brave new world or Malthusian trap?', *Economic History Review*, 2nd series, vol. 35 (1985).

A. L. Beier, 'Poverty and progress in early modern England' in A. L. Beier *et al.* (eds), *The First Modern Society* (Cambridge University Press, 1984) puts the opposite point of view.

The works referred to in this chapter that take a similar pessimistic line are:

P. Bowden's article in J. Thirsk (ed.), *The Agrarian History of England and Wales*, vol. IV 1500–1640 (Cambridge University Press, 1967)

V. Skipp, *Crisis and Development: an Ecological Case Study of the Forest of Arden 1570–1674* (Cambridge University Press, 1978).

So too does K. Wrightson in *English Society 1570–1680* (Hutchinson, 1982).

W. G. Hoskins's (and C. J. Harrison's) analysis of harvests in this period, referred to in this chapter, are summarised in A. G. R. Smith, *The Emergence of a Nation State* (Addison Wesley Longman, 1987).

The best source for the task is:

J. Walter and K. Wrightson, 'Dearth and the social order in early modern England', *Past and Present*, no. 71 (1976) [reprinted in P. Slack (ed.), *Rebellion, Popular Protest and the Social Order in Early Modern England* (Cambridge University Press, 1984)].

9 What were the causes of the English Civil War?

Historical controversy about the causes of the English Civil War

The English Civil War officially began on 22 August 1642, when Charles I ceremonially raised his standard at Nottingham. That has become so well-known by frequent references to it in books on this period, that the extra-ordinary nature of what was happening might be forgotten. The following event that took place in the small Dorset market town of Dorchester four days before that famous event in Nottingham should serve to remind us that we are dealing with a far from ordinary historical episode.

18 August 1642: Dorchester (Dorset)

'A Catholic priest, Hugh Green, who had been convicted at the county assizes of treason, was taken onto a scaffold in the town, where a large hostile crowd had gathered. On the scaffold Green refused to admit his guilt, which inflamed the crowd against him even more. They cheered as the executioner, the town's barber-surgeon, Matthew Barfoot, inflicted on Green the barbaric cruelties of hanging, drawing and quartering, which included cutting out the victim's entrails while he was still conscious. His heart was cut out and (according to a witness) "put upon a spear and showed to the people and so thrown into the fire". The mob then went out of control, swept along by a wave of anti-Catholic hysteria. After Green's body had been quartered and beheaded, some of the crowd got hold of Green's head and played football with it, before eventually putting sticks in the ears, nose and mouth.'

D. Underdown, *Fire From Heaven: Life in an English Town in the Seventeenth Century* (1992).

It is an incident that seems miles away from life in a twentieth-century English community, but the hatred of popery that swept through Dorchester on that summer day in 1642 is closely connected with why the Civil War began. At the same time as the unfortunate priest was being executed, the town authorities in Dorchester were busily taking steps to secure the military control of the town for parliament; in the nearby countryside others were taking equally urgent steps to arm themselves to fight for the king in a civil war that (as will be seen in a later chapter) was more violent, bloody and disastrous in its effects than has often been appreciated in the past.

The aim of this chapter is to start you thinking about the question of why English people should have begun to fight and kill each other in 1642. It is one which has perplexed historians from the seventeenth century down to the present day. The debate between historians on the causes of the English Civil War has been (and still is) as metaphorically bespattered with blood as any civil war battlefield. (For a recent example, see the exchange of views between John Adamson and Mark Kishlansky in the articles listed in the 'further reading' section at the end of this chapter.)

This chapter does not attempt to survey the 'causes of the Civil War' debate from its beginnings in the seventeenth century. It tries instead to make sense of recent contributions to it. The first two sections examine how 'revisionist' historians during the late 1970s and 1980s successfully demolished some older explanations that attempted to show that the Civil War was the inevitable result of *long-term developments* in the later sixteenth and early seventeenth centuries, and how they then attempted to shift the emphasis on to *short-term explanations* of the Civil War. The third section suggests that such revisionism can be carried too far. In that section it is argued that the determination of both Royalists and Parliamentarians to fight each other in 1642 was rooted, not only in short-term pressures arising out of immediate events in the few years before 1642, but also in conflicting ideas that were formed in the period well before 1640.

'Whigs', 'Marxists' and 'Revisionists'

'The search for the origins of the English Civil War', John Morrill has recently written, 'is the early modern historian's Holy Grail.' They remain tantalisingly out of reach and it would be a brave historian who today claimed that he or she had found them. This was not so before the mid 1970s. Many historians thought that they had found the origins in one of two types of long-term causes: 'Whig' and 'Marxist'.

'Whig' explanation of the English Civil War

The Whig interpretation of history originated in Victorian Britain and drew on Charles Darwin's theories of the evolution of mankind – 'the survival of the fittest' – in which mankind was depicted as progressing from an 'inferior', monkey-like creature to a 'superior', well-developed, rational and intelligent being. Whig historians of the later nineteenth and early twentieth centuries assumed that historical development was characterised by a similar inevitable progress towards superior forms of government. They also assumed that these were, in the main, those that practised parliamentary democracy and religious toleration.

When they applied these ideas to seventeenth-century history, the Civil War came to seem to Whig historians to be a key episode in the inevitable progress of Britain from medieval authoritarian monarchical government and religious persecution towards modern constitutional parliamentary monarchy and religious toleration. They also assumed that what brought about the Civil War were progressive political and religious forces that grew so powerful in the later sixteenth and early seventeenth centuries that they made conflict between crown and parliament inevitable.

The two main forces that were thought to have brought this about were the Rise of Parliament and the Rise of Puritanism. Parliament was portrayed as an increasingly aggressive institution that came into frequent conflict with the crown over parliamentary claims to have a greater say in government (see chapter 1). Puritanism was seen as the creed of revolutionaries who wanted not only to change the Church fundamentally but also to redistribute political power (see chapter 4). The inevitable, logical consequence of both these developments (argued Whig historians) was armed conflict between crown and parliament.

'Marxist' explanation of the English Civil War

Like the Whig explanation, this rests on long-term developments. The main difference is that it is *social and economic*, not political and religious, changes that are seen to hold the key to explaining the outbreak of the Civil War. In part at least, this reflected the attraction to a generation of historians who grew up from the 1930s to the 1950s of Karl Marx's idea that social and economic changes were the major determinants of religious and political developments.

Easily the most famous application of this idea to late sixteenth-century and seventeenth-century English history was R. H. Tawney's 'Rise of the Gentry' thesis. From 1941 onwards Tawney and others argued that the increasing wealth and size of a class of landowning gentry in the later sixteenth and early seventeenth centuries was bound to lead one day to a demand for constitutional change to enable the gentry to gain the political power they thought they deserved, given their improved economic wealth and social status. The Civil War came to be seen as a battle for political power in which a rising, progressive social group took on a conservative and reactionary ***ancien regime***.

KEY TERM:

Ancien regime

This was a term first used to describe the regime in France that was overthrown by the French Revolution. It is now used more generally to describe any regime that has been replaced by another.

In the 1950s and 1960s Tawney's thesis became the centre of one of the most celebrated historical debates of all time. Historians tore into each other in print with great ferocity. What shot holes in Tawney's 'Rise of the Gentry' idea was not that there was no rise of the gentry – it is now generally accepted that landed gentlemen were major beneficiaries of the Price Revolution of the sixteenth and early seventeenth centuries (see chapter 2) – but the discovery that in 1642 this prosperous social group split, some opting to fight for the king, some for parliament, and some refusing to commit themselves to either side. The Civil War did not begin as a social conflict between a feudal, reactionary regime and a class of revolutionary-minded, rising gentlemen.

'Revisionism'

By the mid 1970s this and other 'Marxist' explanations for the outbreak of the Civil War had few supporters among historians (the most notable exception is Christopher Hill, who maintained his commitment to an economic and social explanation of the Civil War). But 'Whig' explanations, especially the Rise of Parliament and of Puritanism, were still very influential. In the mid 1970s, however, a marked 'revisionist' reaction against them began, which continued throughout the 1980s.

There is a risk in labelling historians whose work was published in this period as a 'revisionist school', especially since many of them reject the label. Yet it is possible to see characteristics that distinguish their work from that of their predecessors and their successors during the 1990s.

KEY TERM:

Teleological history

Teleological history is written with the assumption that because events took place they were bound to do so.

The principal characteristic of the 'revisionist' explanation of the Civil War is its reaction against long-term 'Whig' and 'Marxist' explanations. Revisionists rejected **teleological history** and the use of hindsight. Instead they argued that historical periods should be looked at in their own right and not in order to look for 'the origins' of later developments. They argued that it was misleading to see the Civil War as an inevitable event. Earlier studies of the period before the Civil War, they believed, had been dominated by those searching for 'the origins' and so had produced distorted accounts of growing conflict between kings and parliaments.

Revisionists instead emphasised the large extent of shared assumptions uniting the crown and its powerful subjects represented in parliament. Some, principally C. Russell, went as far as denying that there were ideological divisions in the parliaments of James I and Charles I from 1604 to 1629. What conflicts there were, it was argued, originated in court factional disputes or in localist misunderstanding of national affairs. Moreover, some revisionists, notably K. Sharpe, portrayed the Personal Rule of the 1630s as a period of relative political calm and stability.

The principal conclusion reached by revisionist historians, therefore, was that the origins of the Civil War were to be found in a short period after the outbreak of Charles I's war with Scotland in the late 1630s and especially after the calling of the Short Parliament and Long Parliament in 1640. The main cause of the Civil War, they argued, was the breakdown of trust between king and parliamentarians between 1640 and 1642 in all three British kingdoms – in England, Ireland and Scotland.

As will be seen, not all of the revisionists' conclusions have met with widespread acceptance. But the revisionists have been successful in demolishing the major Whig and Marxist long-term explanations noted above. As was seen in previous chapters, Elizabethan–early Stuart parliamentary history for much of the period before 1625 does not fit easily into a preconceived framework of persistent confrontational clashes between crown and parliament. Chapter 4 explained why the Rise of Puritanism idea is hard to accept in the light of work by Collinson, Tyacke and others. Puritans did exist in Elizabethan–early Stuart England, but before 1625 these godly men and women found little difficulty in being members of the English Church and few of them showed any inclination to separate from it, and even fewer seemed to be dissatisfied with the status quo in the State. Indeed most of them were conservative upholders of the existing social and political order, especially since many of them were very frightened that it was threatened by the 'many-headed monster' of the poor.

Indeed one of the most surprising discoveries made by revisionist historians was that in 1640, if anyone was a revolutionary who was seeking to bring about innovations in Church and State, it was not MPs, godly Puritans or landed gentlemen but Charles I and his advisers. It was they who since 1625 had introduced new extra-parliamentary financial measures, like forced loans and ship-money, and who had attempted to put into effect Laudian innovations in the Church. This being the case, it gradually dawned on historians that perhaps the best way of describing the situation in 1640 was the reverse of what had once been the orthodox analysis: that the crisis of 1640 was brought about because a conservative-minded political nation was pushed into opposing the king by the anger it felt at the revolutionary changes being attempted by Charles I and his ministers, who by 1640 were politically isolated.

The validity of the revisionist emphasis

Looked at from the perspective of 1640 it is difficult to disagree with the conclusion that the Civil War was 'a surprising and unintended catastrophe'. As many revisionist historians showed, when the Long Parliament met in November 1640 a civil war was not possible, because the aims of the king's opponents were limited and no one envisaged fighting one. Even if they had done so, a civil war would not have been possible in 1640 because the king did not have enough support to wage one.

Yet in the 20 months after the first meeting of the Long Parliament the king's opponents had split. Some moved to a position of indecision and neutralism. Some not only remained committed opponents to the king but also had adopted radical measures that they had not even considered less than two years earlier, including waging war against the king; while others defected from the parliamentary cause and became firm supporters of Charles I.

Many explanations for these contrasting allegiances that produced the Civil War can be found in interrelated events in Britain *between 1640 and 1642*. To that extent the English Civil War was, in effect, 'a British Civil War'. It was 'a War of Three Kingdoms', which began, in part, as a result of *short-term* pressures which pushed people to make different choices by 1642. This will be demonstrated in the next chapter.

Were there, then, no long-term causes of the Civil War?

Since until 1640 many future parliamentarians and future Royalists in the Civil War had a great deal in common, some revisionist historians in the 1980s suggested that there were no long-term causes of the Civil War. Not only did future Royalists and parliamentarians share a common ideology (everyone was a Royalist before 1640) but even on the eve of the Civil War both sides claimed to be fighting for the same causes. Both parliamentarians and Royalists claimed to be fighting for the ancient constitution of king and parliament. Both said that they were intent on defending the true Protestant religion. How then could the Civil War be explained as a conflict between different ideas that had developed in the decades before 1642?

What follows is a suggestion that the answer lies in the fact that the similarities in language used by both sides masked crucial ideological differences between them and that these had developed in the decades before 1640.

The ideology of those who became Royalists

The first element in this was a belief that by 1642 the parliamentary leadership posed a much greater threat to the mixed constitution of king and parliament than did Charles I. To so-called 'constitutional Royalists', like

Sir Edward Hyde and the fourth Earl of Dorset, this was clear from the novel constitutional claims that parliament made in 1641–2. To others this was merely confirmation of a view they had held since the late 1620s: that there was a conspiracy by a few in parliament to undermine the ancient constitution. To people who felt like this, what attracted them to the monarch was a sense of honour and a tradition of service to the crown. This was certainly what led Sir Edmund Verney, a Buckinghamshire gentlemen, to be Charles I's standard bearer at the Battle of Edgehill in October 1642, where he was killed.

For many these considerations of 'constitutional Royalism' and of honour and duty to serve the monarch were inextricably interwoven with a second major ideological principle that drove them to fight for the king in 1642. This was an attachment to the Church as it had developed by 1625: a Church with bishops and with a liturgy centred around a Book of Common Prayer and traditional festivals like Easter and Christmas. For many the direction the Church had taken under Charles I had been abhorrent and in 1640 Laud was impeached and imprisoned by parliament with no opposition. Yet for those who became Royalists the Laudian experiment had not shaken their faith in the **'Jacobethan'** Church. This is partly to be explained in secular terms; as will be seen in the next chapter, many propertied people considered the traditional Church to be a safeguard against social disorder. But by 1640 many also supported the Church in the belief that as it had developed during the reigns of Elizabeth I and James I was now truly reformed and was worthy of being defended against those who wanted to abolish bishops, the Book of Common Prayer, Easter and Christmas. This is an ideology that was rooted in the past, in the slow but gradual acceptance in many English parishes by the later sixteenth and early seventeenth centuries of the reformed Church, which (as will be seen) was strong enough to resist legislative attempts in the 1640s to disrupt it. By 1642 some felt so strongly on this issue that they were willing to fight for it.

KEY TERM:

'Jacobethan'

This is a term, recently invented by the historian David Smith, to mean the English Church as it had developed under Elizabeth I and James I before the rise of Laudianism.

The ideology of those who became parliamentarians

There was an equally strong constitutional element in the beliefs that drove other people to fight for parliament in 1642. A useful phrase to describe this is 'constitutional parliamentarianism', a commitment to a mixed constitution of king and parliament but one that considered royal absolutism as the major threat to it. This was a fear shaped by what Charles I had done in the past, including his contempt for the law in the aftermath of the Five Knights Case (see page 76), his fiscal antiquarianism in the 1630s (see page 89), as well as his actions between 1640 and 1642 (see below). Parliamentarians were driven to fight in 1642 for parliamentary liberties and the rule of law, which the past as well as the present suggested were being threatened by the king.

What comes across much more strongly as a force driving people to fight for parliament is religious zeal of the type that contributed to the gruesome incident in Dorchester described at the beginning of this chapter. It is this zeal that helps to explain, for example, the otherwise surprising commitment to parliament of a social and political conservative like **Sir Simonds D'Ewes**.

PROFILE: *Sir Simonds D'Ewes*

Sir Simonds D'Ewes (1602–50) was a Suffolk MP, a lawyer and antiquarian. He is mainly remembered because his diary of parliamentary proceedings in the early 1640s is a major historical source for this period. What makes D'Ewes interesting in his own right is that his career hardly suggests that he possessed the radical fire to oppose the king as he eventually did during the Civil War. At difficult times in the months before the outbreak of civil war he acted in quite cowardly ways. When the parliamentary debate on the Grand Remonstrance on 22 November 1641 threatened to become violent, D'Ewes left the Commons with the feeble excuse that he had a bad cold. When the king brought soldiers to the Commons on 4 January 1642 attempting to arrest six leading parliamentarians, D'Ewes's courage again failed him and he went home to make his will. Why did D'Ewes not become a Royalist? What distinguished him from many who did was that he was firmly committed to the cause of 'further Reformation'.

Unlike many Royalists, many parliamentarians believed that the Reformation, far from being completed, had made very little progress. For godly men like D'Ewes, now was the time to achieve the true Reformation, to rid the Church of popish remnants and to begin the constructive work of spiritual reformation, by embarking on what became known as 'the reformation of manners'. This was designed to abolish drunkenness, swearing, fornication, adultery and all other sins.

In order to understand the desperate yearning of godly parliamentarians, like D'Ewes (and more prominent parliamentarians in 1642 like John Pym and Viscount Saye and Sele – see profile on page 117), you cannot start in 1640. You need to go back at least to the 1580s, when the first generation of post-Reformation children came of age and some sought to complete the Reformation their parents' generation had only just begun (see chapter 4). So far they had been signally unsuccessful. For many godly men and women who became parliamentarians in 1642, the great excitement of the 1640s was that they believed this was their chance to bring about the true godly reformation through parliament. This is one of the main sources of the vigour and drive of parliamentary activists at Westminster that pushed them into Civil War, as it did individuals in the provinces who emerged in the first few months as committed opponents of the king: Sir William Brereton in Cheshire, John Pyne in Somerset, Oliver Cromwell in East Anglia, Anthony Weldon in Kent and William Purefoy in Warwickshire.

Did these different aspirations make a civil war inevitable?

You must make up your own mind about this question. The view taken here is that these different attitudes to the constitution and Church that were shaped in the period before 1640 did *not* make a civil war inevitable.

As has been seen, the task of ruling Britain was far from easy in the early seventeenth century. Yet James I had coped with it with some, albeit limited, success, at least containing the fears that some had that the crown threatened the future both of parliaments and the reformed Church. Charles I was not able to match his father's achievement. By 1640 he had got himself into a position in which he was almost totally alienated from the political nation, which was deeply mistrustful of the constitutional and religious aims of the king and his closest advisers. Yet not even the king's most ardent critics were contemplating waging war against him in 1640. Moreover, since the king had so few supporters, there could not have been a civil war in 1640.

Therefore, a crucial part of the explanation for the outbreak of the Civil War in 1642 must be found in what happened between 1640 and 1642. As will be seen in the next chapter, during that period the actions and decisions of Charles I ensured that the different constitutional and religious attitudes that have just been examined became of major political importance for the first time.

This need not have happened. If Charles I had been as politically skilful as his father, then it is highly unlikely that it would have done.

Task: class discussion

This chapter has given you information on changing ideas about why the Civil War came about. This is a very big, and quite complicated, topic and it is worth going into in some detail.

Remembering that historians often 'advocate' a particular interpretation, you should divide into groups. Each group should take one possible 'cause', assemble the evidence in support of this factor, and then present its conclusions to the rest of the class. You should use this chapter as the starting-point, but you can use the works in the 'further reading' section, or any other material you know about, to give you extra information. Some material in the next chapter will also be useful. You might find it better to attempt this task after reading it.

When you have heard all the evidence, you should be able to come to an overall judgement about the relative importance of the various factors. To help get the debate going, each group should present the case for one possible 'cause'. For example, the Civil War came about because:

a Long-term constitutional changes were taking place, making conflict between the crown and parliamentarians inevitable.
b Long-term social changes weakened the position of the crown and increased that of wealthy landowners.
c Charles I was an unpopular monarch and his policies from 1629–40 were detested.
d Events in Scotland and Ireland between 1637 and 1642 caused the king and parliamentarians to be deeply mistrustful of each other.
e Religious differences between the king and many of his subjects and between different groups in society could not be resolved peacefully.

Further reading

R. C. Richardson, *The Debate on the English Revolution Revisited* (Methuen, 1988) is the best book on the historical debate on the causes of the English Civil War from the seventeenth century until the present day, including 'the storm over the gentry'.

A. Hughes, *The Causes of the English Civil War* (Macmillan, 1990) also examines various historical explanations, emphasising the importance of long-term factors.

C. Russell's book with the same title and published in the same year by Oxford University Press takes a very different approach to what caused the Civil War, stressing (a) the importance of what happened in Britain after 1637 and (b) Charles's inadequacy as a ruler.

A. Fletcher, *The Outbreak of the English Civil War* (Arnold, 1981) also stresses short-term factors.

The best explanation of why people became Royalists is David Smith, *Constitutional Royalism and the Search for Settlement c. 1640–49* (Cambridge University Press, 1994). [He explains his use of the word 'Jacobethan' in 'Catholic, Anglican or Puritan? Edward Sackville, 4th earl of Dorset, and the ambiguities of religion in early Stuart England', *Transactions of the Royal Historical Society*, 6th series, vol. 2 (1992).]

The best discussion of the religious zeal that drove people to fight for parliament in the Civil War is J. Morrill, 'The religious context of the English Civil War' in J. Morrill, (ed.), *The Nature of the English Revolution* (Addison Wesley Longman, 1993).

The vitriolic argument between Adamson and Kishlansky, referred to in this chapter, took place in the pages of the *Historical Journal*, vols 33 (1990) and 34 (1991) and of the *Journal of British Studies*, vol. 30 (1991).

10 For king or for parliament in 1642?

A popular view of the English Civil War is that it began in 1642 with a nation dividing into 'Roundheads' and 'Cavaliers'. That this is a misleading view has been demonstrated by recent research. Accordingly, the first section of this chapter looks at the extent to which, and the reasons why, some people did not commit themselves to either king or parliament in 1642.

The second section addresses the question of why in the summer of 1642 some English people (perhaps more than the recent emphasis on neutralism has suggested) did take the awesome decision to fight a war against their fellow countrymen. Here the emphasis will be on how the pressure of events between 1640 and 1642 throughout Britain opened up an unbridgeable gulf of distrust between the king and parliamentarians. It will be seen that the Civil War developed out of a question of trust in the hectic twenty-month period *after* the first meeting of the Long Parliament in November 1640: could Charles I be trusted to wield power or not? For some, what happened during that time greatly deepened their distrust of the king; while, for others, those events caused them to distrust parliamentarians more than the king. As a result, each side was forced by the fear of what the other might do to adopt more and more novel, radical tactics – culminating in the decision in 1642 to raise armies to defend themselves.

This chapter ends by returning to the important point made at the end of the last chapter. It is likely that people's differing answers to the question of trust in 1642 were determined largely by the differing religious and constitutional beliefs and aspirations they had formed *before* 1640.

Neutralism and non-commitment

'Oh sweet hart, I am nowe in a great strayght what to doe. Waulkeing this other morning at Westminster, Sir John Potts, with commissary Muttford, saluted me with a commission from the Lord of Warwicke, to take vpon me (by vertue of an Ordinance of Parliament) my company & command againe. I was surprised what to doe, whether to take or refuse.

> *Twas no place to dispute, so I tooke it. And desierd sometime to Advise vpon it. I had not received this many howers, but I met with a declaration point Blanck against it by the King ... I hould it good wisdome and security to keepe my companye as close to me as I can in these dangerous times, And to staye out of the way of my new masters till those first musterings be over ...'*
>
> Sir Thomas Knyvett's letter to his wife, 18 May 1642 in J. Morrill (ed.), *The Revolt of the Provinces* (1980).

This is part of a letter written in London by a Norfolk gentlemen to his wife at home. You are bound to find the language in it difficult. Knyvett's poor spelling (which is typical of this period) does not help, but if you read the letter carefully you will see what he is telling his wife. The letter is justly famous for the way that it lays bare Knyvett's anguish about whether he should obey the orders of king or of parliament to raise soldiers in his locality. Knyvett was expressing the view of many people in England in the spring of 1642 as relations between king and parliamentarians deteriorated and both began issuing orders to raise troops, parliament by authority of the **Militia Ordinance** and the king by **commissions of array**.

Passive neutralism

Knyvett's reaction is a typical illustration of the first of two major types of non-commitment in the months just before and just after the outbreak of the Civil War in August 1642. 'Passive neutralism' is a useful term to describe those who tried to remain uncommitted mainly by doing nothing one way or the other. Few, though, were able to sit on the fence for long. The presence of an army near their homes forced some to contribute men, money, horses and provisions to it. That this was hardly a sign of enthusiastic commitment was seen when such people also 'supported' the army of the other side when the military balance of power in their area changed. In a much fought-over county like Somerset, for example, local gentlemen appeared as 'Royalists' or 'Parliamentarians' in turn. They are more accurately described as 'passive neutrals' as they drifted with the tide, supporting the side that was temporarily the most powerful in their locality.

Active neutralism

Others went further in their non-commitment by adopting a more active neutralist stance. One example of this kind of active neutralism is the 'Treaty of Bunbury', which committed the Cheshire gentlemen who signed it to securing the demilitarisation of the county.

KEY TERMS:

Militia Ordinance

This was passed by parliament in March 1642 without receiving the royal assent. It appointed lord lieutenants and deputy lieutenants, who were to control the militia, thereby challenging the crown's control of the armed forces of the country.

Commissions of array

Charles I responded to parliament's claim in the Militia Ordinance by issuing these commissions, ordering those who received them to raise troops. Such commissions, based solely on the authority of the crown, had not been issued since the early sixteenth century.

> '*It is agreed that there be an absolute cessation of arms from henceforth within this county, and no arms taken up to offend one another but by consent of the King and both Houses of Parliament, unless it be to resist forces brought into the county.*'
>
> The 'Treaty of Bunbury', Cheshire, 23 December 1642.

Another example is the decision made in Staffordshire a few weeks after the start of the war by some local gentry at the quarter sessions to raise a 'third force', that was intended to be used to keep all other armies out of the county.

Some reasons for neutralism

The reasons which led some people to attempt to remain aloof from the war are not hard to imagine. The devastating effects of warfare in Germany in the Thirty Years' War were well known. What also provided a persuasive argument for peace was what was happening nearer home. Between 1640 and 1642 there was another familiar bout of harvest failures and trade depression, that sparked off a wave of food and enclosure riots. No doubt fear of popular rebellion was in the mind of Sir John Hotham, a Yorkshire gentleman, as he vividly put the case for avoidance of a civil war, in which 'the necessitous people of the whole kingdom will presently rise in mighty numbers and whatsoever they pretend for at first, within a while they will set up for themselves to the utter ruin of the nobility and gentry of the kingdom'.

The extent of neutralism

A more difficult task for historians than explaining why people in 1642 were unwilling to commit themselves to a civil war, is that of assessing the extent of genuine neutralism at the start of the war. It is possible that some historians have mistakenly assumed that those who either expressed an unwillingness to take sides in 1642 or a preference for peace rather than for war were deeply committed to non-commitment in the war. That this is not so is seen by the two cases quoted above. Whatever Knyvett's professions of neutrality, his later actions showed his inclinations were to the Royalist side; while Hotham became a committed parliamentarian at the start of the war. It may also be that many of the so-called 'pacification treaties' of 1642 (examples have been found in 22 English counties) were short-term truces made with the intention of providing a breathing space while preparations were made for war.

The presence of neutralism in England at the start of the war has been well-documented in chapter 1 of John Morrill's excellent book, *The Revolt of the Provinces*. Many local studies have also shown – whether in towns or villages, in East Anglia or the North-West – communities dividing into parliamentary and Royalist activists and neutrals. What is worth considering, though, is whether the numbers of activists were greater than the recent emphasis on neutralism in 1642 suggests. It is to the fascinating question of why people chose to support one side or the other in the Civil War that we now turn.

Commitment: for king and for parliament

The best starting-point is the fact that by the first meeting of the Long Parliament in November 1640 most members of the political nation in Britain were united against the policies that Charles I had been pursuing during his Personal Rule. No one, though, as far as one can see, hated the king, his ministers or his policies strongly enough to want to oppose them by force. Nor, it is equally clear, did the king have supporters who were willing to defend him on the battlefield. Therefore, two questions have to be addressed in order to explain why less than two years later some people did commit themselves to a civil war:

1 Why did some of those who were critical of the king and his policies in November 1640 during the next few months begin to advocate more and more radical measures than they had ever previously considered, including waging war against the king?

2 Why did others, who had also been hostile to Charles in 1640, subsequently abandon the parliamentary cause and gradually become such firm supporters of the king that they were willing to fight for him against parliament?

Part of the answers to these two questions can be found in the sequence of events between November 1640 and August 1642 (see time chart below). These events, as will be seen in the following sections, produced dramatically different views about who could or could not be trusted.

Time chart

1640: November The Long Parliament meets
December London Root and Branch Petition demanding abolition of bishops is presented to parliament

1641: February Triennial Act passed
March–April Trial of Strafford collapses

1641: May Rumours are spread of army plots against parliament. Parliament orders every adult male to swear a protestation oath of allegiance to the parliamentary cause

Strafford executed after passage of an Attainder Act (see key term, page 119)

Parliament passes Act making its dissolution without its own consent illegal

July Parliament passes acts abolishing the courts of Star Chamber and High Commission

August Ship-money abolished by parliament

September The king in Scotland tries to imprison the Covenanter leaders ('The Incident')

November News of the Irish rebellion reaches London

Parliament claims the right to appoint the king's ministers

Grand Remonstrance passes Commons by 159 votes to 148

December Militia Bill introduced in the Commons

1642: January King unsuccessfully attempts to arrest parliamentary leaders and leaves London

February Act excluding bishops from the Lords is passed

March Militia Ordinance declared law even though it does not get the royal assent

June King begins to issue commissions of array

The Nineteen Propositions are sent to the king

August King at Nottingham declares war on the parliamentarians

The question of trust: parliamentarianism

PROFILE: *The parliamentary leaders in 1640–41*

The best known of these is **John Pym** (1584–1643), who had been an ardent critic of Charles I's ecclesiastical policies in the later 1620s. During the 1630s his fears of a popish plot to re-establish Catholicism and establish a tyrannical government became stronger and he worked with the Scottish Covenanters in 1639 and 1640 to secure the recall of parliament. He was the foremost opponent of Charles I in the Long Parliament until his death in December 1643. However, he was closely allied with others. In the Commons his principal allies were **Oliver St John** and **John Hampden**. In the Lords he cooperated with peers, notably **Viscount Saye and Sele** and the **Earl of Warwick**, with whom he had been connected in colonising ventures (like the Providence Island and Saybrook Companies) in the 1630s.

What bound this group together was a firm belief that those who were promoting a popish plot were the king's chief ministers. For them, therefore, the key political problem in 1640 was to find means of removing these 'evil councillors' and of ensuring that the king would never again be able to return to the policies they had advised him to follow. One of the major themes that runs through the complicated events summarised in the time chart is their failure, short of going to war against the king, to find means of achieving both these aims. Instead, what happened intensified their distrust of Charles I and their belief that there was a popish plot at court aimed at destroying parliaments and Protestantism in Britain. This can be seen by dividing the 1640–42 period into two:

- November 1640 to May 1641
- June 1641 to August 1642.

November 1640–May 1641: continuing mistrust of the king

During this period the parliamentary leadership followed *a three-fold strategy*. Each element of it failed to achieve its aims.

1 A legislative programme of parliamentary statutes making illegal most of Charles's financial and ecclesiastical policies. The time chart shows how this programme was carried out, as well as the passage of two important acts (the Triennial Act and the Act against dissolving the Long Parliament without its own consent), aimed at safeguarding the future of parliaments. To people who had witnessed Charles I's cynical disregard for the Petition of Right just over a decade earlier, the king's acceptance of these statutes was no guarantee that he would keep his word. It is likely that the parliamentary leadership placed more hope on the second and third parts of their strategy.

2 The second was to remove Charles's major ministers and the judges who had approved the king's right to collect ship-money. Again, the time chart shows that this was done. Like the first part of their strategy, this one also raised difficulties for the parliamentary leaders.

This became clear when they tried to get rid of Strafford. This was achieved at a great political cost. At his trial Strafford was able to tear to shreds the prosecution case that he was guilty of treason, by scornfully questioning how a man who had the support of the king could be guilty of the crime of treason against him. This placed the parliamentary managers of the case against Strafford in a great dilemma: the legal case against Strafford had collapsed but they felt they had to secure his death. Not only was he someone who had manipulated Irish parliaments and who might do the same in England, but he had an Irish army that could be used to prosecute charges of treason against them for negotiating with Scottish Covenanters during the Bishops' Wars. Faced with the prospect of such a threat to their lives, they abandoned Strafford's trial and pushed through parliament an **Attainder Act**. As a result Strafford was executed, but only at the expense of alienating some former supporters who were horrified at this cynical use of a parliamentary statute.

3 Equally seriously, Strafford's death effectively destroyed the third part of the parliamentary leadership's strategy. This was to replace the king's 'evil councillors' by themselves in what became known as the 'bridge appointments scheme'. Not surprisingly, after Strafford's death no more was heard of the scheme. Charles and Henrietta Maria seem to have made little effort to hide their parts in plots by elements in the English army aimed at freeing Strafford from the Tower. Parliament responded by decreeing that a protestation oath should be taken by every adult male in England, indicating clearly that by May 1641 distrust of Charles I was still very great.

June 1641–August 1642: a British crisis

In this period, as in the late 1630s, the connections between events in the three British kingdoms are crucial parts of the explanation for the intensification of mistrust of the king. Parliamentarians were so fearful of Charles's visit to Scotland in the summer of 1641 that they sent a committee to follow him to report on his activities. What they saw, especially his attempt to arrest leading Covenanters ('the Incident'), more than confirmed these fears. When parliament re-assembled after the summer recess, its first action was to appoint a guard to defend its members against a similar attempted coup.

Far more important in raising distrust of Charles, however, was what happened in Ireland in the autumn of 1641. It is difficult to exaggerate the importance of **the Irish Rebellion** in this respect (see Figure 10.1).

In explaining this, what many *believed* was happening in Ireland is more relevant than what *actually* did happen. Many in England (as well as some of the Irish rebels) believed that the revolt had Charles's blessing. Many also interpreted the rebellion as part of the expected Catholic conspiracy against them. This is the reason why many MPs in the immediate aftermath of the news of the rebellion voted for both the radical measures that are summarised in the time chart and for the Grand Remonstrance, appealing for the support of people outside the traditional political nation.

[Picture I]   The Lord Blany forced to ride 14 miles without Bridle or Sadell to save his life. His Lady lodged in Strawe beeing allowed 2d [two pence] a day to releve her & her Children. Slew a kindsman of hers and hanged him up before her face 2 dayes telling her she must expect the same to terrifie her the moore.

[Picture K]   Mr Davenant and his Wife bound in their chaires Striped the 2 Eldest Children of 7 yeares old rosted upon spittes before their Parents faces Cutt their throte and after murdred him.

[Picture L]   Arthur Robinsons daughter 14 yeares old the Rebbels bound her armes a broad, deflowered her one after an other, tell they spoyled her then pulled the haire from her head and cutout her tongue that she might not tell of their Cruelty, but she declared it by writing.

[Picture M]   A Minister and his wife came to Dublin Jan[uary] 30 1641 left behinde him some goods with a supposed frend, sent for them but could not be delivered unlesse he or his Wife came for them. She came and presently they hanged her upe.

[Picture W]   A Woman mangled in so horred a manner that it was not possible shee should be knowne & after the Villaine washed his handes in her bloode, was taken by the Troopers adjudged to be hanged leaped of the lader & hanged Himselfe like a Bloodey Tiger.

[Picture X]   Companyes of the Rebells meeting with the English flyinge for their lives falling downe before them cryinge for mercy thrust theire [blank] into their childrens bellyes & threw them into the water.

[Picture Y]   George Forde hanged on a tree in his owne grownd cut his flesh a peaces, carying it up & downe saynge this is the flesh of one of the traitors against our Holy Father the Pope.

Figure 10.1 Irish massacre scenes, 1641

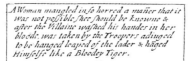

[Picture Z]   a Proclamation that nether English nor Irish should either sell or keepe in their houses any Powder upon the losse of goods & life nether any Armes whatsoever, exept with a license & then but five pound at most at a Shill[ing] ye pound.

As often before, however, Charles's own actions also served to widen the credibility gap between himself and many of his subjects. In the light of what had happened in Scotland, his attempt to arrest leading members of parliament on 4 January 1642 was, to say the least, ill advised. Even if it had succeeded, it is difficult to see any other outcome than the horror among MPs at Charles's use of force against the privileges of parliament.

The result was that (again as can be seen from the time chart) by early 1642 'the parliamentary cause' embraced far more radical demands than it had a year earlier. The parliamentary leaders now demanded that:

- parliament should approve the choice of the king's ministers
- parliament should control the army
- bishops should be excluded from parliament
- parliament had the right to legislate without the king.

Moreover, at varying times during the next few months, under the pressure of events, more and more MPs were converted to the view that only military defeat would force the king to concede these demands.

The question of trust: Royalism

Like the parliamentarians, those who were to become Royalists in 1642, like **Sir Edward Hyde**, developed a conspiracy theory to explain the course of events in the months leading up to the Civil War. The major difference, of course, was that the 'conspiracy' was one centred in parliament not at court.

There is no need to explain in the same detail as in the last section the ways in which the events of 1640–42 seemed to confirm that conspiracy theory. One has only to try to imagine the horrified reactions of wealthy, propertied people to the radical drift of events in those months. There were at least *four major reasons* why those events caused many to decide that they should put their trust in the king rather than in parliament.

1 The first is the fear that, if a settlement was not reached with the king, the result would be parliamentary absolutism and the subversion of the monarchy. The 'illegality' of the means used to get rid of Strafford, the radical constitutional demands made by parliament in 1641–2, and the fact that parliament from March 1642 began to legislate without the king, were all seen as proof of this.

2 The second was the belief that parliament's use in 1641–2 of extra-parliamentary popular pressure, via petitions and demonstrations, was an invitation to 'the many-headed monster' (the poor and unprivileged)

PROFILE: *Sir Edward Hyde*

Hyde, later Earl of Clarendon (1609–74), was a lawyer, who played a leading role against the king in 1640–41 by, for example, supporting the attainder of Strafford. From the end of 1641, however, he became one of Charles I's (and later Charles II's) advisers. His principal role before the Civil War was as draftsman of some of the king's proclamations, which succeeded in portraying Charles I as someone committed to the ancient constitution and the pre-Laudian Church. He left England with Prince Charles in 1646 and remained with the exiled royal court on the continent during the next decade and a half. In 1660 he helped draft the Declaration of Breda (see chapter 20) which contributed to his master's unconditional and peaceful restoration. At the Restoration he was rewarded by being made Earl of Clarendon and Lord Chancellor. He fell from power in 1667 (see chapter 22). In exile again, he completed his *History of the Rebellion*, which is one of the major historical sources for this period. This second period of exile was permanent and he died at Montpellier in 1674.

---

to begin a social revolution. This is one reason, for example, why Sir Edward Dering, a Kent MP, who had been enthusiastically behind the parliamentary leadership in 1640–41 and had even supported demands to abolish bishops in 1641, got cold feet. By the time of the Grand Remonstrance Dering was sneeringly accusing parliament of 'remonstrating downwards, telling stories to the people'. The outbreak of agrarian unrest in this period also made these fears seem more credible.

3 So too did the growth in the early 1640s of religious groups who began to challenge the principle of one uniform national church. What particularly sent chills of horror down the spines of the propertied were petitions (especially the London Root and Branch Petition in December 1640) which demanded the abolition of bishops. To many, religious diversity and the ending of the social control exercised by bishops was a sure recipe for social anarchy and the end of gentry privileges and dominance.

4 What also drove some people towards the king was hatred of the Scots. In a country in which national hostility to 'north Britons' was intense (see page 58) not everyone relished the prospect of a close association with a nation that had just defeated them in war. The Scottish commissioners who came south to negotiate a treaty at the end of that war became the focus of hatred by some in England, especially those who were already fearful of a threat to the episcopal Church. An inevitable consequence of a Scottish alliance would be (and later events in and after 1643 were to prove this) a move towards Presbyterianism and the abolition of bishops.

These were the fears that were played on with great skill by Charles's advisers from late 1641 onwards, principally three converts to the king's cause, Sir Edward Hyde, Lord Falkland and Sir John Culpepper. They produced clever Royalist propaganda in which Charles was presented as the firm upholder of the ancient constitution and the Protestant Church and a bulwark against a social revolution. In the following document, which was drafted by Falkland and Culpepper, they painted a chilling vision of what might happen if the king gave in to the radical demands of the parliamentarians.

> ### *Part of the King's Answer to the Nineteen Propositions, July 1642*
>
> The country would become one in which the common people would destroy 'all rights and properties, all distinctions of families and merits, and by this means this splendid and excellently distinguished form of government [would] end in a dark equal chaos of confusion, and long line of our many noble ancestors in a Jack Cade or a Wat Tyler' [leaders of popular rebellions in 1450 and 1381].

Parliamentarianism and Royalism and the question of principle

In analysing the ways in which the nation divided for and against the king in 1642 there is a danger of missing the fluidity and untidiness of the historical reality. Individuals made allegiances at different times and for many varying reasons; and some made no decision one way or the other. Yet as the normal political processes broke down in 1640 in the wake of events in Charles's three British kingdoms, people were pushed by the pressure of events either towards the king or parliament. The main intention of the last section was to demonstrate that there is much to be said for this account of people being pushed reluctantly in the months before 1642 towards a war they did not want.

Yet it is important to recognise that this is probably only a partial explanation of the outbreak of the English Civil War. Those who took sides in 1642 were not simply conservatives driven by fear to Royalism by the fear of parliament's constitutional innovations, religious radicalism and popular rebellion; and to parliamentarianism by fear and distrust of Charles I and a popish plot. It is likely that some were also motivated by the important religious and constitutional aspirations that were described at the end of the last chapter.

This chapter ends by encouraging you to consider the importance of ideas and beliefs in giving people courage and determination, not only to create the administrative machinery and the armies to fight a civil war, but also in some cases to join armies themselves to fight and kill their fellow countrymen. Were people, as well as being *pushed* by fear and distrust into fighting, also *pulled* towards making allegiances to king and to parliament by principles they believed in? It is highly likely that they were.

Tasks

Answer the following questions on the primary sources reproduced in this chapter.

1 Read the extracts from Sir Thomas Knyvett's letter to his wife, 18 May 1642, and the Treaty of Bunbury in Cheshire, December 1642.

    a What do these sources tell you about the attitudes of some people to the way the country was sliding into civil war at this time?

    b To what extent do these two sources reflect different reactions to the military conflict between the king and parliamentarians?

    c Do these sources provide sufficient information to come to a conclusion about (i) the reasons why and (ii) the extent to which people in 1642 did not commit themselves to either king or parliament in 1642?

    d Why is it difficult to be certain about how many people were neutral at the start of the Civil War?

    e What reasons that are not reflected in these sources can you think of to explain why some people did not commit themselves to one side or the other at the start of the Civil War?

2 Study the pictures of the Irish Rebellion on page 120 and the descriptions beside them. Then read the following extract from the autobiography of Richard Baxter, who was godly Puritan (as defined in chapter 4).

'But of all the rest there was nothing that with the people wrought so much as the Irish massacre and rebellion. The Irish Papists did, by an unexpected insurrection, rise all over Ireland at once ... Two hundred thousand persons they murdered ... Men, women and children were most cruelly used when they killed them, and the infants used like toads and vermin ... Multitudes of them were driven together into rivers, and cast over bridges and drowned ... In a word, scarce any history mentioneth the like barbarous cruelty as this was.'

N. H. Keeble (ed.), *The Autobiography of Richard Baxter* (1984).

a In what ways do these sources depict the Irish Rebellion in similar ways?

b How reliable do you think these sources are as evidence for what happened in Ireland at the start of the Irish Rebellion?

c What might make you think that these sources present an exaggerated view of the Irish Rebellion?

d How useful are these sources for historians who want to understand what happened in England at the end of 1641 and the beginning of 1642?

3 Read the following source, which is part of the king's proclamation, 10 December 1641, together with the extract from the King's Answer to the Nineteen Propositions, July 1642 (page 123). Although both were supposedly written by the king, it is now known that they were written by his advisers.

'His Majesty ... being sensible that the present division, separation and disorder about the worship and service of God, as it is established by the laws and statutes of this kingdom in the Church of England, tendeth to great distraction and confusion, and may endanger the subversion of the very essence and substance of the true religion; hath resolved for the preservation of unity and peace ... obedience to the laws and statutes ordained for the establishing of the true religion in this kingdom.'

S. R. Gardiner (ed.), *Constitutional Documents of the Puritan Revolution* (1906).

a What do these documents tell you about the reasons that might have decided some to become Royalists as the country slid into Civil War in 1641–2?

b Given that many people had felt that Charles's religious policies in the 1630s had produced 'great distraction and confusion', how effective do you think was the king's argument in his December 1641 proclamation?

Further reading

In addition to B. Coward, *The Stuart Age: A History of England 1603–1714* (Addison Wesley Longman, 2nd edn, 1996) pages 185–204 and D. Hirst, *Authority and Conflict* (Arnold, 1985) pages 188–220, see the following more specialised textbooks:

I. Roots, *The Great Rebellion 1640–60* (reprinted by Alan Sutton, 1996)

R. Ashton, *The English Civil War: Conservatism and Revolution 1603–40* (Weidenfeld and Nicolson, 1976), part 2

G. E. Aylmer, *Rebellion or Revolution England 1640–60* (Cambridge University Press, 1986)

J. Morrill (ed.), *The Impact of the English Civil War* (Collins and Brown, 1991).

For neutralism see:

J. Morrill, *The Revolt of the Provinces: Conservatives and Revolutionaries in the English Civil War* (Addison Wesley Longman, 1980), chapter 1.

The best detailed book on this period is:

A. Fletcher, *The Outbreak of the English Civil War* (Arnold, 1981).

11 The English Civil War, 1642–6

It is easy to assume that the parliamentarians' victory in the English Civil War was inevitable. Our knowledge of the overwhelming defeat of royalist forces at major battles in the later stages of the war (like Naseby in June 1645) can lead us to exaggerate the superiority of parliament's war organisation and its resources over those of the king throughout the war. It can also direct attention away from the fact that until 1645 neither side won a battle that proved decisive in winning the war and that for much of the period before 1645 a royalist, rather than a parliamentary, victory seemed the war's more likely outcome.

This chapter is largely about the Civil War from its start in August 1642 until the winter of 1644–5. Its aim is to counter explanations of the parliamentarians' eventual victory in the war that are based on the belief that this was inevitable from the beginning. It will be seen that until early in 1645 the similarities between the war efforts of both sides were more apparent than the differences between them. Both sides created new administrative, financial and military machinery that ensured that the war would be a total war that left few people unaffected. Yet by the winter of 1644–5 the war was deadlocked and its eventual outcome impossible to predict.

This chapter concludes with a class task: the problem of explaining why this situation was transformed by crushing parliamentary victories in 1645 and 1646 that were decisive in forcing the king to concede defeat in the Civil War by May 1646.

Why did neither side win the Civil War, August 1642–December 1644?

Time chart

1642: August Civil War officially starts as the king raises his standard at Nottingham
October Battle of Edgehill ends in a draw
November At Battle of Turnham Green the London trained bands halt the Royalist advance on London

1643: February–April Peace talks ('the Oxford treaty') break up

1643: **February–July** Royalists win military victories in Yorkshire, Lincolnshire and the south-west (battles of Roundway Down and Bristol)

February Parliamentary weekly assessment ordinance

May Parliamentary compulsory loan ordinance

July Parliamentary excise ordinance

Westminster Assembly of Divines begins to discuss a religious settlement

August Parliamentary impressment ordinance

Parliamentarians set up the Eastern Association

September **Solemn League and Covenant** is concluded between England and Scotland

December John Pym dies

1644: **July** Allied parliamentary–Scottish victory at Battle of Marston Moor

August Defeat of Earl of Essex's parliamentary army at Lostwithiel (Cornwall)

September Defeat of Covenanter army at Tippermuir (Scotland) by Montrose and Antrim

October Parliamentary forces led by Manchester and Cromwell fail to press home their advantage after the second Battle of Newbury

November Quarrel in parliament between Manchester (and Political Presbyterians) and Cromwell (and Political Independents)

December Earl of Essex, the Political Presbyterians and the Scots agree to re-open peace talks with the king

KEY TERM:

Solemn League and Covenant

This was the treaty of alliance against the king, made between the English parliamentarians and the Scottish Covenanters.

The character and course of the Civil War, 1642–4

The Civil War was not simply a war fought by a few large field armies. Both sides also had a multitude of small forces often attached to local garrisons. The parliamentarians had as many soldiers in these local armies and garrisons as they had in their three main field armies, commanded by the Earl of Essex, Sir William Waller, and the Earl of Manchester. As a result, the English Civil War did not consist simply of 'set-piece' battles, but also of skirmishes, guerrilla warfare and battles between troops vying for temporary local control. The military history of the war, therefore, is not as straightforward and clear as many accounts that focus only on the major field armies suggest. What is certain, though, is that before the beginning of 1645 neither side held a position of unchallenged military dominance for very long.

The key feature of the *first phase of the war* (August–December 1642), after the indecisive outcome of the first major battle of the war at Edgehill, was the parliamentarians' success in preventing the king's forces from capturing London, which was to be the power base of parliament throughout the war.

However, in the *next phase of the war* (*i.e.* for much of 1643) three of the king's major field armies (the Marquis of Hertford's, Prince Maurice's and Sir Ralph Hopton's in the south-west, the Earl of Newcastle's in the north-east, and the one led by the King in and around his headquarters at Oxford) won a series of remarkable victories that threatened to end in a combined attack on the parliamentary heartland in the south-east of England. The victories of Prince Rupert's royalist army in the midlands and north-west England early in 1644 made that threat seem even more serious.

What put an end to it was the entry into the war in January 1644 of the Scottish army, as a result of the Solemn League and Covenant (see key term opposite). This marked a *third phase in the war* which saw the end of the progress of Newcastle's army into eastern England and a major royalist defeat at the Battle of Marston Moor in July 1644.

That battle, however, was not the decisive military turning-point it has often been said to have been. Marston Moor was followed by a *fourth phase of the war* in the late summer and autumn of 1644, which saw humiliating defeats for all the major field armies. By the beginning of 1645 there was military deadlock.

Why was the war not won decisively and quickly one way or the other? This question is approached from two major directions:

■ a comparison of the war efforts of the two sides
■ an analysis of internal divisions that emerged among both the Royalists and their opponents.

The royalist and parliamentary war efforts, 1642–4

In this period neither side achieved a decisive advantage in the ways it organised its war effort. Both sides succeeded in effecting changes in the ways they raised money and soldiers. Changes in the ways they governed the areas under their control also marked radical departures from traditional methods. Ironically, on the parliamentarians' side, some aspects of

KEY TERMS:

'Assessment'

This new financial measure was first used by the parliamentarians in 1643 and by the Royalists slightly later (they called it 'a contribution'). Assessments were based on the ship-money principle that the money to be raised from each county was stated and so the yield was not dependent on individuals' assessments of their own incomes, as were traditional parliamentary subsidies.

Sequestration

Sequestration meant confiscating the estates and property of their opponents (both sides called them 'delinquents'). Usually both sides allowed the owners to recover their estates on payment of a fine (known as a 'composition'), the rate of which depended on the delinquency of the individual concerned.

Excise

This was a purchase tax on many necessities as well as luxuries.

Free quarter

Free quarter was the compulsory requisitioning by soldiers of horses, food and fuel from private farms and houses in return for a piece of paper promising repayment at a later date.

Impressment

Impressment is the seventeenth-century word for conscription, the compulsory enlistment of men in the army.

their war administration – high taxation, centralised rule, sanctioning of arbitrary imprisonment, for example – were not unlike those that had united many of them against the king by 1640. 'During the course of 1643 almost every clause of the Petition of Right was ignored,' wrote John Morrill. Yet this, though remarkable, is not surprising. As in most wars, civilian and military leaders were pushed by necessity, and especially by the fear of defeat, into taking steps none of them had previously foreseen. What also makes this less surprising than it might otherwise seem is that, as was seen in the last two chapters, parliamentarians (like Royalists) had gone to war to fight for 'a cause'. They were steeled to act in radical ways by their beliefs which had led them to fight in the first place. As a result, during the first few years of the war both sides organised themselves for war in remarkably similar ways.

Both produced similar *financial measures*. The linchpin was a weekly (later a monthly) tax on the areas under their control, called by the parliamentarians an **'assessment'** and by the Royalists a 'contribution'. Both sides raised money by **sequestration**. They also both extracted compulsory loans from wealthy people in exactly the same way that Charles I had done in the 1620s. The Royalists also followed the parliamentarians in collecting a new tax, called the **excise**. Both sides also allowed their troops to have rights of **free quarter**.

All of these new taxes (apart from the excise which was administered centrally) were assessed and collected by local committees of men on whom the king or the parliamentarians could rely. On the parliamentary side these county committees (as they came to be called) developed from the committees formed to administer the new financial measures. On the royalist side the county committees usually began as commissions of array that had been established in 1642 to organise the local militias for the king. But in both royalist and parliamentary areas these county committees were gradually given the wide administrative and judicial powers to run the localities that had traditionally been exercised by JPs.

Soon, too, both sides set about an equally radical *reconstruction of the military system*. **Impressment** was introduced in all the civil war armies, and eventually about 10 per cent of all adult males bore arms in the war. Both sides also formed regional associations of counties in an effort to organise military strategies that were not hindered by localist objections. The most important and successful on either side was the parliamentary **Eastern Association**. Its success was due to the fact that under the dynamic leadership from 1643 of the Earl of Manchester and his second-in-command, Oliver Cromwell, it was given powers to raise and pay a large army. As a result, until mid 1644 the army of the Eastern Association was the most efficient parliamentary army so far in the Civil War.

KEY TERM:

Eastern Association

This was one of a series of regional associations established by the parliamentarians and the king during the Civil War as a means of trying to force people in the localities to support a national war strategy. The **Eastern Association** was established by a parliamentary ordinance passed in December 1642, making the counties of Norfolk, Suffolk, Essex, Hertfordshire, Cambridgeshire and the Isle of Ely (and later also Lincolnshire and Huntingdonshire) into one administrative and military unit.

Yet this ought not obscure similar efforts that were made on the royalist side to organise regional military associations. The king himself, through his Council of War, administered the area around Oxford. Elsewhere in the early months of the war the king appointed six 'warlords' with the official title of lieutenant-general, five of whom were powerful local landowners, who were given wide powers to organise the war efforts in the areas under their control:

Lord Herbert in south-east Wales
the Earl of Carberry in south-west Wales
the Earl of Derby in Lancashire
the Earl of Newcastle in the other northern counties
the Marquis of Hertford in south-west England
Lord Capel, the only outsider, was appointed lieutenant-general of north and mid Wales.

Soon, however, Charles went even further in his efforts to improve the efficiency of his armies by replacing these territorial warlords with professional generals, principally his two nephews, the two sons of Elector Palatine Frederick, Princes Maurice and Rupert. They appointed as subordinates men who, like themselves, had military experience in the Thirty Years' War and who were not restrained by local loyalties from following national war strategies.

As a result of the development of roughly similar war efforts, the two sides were (as yet) more evenly balanced in their effectiveness than has often been assumed.

An equally important effect is that the Civil War had a major devastating impact on the economic and social life of the country. Older accounts of the Civil War often included a story of an astonished Yorkshire farmer, who, on being told in July 1644 to leave Marston Moor because of an impending battle there between king and parliament, exclaimed, 'What, be those two at it again!' It is impossible to believe that anyone could have been so ignorant in 1644, after nearly two years of impressment, high taxation, free quarter, as well as illegal **plundering** of horses and provisions by the armies of both sides. In much fought-over areas like Yorkshire local economies and national trade routes were badly disrupted. Mortality from the indirect (army-borne diseases like typhus, for example) and direct effects of the war may have hit a higher percentage of the adult male population than in both World Wars of the twentieth century. Even in areas well away from the fighting, like Kent, few could have been unaffected by the demands of county committees to support the war effort.

KEY TERM:

Plundering

The word '**plunder**' significantly first entered the English language in the 1640s. It means robbing others of goods or valuables, often using force or the threats of violence.

Not surprisingly, therefore, pressure for a negotiated peace grew between 1642 and 1644. The peace conference at Oxford ('The Oxford Treaty') early in 1643 collapsed, but towards the end of 1644 preliminary negotiations began for another peace conference, which eventually met at Uxbridge early the next year. The demands for peace were most strong among the propertied, but there are signs that they were widely shared. For example, peace petitions and demonstrations in London, often led by women, were common at this time.

By the end of 1644, with no sign of a decisive military victory in sight, it must have seemed as if the king, and not parliament, would be the eventual beneficiary of this situation.

Internal divisions among both Royalists and the king's opponents

A second major reason why no decisive victory occurred is that both sides were increasingly weakened by internal divisions.

> 'Upon the King's return to Oxford [after the military campaigns of 1643], there appeared nothing but dejection of mind, discontent, and secret mutiny; in the army, anger and jealousy amongst the officers, everyone accusing another of want of courage and conduct in the actions of the field; and they who were not of the army, blaming them all for their several failings and gross oversights.'
>
> From *Clarendon's History of the Rebellion* (ed. W. D. Macray, 1888).

The wranglings among the royalists are well-advertised in Sir Edward Hyde's *History of the Rebellion*. This account by a man who was a participant in the political intrigues around the king must be treated with some suspicion about its lack of objectivity. Yet it is likely that it captures the bitter enmities between those around the king. Civilians like Lord Digby hated the king's military advisers like Prince Rupert. There was constant conflict between those, like the queen and Digby, who pressed for an all-out war strategy aimed at an unconditional military victory and those, like Hyde and Lord Falkland, who advocated a limited war strategy combined with efforts to reach a political settlement. Too often Charles, rather than acting as an arbitrator, took sides in these factional disputes, to the detriment of a united royalist war effort.

The parliamentary war effort was, if anything, even more seriously disrupted by internal divisions. The best way of describing these divisions in

KEY TERMS:

War, peace and middle groups

These were not like modern organised political parties. They were loose groups of MPs distinguished largely by their different attitudes to the conduct of the war and to the need for parliamentary unity. The **peace group** (led by Denzil Holles and Philip Stapleton) advocated a defensive war strategy and immediate peace talks. **War group MPs** (e.g. Henry Vane Jr, Arthur Haselrige and Henry Marten) pressed for an offensive war strategy to crush the Royalists before peace talks began. The **middle group** (including John Pym, Oliver St John and Viscount Saye and Sele) were as anxious as the war group to prosecute the war effectively and took a leading part in reforming the war effort. But, unlike the war group, they did not want to break with the peace group. They sought to maintain parliamentary unity.

Presbyterianism

Presbyterianism at this time meant a national Church to which everyone should be forced to belong. Unlike the traditional Church, the Presbyterian Church had no bishops but a government of national and regional synods and local classes, run by deacons and elders. English Presbyterians wanted control of this Church to be in secular hands (this is known as an Erastian Church). But Scottish Presbyterians believed that the Kirk should be superior to the State and have a major say in secular affairs. These differences became clear at the Westminster Assembly of Divines, which from 1643 began to discuss a new religious settlement.

the early stages of the war is by using the terms **'war group'**, **'peace group'** and **'middle group'**.

A major effect of the Scottish alliance was to widen these existing divisions and to bring about new ones. Rather than being a major reason for parliament's victory in the Civil War (which is how it is often portrayed), the Scottish alliance nearly helped parliament to lose it. This is an argument that can be carried too far. The Scottish army did help to extinguish the military threat posed by Newcastle's army in the north in the first half of 1644. But thereafter the Scottish contribution to the war effort was slight and its impact was to weaken the parliamentary cause.

There are three reasons for coming to this conclusion:

1 The first is that for most of the war the Scottish Covenanters' army in England was not able to commit itself wholeheartedly to its task in England because of the constant threat from the anti-Covenanter, royalist forces of Montrose in Scotland, especially after 1 September 1644 when Montrose won a major battle at Tippermuir.

2 By this stage the Covenanters had also lost their enthusiasm for the war in England because huge divisions on religion appeared between themselves and their English allies. Both wanted a Presbyterian national Church, but it became apparent that the Scots and the English meant different things by **Presbyterianism**.

3 The third damaging effect of the Scottish alliance was the most serious of all. It brought about deep religious–political rifts in the ranks of the English parliamentarians. By the winter of 1644 all hopes of maintaining parliamentary unity had vanished. So too had the middle group. English politics were bitterly polarised between Political Independents and Political Presbyterians (see next page).

By the end of 1644 it would have taken amazing powers of foresight for anyone to have prophesied that the parliamentarians would have won the Civil War within less than two years. Neither side had achieved military superiority in the war and both sides were being torn apart by internal squabbles. This makes the problem of explaining the eventual victory of the parliamentarians an extremely fascinating one.

Within a few months after the eruption of the serious quarrels among the king's opponents the military deadlock of 1644 was ended. Unlike the Battle of Marston Moor, the Battle of Naseby in June 1645 did prove to be a major turning-point in the war. As can be seen from the time chart on page 134, it was followed by a series of major parliamentary victories.

Political Independents and Political Presbyterians

The major Political Independents were Oliver St John, Viscount Saye and Sele, Arthur Haselrige and Oliver Cromwell. They were, in the main, members of the former middle and war groups, who had been pushed closer together by:

■ mistrust of Scottish intentions to impose Scottish Presbyterianism on England by negotiations with the king

■ a desire to bring about a more tolerant Independent national Church than either the Scottish or English Presbyterians and to allow some diversity of Protestant religious opinions

■ a common aim to prosecute the war vigorously to prevent the establishment of an intolerant Presbyterian Church.

The main Political Presbyterians were the earls of Essex and Manchester, Denzil Holles and Philip Stapleton. They were, in the main, the members of the former peace group. They were distinguished from Political Independents by:

■ a willingness to ally with the Scots, with whom they worked closely from the end of 1644

■ support of an intolerant religious Presbyterian settlement, in order to prevent any moves towards religious liberty, which they believed would lead to the collapse of the social order

■ a desire for a defensive war strategy, combined with the conclusion of a rapid negotiated peace with the king.

Time chart

1644: December Self-Denying Ordinance proposed in parliament

1645: January–February Break-up of peace talks
February Parliament establishes the New Model Army
April Self-Denying Ordinance passed
June Battle of Naseby (parliamentary victory)
July Battle of Langport (parliamentary victory)
August Parliamentary ordinance establishes Presbyterianism in England
September New Model Army takes Bristol
Royalists are defeated at Rowton Heath (Cheshire)
Montrose is defeated at Philiphaugh in Scotland

1646: March Hopton surrenders to the New Model Army
May Charles leaves Oxford and gives himself up to the Scots
June The Royalists' surrender of Oxford marks the end of the Civil War

KEY TERMS:

Self-Denying Ordinance

By its terms all members of both houses of parliament were to resign their military commands, leaving parliament free to appoint new officers. After a great deal of discussion (see the time chart for the gap between the time the **Self-Denying Ordinance** was proposed and its eventual adoption), some MPs (like Oliver Cromwell) were re-appointed to army commands, but the majority (including the earls of Essex and Manchester) were not.

New Model Army Ordinance

This merged the three largest parliamentary armies – commanded by Manchester, Essex and Waller – into one 22,000-strong army. This consisted of 6,600 horses (in 11 cavalry regiments), 14,400 foot soldiers (in 12 infantry regiments) and one regiment of 1,000 dragoons (these were mounted infantrymen). Sir Thomas Fairfax was appointed as commander-in-chief of this New Model Army and Philip Skippon its major-general. Later Oliver Cromwell became its principal cavalry commander, as Lieutenant General of Horse.

Task

Why did the parliamentarians win the Civil War?

The class activity outlined below is designed to help you work out your own answers to this question. But first you need to know about a relevant episode that has not yet been dealt with: the major reorganisation of the parliamentary armies that took place early in 1645. This was brought about by two measures passed by parliament: the **Self-Denying Ordinance** and the **New Model Army Ordinance**. Provisions were made to pay the New Model Army more effectively than previous armies. These were not totally successful (as will be seen, the New Model Army's wage arrears became a major source of discontent after the war), but for the moment the New Model Army was better paid and better led than previous armies.

Was it also staffed by soldiers who were more committed to the parliamentary cause than ever before? Was the New Model Army 'new' in this respect as well? Since this is a question about which historians disagree, it has been left to the next chapter. You will need to refer to chapter 12 in order to make up your own mind about this important point.

Now you should begin to decide what are the reasons why the king lost the Civil War and which reasons are more important than others. There are two ways of looking at these reasons:

■ by focusing on military (and naval) factors

■ by focusing on developments off the battlefields.

Divide into two groups. The members of each group will have to do some preparatory work considering material in this book (and, if possible, in some of the other books listed below. Use the index to find relevant material.) Meet in groups to pool your knowledge.

Group A should work out a case that argues that parliament's eventual victory is largely explained by military factors. Group B should consider the case for arguing that the Civil War was won (and lost) off the battlefields.

Among the factors Group A should consider are:

— The contribution of parliament's control of the seas. In what ways might that have helped the parliamentary war effort?

— The contribution of the Scottish alliance. Is it possible to exaggerate the military contribution made by the Scottish army?

— The role of the New Model Army. Here there are two major matters to consider:

a Was the New Model Army as 'new' an army as its name implies? What new features did it have and did these help to make it a more effective army than previous ones? [You will need to refer to material in the next chapter when considering whether the officers and soldiers in the New Model Army were different from those in other armies.]

b Is it possible to exaggerate the New Model Army's military contribution to the outcome of the war at the expense of other armies? In addition to the Scottish army, the other principal parliamentary armies still in the field were the Northern Association Army led by Sydenham Poyntz and the Western Association Army led by Sir Edward Massey, together with regional armies commanded by local 'warlords', like Sir William Brereton in Cheshire.

Among the factors Group B should consider are:

— Were parliament's administrative and financial measures more systematic than those of the king? Were they put into effect more ruthlessly by parliamentary county committees and other officials than the Royalist measures?

— How important was parliament's possession of London throughout the war? What could London contribute in terms of men and money to the parliamentary war effort?

Further reading

Begin with one or more of the relevant sections from the following textbooks (the full titles have already been given in previous reading lists):

B. Coward, *The Stuart Age*

D. Hirst, *Authority and Conflict*

R. Ashton, *The English Civil War*

G. E. Aylmer, *Rebellion or Revolution*

See also M. Bennett, *The English Civil War*, Seminar Studies in History (Addison Wesley Longman, 1995).

There are two useful collections of essays:

J. Morrill (ed.), *The Impact of the English Civil War* (Collins and Brown, 1991)

J. Morrill (ed.), *Reactions to the English Civil War* (Macmillan, 1982).

Articles by C. Carlton and I. Gentles in Morrill (1991) and by Hutton in Morrill (1982) summarise the themes of important, detailed books on this topic:

C. Carlton, *Going to the Wars: the Experience of the British Civil Wars 1638–51* (Routledge, 1992)

I. Gentles, *The New Model Army* (Blackwell, 1992)

R. Hutton, *The Royalist War Effort* (Addison Wesley Longman, 1982).

12 Why did the New Model Army revolt in 1647?

Time chart

1646: **July** Parliament's peace terms (the Propositions of Newcastle) are sent to the king

September Earl of Essex dies

1647: **February** Parliament proposes to reduce the New Model Army in size and send it to Ireland. It votes that only Presbyterians should be officers in the army

March Parliament's 'Declaration of Dislike' condemns a moderate army petition as treasonable

March–May Parliamentary commissioners negotiate with the army at Saffron Walden (Essex)

April First election of agitators in the New Model Army

May Parliament's vote to disband the New Model Army with only enough money to pay it 8 weeks' wage arrears prompts the army to begin to march towards London

June Cornet Joyce's seizure of the king from his parliamentary guards is followed by army manifestos (The Solemn Engagement and The Declaration of the Army), setting out its political demands

Why was no settlement made?

The major historical question facing historians at the end of the Civil War – why was no settlement made between the king and the parliamentarians? – looks a simple one. In fact, it is very hard to answer largely because conditions in post-Civil War Britain seemed to make such a settlement inevitable. Dislike of heavy wartime taxation and of the rule of county committees, together with the fear of rebellion from below caused by a resurgence of economic depression (the harvest failed in 1646 and food prices rocketed), made a settlement seem very urgent to anyone with property. Gentry petitions to parliament against the 'arbitrary rule' of 'low-born' county committee men strengthened the political position of the more conservative parliamentarians, the Political Presbyterians (see page 134), who were pushing for a speedy settlement with the king. Nor was war-weariness and a desire to see a return to political and social normality confined to the very wealthy. The latter stages of the war

KEY TERM:

Clubmen

Clubmen were groups of farmers who armed themselves to try to bring the Civil War to an end. In 1645 and 1646 some Clubmen were very organised, raising large armies. Some even attacked the armies of both sides, trying to end the fighting. They were to be found largely in southern England and south Wales.

saw an extraordinary outburst of popular anti-war fervour in parts of southern England and Wales, the **Clubmen**. The country seemed ripe for settlement.

Yet, as can be seen from the time chart, the end of the Civil War saw not a settlement, but an intensification of the crisis which had gripped the country since 1640. The Civil War was followed by another burst of radical events that even the most ardent opponent of the king in 1640 could not have envisaged. This was marked in 1647 by the revolt of a politicised New Model Army.

This chapter examines the reasons why 1647 was a year, not of settlement, but of army revolt. There has been much historical debate about this topic. The first section examines the major ways in which older interpretations of the revolt of the New Model Army have been criticised in recent years. The second section explains how the emergence of the New Model Army as a political force and the dramatic consequences of that in 1647 can be re-interpreted in the light of this debate.

Views about the politicisation of the New Model Army

An older view

For a long time historians had little difficulty in explaining why the New Model Army became politicised in the later 1640s. This older explanation had three main features.

1 *An 'army of saints'* Firstly, it was thought that the circumstances in which the army was formed in 1645 ensured that it would be a powerful political, as well as military, force. The formation of the New Model Army was seen as a victory for the radical wing of the parliamentarians, the Political Independents, in the grim political in-fighting that characterised parliamentary politics in the winter of 1644–5 (see pages 133–4). The victorious Political Independents staffed the new army with officers chosen primarily for their military professionalism and their commitment to a godly reformation rather than their social origins. Most of the rank-and-file soldiers in the New Model Army were also thought to have been godly men, who had volunteered to fight for their cause on and off the battlefield. The New Model Army was, in short, 'an army of saints', that, having defeated the king's armies, was bound to take an active political role in order to ensure that the cause they believed in should be secured in the postwar settlement.

Agitators

Agitators were representatives elected by soldiers in the New Model Army in the spring of 1647 to communicate their views to the army's senior officers. They were called agitators because (as they said) their function was to agitate on behalf of their fellow soldiers. They first appeared in cavalry regiments, but soon agitators were elected throughout the New Model Army. For a time in 1647 (see the next chapter) agitators sat with officers in the New Model Army's General Council.

2 *An army dominated by Levellers*   The second explanation for the New Model Army's political activism seemed equally as persuasive. Few doubted that during the latter stages of the war, the army was infiltrated by London political radicals, known as Levellers, who gained a massive success in promoting their radical ideas among junior officers and rank-and-file soldiers. The election of **agitators**, was seen as proof of this injection into the New Model Army of Leveller political militancy.

3 *A republican army*   Thirdly, the New Model Army's political programme – set out in the documents it issued during the next few months – calling for political reform and religious toleration, was seen not only as the inevitable outcome of the army's religious zeal and Leveller political radicalism; it was also the beginning of a campaign that was bound very soon to demand the overthrow of the monarchy in Britain.

A newer view

In recent years the validity of each of these three features has been questioned, largely by an American historian, Mark Kishlansky.

1 *An army of saints?*   Kishlansky claimed that the New Model Army was not the outcome of a Political Independent victory over their Political Presbyterian opponents. In Kishlansky's interpretation, politics at Westminster in 1644–5 were characterised (using terms he drew from American political science) not by 'adversarial' but by 'consensus' politics. What brought about the major military organisation of 1645, Kishlansky argued, was a *common* desire among many parliamentarians for military reform. Godly MPs were united by a conviction that the defeat of their armies and the bickering among their generals in the autumn and winter of 1644 were caused by God's displeasure at their sinfulness in prolonging the war for their own self-advancement. So there developed a powerful movement among the majority of MPs to regain God's blessing, which they believed had won them great victories at Marston Moor and elsewhere. This would be achieved by ridding themselves of their military offices in a display of godly self-denial (hence the Self-Denying Ordinance – see previous chapter).

Kishlansky also pointed out that the army that was created at the same time by the New Model Army Ordinance was simply made up of regiments from the old parliamentary armies, previously led by Waller, Essex and Manchester. Like the old armies, it was staffed by many officers who had been promoted mainly because they were gentlemen and soldiers who had been conscripted. The only aspects that were new about the New Model Army, as Kishlansky saw it, was that under its new leaders it was better trained and led. Professionalism, not religious radicalism, accounted for its military victories at the end of the Civil War. There was little about the origins of the New Model Army that ensured that it would seek to emulate its military record in the world of postwar politics.

2 *The army and the Levellers*   The connections between the New Model Army and the Levellers were denied equally firmly by Kishlansky. He claimed that before the summer of 1647 London radicals were too few in number and too disorganised to infiltrate the New Model Army. Their concerns, set out in documents like the *Remonstrance of Many Thousand Citizens* (1646) and the *Large Petition* (March 1647), although similar to those of the army, had developed independently. The Levellers frequently tried to get army support, but their appeals got very little response before the middle of 1647.

3 *The army and its sense of honour*   Kishlansky's main explanation for the political activism of the New Model Army lay, not in the impact on it of radical ideas from outside, but in conditions within the army that made it ripe for revolt. But these conditions were shaped, not by any religious zeal of its soldiers, but by a sense of bitter injustice felt within the army at the attacks made on the army's honour by parliament. These intensified early in 1647 when parliament announced it intended to disband the army without either paying the bulk of its wage arrears or providing any **indemnity** that soldiers would not be prosecuted for anything they had done during the war.

KEY TERM:

Indemnity

Indemnity means exemption from legal penalties. The demand for indemnity was given great importance by the agitators in 1647, because soldiers had frequently requisitioned horses and other property during the war (see key term 'free quarter', page 130). They now feared that, unless they were given indemnity, they would be charged with horse-stealing and other crimes.

When parliament also condemned as treasonable an army's petition for the redress of these grievances, the soldiers were provoked into political action. In this way, Kishlansky argued, what began as an army mutiny over material grievances became a revolt to secure the army's rights to petition and take part in the political process. On this view, the politicisation of the New Model Army came about very late and very quickly. It was not caused by any deeply-held political or religious ideologies. It was, therefore, not inevitable that the revolt of the army would end less than two years later in the abolition of the monarchy.

A re-interpretation of the New Model Army

Widely differing interpretations by professional historians like these mean that there are no 'correct' answers to questions about the role of the New Model Army in the later 1640s. But the debate has made possible a re-interpretation of the New Model Army's role.

Its origins

As has been seen, historical revisionism can sometimes be carried too far. This is true of Kishlansky's account of the origins of the New Model Army. The most convincing part of his account is the evidence that it was not just Political Independent MPs who were converted to supporting military reorganisation early in 1645. The common reaction of seventeenth-century godly men and women to defeat and disasters of all kinds was to assume that the reason for their plight was the loss of God's blessing, which was, in turn, caused by their own sinfulness (see chapter 4). In the dire circumstances facing parliamentarians at the end of 1644, it does seem likely that when Oliver Cromwell and Zouch Tate floated the idea of a Self-Denying Ordinance, demanding that MPs lay down their military commands and 'not perpetually continue themselves in grandeur', they gained widespread support from *both* Political Presbyterians and Political Independents. What makes this even more likely is that coupled with this plea to godly self-denial was a nationalistic appeal to all with 'true English hearts and zealous affection towards the general weal of our Mother Country'. What also must have given the proposal general support in the next few months was the slow progress and eventual collapse of the peace negotiations early in 1645. The end of 'the Treaty of Uxbridge' closed the door to further negotiations, making the effective prosecution of the war the only viable political strategy at this time.

Yet what seems highly unlikely is that the subsequent military reorganisation caused no political controversy. This flies in the face of overwhelming evidence of bitter political disagreements between Political Presbyterians and Political Independents in the early months of 1645 over the shape of the new army. Even the appointment of Thomas Fairfax as its commander-in-chief was only approved by the Commons by a vote of 101 to 69, in which the **tellers** on both sides were prominent political activists: Political Independents, Oliver Cromwell and Henry Vane, for the 'ayes' and Political Presbyterians, Denzil Holles and Philip Stapleton, for the 'noes'. This division was followed by a prolonged battle in the Lords over the appointments of most of the other officers of the new army, in which conservatives in the Lords failed to block the appointment of many more officers from Manchester's old army (in which there was a greater concentration of godly men) than from regiments once commanded by Waller and by Essex. Moreover, the vast majority of officers of whom the Lords disapproved were radical Independents; while those they favoured were moderate Presbyterians, often men associated with the Earl of Essex.

KEY TERM:

Tellers

Tellers, then as now, were those MPs appointed (two from each side) to count votes in the Commons when decisions were being taken at the end of debates.

Its religious character

These unsuccessful efforts also make it hard to accept Kishlansky's picture of a New Model Army in which religious zeal was unimportant. Not only were officers with radical Independent views appointed to command the new army, but Ian Gentles's work on the composition of the army reveals a very high proportion of volunteers, drawn from the sons of yeomen and craftsmen, among the cavalry regiments. These were men who had joined to fight for a cause, in contrast with the conscripts in the infantry regiments, who were poorer and less committed and many of whom deserted before the end of the war. It has to be conceded that some of the evidence for radical religious zeal among many of the officers and cavalry comes from hostile sources, like *Gangraena*. This was a huge book published in 1646 by a conservative Presbyterian, Thomas Edwardes, whose reports of the New Model Army were distorted by fears that religious zeal would lead to political radicalism and worse.

'A godly Minister ... told me June 12 1646 that ... a Major belonging to the Army ... told him plainly that they were not such much against Presbyteriall Government (though many thought them so) as against the being tyed to any Government at all.

A godly young man of Summersetshire, or Dorsetshire, at whose house a Lieutenant of a Company of Sir Thomas Fairfax Army quartered, told me that this Lieutenant maintained these opinions: 1 That women might preach ... 2 That if a womans husband was asleep or absent from her, she might lye with another man, and it was lawfull; for sleep was a death.'

From Thomas Edwardes's *Gangraena*, 1646.

Yet such accounts should not be totally discounted. Oliver Cromwell's letter, pleading for religious toleration, after the New Model Army's victory at Bristol captures the religious enthusiasm of many of his men.

'Presbyterians, Independents, all had here the same spirit of faith and prayer; the same presence and answer; they agree here, know no names of difference: pity it should be otherwise.'

Cromwell's letter to the Speaker of the Commons, September 1645 in W. C. Abbott (ed.), *The Writings and Speeches of Oliver Cromwell*, vol. 1.

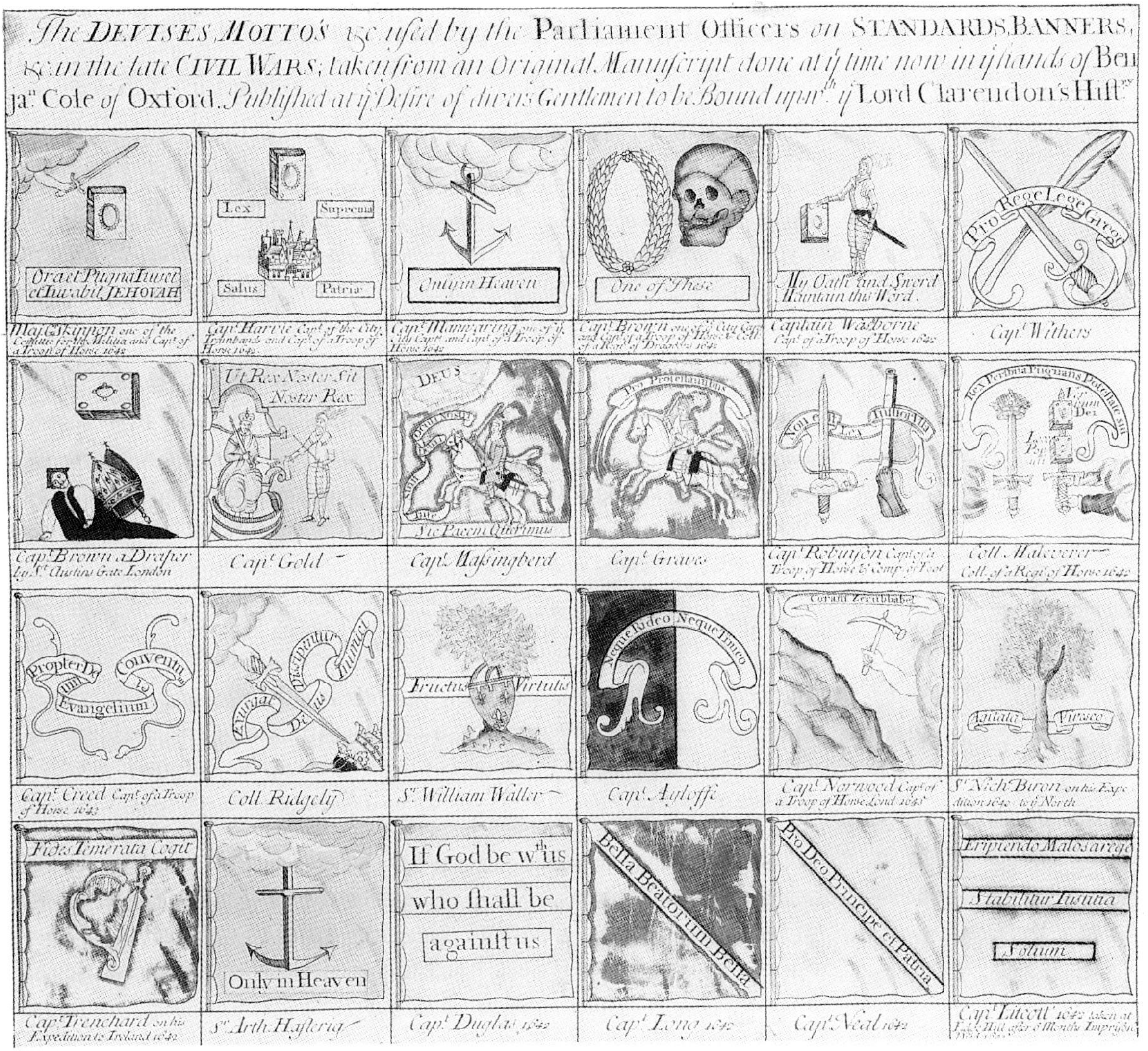

The DEVISES MOTTOS &c. used by the Parliament Officers on STANDARDS, BANNERS, &c. in the late CIVIL WARS; taken from an Original Manuscript done at y^e time now in y^e hands of Benjaⁿ Cole of Oxford. Published at ye Desire of divers Gentlemen to be Bound up wth ye Lord Clarendon's Hist^y

Figure 12.1 *The banners and standards of Parliamentarian regiments from an engraving of 1722*

Not all army chaplains were as charismatic as Hugh Peter and William Dell, but most of them were religious Independents. Lay preaching, fasting and days of humiliation, too, were common in the New Model Army. The best visual signs of its religious zeal, apart from the damage that its soldiers did to many English cathedrals (continuing the godly iconoclasm of the sixteenth century – see chapter 4), are the army's regimental banners with their stirring religious mottoes (Figure 12.1).

Of course, the New Model Army was not without rank-and-file conscripts and officers who shared their desire to end the war rapidly. Indeed Royalist sentiment was not unknown in the ranks of the New Model Army. But it was not just its professionalism that was new about the New Model Army.

The reasons for its politicisation

Did the religious commitment of many of its soldiers in 1645–6 provide the drive that made inevitable its emergence as a major political force in 1647? Its grievances at the beginning of that year, that were voiced from its headquarters in and around Saffron Walden in Essex, suggest that this was not the case. They were moderate ones that ought to have been fairly easy to satisfy, paving the way for its speedy demobilisation. All that was required was a parliamentary guarantee of indemnity protecting demobilised soldiers from legal prosecutions for actions they had taken during the war, together with the settlement of their wage arrears. These were not large. Although the total arrears of all the parliamentary armies at the end of the war totalled about £3 million, only half that sum was owed to the New Model Army. Moreover, even the most militant regiments did not demand a once-and-for-all settlement. There is no reason to doubt a later New Model Army claim that all that was demanded was four months' arrears of pay, which would have cost only about £200,000. These limited aims do not suggest that this was an army that was inevitably destined to explode into revolutionary action.

That it did so is to be explained by the fact that Holles and Stapleton, the leaders of the Political Presbyterian majority in parliament, decided not to grant the army's limited demands but to conduct a sustained, aggressive campaign against it. The key anti-army measures of that campaign between February and May 1647 are noted in the time chart. It is not necessary to explain in detail the reactions of an army, in which religious and political debate was common, to measures like the parliamentary 'Declaration of Dislike', which condemned army petitioners as 'enemies of the state'. Nor does it need much imagination to understand the reactions of soldiers who, rather than being rewarded for their sufferings in helping to win the war for parliament, were presented with the unattractive option of disbandment without pay or military service in Ireland. It is an open question whether the Earl of Essex, if he had lived, would have advised his civilian Political Presbyterian allies against offending the army in this way. But Essex died in September 1646, and no one was there to prevent Holles from committing a serious political error, which had explosive consequences.

Conclusion

Not for the first time in the history of seventeenth-century Britain it is necessary to emphasise that it was a combination of 'functional' and 'ideological' pressures that pushed people into taking radical actions. One aim of this chapter has been to show that the New Model Army was not apolitical when it was first established. Yet it was the political attack on the soldiers by Holles and the Political Presbyterians early in 1647 that transformed the army's latent political awareness into open political activism.

That is why the New Model Army had become a major political force by June 1647. What it was not, however, was a political force with a Leveller, republican programme. Grasping that fact is essential in order to deal with the historical problem raised in the next chapter.

Task: source evaluation

Here are extracts from two of the many documents produced by the New Model Army in the spring and early summer of 1647. The complete documents are printed in A. S. P. Woodhouse (ed.), *Puritanism and Liberty* (Dent, 1992). Read both extracts and then answer the questions at the end.

Source A   A Second Apologie of All the Private Soldiers

[This was presented to Sir Thomas Fairfax by three leading agitators, Edward Sexby, William Allen and Thomas Shepherd on 28 April 1647, when the army was camped in and around Saffron Walden, Essex. It was printed on 3 May 1647.]

'Sirs: We your soldiers, who have served under your commands, with all readiness, to free this our native land and nation from tyranny and oppressions whatsoever, and that by virtue and power derived from this present Parliament ... But we see the oppression is as great as ever ... Is it not better to die like men than to be enslaved and hanged like dogs? ... We have been quiet and peaceable in obeying all orders and commands, yet not, we have a just cause to tell you, if we be not relieved in our grievances:
(1) That the honour of this Army may be vindicated in every particular, especially about the late petition, and reparations given, and justice done upon the fomenters.
(2) That an Act of Indemnity may be made for all things done in time and place of war.
(3) That the wives and children of those who have been slain in the service, and maimed soldiers, may be provided for.
(4) Our arrears, under this General, to be paid us ...
(5) That we that have served the Parliament freely may not be pressed out of the kingdom.
(6) That the liberty of the subject may no longer be enslaved, but that justice and judgements may be dealt with to the meanest subject according to the old law.'

Source B   A Representation of the Army

[This was drafted by Henry Ireton and other officers and probably approved by agitators in the new General Council of the Army. It was published on 14 June 1647 at Triplow Heath, near Cambridge, as the army marched towards London.]

'We were not a mere mercenary army, hired to serve any arbitrary power of a state, but called forth and conjured by the several declarations of Parliament to the defence of our own and the people's just rights and liberties and so we took up arms in judgement and conscience to those ends ... We do humbly desire for the settling and securing of our own and the kingdom's right, freedom, peace and safety, as followeth:

(1) That the House may be speedily purged of such members as for their delinquency, or for corruption, or abuse to the state, or undue election, ought not to sit there.

(2) That those persons who have, in the late unjust and high proceedings against the Army, appeared to have the will, the confidence, credit, and power to abuse the Parliament and the Army, and endanger the kingdom in carrying on such things against us while an army, may be some way speedily disabled from doing the like or worse to us, when disbanded or dispersed ...'

[The army also made demands for:
– regular parliamentary elections
– the abolition of the royal power to adjourn and dissolve parliaments
– the people's right to petition parliament.]

'These proposals aforegoing being the principal things we bottom and insist upon, we shall ... acquiesce for other particulars in the wisdom and justice of Parliament. And whereas it hath been suggested, or suspected, that ... our design is to overthrow Presbytery ... and to have the Independent government set up, we do clearly disclaim and disavow any such design. We only desire that, according to the declarations promising a privilege for tender consciences, there may be some effectual course taken, according to the intent thereof, and that such who upon conscientious grounds may differ from the established forms, may not for that be debarred from the common rights ... while they live soberly, honestly, inoffensively towards others, and peacefully and faithfully towards the state.'

Questions

1 What is the specific reason referred to in source A for the demand that the honour of the army be vindicated?

2 Why do the soldiers in source A want an Act of Indemnity?

3 What do the soldiers mean in source B when they claim that they 'were not a mere mercenary army'?

4 Make lists of the demands made in these two documents. What are the major differences between the two lists? Why was the army making more sweeping demands in source B than in source A?

5 What do both these sources suggest were the main reasons why the New Model Army became politicised?

Further reading

The textbooks by Coward, Hirst, Ashton, Aylmer and Roots have additional information on this topic.

Kishlansky's views are summarised in his article, 'Ideology and politics in the parliamentary armies 1645–9' in J. Morrill (ed.), *Reactions to the English Civil War* (Macmillan, 1982). [Fuller versions are in his book, *The Rise of the New Model Army* (Cambridge University Press, 1975) and in 'The army and the Levellers: the road to Putney', *Historical Journal*, vol. 22 (1979).]

The best alternative accounts of the origins and politicisation of the New Model Army are by I. Gentles and A. Woolrych. Gentles summarises his views in his article 'The impact of the New Model Army' in J. Morrill (ed.), *The Impact of the English Civil War* (Collins and Brown, 1991). The book-length version is *The New Model Army* (Blackwell, 1992). Woolrych's book, *Soldiers and Statesmen: the General Council of the Army and its Debates 1647–8* (Oxford University Press, 1987), is best used as a work of reference to dip into.

13 Why was Charles I executed in 1649?

Earlier chapters should have made it fairly obvious that it is difficult to say why Charles I was executed in 1649. Given that there were no 'historical forces' at work making even the outbreak of a Civil War inevitable, it is highly unlikely that there are any long-term reasons why Charles I should have been executed.

Moreover, what makes this outcome even more surprising is that, as has been seen, a strong theme of British politics during and immediately after the Civil War was a growing desire for a settlement that would restore Charles I to power, not lead to his trial and execution. This chapter attempts to explain why, despite this situation, Charles I did end his life on the executioner's block on 30 January 1649.

It is a task, however, that does not get any easier by examining the events which followed the politicisation of the New Model Army during the first half of 1647. The army's political programme included no design to execute the king. On the contrary, there was a large degree of agreement on the need for a monarchical settlement between army officers and the agitator representatives of the rank-and-file soldiers. During the summer and autumn of 1647 the New Model Army was united in seeking a settlement with the king.

The search for the explanation for the king's execution, therefore, must begin by looking at why the army's hopes for a settlement with Charles I collapsed, as they had done by the end of 1647. Early in January 1648 parliament even decided (in the Vote of No Addresses) never again to negotiate with the king. This, however, will not provide the only explanation for the execution of the king in January 1649, because the Vote of No Addresses was soon overturned. It was followed during much of 1648 by a series of events, called the Second Civil War, that showed that hopes of restoring Charles I to power had become stronger in the country and at Westminster than ever.

The searcher for the causes of Charles's execution is, therefore, faced with another major question: why was no settlement reached with the king in 1648 and why did a minority make the awesome decisions to bring the king to trial and then to execute him? The second part of this chapter addresses that fascinating question.

Time chart

1647: June Cornet Joyce's seizure of the king from his parliamentary guards in Northamptonshire is followed by army manifestos setting out its political demands

July Army council at Reading agrees proposals to be put to the king (The Heads of the Proposals) and the negotiations on them with the king begin

Political Presbyterians attempt a counter-revolution in London as mobs invade the Commons forcing MPs to reinstate Presbyterian control of the City militia and to invite the king to the capital

August The army occupies London and the leaders of the counter-revolution flee

October New Leveller agitators emerge in some regiments. Levellers and new agitators publish *The Case of the Army Truly Stated* and *The Agreement of the People*

Debates of the army council at Putney begin

November King escapes from Hampton Court

Putney debates end and an army mutiny at Ware (Hertfordshire) is crushed

December King allies with the Scots (the Engagement)

1648: January Parliament passes the Vote of No Addresses, declaring the end for ever of negotiations with the king

Why did the army's negotiations with the king fail?

Before explaining why the army's negotiations with the king failed in 1647, it is necessary to establish two important features of the political activities of the army that remained constant during the exciting period from June to October 1647:

1 Agitators and senior army officers were agreed on a political programme that would have restored the king to power.

2 Links between the army and Political Independent leaders in parliament were stronger and more influential than those between the army and Leveller radicals.

What facilitated the closeness of officers and agitators in the army after June 1647 is that in the previous few weeks many conservative officers, whose sympathies lay with the Political Presbyterians, left the army. Fifty-seven – one-quarter of officers of the rank of captain-lieutenant and above – departed in May–June 1647. These were mainly senior officers, who were replaced by men with more militant political and religious views, such as Thomas Harrison (see profile, page 180), Thomas Pride and William Goffe.

Much that happened during the next few months suggests that officers and agitators collaborated fairly closely. In removing the king from his parliamentary guards at Holmby House and bringing him to the army's headquarters at Newmarket on 4 June 1647, Cornet Joyce and his men might have gone further than officers like Fairfax and Cromwell wanted, but the latter almost certainly gave their blessings to Joyce's plans to seize the king's person. The financial account books of William Clarke, Fairfax's secretary, revealingly show payments being authorised by senior officers to agitators or their representatives, who were sent to explain the army's actions to potential supporters elsewhere in Britain, especially in the northern parliamentary army.

This collaboration is also confirmed by the first political manifestos issued by the army in June. As well as calling for the purge of its enemies from parliament (notably the **Eleven Members**), regular parliaments and measures of religious toleration, the drafters of the manifestos (of whom the most important was Henry Ireton) made provision for a general council of the army which contained both officers and agitators.

Early in July the army, after marching from Essex through Hertfordshire towards London, fell back on Reading, 35 miles to the west of the capital. There Ireton (who was the foremost political theorist in the army) began work on a blueprint for a postwar settlement, *The Heads of the Proposals*. It is now known that, when drafting this document, Ireton worked closely with civilian Political Independents, including Oliver St John and a group of powerful peers, the earls of Northumberland and Pembroke, Lord Wharton and Viscount Saye and Sele. Both Wharton and Saye and Sele were at Reading in July and *The Heads of the Proposals* received their full support.

It was also backed by the agitators in the army council. In the council debates on *The Heads of the Proposals* at Reading the only sign of divisions between agitators and officers was over tactics: the agitators urging an immediate march on London, the officers sounding a cautionary note. Cromwell is recorded as arguing for the superiority of a negotiated settlement over one imposed by force: 'whatsoever you get by a treaty ... will be firm and durable ... we shall avoid the great objection that will lie against us, that we have got things of the parliament by force ... that which you have by force, I think of it as nothing'. There was no similar disagreement over the provisions of *The Heads of the Proposals*, which in some respects were more lenient than the parliamentary Propositions of Newcastle that had been sent to the king in July 1646.

> ### *The Provisions of* **The Heads of the Proposals**
> *(comparable provisions in the Propositions of Newcastle are in brackets)*
>
> - Chief officers of state to be nominated by parliament for 10 years (for ever)
> - The militia to be controlled by parliament for 10 years (20 years)
> - Bishops were to lose their powers to coerce everyone to attend the national Church (bishops were to be abolished and an intolerant Presbyterian Church established)
> - 7 Royalists to be exempted from general pardon (58 Royalists)
> - Biennial parliaments with seats redistributed to match the localities' wealth (triennial parliaments)
> - Parliament to remedy Leveller grievances, including the excise, and legal reform.

The attempted 'counter-revolution' on 26 July, organised by Holles and the Political Presbyterians in London, forced Fairfax and Cromwell to order the military occupation of the capital. But all the signs are that the army's occupation of London did not change its basic strategy: during August and September negotiations with the king, which had begun in Reading in July, continued with the support of soldiers and civilian Political Independents alike.

Why did *The Heads of the Proposals* fail?

There are two main answers to this question:

- the role of the Levellers
- the attitude of the king.

The role of the Levellers

KEY TERM:

Grandees

This is the scornful term for the senior army officers that, significantly, only began to be used by Levellers and army agitators at this time. Its use is a symptom of the new divisions that appeared in the army.

The influence of the London Levellers on the army only became significant after the army occupied London in August. One effect was to cause the disintegration of army unity. From his prison in the Tower one of the Leveller leaders, **John Lilburne**, joined other Levellers, like Richard Overton and John Wildman, in writing pamphlets that questioned the motives of 'the **grandees**' in negotiating with the king and which urged the army to adopt the radical religious and constitutional programme of the Levellers (see chapter 14). They also played on the soldiers' grievance that the bulk of their wage arrears were still unpaid.

PROFILE: *John Lilburne*

Lilburne's imprisonment in the Tower in 1647 was not an unusual event in his life. The younger son of a Durham gentry family, he came to London to serve as apprentice to a London clothier. From his mid-twenties he spent his life attacking the government of the day and suffering the consequences. In 1638 he was imprisoned by Star Chamber for writing pamphlets against bishops. He was released from prison by the Long Parliament in 1640 and during the Civil War fought in the parliamentary army of the Eastern Association, rising to the rank of Lieutenant Colonel. In 1645 he left the army and began writing pamphlets against Presbyterian religious intolerance and in favour of freedom of speech and conscience, for which he was frequently imprisoned by the Presbyterian-dominated parliament. His imprisonment, however, did not stop him writing pamphlets and taking part in the organisation of the campaign of the London Levellers. Like his fellow Levellers, Lilburne became as mistrustful of the army leaders as he had been of parliament. He took no part in the execution of the king and, after it, launched savage attacks in print on the new republic and was imprisoned yet again. He successfully defended himself at his trial in 1649, but in 1651 found himself again in trouble with the Rump Parliament, which banished him to exile in the Netherlands. In 1653 he returned, was arrested and again was acquitted. But this time he was not released but imprisoned for a time in Jersey. He was eventually released in 1655 and spent his last years as a Quaker (see chapter 20). He died two years later, aged about 43.

By the end of September the Leveller campaign began to bear fruit, when in five cavalry regiments new agitators emerged. During the next few weeks others appeared in infantry, as well as cavalry, regiments. It is not clear whether these new agitators were elected, but what is certain is that they were closely connected with civilian Levellers and very active. Some even travelled to Lambert's regiment in Yorkshire, urging their comrades to choose new agents 'for that the officers had broken their engagements'. Their main power base, however, was the capital. There, together with their Leveller allies, they drafted in the first weeks of October a swingeing indictment of the grandees, *The Case of the Army Truly Stated*, which was presented to Fairfax on 18 October. Just over a week later they published *The Agreement of the People*, a detailed plan for a constitutional and religious settlement that was a radical alternative to the army's *The Heads of the Proposals*.

In order to try to defuse this Leveller attack on army unity, Fairfax and

Cromwell decided to invite the new agitators and their civilian friends to the army council meeting at Putney on 28 October 1647. What has not surprisingly fascinated later generations about the subsequent Putney Debates is the great discussion that took place on the franchise, as army Levellers like Colonel Thomas Rainsborough challenged Ireton's claim that only the rich should be allowed to vote (see chapter 14). However, at the time the main importance of these debates was that they deepened divisions within the army, as opposition to negotiations with the king grew. In this respect, the Putney Debates failed. Although (as can be seen from the time chart) the officers restored military discipline by ending the debates, by sending the agitators back to their regiments, by ruthlessly crushing army mutinies, and by purging prominent radicals from the army, the attempt to reach a settlement with the king was now seriously damaged.

The attitude of the king

The role of the Levellers in bringing about the failure of a settlement on *The Heads of the Proposals* has not always been appreciated. The second major cause of this failure, the role of Charles I, is more obvious and therefore needs less discussion. Charles I brought about the failure of settlement in two ways.

1 The first was not apparent at the time, but historians can read documents that show conclusively that at no time after 1646 had the king any intention of reaching a settlement with anyone. In his private letters to his wife, Charles made clear that he was convinced that if he delayed the conclusion of negotiations long enough his opponents would fall out among themselves, resulting in the king's restoration to power. The memoirs of one of the royal intermediaries between the king and the army leaders, Sir John Berkeley, in 1647 also reveal that Charles had no intention of agreeing to *The Heads of the Proposals*.

2 Charles's private intransigent attitude was known to only a few at the time. What Charles did, though, was known to everyone. The result was very damaging to the prospects of a settlement with the army. By escaping from army custody at Hampton Court, fleeing to the Isle of Wight, and then allying with the Scots (the Engagement), promising to establish Scottish Presbyterianism in England, Charles, as on many occasions in the past, revealed his untrustworthiness. The reaction of army officers and their Political Independent allies to what they considered to be treacherous behaviour was to break off negotiations with the king and to plan a parliamentary campaign that resulted in the passage of the Vote of No Addresses. This pledged that parliament 'will make no further addresses or applications to the king'.

Why did the Second Civil War not restore the king to power?

Time chart

1648: March Revolt in south Wales against the New Model Army begins

May–June Revolts against the army in Kent, Essex and the navy

July Scottish army invades northern England

Surrender of the south Wales rebels at Pembroke (the rebel leaders are sent to London for execution)

August Cromwell and Lambert defeat the Scottish army at Preston

Fairfax defeats the Essex and Kent rebels (two rebel leaders are executed)

Vote of No Addresses overturned in parliament

September Parliament begins negotiating with the king at Newport (Isle of Wight)

November The army's Remonstrance demands the trial of the king

December The army occupies London again

The Commons vote to continue the Newport negotiations which prompts the army's purge of parliament (Pride's Purge)

1649: January The trial and execution of the king

The Second Civil War and the Treaty of Newport

Within weeks of its passage the Vote of No Addresses was a dead letter. The principal reason is that (as before) for many people distrust of the king proved to be less powerful than fear and hatred of the army, county committees, high taxation and religious radicalism. For a few months after December 1647 part of south-east England and south Wales erupted into revolt against all these things and for a speedy settlement with the king. That MPs at Westminster were not insulated from this powerful desire to return speedily to old ways is witnessed by parliament's decision to reject the Vote of No Addresses and to re-open negotiations with the king at Newport on the Isle of Wight (The Newport 'Treaty').

As in the months immediately after the end of the First Civil War, a powerful 'counter-revolution' got underway. The main difference is that this time it was also supported by influential Political Independents, like Oliver St John and Viscount Saye and Sele, who had allied with the army in successfully blocking the 'counter-revolution' of 1646–7. As the New Model Army turned its attention to the task of crushing the revolts in the provinces and in the navy and an invading Scottish army, the prospects of a monarchical settlement seemed brighter than they had ever been.

The English Revolution, December 1648–January 1649

Why was no such settlement made? Why was there instead an English Revolution?

The starting-point for answering these questions is understanding that one feature distinguishes the English Revolution from other revolutions. Unlike the French Revolution in 1789, the Russian Revolution in 1917 and revolutions in many countries in eastern Europe in 1989, there was no hint of any mass popular enthusiasm for the English Revolution of 1648–9. It had no event like the storming of the Bastille in Paris, the popular attack on the Winter Palace in St Petersburg, or the tearing down of the Berlin Wall. There was no popular rejoicing in England on 30 January 1649 when Charles I was executed on a platform erected outside the Banqueting Hall in Whitehall in London. Instead, according to one eyewitness of the scene, when the executioner's axe fell and the king's head was displayed, the watching crowd let out a great groan. Ironically Charles I was more popular at the moment of his death than at any other time in the 1640s. Whereas in November 1640 he had been opposed by most people represented in parliament, on 5 December 1648, even though a hostile regiment of soldiers was outside the House, a majority of MPs voted that negotiations with the king, aimed at restoring him to power with minimal conditions, should continue.

One of the key features of the English Revolution is that it was carried out by a minority, whose decisions to become regicides were taken at a very late stage. The two men who took the lead in bringing the king to trial, Ireton and his father-in-law, Cromwell, had been fully committed only a year before to securing a monarchical settlement.

The searcher for the explanation for the execution of the king in 1649 is, therefore, faced with the most important question of all. What caused them and a few others to abandon settlement and to try to bring about the king's death?

It is suggested in this final section that, like others on different occasions in the 1640s, they were driven to take this difficult decision by a combination of 'functional' and 'ideological' pressures. This is what Cromwell meant when he said he had been forced to take this extreme course by 'providence and necessity'.

> *'When it was first moved in the House of Commons to proceed capitally against the King, Cromwell stood up and told them, That if any man moved this upon design, he should think him the greatest Traytor in the world, but since providence and necessity had cast them upon it, he should pray God to bless their Councels ...'*
>
> A contemporary report of Cromwell's speech in the Commons, 26 December 1648.

Necessity

This first ('functional') reason is easier to understand and explain than the second. It derives from themes that have been seen many times already in the history of the English Revolution: distrust of Charles I and the importance of events in Scotland. There had been many occasions in the past when Charles I had demonstrated his untrustworthiness. But it was Charles's escape from Hampton Court, thereby turning his back on what many had considered a reasonable package of measures, set out in *The Heads of the Proposals* that convinced some that Charles I would never agree to any kind of settlement.

What helped them reach this decision was the Scottish dimension, which, as it had done in 1640–41 and in 1644, pushed events in England in a more radical direction than ever before. Charles's alliance with the Scots and his approval of the use of a Scottish army against his English subjects was vital in persuading some that, on practical grounds alone, an agreement with Charles I was now impossible and they therefore must look for an alternative type of postwar settlement.

Providence

What drove them on was also an ideological zeal: 'providence'. To understand this you should re-read the sections on the aims and mentality of the godly that were discussed in chapter 4, and on the religious zeal of some men who became parliamentarians in 1642 in chapter 9. Many of the king's opponents had lost that zeal during the course of the 1640s. Many of those who put the king on trial in 1649 had not.

This religious zeal can still be seen in 1648–9 among a few civilian radicals at Westminster, like Edmund Ludlow, as well as in the London and county petitions to parliament at this time, supporting the trial of the king. It was most visible in the army's ranks, largely because, like other armies that have fought long wars, the New Model Army had developed an *esprit de corps*, forged by a common feeling of suffering and achievement. For many in the army (including Cromwell) their victories in battle were considered to be signs of God's favour. As they saw it, their victory in the Civil War had been decided by God's judgement. In these circumstances they considered that those who fought against them in 1648 were guilty of the heinous crime of flying in the face of God's judgement.

> *'Their fault who have appeared in this summer's business [the Second Civil War] is certainly double to theirs who were in the first, because it is a repetition of the same offence against all the witnesses that God has borne, by making and abetting a second war.'*
>
> Cromwell's letter to the Speaker of the Commons, July 1648.

Gradually during the course of 1648 people like Cromwell began to put the king himself in this category, as well as leaders of the rebellions against the army. Like them, Charles I was accused of being guilty of the war crime of plunging the country into an unnecessary bout of blood-shed. What was worse, he was also (as they put it) 'a man of blood', whose death God demanded before He would continue to support them. This providential mentality was also reflected in the army Remonstrance of November 1648, which was drafted by Ireton and which declared that the king was 'guilty of the highest treason against law amongst men ... guilty ... of all the innocent blood spilt thereby'.

> *'Ye shall not pollute the Land wherin yee are; for bloud, it defileth the Land, and the Land cannot be cleansed of the bloud that is shed therin, but by the bloud of him that shed it.'*
>
> The Old Testament Book of Numbers, chapter 35, verse 33.

It can be seen even more clearly in this biblical text that Thomas Brook attached to the printed version of the sermon he delivered before the Commons on 27 December 1648, when the House was steeling itself to take the decision to establish a special court to try the king.

This chapter ends by suggesting that at the heart of the explanation for Charles's execution in 1649 was not republican enthusiasm, but religious zeal. It was this that in 1649 drove men who were social and political conservatives to become revolutionaries.

Task: evaluation of the role of an individual

A major function of historians is to evaluate the role played by individuals in historical events. Historians, however, differ in the way they approach this function. Some historians take the line that, in general, the role of individuals is less important than other factors. Individuals, they assume, were generally helpless in the face of powerful forces that were largely beyond their control. Other historians start from the assumption that the roles played by individuals were decisive in shaping the course of events.

This task gives you an opportunity to decide which of these two approaches is better by evaluating the role of Charles I in what happened between November 1640 and January 1649.

Here are two hypotheses:

A 'Charles I is the main reason why there was no settlement'

B 'Even if Charles I had acted differently proposals for a settlement would have collapsed'

Which hypothesis do you prefer as an explanation of the failure to reach a negotiated settlement between:
a November 1640 and August 1642
b August 1642 and July 1646
c July 1646 and January 1649?

Write a mini-essay (no more than two sides of A4 paper) on each part of the question.

You may, if you wish, devise an alternative hypothesis of your own. Whichever hypothesis you choose, you must support it with relevant historical arguments and analysis.

NB To tackle this task you will need to use material in chapters 9–12, as well as this chapter.

Further reading

In addition to the relevant pages of the textbooks listed at the end of the last chapter, the best detailed book on 1647–9 is D. Underdown, *Pride's Purge: the Politics of the Puritan Revolution* (Oxford University Press, 1971), chapters 4–6.

The best book on the Levellers is G. Aylmer, *The Levellers and the English Revolution* (Thames and Hudson, 1973).

See V. Pearl, 'London's counter-revolution' in G. E. Aylmer (ed.), *The Interregnum: the Quest for Settlement 1646–60* (Macmillan, 1973) for the conservative reaction in London in 1646–7.

See J. Morrill, *The Revolt of the Provinces* (Addison Wesley Longman, 1980) pages 125–31 for the Second Civil War in 1648.

See B. Coward, *Oliver Cromwell* (Addison Wesley Longman, 1991) pages 58–65 for a suggested explanation for Cromwell's actions at this time.

14 Levellers, Diggers and Ranters: the world turned upside down?

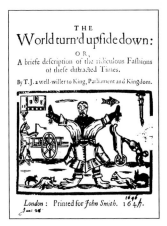

Figure 14.1 *'The World turn'd upside down' – from a pamphlet produced in 1647*

During the later 1640s and early 1650s the dramatic political and military events, that have been the subject of previous chapters, were accompanied by a remarkable explosion of new radical groups, demanding revolutionary changes. The cartoon (Figure 14.1), depicting a world in which fishes fly and so on, is a lighthearted comment on what was happening. But beneath the humour was the horrified fear of propertied people at the trend of events. Might not the attack on the established political and ecclesiastical order be followed by the overturning of the existing social order? Was their world about to be turned upside down?

This chapter looks at three of the most famous radical groups of this period and raises a major historical problem about them for you to consider when you read the sources at the end of the chapter: to what extent did their ideas and activities justify the fears of many contemporaries that the world was about to be turned upside down?

The ideas of the Levellers, Diggers and Ranters

Until fairly recently historians generally agreed that the ideas of these three groups – the Levellers, Diggers and Ranters – represented an important and powerful radical, but popular, challenge to the traditional social and political order.

The Levellers

This was the most important radical group to appear during the English Revolution. From 1645 onwards John Lilburne (see profile on page 152), John Wildman, William Walwyn and Richard Overton began to publish in London a stream of pamphlets and tracts that gained them the nickname 'Levellers'. Leveller pamphlets between 1645 and 1647 had stirring titles like *England's Birth-Right Justified* (1645), *A Remonstrance of Many Thousand Citizens* (1646), *Regal Tyranny Discovered* (1647) and *The Large Petition* (1647). In the summer and autumn of 1647, as has been seen, Levellers collaborated with militant army agitators in producing the radical demands set out in *The Case of the Army Truly Stated* and the first *Agreement of the People* (see chapter 13). In 1648–9 the output of Leveller writings continued, notably Lilburne's *England's New Chains Discovered* (1649), reflecting the Levellers' dissatisfaction with the army after the execution of the king.

The Levellers also proved adept at collecting thousands of signatures for their petitions and at organising mass popular demonstrations in support, for example, of Lilburne at his various trials and at the funeral of the army Leveller, Colonel Thomas Rainsborough in 1648. In the winter of 1648–9, Leveller local committees were established in some London wards, organising meetings in taverns and collecting subscriptions that were sent to two Leveller treasurers. At this time also the Levellers used a newspaper, *The Moderate*, to print material in support of the Leveller cause.

What was 'the Leveller cause'? As will be seen, it is doubtful whether there was 'a party political programme' on which all Levellers were agreed. But in many Leveller publications can be found demands that:

1 The existing constitution be swept away and be replaced by a new one, to which all who wanted political rights should agree. (This is why it was called 'The Agreement of the People'.)

2 The new constitution should be based on the belief that all men were equal and that government should be founded on the consent of the people.

3 The House of Commons (which they called the Representative) should be the supreme legislature in the new constitution (many Levellers advocated the abolition of the monarchy and the House of Lords) and measures should be taken to ensure that it reflected the will of the people. They demanded, for example, that there should be frequent elections, a redistribution of parliamentary seats and an extension of the franchise.

4 Fourthly, that the power of parliaments should be limited in two major ways:

■ by defining individual rights over which parliaments had no authority. The principle ones were people's freedom to hold whatever religious views they chose and to be considered equal before the law.

■ by decentralising power wherever possible. Accordingly, the Levellers demanded that local magistrates (including JPs) and all local officials should be elected, so that they were subject to local democratic control. The Levellers also wanted local law courts, run by locally-elected judges, and local militias to replace, respectively, the central law courts in London and a centralised, professional army.

5 There should be fundamental reform of the legal and judicial system and the abolition of trading and industrial monopolies.

It is likely that many of these demands were shaped by recent experiences, which had made Levellers wary of giving unlimited powers to a parliament that imprisoned its leaders and condemned its petitions. It is also probable that the model of decentralised democracy was influenced by the experience of many Levellers, who were members of Independent gathered churches, which elected their ministers and tried to reach agreement by discussions among the congregation. Whatever their origins, there is no doubt that the Leveller proposals for religious liberty, popular sovereignty and decentralised democracy were the most comprehensive and radical reform programme to appear during the English Revolution.

The Diggers or True Levellers

These were the followers of **Gerard Winstanley**. They called themselves the True Levellers, but were nicknamed the Diggers, because they attempted to set up communities that cultivated the land in common. The first Digger commune was established on 1 April 1649 by Winstanley and his followers at St George's Hill, near Walton in Surrey. In August they were forced by hostile locals to move to Cobham Heath in Surrey, where they stayed until they were dispersed in the following year. Other scattered Digger communes, including one at Iver in Buckinghamshire, were established in some Midland and south-eastern counties of England, but, like the ones in Surrey, they were quickly quashed by violent local opposition.

The Ranters

The Ranters is a term first used in pamphlets and newspapers in 1650–51. The pamphlets had eye-catching titles, like *The Ranters Religion, Or a Faithfull and Infallible Narrative of their Diabolicall Opinions*, or The *Ranters Ranting* (see page 167 – complete with woodcut drawings of naked men and women). Ranters were said to hold two distinctive beliefs: **antinomianism** and **pantheism**. These led Ranters to deny the existence of sin, on the grounds that, since God was the author of all things, sin, which was the negation of God, could not exist. In the works of a few men, notably in Abiezer Coppe's *A Fiery Flying Roll* (1650), this case was developed to demonstrate that, theoretically at least, all activities – including sexual promiscuity, swearing, drunkenness and theft – were legitimate. Newspapers and pamphlets in the early 1650s described the

KEY TERMS:

Antinomianism

This is a theological term used to describe a development of the Calvinist doctrine of predestination (see key term, page 48). This was the belief that those who were to be saved from damnation and an afterlife in Hell had already been determined by God. It was, therefore, possible to argue that those who were saved (the Elect) were free on earth to do anything they liked. This interpretation of Calvinist predestination was called **antinomianism** and was denounced by orthodox Calvinists.

Pantheism

Pantheism is the belief that God is in all creatures, plants and everything.

PROFILE: *Gerard Winstanley*

Winstanley was a Lancastrian from Wigan. In 1630, when he was about 21, he came to London as an apprentice in the cloth trade. He later became a cloth merchant and in 1637 a freeman of the Merchant Taylor's Company. In the early 1640s his business collapsed and for much of the 1640s he lived in Cobham, Surrey, working as a cowherd. In 1648–9 he began to write and publish religious tracts, in which he developed the idea that was central to Digger philosophy: that God was not a personal deity but the spirit of reason and cooperation that would one day be found in everyone. In his tract *The New Law of Righteousness* (1649) he claimed that, when in a trance, he had received a message from God that the eventual triumph of reason would only come about if the earth was returned to common ownership. Winstanley believed that this had been destroyed at the Norman Conquest, when private property had been introduced. In later tracts, notably *The Law of Freedom in a Platform* (1652), Winstanley went on to develop a vision of an ideal society, in which there would be common ownership of all the means of production and distribution, complete freedom of worship, compulsory education for boys and girls, and in which the monarchy, the clergy and lawyers would be abolished. He envisaged a transitional stage with elected parliaments and magistrates, but he believed that eventually, as the voice of God triumphed within everyone, the formal authority of a state would not be needed.

After this brief episode (1649–52) as an author and Digger activist, Winstanley's career is clouded in doubt. He seems to have played no further part in public life. He returned to London, where his economic fortunes, as a corn merchant, revived. He became a Quaker and died in 1676, aged 67.

---

ways in which Ranters put these beliefs into practice, as did Lawrence Clarkson in his autobiography, *The Lost Sheep Found* (1660).

Revolutionary and well-supported?

Were the ideas of Levellers, Diggers and Ranters as revolutionary and as well-supported as some contemporaries (followed by later historians) assumed? Much recent writing by historians of seventeenth-century England has maintained that the answer to this question is 'no'. What are the grounds that have been put forward for reducing considerably the significance of these radical groups in the history of the English Revolution?

The Levellers

Four main reasons for reducing the significance of the Levellers have been suggested:

1 The positive influence of the Levellers on contemporary events was very limited. Except for a brief period in the late summer of 1647, the Levellers' influence on the New Model Army was slight. It could, therefore, be that the main political impact of the Levellers was a negative one, encouraging the growth of conservatism in the Second Civil War (see chapter 13) and during the rule of the Commonwealth between 1649 and 1653 (see chapter 15).

2 The commitment of the Levellers to democracy was not as revolutionary as was once thought. Not only did no Leveller advocate giving the vote to women, but some Levellers (including Maximilian Petty at the Putney Debates) excluded servants and those in receipt of alms from the franchise. The first *Agreement of the People* left the question of who should have the vote undefined, but subsequent versions of the agreement (in December 1648 and May 1649) gave the vote only to adult, male heads of households.

3 In addition to the question of who should have the vote, there were other disagreements between individual Levellers. The principal Levellers not only differed in temperament (the fiery, excitable, charismatic Lilburne and Walwyn, the solid, London citizen, for example), but also in religious beliefs (Lilburne, until he became a Quaker at the end of his life, believed in Calvinist predestination, while Walwyn's theology was one of free will). Moreover, their pamphlets stressed different social and economic reforms that reflected their individual interests, casting doubt on the idea that there was a Leveller 'movement'.

4 Permanent popular support for the Levellers was not as great as is sometimes suggested by the massive support they received on specific occasions. This is shown, it is argued, by the fairly narrow audience to which Leveller pamphlets and manifestos appealed, especially those calling for legal, social and economic reforms. Leveller demands for the abolition of trading and industrial monopolies and reform of the law, as well as their attacks on the professions, were designed to appeal to the 'middling sort' – small-scale craftsmen and traders. This was the group that would have been most likely to have benefited from the Leveller political reforms. The Levellers hardly mentioned the social and economic grievances of the mass of English people, who (as was seen in chapter 2) lived and worked on the land as smallholders and agricultural labourers. Was not the Leveller message irrelevant to their condition?

The Diggers

The case for not exaggerating the contemporary significance of the Diggers needs less emphasis. Winstanley clearly represented a tiny number of people. Moreover, although unlike the Levellers, the Diggers had ideas that were relevant to the agrarian society of the country, they were too revolutionary to have much impact. It is significant that the tiny Digger communes aroused the anger of local farmers and smallholders, as well as landowners. It may be that more typical of popular rural opinion in the mid seventeenth century than the ideas of the Diggers was the conservatism of the Clubmen (see chapter 12).

The Ranters

The Ranters have been the subject of the most extreme form of historical revisionism: one historian has argued that they never existed! This is a case that rests on three main arguments:

1 That all the sources for studying the Ranters are hostile reports written by their enemies. Even Lawrence Clarkson's account of his activities as a Ranter was written when he had become a Quaker, making it a possibility that he distorted what he had done in order to dramatise his conversion. The implication of this argument is that the Ranters were invented, partly by enterprising journalists in order to sell newspapers and pamphlets to a sensation-seeking public, and partly by conservative ministers and laymen who used the Ranter myth to frighten back to the fold anyone tempted to stray from the path of orthodox Protestantism.

2 That 1649–51 was a time when many people were especially likely to believe in Ranter stories. Not only were they frightened by the prospects of more revolutionary events that might follow the execution of the king and the establishment of the republic, but the period was one of successive harvest failures and rising food prices. In this atmosphere fear of popular rebellions spread like wildfire.

3 That no contemporary writings exist that put forward a *full-blown* Ranter philosophy – that is, one that combines all the main elements of antinomianism and pantheism and advocates the practical expression of this libertine philosophy.

Task: evaluation of sources

One way of formulating your own ideas about the significance of these radical groups is by reading the following sources and then attempting to answer the questions which follow.

Source A

An extract from the Blasphemy Act, 1650. [The full title of the Act is 'An Act against several Atheistical, Blasphemous and Execrable Opinions, derogatory to the honor of God, and destructive to Humane Society'. It established punishments of six months' imprisonment for the first offence and banishment from the country for the second offence for those who held certain views. This extract includes a sample of these views.]

'All and every person ... who shall ... proceed to ... maintain him or her self, or any other meer Creature, to be very God ... or that the true God, or the Eternal Majesty dwells in the Creature and no where else: Or whosoever shall presume ... to profess That these acts of Denying and Blaspheming God ... or the acts of Lying, Stealing, Cousening and Defrauding others; or the acts of Murther, Adultery, Incest, Fornication, Uncleanness, Sodomy, Drunkenness, filthy and lascivious Speaking, are not things in themselves shameful ...; Or whosoever shall ... profess, That whatsoever is acted by them (whether Whoredom, Adultery, drunkenness or the like Wickedness) may be committed without sin ... or that such men and women are most perfect ... which do commit the greatest Sins with least remorse.'

(Quoted in C. H. Firth and F. R. Rait (eds), *Acts and Ordinances of the Interregnum*, vol. 2, 1900.)

Source B

Thomas Rainsborough's and Maximillian Petty's speeches at the Putney Debates, 29 October 1647. [On this day there took place the most famous part of the Putney Debates in the army council, consisting of army officers, agitators and Leveller representatives, on the question of who should have the vote. Both Rainsborough and Petty were Levellers.]

Rainsborough: 'I thinke that the poorest hee that is in England hath a life to live as the greatest hee; and therefore truly, Sir, I thinke itt's cleare, that every man that is to live under a Government ought first by his owne consent to putt himself under that Government; and I doe thinke that the poorest man in England is nott att all bound in a stricte sence to that Government that hee hath not had a voice to putt himself under ... I doe nott finde any thinge in the law of God, that a Lord shall chuse 20 Burgesses, and a Gentleman butt two, or a poore man shall chuse none.'

Petty: 'I conceive the reason why wee would exclude apprentices, or servants, or those that take almes, is because they depend upon the will of other men and should be afraid to dispense [them]. For servants and apprentices, they are included in their masters, and soe for those that receive almes from doore to doore; butt if there bee any generall way taken for those that are nott [so] bound [to the will of other men] itt would doe well.'

(Quoted in C. H. Firth (ed.), *The Clarke Papers*, vol. 2, 1992.)

Source C

Clause 4 of *The Agreement of the People*, 1647. [*The Agreement of the People* was the constitution proposed by the Levellers in October 1647.]

'That the power of this and all future representatives of this nation is inferior only to theirs who choose them, and doth extend ... generally to whatsoever is not expressly or implicitly reserved by the represented to themselves Which are as followeth:

1 That matters of religion and the ways of God's worship are not at all entrusted by us to any human power ...
2 That the matter of impressing and constraining any of us to serve in the wars is against our freedom ...
3 That after the dissolution of the present parliament no person be at any time questioned for anything said or done in reference to the late public differences ...
4 That in laws made or to be made every person may be bound alike ...
5 That as the laws ought to be equal, so they must be good, and not evidently destructive to the safety and well-being of the people.
   These things we declare to be our native rights, and therefore are agreed and resolved to maintain them with our utmost possibilities against all opposition whatsoever; being compelled thereunto not only by the examples of ancestors ... but also by our own woeful experience.'

(Quoted in J. P. Kenyon (ed.), *The Stuart Constitution* (1986).)

Source D

Gerard Winstanley, *The True Leveller Standard Advanced*, April 1649. [This extract is from the beginning of this pamphlet.]

'A declaration to the powers of England and to all the powers of the world, shewing the cause why the common people of England have begun and gives consent to dig up, manure and sow corn upon George Hill in Surrey; by those that have subscribed, and thousands more that gives consent.

   In the beginning of time, the great creator Reason made the earth to be a common treasury ... Not one word was spoken in the beginning, that one branch of mankind should rule over another. And the reason is this, every single man, male or female, is a perfect creature of himself; and the same spirit that made the globe dwells in man to govern the globe; so that the flesh of man being subject to reason, his maker, hath him to be his teacher and ruler within himself.'

Source E

a Title page of *The Ranters Ranting*, November 1651

The Ranters Ranting

WITH

The apprehending, examinations, and confession of *John Collins*, *I. Shakespear*, *Tho. Wiberton*, and five more which are to answer the next Sessions. And severall songs or catches, which were sung at their meetings. Also their several kinds of mirth, and dancing. Their blasphemous opinions. Their belief concerning heaven and hell. And the reason why one of the same opinion cut off the heads of his own mother and brother. Set forth for the further discovery of this ungodly crew.

Behold our love to our Fellow-Creature.

Welcome Fellow-Creature.

Let us eat while they dance.

Decemb: 2   LONDON
Printed by B. Alsop, 1651

b An extract from Lawrence Clarkson, *The Lost Sheep Found: Or The Prodigal Returned to his Fathers House, After Many a sad and Weary Journey Through Many Religious Countreys*, 1660. [In this extract Clarkson describes how he preached the Ranter philosophy in London when he was a preacher in the New Model Army.]

'I affirmed that there was no sin, but as man esteemed it sin, and therefore none can be free from sin till in purity it be acted as no sin ... I pleaded the words of Paul, That I know and am persuaded by the Lord Jesus, that there was nothing unclean, but as man esteemed it ... therefore till you can lie with all women as one woman, and not judge it sin, you can do nothing but sin ... Sarah Kullin being then present, did invite me to make trial of what I had expressed ... She invited me to Mr Wats in Rood-lane, where was one or two more like her self, and as I take it, lay with me that night.'

Questions

1 a What groups do you think are being referred to specifically in source A?

b Why did their activities prompt such a violent reaction?

2 Read source B. Compare the political ideas put forward by Rainsborough and Petty in this source.

3 Read source C. Explain the Levellers' proposals, and the ideas on which they were based.

4 Explain the importance of source D in the philosophy of Winstanley and the Diggers.

5 Look at source E (a). What main features of the Ranters do you think that the author of *The Ranters Ranting* wanted to convey to those who read the pamphlet?

6 a Which of the features might the extract from Clarkson's autobiography in source E (b) seem to support?

b What are the limitations of these sources as evidence for the history of the Ranters?

c Are the limitations conclusive proof that the Ranters did not exist?

Further reading

The best short books on this topic are:

D. D. Dow, *Radicalism in the English Revolution* (Historical Association Studies, 1985)

H. Shaw, *The Levellers*, Seminar Studies in History (Addison Wesley Longman, 1968)

B. Reay and L. McGregor (eds), *Radical Religion in the English Revolution* (Oxford University Press, 1975)

G. Aylmer, *The Levellers and the English Revolution* (Thames and Hudson, 1986).

Easily the best book that has the traditional views of radical groups in the English Revolution is:

C. Hill, *The World Turned Upside Down: Popular Beliefs during the English Revolution* (Penguin, 1971).

The book that argues that the Ranters did not exist is:

J. C. Davis, *Fear, Myth and History: the Ranters and Historians* (Cambridge University Press, 1986).

15 The Commonwealth, 1649–53

Time chart

1649: January Trial and execution of the king

March Acts passed abolishing monarchy and the House of Lords

Leveller leaders are arrested

April Digger communities established in Surrey

Sales of crown estates begin (proceeds are used to begin the reconstruction of the navy)

May Act declaring England a republic ('Commonwealth') is passed

Army mutinies suppressed at Burford (Oxon.) and elsewhere

August Cromwell's expeditionary force to Ireland sets out

September Parliament imposes press censorship

New Model Army massacres civilian and soldiers at Drogheda (Ireland)

October Another massacre committed by the New Model Army at Wexford (Ireland)

1650: January Rump Parliament orders that all adult males take an Oath of Engagement, declaring their loyalty to the republic

February Act for the Propagation of the Gospel in Wales passed

May Rump passes Act decreeing the death penalty for adultery

June Government weekly newspaper, *Mercurius Politicus*, launched

After his return from Ireland Cromwell is appointed as commander of expeditionary force to Scotland, where Charles II has landed

August Rump passes Blasphemy Act against religious nonconformists

September Cromwell defeats Scots at Dunbar

Rump repeals all laws compelling attendance at the national Church

October Rump passes Act aiming to make the law more open to all by declaring that all legal proceedings should be in English and not Latin and should be written in ordinary handwriting not court hand

1651: July Rump passes first of three Acts for sale of estates confiscated from principal Royalists

1651: September Cromwell defeats Scottish-Royalist army at Worcester
October Charles II flees to continent
Navigation Act passed

1652: January Hale Commission on law reform appointed
May Anglo-Dutch war begins

1653: April Cromwell takes soldiers to Parliament and forcibly expels MPs to end the rule of the **Commonwealth**

KEY TERM:

Commonwealth

This is the name given at the time to the republican government of the country between 1649 and April 1653. It consisted of the Rump Parliament and the Council of State. The Rump Parliament is the nickname given to the parliament containing those MPs who continued to sit after Pride's Purge of December 1648. In February 1649 the House of Lords was abolished and so the Rump became a single-chamber parliament. It exercised the traditional legislative role of parliaments, but it also took over most of the executive powers previously exercised by monarchs. It elected annually a Council of State of 41 members to carry out these executive powers for it, though in practice it interfered regularly in its proceedings.

Most revolutions have followed a common pattern, in which the overthrow of the old regime by a revolution was only *eventually* followed by the establishment of a new regime that disappointed the hopes of those who wanted further revolutionary change. The English Revolution of 1648–9 differed in the speed with which the hopes of further revolutionary changes were dashed. That the Commonwealth that was established *immediately after the English Revolution* was a conservative one was widely recognised at the time, and since.

Why did the English Revolution not follow a 'normal' revolutionary pattern?

In order to answer that question this chapter examines two related questions about the Commonwealth. The first is about change and continuity: how much was changed by the establishment of the Commonwealth? The second is about causation: why did the Commonwealth not produce more extensive changes than it did?

How much was changed by the establishment of the Commonwealth?

What was changed?

The first point to make is that, although the Commonwealth thoroughly deserves its reputation as a conservative government, this should not obscure the fact that 1649 marked a major change in the government of Britain in two major respects.

1 *From monarchy to republic* This is the most obvious of the two aspects. What happened between December 1648 and May 1649 amounted to the most revolutionary change in the nature of the English state that had ever occurred. There took place:

- the overthrow of monarchy and the establishment of a republic
- the abolition of the House of Lords and the establishment of a single-chamber parliament

▧ the replacement of the royal prerogative courts, the Privy Council and administrative departments – like the Exchequer and the Admiralty – by a parliamentary Council of State and numerous sub-committees.

In January 1650 it was decreed that all males over 18 years of age were to take an oath of engagement, promising obedience to 'the Commonwealth, as it is now established, without a King or House of Lords'. There was even an attempt to introduce a revolutionary calendar, beginning with 1649 as 'the first year of freedom'.

There was also a change in the type of people who ran government. Periodic purges of commissions of the peace in the early 1650s excluded gentry who it was thought might be hostile to the new republic. But more often than not the traditional governing classes voluntarily withdrew from an active part in government in horror at the execution of the king. The publication in the early 1650s of books, like Isaac Walton's *The Compleat Angler*, celebrating the joys of rural isolation, is no coincidence. For a time the Commonwealth had to rely for its local government on new men, who, though gentlemen, were lesser gentry who had not figured prominently at the head of pre-Civil War county and borough governments.

2 *The achievement of national security and international respectability* There also rapidly took place a change in the security and international standing of the country. In 1649 the new republic was fragile and insecure, beset by the threat of a Royalist invasion in collaboration with the opponents of the republic either in Ireland (where the rebellion that had begun in 1641 was still in progress) or in Scotland. It also faced severe international hostility – one illustration of which was the assassinations of two of its ambassadors when they went to take up their new diplomatic posts in the United Provinces and Spain.

Within a few years there took place a dramatic change in that situation. During 1649–50 the rebellion in Ireland was crushed. Cromwell's campaign there was conducted with a brutal efficiency that included the horrific massacres of civilians as well as soldiers at Drogheda and Wexford. Cromwell's justification for these was one used for the bombing of Hiroshima in Japan in 1945: that they 'will tend to prevent the effusion of blood for the future'. But behind his actions also lay the desire for revenge for what he (and many other English Protestants) thought had happened in Ireland in 1641 (see chapter 10).

> '*You, unprovoked, put the English to the most unheard of and most barbarous massacre (without respect of sex or age) that ever the sun beheld, and at a time when Ireland was in perfect peace ... You are a part of Antichrist, whose Kingdoms the Scriptures so expressly speaks should be laid in blood ... and ere it be long, you must all of you have blood to drink; even the dregs of the cup of the fury and wrath of God, which will be poured out unto you.*'
>
> Cromwell's Declaration to the Irish clergy, January 1650, in W. C. Abbott (ed.), *The Writings and Speeches of Oliver Cromwell*, vol. 2.

The republic also faced military opposition in Scotland. The threat of invasion from Scotland became great in June 1650 when Charles I's son, Charles Stuart, went there and accepted Presbyterianism as the price for Scottish armed support. This threat was dealt with by Oliver Cromwell's army on its campaigns there in 1650–51 as efficiently but with less brutality than in Ireland. The attitude of the English republicans to the Protestant Scots was very different to their view of the Irish. Compare this army declaration to the Scots at the start of the Scottish campaign with Cromwell's declaration to the Irish clergy.

> '*We do and are ready to embrace as much as doth, or shall be made appear to us to be according to the Word of God. Are we to be dealt with as enemies because we come not your way? Is religion wrapped up in that or any one form?*'
>
> The English army's declaration to the Scots, in W. C. Abbott (ed.), *The Writings and Speeches of Oliver Cromwell*, vol. 2.

When the Scots rejected these overtures, Cromwell resorted to military action. After decisive battles at Dunbar and Worcester ended the Royalist-Scottish threat, Scotland, like Ireland, was subjected to English rule.

Military conquest was followed by plans to bring Scotland, as well as Ireland, into a closer formal union with England. This was not achieved until after the dissolution of the Commonwealth in April 1653, but the foundations were laid during the rule of the Commonwealth.

Not only was the British problem solved (if only temporarily) shortly after 1649, but there was an equally remarkable transformation in the country's international standing. In great contrast to the commercial and foreign policies of early Stuart monarchs, which had been ineffectual, the Commonwealth followed dynamic policies, laying the foundations for the subsequent diplomatic achievements of the Protectorate.

These policies originated in the Rump's reaction to the current trade depression. A Council of Trade was appointed in August 1650 to find remedies for it. Its most notable proposal was the Navigation Act of October 1651, which declared that all imports to England had to be in English ships or in ships of the country where the imported goods originated. Although this was not the only cause of the war with the Dutch that began in 1652 (the English and Dutch had a long history of commercial rivalry), it was its major one. Largely due to the beginnings of the development of a powerful navy by the Commonwealth, it was a war in which the English were very successful. Behind its success, too, was the efficient administration of committed republicans, like Henry Marten and Thomas Challenor, who raised money by taxes, sales of dean and chapter lands and borrowing to pay for the war, belying (in part) the reputation that the Commonwealth later got as a corrupt and inefficient regime.

What did the Commonwealth not change?

Cromwell 'told the House, that they had sat long enough ... that some of them were whoremasters ... that others of them were drunkards, and some corrupt and unjust men and scandalous to the profession of the gospel, and it was not fit that they should sit as a parliament any longer.'

A report of Cromwell's speech on 20 April 1653 when dissolving the Rump Parliament, quoted in B. Worden, *The Rump Parliament* (1974).

One of the origins of the Commonwealth's reputation as a corrupt regime was the complaints of disappointed radicals in the army (including eventually Oliver Cromwell) and elsewhere at its failure to carry out further reforms after the political revolution of 1649. They were justified in their disappointment: the English Revolution came to a halt in 1649.

The conservatism of the Rump and Council of State was evident from the very beginning in the suppression of the Levellers. By March 1649 Lilburne, Walwyn and Overton were in prison and in the following weeks army mutinies were efficiently suppressed by Cromwell and Fairfax at Burford and elsewhere. Lilburne's angry, sarcastic outburst against the Commonwealth's 'new kind of liberty' is hardly surprising.

> *'A Councel of State is hastily erected for Guardians thereof, who to that end are possessed with power to order and dispose all the forces appertaining to England by Sea or Land, to dispose of the publicke Treasure, to command any person whatsoever before them, to give oath for the discovering of Truth, to imprison any that shall dis-obey their commands, and such as they shall judge contumacious. What now is become of that liberty that no mans person shall be attached or imprisoned, or otherwise dis-eased of his Free-hold, or free Customs, but by lawful judgement of his equals?'*
>
> J. Lilburne, *Englands New Chains Discovered*, 1649, quoted in G. Aylmer (ed.), *The Levellers in the English Revolution* (1975).

The Rump's conservatism was confirmed by the restrictions it placed on the press in September 1650 and its establishment of a monopoly for a government newspaper, *Mercurius Politicus*. This newspaper was launched in June 1650 and, under the editorship of Marchamont Needham, became a superb propaganda vehicle for the regime.

However, the most convincing evidence of the Commonwealth's conservatism both at the time and since was its dismal record on reform. Only when army pressure for reform became intense (especially after victories, like that at Dunbar) did the Rump make any significant progress.

Reform of the law

An example of this is the way that the Rump passed one of its few significant law reforms (the Act of October 1650 – see time chart) shortly after receiving Cromwell's letter from Dunbar urging reform. In January 1652, again under army pressure, with Colonel Pride and some soldiers outside the chamber, the Rump appointed a commission on law reform under Matthew Hale. Yet, although the Hale commission had drafted a series of reforms within six months, none of them was put into effect.

Social reform

Here, although there was no shortage of reform ideas, the Rump achieved even less. Ever since the early 1640s, pamphleteers like Samuel Hartlib had been producing plans for the reform of all walks of life, including state hospitals, school-building projects, state-run workhouses and banks. Hartlib even proposed what he called 'an Office of Addresses', a national body that would act as a labour exchange and as a coordinator of social reform projects. None of these proposals made any impact on the Rump, which passed no significant measure of social reform.

Religious reform

Here the most important measures passed by the Rump were: the Act of September 1650 that repealed all previous statutes that compelled people to attend the national Church; and, later, Acts for the Propagation of the Gospel in Wales, Ireland and parts of England, that were meant to provide well-paid and educated clergy to spread the gospel in 'the dark corners of the land'. But these did little to satisfy the demands of radicals who hoped that the political revolution of 1649 would be the prelude to a godly reformation, the centrepiece of which would be liberty of conscience. To their fury the Rump seemed intent on imposing religious intolerance not further toleration. In 1649 a parliamentary vote in favour of Presbyterianism was only defeated by the casting vote of the Speaker. Moreover, in 1650 it passed Acts (see the time chart) against religious nonconformity, adultery, fornication, incest and swearing, reflecting the belief of many in the Rump that the relaxation of the penalties enforcing religious uniformity was leading to the spread of extremist views, like those of the Ranters. Religious liberty was obviously very low on the Rump's agenda.

Constitutional reform

The Rump cannot be accused of not considering constitutional reform. Much parliamentary time was spent discussing schemes for the redistribution of parliamentary seats and for making arrangements for new elections and the transference of power to a new assembly. But not until its last few weeks did the Rump make any decisions on constitutional change. Consequently, suspicions grew in the army that the Rump was intent on perpetuating itself in power, especially when one of the schemes being discussed was merely for by-elections to fill vacant seats.

Why was the Commonwealth not a revolutionary regime?

There are two major reasons, the second of which is easily the more important.

1 It is a possibility that the day-to-day pressures of government were too urgent to allow time for plans for fundamental reform to be carried out. This is not without some substance. As has been seen, the early years of the Republic were fraught with perils for the new regime. There was an urgent need to put most of its efforts into meeting the threat to its security from Ireland, Scotland and the Royalists. The early years, too, were a period of severe economic depression, with fears of riots and rebellions (as well as Ranters, Diggers and Levellers). Reform took a poor second place to those kinds of considerations.

2 There is little doubt that there were few revolutionaries in the Commonwealth government. This is obviously a more fundamental reason why the Commonwealth was not a revolutionary regime!

But until the publication of the books on the Rump by Underdown and Worden (see 'Further reading', page 178), it was a reason that was missed by historians. Previous historians made two mistaken assumptions about the Rump:

■ that those who supported the purge of parliament in December 1648 were political radicals

■ that the Rump was purged of all conservative Presbyterians.

Underdown's detailed comparison of the supporters and the victims of the Purge suggest that the former were of slightly lower social status than the latter, but both were gentlemen. Moreover, even the most committed supporters of the regicide were not ideological republicans, the most startling illustration of which is that 22 of the original 41 members of the Council of State in 1649 would not take an oath which declared that they approved of the regicide. Theoretical justifications for taking the Oath of Engagement to the Republic were based on pragmaticism – that the regime demanded loyalty because it provided security against rebellion and invasion – and not the ideological superiority of republics over other forms of government.

In the early months of 1649 many MPs secluded in December 1648 returned to the Rump. In their hostility to the army and in their desire to woo the support of the traditional governors of the country, they were indistinguishable from those who had not been purged in 1648. For many of them their hostility to the army and reform grew greater with the passage of time. Even the cause of moderate reform was shunned because of its association with the army and with extremism. By 1652–3 there were all the ingredients for the kind of confrontation between parliament and army that had provoked army militancy in 1647 (see chapter 12).

Why was the Rump dissolved in April 1653?

Although the key lies with Oliver Cromwell, the Rump was not dissolved, as was once thought, because Cromwell discovered in April 1653 that parliament was about to pass a bill providing merely for by-elections and that this provoked his anger that the Rump was intent in keeping itself permanently in power. Although the bill does not survive (Cromwell destroyed it), it is highly likely that the bill provided for elections in November and made arrangements for new MPs to be vetted by the out-going parliament.

Why, then, did Cromwell dissolve the Rump? A possible answer is that by April 1653 he realised that it was no longer possible to maintain what he had been doing since 1649 – that is, keeping both the loyalty of the army and his contacts with the parliamentarians of the Rump. For much of the time he had been successful in straddling the world of the army and parliament. Like his allies in the Rump, he had worked assiduously to persuade secluded MPs to return to parliament, suppressed army mutinies and taken a firm anti-Leveller stance. But his campaigns in the army in Ireland and Scotland had kept burning brightly his yearning for reformation.

> 'After it had pleased God not only to realise Ireland and give in Scotland, but so marvellously to appear for the people at Worcester ... the Parliament had opportunity to give the people the harvest of all their labour, blood and treasure, and to settle a due liberty both in reference to civil and spiritual things ... it was a matter of much grief to the good and well-affected of the land, to observe the little progress which was made therein.'
>
> A declaration by Cromwell and the Council of Army officers, 22 April 1653, in W. C. Abbott (ed.), *The Writings and Speeches of Oliver Cromwell*, vol. 2.

Although after Worcester Cromwell still hoped that this might be achieved through the Rump, by April 1653 this hope had been aban-doned. What caused him to believe this? There is little doubt that the Rump's continued obstruction of reform in the winter of 1652–3 began to cause Cromwell to lose patience with parliament. It is very likely that he gradually became convinced that any parliament elected without the army imposing qualifications on its members would be hostile to reform and that for this reason alone he must act.

Was he also (as in 1648) driven by providential zeal? There can be no certain answer to this question, but it is possible that he was. In November 1652, according to Bulstrode Whitelocke, Cromwell said that 'there is little Hope of a Settlement to be made by them [the MPs of the Rump], really there is not ... We all forget God, and God will forget us, and render us up to Confusion.' As in 1648, Cromwell took part in prayer meetings in the Army Council in January 1653 to seek God's guidance and to find the source of the army's problems. At one of them the officers concluded that they were failing because they were losing God's support: 'our hearts have been looking after the things of the world and our present affairs, more than the things of Jesus Christ and His people'. For nearly the whole of March 1652 Cromwell was absent from parliament and the Council of State – a period of introspection and withdrawal, which preceded the decisive action he took on 20 April 1653. You might consider whether you think that during that time religious zeal, as well as the more practical realisation that army–parliament cooperation was no longer possible, gripped Cromwell and eventually pushed him to expel the Rump so violently on 20 April 1653.

Further reading

In addition to the textbooks that cover this period, see R. Hutton, *The British Republic* (Macmillan, 1990).

More detailed books are:

D. Underdown, *Pride's Purge: Politics During the English Revolution* (Oxford University Press, 1970).

B. Worden, *The Rump Parliament* (Cambridge University Press, 1975).

16 Image and reality: Barebones Parliament

Does Barebones Parliament deserve its poor reputation?

Following the dissolution of the Rump Parliament in April 1653, the history of the English Republic enters what has always seemed to be a bizarre and extraordinary interlude: the rule of a nominated assembly, variously ridiculed by contemporaries and historians alike as 'a parliament of saints' or **Barebones Parliament**. One does not have to look far for sneering comments on it by contemporaries.

> '*A pack of weak, senseless fellows; much the major part of them consisted of inferior persons, of no quality or name, artificers of the meanest trades, known only by their gifts in praying and preaching.*'
>
> Clarendon's *History of the Rebellion* (ed. W. D. Mackay, 1888).

> '*Abject and mean people*'
>
> James Heath, *Flagellum* (1660).

> '*Pettifoggers, Innkeepers, Millwrights, Stockingmongers and such a rabble as never had hopes to be of a Grand Jury.*'
>
> A contemporary letter from England to the exiled royalist court.

KEY TERM:

Barebones Parliament

Barebones Parliament is the label used here because it has been the one most commonly used from the time when the assembly was sitting until the present day. It was, though, not an elected parliament but an assembly of men chosen largely by the council of officers of the army. Also unlike normal parliaments before 1707, it contained representatives from Scotland and Ireland as well as England and Wales. It got its nickname from one of its members, Praise-God Barebone, a London leatherseller and lay preacher, who addressed his congregation in his warehouse. Yet Barebones was not a leading member of the Parliament, although he sat on a number of its committees. In the Common Council in January 1660 he spoke against sending the City's congratulations to General Monck, who (it will be seen) was paving the way for the restoration of the monarchy.

Even though these judgements all came from Royalist sources that were extremely hostile to the regicide republic, later writers have (until recently) generally accepted them, especially since these damning verdicts were shared by other, less hostile, observers. For example, Oliver Cromwell, who had a major role in summoning Barebones Parliament, later condemned it as leading to 'the subversion of the laws and of all the liberties of the nation, the destruction of the Ministry of this nation; in a word the confusion of all things'.

Does Barebones Parliament deserve this kind of reputation? One of the principal tasks of historians is to discover the extent to which the image that is commonly presented of individuals and episodes is a distortion of what actually happened. This chapter focuses on the contrast between the way Barebones Parliament was (and has been) portrayed and what later historical research has revealed.

The next section compares the historical 'reality' (what historians believe actually happened) with the 'image' (what people at the time believed happened). It will be seen that the two differ and that Barebones Parliament does not deserve its reputation.

Why, then, did it collapse after only five months? The final section of the chapter shows that (as on other occasions) what people believed to be true was more important than what actually happened.

Barebones Parliament: image and historical reality

Image

Barebones Parliament's image is based on three principal criticisms.

1 That it was the product of aims that were bound to fail, because they were impractical and idealistic, dreamed up by visionaries like **Major-General Thomas Harrison** and his **Fifth Monarchy** friends. Barebones Parliament was thought to have originated as part of their grand scheme for the rule of a godly elite, who were to prepare the ground for the imminent day when King Jesus should return to earth.

KEY TERM:

Fifth Monarchy Men

The **Fifth Monarchy Men** flourished in the early 1650s, especially among clothworkers in London. Fifth Monarchy Men, like John Rogers, interpreted prophecies in the Old Testament (especially in the books of Revelation and Daniel) to mean that the four great empires, after which it was foretold Christ's perpetual kingdom on earth (the Fifth Monarchy) would be established, were the four empires of Babylon, Persia, Greece and Rome. The Fifth Monarchy Men believed that the execution of Charles I was the sign that the establishment of the Fifth Monarchy, King Jesus' reign on earth, was imminent. In the meantime, they demanded that an interim body of godly men should rule according to the biblical laws of Moses (the Mosaic law).

PROFILE: *Major-General Thomas Harrison*

Harrison was possibly the son of a butcher from Newcastle-under-Lyme in Shropshire. Like Cromwell, he rose to prominence primarily as a soldier during the Civil War and he signed the king's death warrant in 1649. But unlike Cromwell his links with the army and radical religious sects were not counterbalanced by strong alliances with civilian politicians. After the collapse of Barebones Parliament, he refused to support the Protectorate and retired to private life in Shropshire and remained opposed to Cromwell. He was periodically arrested on suspicion of plotting against him. At the Restoration he was executed as a regicide. On the scaffold he was reported to have met his death courageously, answering someone in the crowd who called out, 'where is your good old cause now?' with the reply, putting his hand on his heart, 'here it is, and I am going to seal it with my blood'.

---

2 The second criticism is that Barebones Parliament, as befitted its origins, was composed of men who were quite unfitted to rule. Like Praise-God Barebone (see key term, page 179), most members of Barebones Parliament were said to have been drawn largely from outside the traditional governing landed class – men who were poorly educated, lacked political and administrative experience, and who were driven by religious fanaticism.

3 The final criticism is that Barebones Parliament spent its time discussing reforms that were too wild and impractical to have any chance of working. Like its origins and composition, Barebones Parliament's record made its collapse inevitable.

The historical reality

Recent studies of Barebones Parliament, however, have convincingly shown that each part of this image is a distortion of what actually happened in 1653.

1 *Its origins* It is undoubtedly true that millenarian expectations were high in the immediate wake of the dissolution of the Rump Parliament. Cromwell and many of his fellow senior army officers were desperate to find a means of achieving the kind of reforms that the Rump had been incapable of carrying out. The most dramatic example of this mood is Cromwell's speech at the opening of Barebones Parliament on 4 July 1653. It was peppered with fiery passages of enthusiastic millenarian expectation, delivered with tears, at times, rolling down Cromwell's cheeks, and in a style reminiscent of Martin Luther King's 'I have a dream' speech three centuries later.

> '*I confess I never looked to see such a day as this – it may be nor you either – when Jesus Christ should be so owned as He is, at this day, and in this work . . . I say you are called with a high call. And why should we be afraid to say or think, that this may be the day to usher in the things that God has promised; which hath been prophesied of; which He hath set the hearts of His people to wait for and expect? . . . Indeed I do think something is at the door; we are at the threshold.*'
>
> Cromwell's speech at the opening of Barebones Parliament, 4 July 1653, quoted in W. C. Abbott (ed.), *The Writings and Speeches of Oliver Cromwell*, vol. 3.

There is no evidence that Cromwell and other senior army officers intended to use military power to impose a full-scale, Fifth Monarchy-

PROFILE: *Major-General John Lambert*

Born into a minor Yorkshire gentry family, **Lambert** rose to importance solely as a successful soldier in the First and Second Civil Wars and in Scotland in 1650–51. Like Cromwell, he made the transition from soldier to politician and was the main architect of the Instrument of Government, that established the Protectorate in December 1653. From then until 1657 he was 'Cromwell's understudy'. If Cromwell had died before 1657 he may well have been his successor as Protector. But in 1657 his political fortunes collapsed. He opposed Cromwell's acceptance of a new constitution, the Humble Petition and Advice, and retired to private life at his house in Wimbledon, a former palace belonging to Queen Henrietta Maria. After Cromwell's death his political career briefly recovered and he was a major figure in the politics of the period that preceded the Restoration (see chapter 20). At the Restoration he was arrested and spent the last 14 years of his life as a prisoner on Guernsey and on St Nicholas Island in Plymouth Sound.

style millenarian rule of the saints. On the contrary, the available evidence suggests that they had no specific idea what to do after the sudden dissolution of the Rump.

They were more certain about what they did *not* want to do. They vigorously denied that they intended to establish a military dictatorship. In a printed letter, dated 3 May, written by a journalist employed by Cromwell, they countered the charge that their use of naked military power on 20 April had stifled 'the liberty of the people'. 'I must tell you again', the letter declared, 'it is only suspended, 'tis a sword taken out of a mad man's hand, till he recover his senses.' Such claims need, of course, to be treated with some scepticism, but they receive support from the fact that immediately after 20 April Cromwell and his senior army officers spent a lot of time discussing with civilian ex-Rumpers, including Oliver St John, means of drawing up 'some instrument of government that might put the power out of his [Cromwell's] hands'. The debate was not about whether or not the army should continue to hold power, but about the kind of body to which power should be transferred.

Two main proposals by leading army officers were discussed: **John Lambert**'s for the appointment of a small council of 12 men, chosen by the army, to fill the power vacuum temporarily; and Thomas Harrison's for an assembly of 70 men, appointed by the Independent **gathered churches**, modelled on the **Jewish Sanhedrin**, and ruling until Jesus'

KEY TERMS:

Gathered churches

These were Independent churches that had appeared since 1640, consisting of congregations that had broken away from the parish church. The congregations of **gathered churches** decided on their own form of worship, conducted by ministers they had chosen.

Jewish Sanhedrin(m)

This was the highest court of justice and supreme council in ancient Jerusalem between the 5th century BC and 70 AD.

earthly kingdom was established. Many have concluded (as did Lambert) that the Council of Officers' announcement on 30 April that power should be devolved on a small Council of State and a larger assembly of about 140 nominated men of 'approved fidelity and honesty' from all parts of Britain was a victory for Harrison. They (and he) were wrong. Harrison was equally as unhappy at the outcome and both men withdrew temporarily from the centre of the political stage.

Although power was passed to an assembly of godly men, it was made clear that this did not herald the permanent rule of an elite as the Fifth Monarchists intended. Cromwell and some of his officers shared Harrison's yearning for a godly reformation, but not at the expense of losing touch with political reality. They realised that Harrison's proposal would have further alienated the regime from conservative opinion. They also realised that to have called an elected parliament at that time would inevitably have resulted in a large anti-army majority and the collapse of their hopes of reform for ever. But they made it clear that they were in favour of calling elected parliaments in the future, as did Barebones Parliament. Shortly after it assembled it declared that 'our posterities . . . we expect still to be governed by successive parliaments'.

That Barebones Parliament originated in a spirit of pragmatism as well as of idealism is also shown by the limited role in the nomination of its members given to the gathered churches, which recommended only 15 of the 144 members of Barebones Parliament. The selection process was kept strictly in the hands of members of the Council of Officers, who believed that godliness was not the only necessary attribute of those chosen.

2 *Its composition*   As a result the membership of Barebones Parliament was very different from the image projected of it by Clarendon (see quote on page 179). It is true that those chosen were generally of slightly lower social status than those normally elected to parliaments in the seventeenth century. But the vast majority were gentlemen, including two titled noblemen (Lord Eure and Viscount Lisle) and representatives of leading county landed elites (like Anthony Ashley Cooper, Sir Charles Wolseley and three future earls). Most were from the lower end of the gentry, but very few were tradesmen. Moreover, few of them lacked an education or political and administrative experience. Around 60 had been educated at a university or Inn of Court, 14 or 15 were barristers, 119 were JPs (including 89 who had been JPs before 1650), and even more had served on parliamentary commissions in their localities.

Clearly Barebones Parliament was not 'a rabble as never had hopes to be of a Grand Jury'. Nor do its members fit comfortably into the image of religious fanatics. Detailed research by Capp and Woolrych has uncovered only 13 Fifth Monarchists in Barebones Parliament and many of them (including Harrison) played only a small part in its proceedings. Very few were out-and-out religious radicals, and most were moderate religious Independents, who wanted liberty for individual consciences within a broad national Church.

3 *Its record*   What is also surprising to those accustomed to the image of Barebones Parliament as a complete flop is both the efficiency with which it went about its business and its practical achievements. In some respects it acted like a normal seventeenth-century parliament. It met in St Stephen's Chapel, Westminster, the home of normal parliaments; and it chose a Speaker (Francis Rous, who had sat in every parliament since 1626) and a Clerk (Henry Scobell, who had held that post in the Rump). In other respects it acted more efficiently than normal parliaments, few of whom met (as did Barebones Parliament) regularly from 8 a.m. and on six days a week. Nor did its habit of occasionally setting days aside for prayer (as did the Long Parliament) interfere unduly with its business, which was streamlined by a structure of standing committees, devised by a 'committee for committees'.

In this context its legislative record is not surprising. In just over five months it passed over thirty statutes and many other bills were in the pipeline when it ended in December 1653. Most progress was made on law reform. Acts were passed for the relief of creditors and poor prisoners, and civil marriages carried out by JPs were legalised. To fill the gap left by the collapse of the church courts, machinery was established for the probate of wills and for registering births, marriages and deaths.

Even more wide-ranging law reforms were being drafted, taking up many of the Hale Commission's recommendations (see chapter 15). Measures were also proposed to rationalise the revenue system, including abolition of the hated excise, and an act was passed to regulate the conditions under which idiots and lunatics were kept. Barebones Parliament, too, continued the Rump's work in bringing Scotland even further than ever under English control, making the government of 'Britain' a reality for the first time since the union of the crowns in 1603.

The end of Barebones Parliament

Why, then, did Barebones Parliament come to an end in December 1653 after a mere five months' session?

The answer is more complicated than simply the inevitable collapse of an assembly of idealistic, inept religious fanatics. Far from being inevitable, Barebones Parliament came to an end suddenly. On 12 December a group of conservative members (led by Sir Charles Wolseley, Ashley Cooper and others) met even earlier than usual by prior arrangement (perhaps in collusion with John Lambert, who had returned to London a few weeks before and had spent the time discussing constitutional proposals). They proposed that Barebones Parliament abdicate its power to Cromwell. The Speaker refused to hear any objections and a group of 50 (later swollen to about 80) marched to Whitehall to present a paper of abdication to Cromwell. He accepted it and soldiers were sent to eject those who had remained behind.

It is true that, before that date, opinion in Barebones Parliament had polarised on radical–moderate lines on issues like proposals to abolish tithes and impropriated livings, but such divisions had only rarely disrupted the assembly's business and the radicals never gained over-whelming control. Indeed in November the assembly elected more moderate members to the Council of State than ever.

Why, then, very shortly afterwards did a majority of its members make the offer to abdicate and why did Cromwell accept it?

The broad answer is that by December both they and he had come to share the view of conservative opinion in the country at large that if Barebones Parliament continued the world would be turned upside down. Barebones Parliament came to be *seen* (even by the man who had brought it into being and by some of its members) as something that it was *not*.

To many, Barebones Parliament appeared to be a major threat to the hierarchical social order. Although many of its members were not low-born revolutionaries intent on subverting society: what aroused fears that they were is that many were drawn from the lesser gentry. When Barebones Parliament continued the wide-ranging purges of the commissions of the peace begun by the Rump, in which many wealthy men were ejected from what they considered to be their rightful places on the bench, these fears were confirmed. To a gentry governing class whose fears of social revolution had already reached high levels of paranoia (see chapter 14) such measures were ominous. Even though Barebones Parliament demonstrated its conservatism by arresting and bringing to trial the Leveller leader, John Lilburne, this rebounded against it. The huge, popular demonstrations in London that greeted Lilburne's acquittal were unfairly slotted into the image of Barebones Parliament as a regime that encouraged radicalism.

This was reinforced by the way Barebones Parliament seemed also to be fostering religious radicalism. Although there were very few religious extremists in the assembly, many came to believe that religious liberty was being abused and that taking place before their eyes was what ortho- dox clergy had always predicted: that religious freedom would produce social disorder. Though they were few in number and not members of Barebones Assembly, some religious radicals were very outspoken in their condemnation of established clergy. In October 1653 in a debate with orthodox ministers one religious radical, William Erbery, denounced his opponents as 'Monsters, Beasts, Asses, greedy dogs, False Prophets'. The upshot was a riot. Although the Council of State published declarations forbidding such events, it was the regime that was given the blame.

When Cromwell much later said of Barebones Parliament, 'what did they? Fly at liberty and property', he was merely reflecting a common view. What, above all, reinforced it were the attempts by radicals in the assembly to push radical proposals regarding two matters: reform of the law and the interlinked issue of tithes and lay patronage of church livings. Although there was much common ground on reforming the law as the Hales Commission had recommended, a few radicals pressed for even more fundamental changes, some even proposing the Fifth Monarchist idea of the establishment of the Mosaic law instead of the English common law. To some, the radicals' victory on 5 August in securing a vote in favour of abolishing the court of Chancery was seen as a terrifying move in that direction. Even more horrendous to conserva- tive opinion were the proposals that were made to abolish tithes and advowsons (right to appoint church ministers). As was seen in chapter 4, both had generally become recognised by many landed gentlemen as parts of their property rights and such proposals threatened them directly. Not surprisingly, a narrow vote on 10 December (56 : 52) reject- ing a committee's report to retain tithes was the event which convinced many in the assembly as well as outside it that the image of a regime intent on subverting property and society as they knew it was correct.

Conclusion

It is not without irony that, whereas the Rump was brought to an end because it dragged its heels on reform, Barebones Parliament collapsed because it attempted to carry out reform with too much enthusiasm. As a result, it came to be seen as a revolutionary threat, mounted by low-born religious fanatics, to the social order and the political fabric of the state. That image is not borne out by historical reality, but it was its image that ensured that it lasted for only five months.

Task

This task covers the topic in chapter 15 as well as Barebones Parliament. It asks you to explain why both regimes that were established in the first years of the English republic (the Rump Parliament and Barebones Parliament) failed to provide the basis for permanent republican rule.

This is not an easy historical problem to tackle, because (as we have just seen) both the Rump Parliament and Barebones Parliament were very different in character; despite the qualifications made in this chapter, Barebones Parliament was a much more radical regime than the government of the Rump Parliament.

Why, then, did both regimes fail? Working out your answer to this question will give you some idea of the enormity of the problems Cromwell faced when he became Protector of Britain in December 1653 and tried to establish a workable constitutional settlement.

The task is to write an essay on the following question: 'Why did the Rump and Barebones parliaments fail to provide the basis of permanent Republican rule?'

Here are some ideas – by no means the only ones – for how the structure of an answer might look:

1 England in 1649: deeply divided.
   (a) Most of the traditional governing class terrified of radicalism and reform, in religion (toleration), in politics (wider franchise), and wanted order.
   (b) Army was focus of those determined to achieve the reforms they had fought for.
   Republican regimes had to try to satisfy both.

2 Republican government seeking for legitimacy, in absence of king. This lay with the Rump, as remnants of elected parliament. But Rump reluctant to countenance any reform – give some details of legislative programme here (see chapter 15). So removed by army.

3 Barebones. Not as radical or crazed as myth (see this chapter). Give details of legislative programme here. But Barebones perceived to be dangerously radical. So dissolved by actions of its more conservative members.

4 Conclusion. Same problem of having to satisfy conservative and radical elements landed on Cromwell.

Further reading

In addition to the textbooks listed at the end of previous chapters, the Longman Seminar Studies in History volume by T. Barnard, *The English Republic* (1982) and the Lancaster pamphlet by A. Woolrych, *England Without a King* (1983) cover this topic.

The best detailed book on it is:

A. Woolrych, *From Commonwealth to Protectorate* (Oxford University Press, 1983).

See also B. Capp, *The Fifth Monarchy Men: a Study in Seventeenth-Century Millenarianism* (Faber, 1972).

17 What were Cromwell's aims for Britain, 1653–8?

Time chart

1653: December Cromwell inaugurated as Protector under the constitution known as the Instrument of Government

1654: January The Oath of Engagement is abolished
March Protector and council issue the triers ordinance; (in **April**) an ordinance uniting England and Scotland; (**August**) ordinances establishing ejectors and reforming chancery
September Cromwell's first parliament meets after MPs are forced to sign a 'Recognition' of the legality of the Instrument of Government, or resign
November George Cony imprisoned for refusing to pay customs duties that have not been approved by parliament
December The 'Western Design' leaves for the Caribbean

1655: January Cromwell angrily dissolves his first parliament
March Penruddock's royalist rebellion in Wiltshire is put down
April 'Western Design' defeated at San Domingo
May Cony's lawyers are imprisoned
June Lord Chief Justice Rolle resigns over his part in Cony's case
August The Major-Generals are appointed

1656: September Second Protectorate Parliament begins after exclusion of over 100 MPs

1657: January Cromwell decides to abandon the Instrument of Government and the Major-Generals
March A new constitution (the Humble Petition and Advice) and the crown is offered by parliament to Cromwell
May Cromwell accepts the Humble Petition and Advice but not the crown
June Cromwell re-installed as Protector

1658: February Cromwell dismisses his second parliament
September Oliver Cromwell dies and is succeeded as protector by his son, Richard.

On 16 December 1653, four days after the sudden end of the Barebones Parliament, **Oliver Cromwell** was installed as Lord Protector of England, Wales, Ireland and Scotland.

PROFILE: *Oliver Cromwell*

For the next five years Britain was ruled by someone very different from Stuart monarchs. **Oliver Cromwell** owed his position not to hereditary right but to his brilliant military career. Born in 1599, his life before 1640 is very obscure. He rarely left his native East Anglia, where he was a working farmer who eventually inherited enough land to be considered a minor gentleman. When the Long Parliament met in 1640 he was returned as MP for Cambridge, but despite his distant family connections with some of the parliamentary leaders, he did not become of significant political importance until his well-reported victories as a cavalry commander in the army of the Eastern Association in 1643–4 (notably at the Battle of Marston Moor) made him known nationally. From that point on (as seen in earlier chapters) he played an important role in the postwar political events that culminated in the establishment of the republic in 1649. It is likely, though, that he never was as prominent in these events as is sometimes assumed (Henry Ireton's role in 1648, for example, was at least as important as his). But, his military achievements in defeating the republic's enemies in Ireland (1649–50) and in Scotland (1650–51) again catapulted him to the forefront of politics as disillusionment with the Rump grew. One of the many remarkable aspects of his career is the rapidity of his rise from a fairly humble East Anglian farmer to the dizzy heights of ruler of Britain. Oliver Cromwell died in 1658.

Nothing better underlines the break with British monarchical tradition that took place in the 1650s than the contrast between elaborate royal coronations of the past and the brief, simple ceremony in Westminster Hall in December 1653. Cromwell, wearing a plain black suit, swore an oath pledging that as Protector he would settle Britain 'upon such Basis and Foundation as, by the blessing of God, might be lasting, secure Property, and answer those great Ends of Religion and Liberty so long contended for'. Yet the Protectorate of Oliver Cromwell has often been portrayed as a regime that gradually became more traditional, making the restoration of monarchy in 1660 unsurprising and inevitable. This and the next three chapters present material that will enable you to question the view that the restoration of the monarchy was indeed inevitable.

This chapter focuses on Cromwell's aims as Protector of Britain, a subject about which historians have never agreed. It will be argued here that Cromwell's aims were not those of a conservative figure (rather like Napoleon and Stalin in the later revolutions in France and Russia) presiding over a regime that ditched the revolutionary ideals of the 1640s. Cromwell is portrayed as a man for whom these ideals remained alive.

The first section of this chapter shows that the view of Cromwell as a conservative ruler is not *totally* erroneous. One of his main aims as Protector was to try to win the support of the traditional ruling classes of the country and to heal the divisions (he often called them 'the wounds') caused by the Civil War. Pursuing that aim of 'settlement' often made the Protector seem to be a very conservative figure.

In the second part of the chapter it will be seen that Cromwell had another important aim as Protector that ran counter to, and at times of crisis took precedence over, his desire for 'settlement'. This was his yearning for the godly reformation that had driven him and other militant activists to fight against the king in the Civil War. The fact that Cromwell's zeal for 'reformation' remained undimmed is the key to explaining three of the major episodes of the history of the Protectorate:

■ the failure of the two Protectorate Parliaments (1654–5 and 1656–8)

■ the authoritarian policies pursued in the mid 1650s (including the rule of the Major-Generals) and

■ Cromwell's refusal of the crown in 1657.

Cromwell and 'settlement'

'I am hugely taken with the word Settlement, with the thing and with the notion of it', Cromwell told a parliamentary delegation in April 1657, repeating a point he made on many other occasions during the Protectorate. What he meant by 'settlement' was a government as similar as possible to a traditional one. Cromwell was not a republican ideologue. As was seen in chapter 13, in the late 1640s he had tried to reach a settlement with Charles I on the basis of *The Heads of the Proposals* in association with Political Independent allies like Lord Saye and Sele and Oliver St John. Only reluctantly and belatedly had he taken the decision to execute the king. Even after that, he often made it clear that he was not opposed in principle to monarchy. In 1651 he was reported as saying that 'if it may be done with safety, and preservation of our Rights, both as Englishmen and Christians, a Settlement with somewhat of Monarchical power in it would be very effectual'.

The Instrument of Government, which from 1653 to 1657 was the constitution of the Protectorate (probably written by John Lambert), embodied many of the aspirations Cromwell had shared with civilian Political Independent parliamentarians in the late 1640s. Government was to be by 'one single person' called a Protector, who was to share control of the army with parliaments that were to be elected every three years and which sat for a minimum of five months. The Protector (like monarchs as envisaged by *The Heads of the Proposals*) was to act in financial and military matters and in the appointment of senior officers of state with a Council of State. Eight of the original 15 members of the Council were civilians and only four (John Desborough, Charles Fleetwood, John Lambert and Philip Skippon) can definitely be labelled as 'soldiers'.

What must also have seemed reassuringly unrevolutionary to propertied people was Cromwell's abandonment of the Rump's Oath of Engagement, which forced men to swear allegiance to the republic and to recognise the abolition of the monarchy and the House of Lords. When Cromwell opened the first Protectorate Parliament in September 1654 he stressed the importance of 'healing and settling'. 'Remembering transactions too particularly,' he said, referring to the violence and conflicts of the recent past, 'may set the wound fresh a-bleeding.' In an effort to heal those wounds and win support for the Protectorate, he emphasised his attachment to the traditional hierarchical social order: 'a nobleman, a gentleman and a yeoman (That is a good interest of the nation and a great one)'. Remarkably, he added that 'property [was one of] the badges of the kingdom of Christ'. John Lilburne remained securely locked in the Tower and Cromwell poured scorn on 'Levelling principles [that] tend to the reducing of all to equality'.

Later in the Protectorate Cromwell went even further in his attempt to make the regime acceptable to conservative opinion. In 1657, in the face of severe opposition from within the army, he gave way to the pressure of his civilian advisers, principally **Roger Boyle (Lord Broghill)** to ditch the army's constitution, the Instrument of Government, and accept a new parliamentary constitution, the Humble Petition and Advice. Although he refused the associated offer of the throne, he accepted all the other parts of the new civilian constitution. These included parliamentary approval of the great officers of state and the appointment of a second, House of Lords-like, parliamentary chamber – 'the Other House' – whose members were to be nominated by the Protector and Council.

Though he was not King Oliver, by this time Cromwell as Protector often looked and acted like a king. Throughout his Protectorate he was officially called 'Your Highness' and signed documents as 'Oliver P' in imitation of the royal 'Charles R'. The Cromwellian court, whether at Whitehall or Hampton Court, was not unlike that of a monarch. Tapestries, paintings and fountains, that had been removed during the Civil War, were restored. Even the Royalist diarist, John Evelyn, after visiting Whitehall in 1656, had to concede that it was 'very glorious and well furnished'. Like monarchs, Cromwell knighted people, and even created two life peers. Two of his daughters married noblemen. His reinvestiture as Protector in June 1657 under the Humble Petition and Advice, unlike his

PROFILE: *Roger Boyle, Lord Broghill*

Boyle (1621–79) was the third son of Richard Boyle, first Earl of Cork, a leader of the Protestant 'New English' (see chapter 7) in Ireland. In the 1640s he served with the royalist army against the Irish rebellion. But, after the execution of the king in 1649, he was persuaded by Cromwell to join him on his Irish military campaign of 1649–50. During the Protectorate he became one of Cromwell's chief civilian confidants. He was Lord President of the Council of Scotland in 1656, helping to create an orderly administration there. In England he consistently tried to persuade Cromwell to follow conservative policies that would win the support of the traditional ruling elite. He was behind the offer of the crown to Cromwell in 1657. After Cromwell's death he returned to Ireland and helped secure the country for Charles II. At the Restoration he was rewarded with the earldom of Orrery and he became Lord President of Munster in Ireland.

first inauguration in December 1653, was regal in splendour. Surrounded by leading national and international dignitaries, Cromwell, dressed in an ermine-lined robe, took the oath as Protector, after being given the sword of state and a sceptre of gold.

Cromwell and 'reformation'

What makes Cromwell such an interesting and complex character is that alongside his conservative desire for 'settlement' he also had a driving zeal for 'reformation'. What he meant by that, it has to be admitted, is far from clear. It undoubtedly did *not* mean the imposition of a gloomy, 'puritanical' society by a man who was hostile to fun and enjoyment, as well as music, art and literature, as has sometimes been imagined. A book of Cromwellian jokes would be a slim volume, but his employment of a master of music at Hampton Court and his patronage of artists, dramatists and poets, including Milton and Dryden, is enough to explode the image of Cromwell as a cultural philistine.

One of the reasons why it is difficult to be equally definite about what Cromwell *did* mean by 'reformation' is that he rarely put his vision of a reformed Britain into words. Frustratingly, his references to it are vague, as when he said that his aim was 'to reap the fruit of all the blood and treasure that has been spent in this cause'. Yet two main themes can be seen running through his speeches, writings and actions: a concern for social justice and a yearning for a godly 'reformation of manners'.

Cromwell and social justice

The first is clearly seen in this letter that he wrote, still in a state of euphoria, on the day after he had led the English army to a miraculous victory over a much larger Scottish army at Dunbar on 3 September 1650.

> 'Relieve the oppressed, hear the groans of poor prisoners in England; be pleased to reform the abuses of all professions; and if there anyone that makes many poor to make a few rich that suits not a Commonwealth.'
>
> Cromwell's letter to the Speaker of the Commons, 4 September 1650, quoted in W. C. Abbott (ed.), *The Writings and Speeches of Oliver Cromwell*, vol. 2.

Cromwell's ideal 'commonwealth' had no place for ideas of social equality, but he did believe that the rich, as well as having rightful privileges, also had responsibilities to care for those less well-off than themselves. From this stemmed Cromwell's consistent interest in reform of education, government and the law. During the Protectorate he backed an unsuccessful attempt to found a third English university at Durham, and he urged JPs to administer local matters, like poor relief, effectively and fairly. He always gave law reform a high profile. Before the first Protectorate Parliament met, he and his Council used the powers given them by the Instrument of Government to issue an ordinance making access to the court of Chancery easier and cheaper. He brought to London a Gloucestershire law reformer, William Sheppard, 'to consider (as he told the first Protectorate Parliament) how the laws might be made plain and short, and less chargeable to the people, how to lessen expense, for the good of the nation'.

Cromwell and 'a godly reformation'

It is not necessary to explain in detail the second theme of Cromwell's vision of a reformed country – the reformation of manners – since this was done in chapter 4. Like godly men and women since at least the 1580s, Cromwell believed that the Reformation that had been begun in the mid sixteenth century would not be achieved until there had been a spiritual reformation of people's lives. Only then would God give the nation His blessing and enable the country to become truly reformed.

Like his godly comrades, he saw an alliance between magistrates and ministers as the best way of achieving this reformation of manners. During the first months of the Protectorate, therefore, officials were to be appointed – **Triers and Ejectors** – who were to ensure that the Church was staffed by godly men. Apart from that, Cromwell envisaged that

KEY TERMS:

Triers and Ejectors

Triers were men appointed to a central commission, which was to assess all applications to the ministry. **Ejectors** were appointed to local commissions, which were to weed out unsuitable ministers.

there would be little state control over people's religious beliefs. There was to be, Cromwell said, 'no compulsion but that of light and reason'. By that he certainly did not mean there should be an unlimited religious liberty that would destroy the unity of Protestantism. Not only Catholics, therefore, were excluded from Cromwellian 'toleration'. Protestants, like Quakers (see chapter 20), who often violently interrupted church services, were also not welcome.

Yet Cromwellian 'toleration' was far more tolerant of different religious groups, including Presbyterians, Independents and Baptists, than was the Church presided over by Archbishop Laud in the 1630s (see chapter 7) or the Church that was to be restored in the 1660s (see chapter 21).

> *'If men will profess – be those under Baptism, be those of the Independent judgement simply, and of the Presbyterian judgement – in the name of God encourage them … to make use of their own consciences.'*
>
> Cromwell's speech to parliament, 17 September 1656, quoted in W. C. Abbott (ed.), *The Writings and Speeches of Oliver Cromwell*, vol. 3.

As will be seen, few who heard Cromwell's speech were willing to go as far as him, fearing, as many who became Royalists in the early 1640s had done, that religious liberty would lead to social revolution. Yet 'liberty for tender consciences' was central to Cromwell's desire for 'reformation' and, unlike many other godly gentlemen, he consistently refused to abandon it. He was not willing to sacrifice that principle even though it would have brought him much political popularity.

One of the clues that helps to explain the puzzle of why Cromwell gave a higher priority to the principle of religious liberty than to political expediency is that for him the biblical parallel between the English of the 1650s and the Israelites of Old Testament days remained a powerful influence (see chapter 4). As the Israelite example showed, victory over their Egyptian oppressors at the Battle of Jericho depended on their first purging themselves of sin. Only then did they win God's blessing and thereby inherit the Promised Land of Jerusalem. Like the Israelites, Cromwell believed the English needed to undergo a 'reformation of manners', because only then would the creation of a godly society be made possible.

> [We do not want] 'a captain to lead us back into Egypt, if there be such a place – I mean metaphorically and allegorically so – that is to say, returning to all those things that we think we have been fighting against … I am confident that the liberty and prosperity of this nation depends upon reformation … make it a shame to see men to be bold in sin and prophaneness and God will bless you.'
>
> Cromwell's speech to parliament, 17 September 1656, quoted in W. C. Abbott (ed.), *The Writings and Speeches of Oliver Cromwell*, vol. 4.

It is fundamental to an understanding of Cromwell's political position in the 1650s to realise that such views, though not unique, were not shared by many politically-powerful people. Unlike many others, Cromwell's zeal for reformation remained undimmed. One effect was to weaken his political position and to increase his reliance on the army. The army became more than ever his main hope for securing his hoped-for godly reformation.

Cromwell and his parliaments

This is one of the main reasons why both Protectorate Parliaments ended in failure. For most MPs hatred of the army was indistinguishable from their loathing of religious liberty, and during his Protectorate Cromwell was closely identified with both.

Cromwell did not help matters by his failure to provide a political lead for MPs. He once said that he had chosen to adopt as Protector the role of a 'good constable to keep the peace of the parish', and by and large he does not seem to have indulged in tactics of parliamentary management. To that extent Trevor-Roper's diagnosis of the failure of parliamentary rule during the Protectorate is correct (see 'Further reading' on page 199). But it is unlikely that any amount of behind-the-scenes preparations would have prevented the ferocious attack made on Cromwell at the opening of the first Protectorate Parliament by **Commonwealthsmen**, whose memory of 20 April 1653 was still very much alive. Their anger at the army's interference with parliamentary privileges was increased by the legislative powers given to the Protector and Council by the Instrument of Government.

A few days after the start of the session in September 1654 these vocal opponents and others (about 100 MPs in all) withdrew from parliament after refusing to sign a declaration that they would adhere to the principle

KEY TERM:

Commonwealthsmen

Commonwealthsmen were those who had keenly supported the rule of the Rump (1649–53). Prominent Commonwealthsmen were Arthur Haselrige, Edmund Ludlow, Henry Marten and Thomas Scot, who were united in the belief in parliamentary liberties. From the army's expulsion of the Rump on 20 April 1653 onwards the Commonwealthsmen were consistent opponents of the Protector and the army.

of government by a single person and a parliament. Two years later the Council excluded a similar number of MPs from the first session of the second Protectorate Parliament. Nevertheless, despite the absence of Commonwealthsmen in both parliamentary sessions of 1654–5 and 1656–7, differences between Protector and the remaining MPs on the allied issues of the army and religious liberty were still very much alive. Both sessions saw sustained outbursts of religious intolerance and anti-army feeling, that reached heights not seen since the days of Holles's 'counter-revolution' of 1647 (see chapter 12). Cromwell's sudden dissolutions of both parliaments in January 1655 and in February 1658 were largely motivated by his anger at the ferocity of these attacks which threatened to kill his hopes for 'reformation'.

Cromwell's 'personal rule' and the Major-Generals, 1655–6

As can be seen from the time chart on page 188, the period in between the meetings of Oliver Cromwell's two parliaments is marked by a period of unparliamentary, authoritarian rule. This is illustrated principally by **Cony's Case**, Cromwell's treatment of leading judges, and the appointment of eleven Major-Generals to rule the English provinces.

In part, the reasons for this departure from parliamentary rule were pragmatic: the collapse of the first Protectorate Parliament and Cromwell's increasingly isolated political position made any other course difficult. But it is likely that Cromwell's commitment to 'reformation' provides the most important explanation.

One principal event in 1655 led him to believe that 'reformation' was in danger and that severe, drastic measures were needed to save it. The effect of the failure of the **'Western Design'** on Cromwell was devastating. When in July 1655 he heard of its defeat at San Domingo in the Caribbean, he shut himself away alone in his room for a whole day. Just as military victories in the past had convinced him that he had God's support, so he felt that the humiliating defeat of his forces in the Caribbean had been caused by God's rebuke. For Cromwell the cause was clear: 'we have cause to be humbled for the reproof God gave us at San Domingo, upon the account of our sins, as well as others', he wrote to one of his commanders in the Caribbean. He was equally as certain about the remedy: steps needed to be taken urgently, he ordered, to ensure that 'all manner of vice may be thoroughly discountenanced and severely punished; and that such a form of government may be exercised that virtue and godliness may receive due encouragement'.

KEY TERMS:

Cony's Case

This case was brought in November 1654 in the Court of Upper Bench by the Council of State against George Cony, a merchant who refused to pay customs duties on imported silk on the grounds that they had not been approved by parliament. A few months later, Cony's lawyers were imprisoned for questioning the Protector's prerogative and a senior judge was forced to resign for having allowed the case to proceed.

'Western Design'

This was an English military-naval expeditionary force sent by Cromwell to attack Spanish trade and colonies in the Caribbean. Like the promoters of the Providence Island Company in the 1630s (see page 117), Cromwell hoped to strike a blow at Catholicism in the New World, as well as to capture valuable Spanish possessions. The expedition was a total disaster. The Spanish forces on Hispaniola (modern Haiti and the Dominican Republic) were too strong and defeated the expedition at San Domingo on 25 April 1655. After retreating to Jamaica, where about half the expeditionary force died from disease, the commanders of the 'Western Design' (William Penn and Robert Venables) returned home, where they were imprisoned in the Tower.

KEY TERM:

Decimation tax

This was the nickname given to a fine, first levied in 1655, of 10 per cent on wealthy men who had fought for the king in the Civil War. The money was to be used to pay for new local militias.

There were many reasons for the appointment of the Major-Generals in August 1655 – security was undoubtedly one, in the wake of the Royalist Penruddock Rising – but Cromwell's zeal for 'reformation' was the principal one. In October revised instructions were sent to the Major-Generals that stressed moral reform as one of their prime tasks: the vigorous prosecution of drunkenness, blasphemy, swearing and adultery and the suppression of gaming houses, alehouses and brothels. As in 1648 (see chapter 13), Cromwell vented his anger on those who he felt were standing in the way of a national reformation. The **decimation tax** was justified on the grounds that the taxpayers were major obstacles to the 'hopes we have conceived of seeing this poor nation settled and reformed from that spirit of prophaness which these men do keepe up and countenance'. He later went even further, denouncing 'Papists and Cavaliers' as 'un-Christian' and 'un-English-like'.

Many of Cromwell's actions during this period of 'personal rule' in 1655–6 suggest that 'reformation' had taken precedence over 'settlement' in his mind.

Why did Cromwell refuse the crown in 1657?

Cromwell rarely allowed such a situation to continue for long. His instincts were to try to reconcile the tensions between his aims of 'settlement' and 'reformation'. This is one reason why he did not oppose the end of the rule of the Major-Generals and the moves towards a new civilian constitution in the winter of 1656–7. 'He sings sweetly that sings a song of reconciliation betwixt these two interests [of settlement and reformation],' he said in April 1657 to a parliamentary committee that urged him to accept the Humble Petition and Advice. 'I think in this government [the proposed constitution] you have made them consist.' The only major part of it he would not accept was its offer to him of the crown. After agonising over the offer for weeks in the spring of 1657 he finally turned it down. Why?

It is unlikely that he had only one reason for doing so. Maybe, as many in the past have supposed, he was afraid of losing the support of the army if he took the crown. Maybe, too, he did not want to give too much influence to civilian advisers. Perhaps he suspected that people, like Lord Broghill, who pressed him to accept the crown and who were not sympathetic to his plans for a godly reformation would have too much influence if he became King Oliver.

As always, though, a major consideration in Cromwell's calculations was his providential zeal for reformation. To a man who was already worried, by the evidence of the 'Western Design', that he had lost God's support, it is possible that what Cromwell feared most at this crucial time was not the army but God. Would not his acceptance of the kingship be seen as a sign of his own sin of pride, ambition and self-advancement? Voicing these fears to a parliamentary delegation at the height of the kingship crisis, he said that if the crown was given to someone 'that God has no pleasure in, that perhaps may be the end of this work'. In any case, had not God's will been to destroy the monarchy in 1649. Would not the consequence of flying in the face of God's judgement be disastrous? This was the key point Cromwell made when he explained his reasons for rejecting the crown in April 1657:

> 'Truly the providence of God has laid this title [monarchy] aside providentially ... God ... hath not only dealt so with the persons and the family [the Stuarts] but he hath blasted the title ... I would not seek to set up that that providence hath destroyed and laid in the dust, and I would not build Jericho again.'

There could be no better demonstration of the main argument of this chapter, that when the task of reconciling his two major aims – settlement and reformation – became impossible, Cromwell always chose the more politically hazardous cause of reformation.

Task

Working in groups, decide whether or not you agree with the interpretation of Cromwell's aims given in this chapter. (For a different one, read the section on Cromwell in R. Hutton's *The British Republic*.) Cromwell is a man about whom historical opinion is divided and there is no 'correct' historical interpretation of him. You are free to come to your own conclusions. Remember, though, that you must back them up with evidence and reasoned argument.

As you work, bear in mind the following questions:

1 Settlement
  a What did Cromwell mean by 'settlement'?
  b Why did he want a 'settlement'?
  c What does this tell us about his aims?

2 Reformation

    a What did Cromwell mean by 'Reformation'?

    b Why did he want 'Reformation'?

    c What does this tell us about his aims?

3 What were the reasons for:

    a the failure of Cromwell's parliaments?

    b the appointment of the Major-Generals?

    c Cromwell's refusal of the crown?

Note that in dealing with these three questions, this chapter has emphasised one particular reason. You should consider other possible causes.

4 What do your answers to all parts of question **3** tell you about Cromwell's aims? Use these headings to write notes on Oliver Cromwell and his character and aims.

Further reading

In addition to the textbooks listed at the end of previous chapters, see also:

R. Hutton, *The British Republic* (Macmillan, 1990)

B. Coward, *Oliver Cromwell* (Addison Wesley Longman, 1991)

D. Smith, *Oliver Cromwell: Politics and Religion in the English Revolution 1640–58* (Cambridge University Press, 1991)

J. Morrill (ed.), *Oliver Cromwell and the English Revolution* (Addison Wesley Longman, 1990).

There is a handy edition of Cromwell's speeches edited by I. Roots (ed.), *Cromwell's Speeches* (Dent, 1989).

H. Trevor-Roper's argument that the explanation for the failure of Cromwell's parliaments is to be found in Cromwell's lack of parliamentary management is set out in his article 'Oliver Cromwell and his parliaments' in I. Roots (ed.), *Cromwell: a Profile* (Macmillan, 1973).

18 Was the rule of Oliver Cromwell a failure?

Hindsight is sometimes a blessing for historians. In attempting to make sense of what happened in the past, the knowledge of how historical stories ended puts historians at a tremendous advantage over people who lived at the time.

Yet hindsight can also be a historian's curse. This chapter emphasises the disadvantages that hindsight can have for historical studies. In the case of the rule of Oliver Cromwell it has produced distorted accounts of what happened during the Protectorate. The knowledge that the Protectorate was short-lived and that the monarchy was restored in 1660 has caused some historians to give too much emphasis to opposition to the republic, leading to assumptions that Cromwell's rule in England was a failure and that the eventual collapse of the republic was 'inevitable'.

The argument of this chapter is that this is a misleading interpretation of Oliver Cromwell's Protectorate between 1653 and 1658. England in the 1650s was not a country seething with a growing hostility to Cromwell and the republican regime that culminated in an anti-republican, pro-Royalist explosion shortly after his death.

Was, then, Cromwell's rule a success? As in similar cases in which historians (or examiners) ask this kind of question, the answer depends on what is meant by 'success'. In the first section of the chapter evidence will be presented to show that, if by 'success' is meant the full realisation of Cromwell's own ambitions and the achievement of *enthusiastic* support in the country for the regime, then the answer is a definite 'no'.

The second section of the chapter, however, demonstrates that if the Protectorate's 'success' is judged by the extent to which it was accepted by England's traditional ruling elites, a different answer can be given. When Oliver Cromwell died in September 1658, not only was there no sign of any demand for the restoration of the Stuarts, but the Protectorate had succeeded in becoming accepted by many as a regime that promised stability and security.

The failure of godly reformation

Cromwell's calls for 'reformation' (examined in the last chapter) did not go totally unheeded in the English provinces. In some English towns and villages there were a few men and women who were as avid as Cromwell in their zeal for a 'reformation of manners' and who were given encouragement by the signals coming from London. In York, Worcester, Oxford, Gloucester and Coventry, for example, groups of godly governing elites pushed ahead with programmes for the imposition of moral discipline that they had developed before the Civil War.

> *'Curb and restrain more and more all prophaneness and ungodliness on the one hand, so also discriminate a true stated christian liberty from the practice of damnable errors and blasphemy . . .'*
>
> A petition to Cromwell in 1657 or 1658, signed by 1,100 Coventry householders, quoted by A. Hughes, 'Coventry and the English Revolution' in R. C. Richardson (ed.), *Town and Countryside in the English Revolution* (1992).

In 1656 the Mayor of Coventry, Robert Beake, put into effect measures against an excess of alehouses, drunkards and sabbath-breakers. On successive Sundays in March 1656 he even sent out troopers into the countryside around Coventry to arrest anyone travelling on the Sabbath. Captain John Pickering's notebook for 1656–60 shows a Yorkshire godly magistrate similarly obsessed with bringing to book those accused of swearing, drunkenness and fornication. On the other side of the Pennines in 1656 Edmund Hopwood, a south-east Lancashire JP, convicted 22 alehouse-keepers, 33 'tipplers', 15 drunkards, 13 swearers and 10 sabbath-breakers.

The time when this kind of people came into their own was during the rule of the major-generals, many of whom shared Cromwell's intense zeal for a godly reformation. Without much doubt the major-general for Lancashire, Cheshire and Staffordshire, Charles Worsley, was the most zealous moral reformer of the lot, driven (like Cromwell) by the shame he felt at the failure of the 'Western Design'. 'The Lord help us', Worsley once wrote, 'to know what our sin is, or what His pleasure is, that we are so crossed and visited in Jamaica.' He consequently embarked on an attempt to purge the north-west of sin. In a short time he had closed 200 alehouses in one part of Lancashire alone (around Blackburn) – part of an uninhibited, energetic campaign that contributed to his own death. He died in his early thirties in 1656.

Less spectacularly, but no less energetically, other like-minded godly people, like **Richard Baxter**, forged networks designed to put Cromwell's vision of a godly society into effect. Yet energetic though these efforts of the godly were in the 1650s, their campaigns met with very limited success. There are three main reasons why this was so.

1 The first is that the godly were a tiny minority. As we saw in chapter 4, this had always been the case. During the 1640s and 1650s their numbers dwindled even more, as many godly men and women (unlike Cromwell) broke away from the cause of godly reformation as it became associated with political extremism.

2 The second reason for their failure is that their campaign was very unpopular. It was not just that (as is easily imagined) efforts to stop excessive drinking and fornication were resisted (in January 1656 Mayor Beake's order to close alehouses in parts of Coventry provoked a riot), but by the mid seventeenth century the English Church as it had developed between 1559 and 1625 (*i.e.* before the Laudian changes) had become widely accepted. 'Half-reformed' though it might be, the Church with its traditional festivals, like Christmas and Easter, had sunk deep roots in English popular life. Godly ministers, like Adam Martindale in Gorton, Manchester, reported dismally on the failure of their attempts to educate people by catechising.

> *'I met with great discouragement through the unwillingness of the people (especially the old ignoramuses) to have their extreme defects in knowledge searched out, the backwardness of the prophane to have the smart plaster of admonition applied ... to their sores.'*
>
> R. Parkinson (ed.), *The Life of Adam Martindale* (Chetham Society, vol. 4, 1845).

Martindale may have been right in assessing the cause of his problems, but there is enough evidence of positive commitment to the 'half-reformed' Church by the 1650s to suggest that this, as well as popular apathy and ignorance, was another major obstacle to the kind of godly reformation Cromwell wanted to achieve.

3 Ironically, the third reason for the slow progress made towards godly reformation is that Cromwell himself gave it little *active* support. As has been seen, his preferred method of government was confined to pursuing reformation by exhortation and by relying on local initiatives, not to do so by compulsion. The consequence was to allow what Cromwell did not want: the splintering of the godly cause, as different religious sects, instead of uniting to fight a common enemy, sniped at each other. In his Manchester congregation Martindale found Presbyterians at the throats of Independents. 'I was', he once wrote, 'resolved to remove into another place where there would be no occasion for like bickering.' No doubt Cromwell occasionally felt the same sense of disillusion. The man who yearned for a godly reformation saw instead a nation dissolving into godly quarrels.

There is one other way in which the campaign for godly reformation can be judged to have failed: it damaged Cromwell's attempts to secure 'settlement' – to make the Protectorate acceptable to the traditional rulers of the country. For them the consequences of allowing even limited religious toleration were bad enough. What was at least as frightening was that, in order to try to achieve this, Cromwell also needed the army. Consequently, throughout the 1650s most commissions of the peace and local assessment commissions, responsible for raising taxes, included military men. Permanent garrisons also were maintained all over the country. All this did little to reconcile propertied people to the republic.

Cromwellian stability and security

There is, then, little evidence that Cromwell ever succeeded in gaining *enthusiastic* support for the Protectorate from more than a tiny minority of his fellow countrymen. This, though, should not be taken as a cue to launch into an argument that hostility and opposition to Cromwell was *the keynote* of the Protectorate. There is much evidence against such a view. Royalist attempts to organise armed uprisings in England in the 1650s were always cold-shouldered by the vast majority of people. The most serious, Penruddock's Rising in 1655, caused Cromwell and the Council great alarm, but it was in reality a damp squib that was easily extinguished. Furthermore, a strong theme of English provincial life in the 1650s is the resumption of active roles in local government by the traditional ruling classes, after their withdrawal (and, in some cases, expulsion) during and after the Civil War. Everywhere, alongside men of lesser gentry origins, representatives of pre-Civil War ruling elites can be found again as JPs during the Protectorate.

Why did such people not support Royalist rebellions, but instead give their support to the republic?

The consequences of taking on Cromwellian soldiers must have been enough to dissuade some from rebellion. So, too, was the amateur and incompetent way in which Royalist **émigrés** groups, like the Sealed Knot (founded in 1653), attempted to pull together many of the disaffected elements in England – Political Presbyterians and Levellers, as well as Royalists. Some, like Thomas Edgar, a Suffolk JP, admitted that one reason for supporting the republic was the lack of a viable alternative.

KEY TERM:

Emigrés

Emigrés is a word originally used to refer to those who fled from France during the French Revolution in 1789. It is now also used to refer to anyone who is a political or religious exile from his or her native country.

> *'Those in public employment in a Commonwealth must not desert government because the way or form doth not like them. Though one kind of government be better than another, yet take that is next [i.e. the present government] rather than none.'*
>
> The speech of Thomas Edgar to fellow JPs, April 1650, quoted in D. Underdown, *Pride's Purge: the Politics of the Puritan Revolution* (1971).

For many, too, Cromwell's 'healing and settling' policies and the traditional style of his government (seen in the last chapter) helped to make his regime respectable and attractive. Many realised that it suited them and their interests too well to risk all on a desperate, reckless gamble in support of a penniless Charles Stuart. The Protector often intervened personally to prevent local sequestration commissioners from taking excessive vengeance on ex-Royalists, so allowing them to recover their estates. Even during the rule of the major-generals, when Cromwell in public was urging them to tax ex-Royalists for what he called 'un-Christian and un-English-like' behaviour, the Protector privately ordered leniency in the collection of the decimation tax in individual cases. Major-General Worsley complained bitterly (and ungrammatically) to Cromwell's secretary of state, John Thurloe, about 'the many references, that is [sic] sent to us by his highness in behalf of those that are decimated'.

What also helped in the process of reconciliation was that the Protectorate had neither the bureaucratic machinery nor political will necessary to mount a coordinated 'policy' of centralisation that might hurt local interests. Cromwell's 'good constable' approach to government allowed much room for local initiative. Even during the rule of the Major-Generals the traditional local government machinery remained in place, staffed by local men who were able to ensure that most of the orders given to the major-generals remained dead letters.

Above all, republican government was attractive because it worked. It carried out the main function expected of all early modern governments: the maintenance of social order and stability. As was seen in chapter 14, the early years of the republic were a period of severe crisis for propertied people. The tearing down of monarchy and the House of Lords was accompanied by one of the worst economic depressions of the seventeenth century, exacerbated by a flood of unemployed, demobilised soldiers and a poor law system weakened by the effects of the Civil War. During the Protectorate, local governors everywhere responded to this crisis with impressive efficiency. During the 1650s the JPs in Warwickshire issued three times the number of poor relief orders than had been done in the 1630s. Elsewhere, too, grain prices were reduced, grain stocks distributed efficiently and a greater fairness introduced in the collection of taxes. It is likely that, looked at from the perspective of the English provinces, the government of England seemed to be working at least as well (and in some cases better) than it did at other times in the seventeenth century.

As the 1650s progressed, 'the wounds' opened up by the Civil War, that Cromwell often referred to, began to heal. In 1658 a Cheshire gentleman, Thomas Mainwaring, as he recorded in his diary, held dinner parties at which former enemies during and after the Civil War sat round the same table. Such gatherings are a small illustration of a big, important theme in the history of the Protectorate: the drift back towards normality and towards acceptance of a regime that offered stability and was a guarantee against those who seemed intent on turning the world upside down.

Further reading

See list at end of previous chapter.

19 Cromwellian foreign policy

Time chart

1653: February English naval victory over the Dutch in the Channel off Beachy Head

June Another Dutch naval defeat off Gabarde. Dutch commissioners arrive in London to negotiate peace

July Dutch admiral Trompe is killed in naval battle off the Texel

1654: April Treaty of Westminster ends the Anglo-Dutch war. Debates in the next few months in the Council about declaring war on Spain in the Caribbean

December The 'Western Design' expeditionary force sets off for the Caribbean

1655: April 'Western Design' force humiliated at San Domingo

May 'Western Design' force lands in Jamaica

October Anglo-French treaty made and war with Spain in Europe begins

1656: September Naval victory over Spanish off Cadiz

1657: May Admiral Blake captures Spanish treasure fleet at Santa Cruz (Canary Islands)

English troops arrive in Flanders

Swedish-Danish war begins

October English capture Mardyke (Spanish Netherlands port)

1658: February Treaty of Roskilde temporarily ends Swedish-Danish war

June Anglo-French allies defeat Spanish force at Battle of the Dunes

Jamaica is secured against Spanish attacks

English occupy Dunkirk (Spanish Netherlands port)

Historical opinion on the foreign policy of Oliver Cromwell is as divided as it is on most other aspects of the man's life and career. Debate about it began almost immediately after Cromwell's death. One could hardly imagine two more different assessments of Cromwell's record in foreign affairs than these by Clarendon and **Slingsby Bethel** (see Figure 19.1), both written in the 1660s.

PROFILE: *Slingsby Bethel*

Bethel was the third son of a minor Yorkshire landed gentleman. Like many younger sons from this social group he was apprenticed to a merchant and he lived in Hamburg from 1637 to 1649. Although he held republican views and was a religious Independent, he disapproved of the Protectorate's reliance on the army. After the Restoration, as a wealthy merchant he became associated with the Whig cause and in 1680 he was chosen as a Whig sheriff of London. In the Tory reaction that followed the Exclusion Crisis (see chapters 22 and 23) he decided to leave England, returning to Hamburg in 1682. He only felt it safe to come back to London in February 1689 after the Glorious Revolution. Bethel died in 1697, aged 80.

'His [Cromwell's] greatness at home was but a shadow of the glory he had abroad. It was hard to discover which feared him most, France, Spain, or the Low Countries, where his friendship was current at the value he put on it. And as they did all sacrifice their honour and interest at his pleasure, so there is nothing he could have demanded that either of them would have denied him.'

From *Clarendon's History of the Rebellion* (ed. W. D. Macray, 1888).

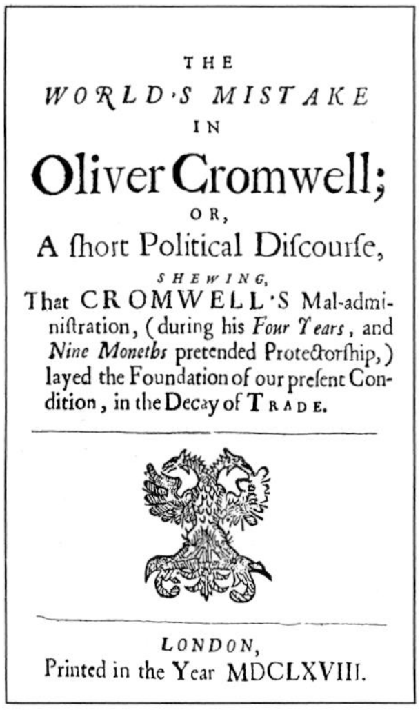

'It may well be Concluded that he lay the Foundation of our present want of Trade, to what we had formerly enjoyed; ... When I contemplate these great Failings, I cannot but apprehend the sadd Condition any people are in, whose Governour drive on a distinct contrary Interest to theirs; for doubtless Cromwell's over-weening Care to secure his particular Interest, against His Majesty (then abroad) and the Long Parliament, whom he had turned out, with a prodigious Ambition of acquiring a glorious Name in the World, carried him on to all his Mistakes and Absurdities, to the irrepairable losse and dammage of his famous Kingdom.'

Slingsby Bethel, *The World's Mistake in Oliver Cromwell* (1668).

THE
WORLD·S MISTAKE
I N
Oliver Cromwell;
O R,
A fhort Political Difcourfe,
S H E W I N G,
That C R O M W E L L 'S Mal-admi-
niftration, (during his *Four Years,* and
Nine Moneths pretended Protectorfhip,)
layed the Foundation of our prefent Con-
dition, in the Decay of T R A D E.

LONDON,
Printed in the Year MDCLXVIII.

Figure 19.1 Title page of 1972 facsimile reprint of Slingsby Bethel's political discourse

Slingsby Bethel's comment is one of the earliest examples of what was to become a common charge levelled at Cromwell's foreign policy: that Cromwell sacrificed the country's present and future national interest in pursuit of his own personal, religious aims, which were shaped by the past.

The task at the end of this chapter is to write an essay on a question that amounts to asking whether Slingsby Bethel got it right. To enable you to do that, this chapter looks at the most important allegations made about Cromwell's foreign policy in Bethel's pamphlet. As will be seen, there is something to be said *for and against* each of them. You will need to bear in mind the possibility that, as with many historical questions, there is no clear-cut 'correct' answer to this question *one way or the other*. You will have to decide the extent to which Slingsby Bethel got it right.

Cromwell's relations with the Dutch

'This Nation being in this flourishing and formidable posture, Cromwell began his Usurpation, upon the greatest advantages imaginable, having it in his power to have made peace, and profitable Leagues, in what manner he had pleased withall our neighbours, everyone courting us then, and being ambitious of the friendship of England; But as if the Lord had infatuated, and deprived him of common sence and reason, he neglected all our golden opportunities, misimproved the Victory God had given us over the United Netherlands, making peace (without ever striking stroak) so soon as ever things came into his hands, upon equal tearms with them.'

Slingsby Bethel, *The World's Mistake in Oliver Cromwell*.

Was Slingsby Bethel right in claiming that Cromwell's religious affinity with the Protestant Dutch caused him to make peace on terms unfavourable to England in the Treaty of Westminster in 1654?

There are some grounds for believing that he was. Although Cromwell did not go as far as some of those councillors who proposed a union of the two countries, he did work for an end to the Anglo-Dutch war even before the Protectorate began. In July 1653 the Dutch peace envoy said that Cromwell had told him that 'the interests of this nation [England] and ours to [the United Provinces] consisted in the welfare of commerce and navigation ... The world was wide enough for both.' This was an attitude unlikely to have caused Cromwell to use England's naval strength to squeeze the Dutch into making major commercial conces-sions. Even one of the key possessions conceded to England by the Dutch in 1654 (Pula Run in the East Indies, a source of valuable spices) was never in fact handed over. It could be that Cromwell's hopes of forming an Anglo-Dutch Protestant crusade against European Catholicism ensured that the Treaty of Westminster was more lenient to the Dutch than it might otherwise have been.

KEY TERM:

House of Orange

This was the family which had led the United Provinces to freedom in their revolt against Spanish rule in the later sixteenth and early seventeenth centuries. Prince William II of Orange, who died in 1650, had been married to Mary, daughter of Charles I, king of England. Their son was William of Orange, who became King William III of England in 1689.

Yet some of the Treaty's terms suggest that Cromwell and the Council were not driven only by religious zeal. Concern for England's security and commercial interests are also reflected in the Treaty's terms. Successful efforts were made to prevent the Stuarts gaining the powerful support of the **House of Orange**, with whom they had close links. In the treaty the Dutch guaranteed that they would never allow a member of the Orange family to become the head ('Stadholder') of their country.

In making the treaty, the English negotiators also had their country's commercial interests in mind since, if the war had continued, it was possible that the Dutch would have allied with Denmark and secured trading privileges in the Baltic to the detriment there of English merchants. The Anglo-Dutch peace treaty re-opened the Baltic to English shipping, and this success was consolidated soon afterwards by an Anglo-Danish commercial treaty that gave English merchants equal rights with the Dutch in Baltic trade.

Cromwell and the Baltic

'Whereas, it had in all Ages been the policies of the Northern States and potentates, to keep the Dominion of the Baltick Sea, devided amongst several pettie Princes and States, that no one might be sole Master of it; because otherwise, most of the necessary Commodities for shipping, coming from thence and Norway, any one Lord of the whole, might lay up the shipping of Europe, by the walls, in shutting only of his Ports, and denying the Commodities of his Country to other States. Cromwell contrary to this wise Maxime, endeavoured to put the whole Baltick sea in the Sweeds hands ... If he had understood the importance of the Baltick Sea to this Nation, he could not have been so impolitick, as to have projected so dangerous a design against his new Utopia, as giving the opening and shutting of it to any one Prince.'

Slingsby Bethel, *The World's Mistake in Oliver Cromwell*.

Was Slingsby Bethel right in claiming that Cromwell misunderstood the importance of not allowing Sweden to dominate the Baltic, which was a vital source of England's naval supplies?

There are some grounds for believing that he was. It sometimes seemed as if Cromwell forgot England's commercial interests and that he was obsessed by the unrealistic dream of forming a pan-Protestant religious crusade with Charles X of Sweden that might one day crush Catholicism in southern Europe and perhaps even reach the gates of Rome. One of Cromwell's heroes was an earlier Swedish king, Gustavus Adolphus, who Cromwell, like many English protestants of his generation, had seen leading a Protestant military crusade against Catholic tyranny in Germany in the Thirty Years' War in the late 1620s and early 1630s. There were times, as this report by the Swedish ambassador in London indicates, when Cromwell seemed to allow nostalgia to determine his attitude to Charles X.

> '*He [Cromwell, the Swedish ambassador reported Cromwell as saying] had always followed his [Gustavus Adolphus's] great campaigns with the greatest pleasure, had many times thanked God, with tears of joy in his eyes, for His gracious mercies, and when the tidings came of his death [at the Battle of Lutzen in 1632], had so mourned it that he could scarcely believe that any Swede could mourn it more bitterly, for he saw that a great instrument to quell the power of the papists had been taken away.' [Cromwell went on to say he hoped that Charles X] 'would repair that loss ... he made no doubt that on his side there was readiness to contribute all possible means to the securing of his work.'*
>
> The report of the Swedish ambassador in London, 1655–6, quoted in M. Roberts (ed.), *Swedish diplomats at Cromwell's Court 1655–6: the Missions of Peter Julius Coyet and Christer Bonde* (Camden Society, vol. 36, 1988).

It is possible that such sentiments prevented Cromwell from seeing that the Swedes were intent on securing supreme power in the Baltic. Yet there is a case for believing that Cromwell and his councillors rarely allowed religious enthusiasm to dominate their Baltic policies. They resisted tempting offers to enter a full alliance with Sweden, but instead made a commercial treaty with Sweden in July 1656, confirming English trading rights in the Baltic. Furthermore, they refused to take sides in the Swedish–Danish quarrel that exploded into open warfare in 1657, and the English ambassador in Sweden, Philip Meadowes, played a key role in negotiating the Treaty of Roskilde, which brought that war to an end in February 1658. This brought peace to the Baltic, which was essential for the prosperity of English trade there.

Cromwell and Spain and France

> 'Contrary to our Interest [Cromwell] made an unjust Warr with Spain,
> and an impolllitick League with France, bringing the first thereby under,
> and making the latter too great for Christendome, and by that means,
> broke the ballance betwixt the two Crowns of Spain, and France, which
> his Predecessors the Long Parliament, had always wisely preserved. In
> this dishonest Warr with Spain, he pretended and indeavoured, to impose
> a belief upon the world, that he had nothing in his eye, but the
> Advancement of the Protestant Cause, and the honour of this Nation; but
> his pretences, were either fraudulent, or he was ignorant of Forreign
> affairs (as I am apt to think, that he was not guilty of too much knowledge
> in them) ... Cromwells designs must ... appear ... contrary to the Interest
> of this Kingdome, so the Issue of them was dammageable to the people of
> England: As ... in his War with Spain, by the losse of that beneficial
> Trade to our Nation, and giving it to the Hollanders ... and in spending
> the great Publick stock he found, and yet leaving a vast debt upon the
> Kingdom.'
>
> Slingsby Bethel, *The World's Mistake in Oliver Cromwell.*

The most important focus of European affairs in the middle of the seventeenth century was the relationship between the two Catholic powers
that stood head and shoulders above all the rest, Spain and France. In *The
World's Mistake in Oliver Cromwell* Bethel made three major allegations
against Cromwell's policies with these two superpowers:

1 That they were based on Cromwell's ignorance of the complicated
details of the world of international diplomacy ('I am apt to think, he
was not guilty of too much knowledge of them', as Bethel quaintly put
it). This charge has an element of truth. Cromwell, like many of those
around him, had no previous experience of international diplomacy. In
1656 the Swedish ambassador, Christer Bonde, was shocked to learn that
few in the Cromwellian entourage were proficient in one of the main
languages of diplomacy, Latin. 'It is a scandal', he wrote, 'thay have no
one who can write a decent line in Latin, but the blind Miltonius [the
poet John Milton, who was a government official in the Protectorate]
must translate anything they want done from English to Latin, and one
can easily imagine how it goes.'

2 That this ignorance led them to fail to see that the major threat to
international stability was no longer Spain, as it had been in the later
sixteenth and early seventeenth centuries, justifying, for example, the

211

Elizabethan wars against Spain. Bethel insisted that by the 1650s France was the rising power in Europe and that England's international duty should have been to maintain the balance of French–Spanish power by putting its weight against France. In this respect Cromwell's decisions to ally with France and declare war on Spain, Bethel alleged, destroyed the international balance of powers on which European stability depended.

3 That it was Cromwell's religious zeal, as well as ignorance, that blinded him to the realities of international diplomacy. As in his relations with the Dutch and the Baltic powers, Bethel believed that Cromwell saw the map of Europe in the religious terms of the past. There are some reasons for believing that this was so. Cromwell's speeches in the 1650s are peppered with a loathing of Catholic Spain. That is not surprising in a man whose formative years had been those when memories of epic struggles of Elizabethan seamen in the Spanish Main were very recent, and when there had been talk in parliament and among groups like the Providence Island Company of mounting privateering crusades against Spanish power in the Caribbean. When the 'Western Design' (see chapter 17) was being debated in the Protectorate Council, a rare report of what was said shows Cromwell using religious arguments against those, like John Lambert, who warned of the high cost of an expeditionary force across the Atlantic.

> *'Providence seemed to lead us hither. We consider this attempt, because we thinke God has not brought us hither where wee are but to consider the worke that we may doe in the world as well as at home.'*
>
> Cromwell's speech in the Council, 1654, quoted in W. C. Abbott (ed.), *The Writings and Speeches of Oliver Cromwell*, vol. 4.

If Cromwell hoped for a cheap war against Spain that would be restricted to the Caribbean, such hopes were soon shown to be unrealistic. Not only was the 'Western Design' a disastrous failure, but its one minor gain, Jamaica, was ruinously expensive to maintain. Moreover, the war soon spilled over into Europe, involving expensive naval campaigns led by Admiral Robert Blake in the Mediterranean and the Atlantic, as well as war in Flanders after 1657, when England joined in an offensive anti-Spanish alliance with France. As a result, the government's debts soared and the cloth trade with Europe was badly disrupted.

Yet there are three major arguments to counter Bethel's pessimistic assessment of Cromwell's relations with France and Spain:

1 That considerations of English security, as well as religious zeal, dictated the decision to go to war with Spain. Like all regimes that seize power by a military coup (the Tudor monarchy after 1485 is a good example) fear of invasion and rebellion by those who have been dispossessed was a constant consideration behind policy-making during the Protectorate. France's close proximity across the English Channel made it a more potentially dangerous launching-pad for a Stuart invasion of England than the distant shores of Spain. This was a powerful motive for the drift of the Protectorate's relations towards France and against Spain. In this respect the Anglo-French capture from Spain of Dunkirk in June 1658 was an important success in this aim of countering a Stuart-Spanish threat to English security.

2 That it was far from obvious in the 1650s that France would become England's major rival in Europe during the later seventeenth century. Only the benefit of hindsight gives any credence to the charge that Cromwellian foreign policies destroyed a European balance of power to the subsequent advantage of France.

3 That, though expensive, Cromwellian foreign policy was remarkably successful, not only in its basic task of preserving the country from foreign invasion, but in enhancing its international reputation. During the period covered by this book so far, England had played a fairly ineffectual role in European affairs. Moreover, between 1660 and 1688 neither Charles II or James II were able, even if they had wanted to, to break free from that pattern. During the 1650s, however, the republican governments did so. During the early part of the Protectorate both major European superpowers sought to gain the republic as a friend and ally. For the last time before the wars against France in the 1690s–early 1700s the country possessed a navy that was capable of giving teeth to its diplomatic influence in international affairs. The history of the Cromwellian navy under the leadership of Admiral Robert Blake is one of dazzling victories against north African pirates in the Mediterranean, as well as more renowned events, like its destruction of the returning Spanish treasure fleet at Santa Cruz in the Canary Islands in 1657. Moreover, again as a brief, temporary foretaste of what was to become permanent by the last decade of the Stuart age, 'Britain' became a reality, as the English Republic slowly secured its control over Ireland and Scotland. Though he obviously hated what he saw, the Royalist diarist John Evelyn could not ignore the symbolism of British international power in the figurehead of a new ship, *The Naseby*, which he saw launched in 1655. It was an image portrayed also on coins issued in the 1650s.

Figure 19.2 *Cromwellian coin*

> *On the prow of the new ship, noted Evelyn, was a figurehead of 'Oliver, on horseback, trampling six nations under foot, a Scot, an Irishman, Dutch, French, Spaniard and English ... a Fame held with a laurel over his insulting head, and the Words, "God with Us".'*
>
> B. Capp, *Cromwell's Navy: the Fleet and the English Revolution* (1989).

It was image that was, one can argue, not without some foundation in reality.

Task: essay writing

Write an essay on the following:

'Cromwell's foreign policy was dominated by religious ideals at the expense of England's national interests.' Do you agree?

Some hints on answering it:

Examiners are fond of asking questions that are based on quotations, like this one. Sometimes the central point of these quotation-questions is not as easy to see as it is in other types of questions. Therefore the first thing you need to do, before answering it, is to decide what the question is about. In this case, it is relatively easy. This is a question about the major principles or aims that shaped the making of foreign policy during Oliver Cromwell's Protectorate.

Nevertheless, you must not simply give a catalogue of various kinds of motives behind Cromwell's foreign policy. You must construct your answer so that it is a direct reply to the quotation in the title. One way of doing this is to focus your answer around the various assumptions that are made by the author of the quotation. For example, you could give your essay a two-part structure:

1 Was Cromwell's foreign policy, in fact, dominated by religious ideals?

2 Did the religious ideals behind Cromwell's foreign policy conflict with England's national interests?

Another point you might consider (possibly in the introduction) is the difficulties that face historians in answering this question. Historians (like contemporaries) differ about what the answer to it is. Even more importantly, the primary source material that survives does not give one clear answer. Rarely do historians in this period have records of debates between Cromwell and his advisers about what they were aiming to achieve. Often, therefore, why particular policies were decided on has to be based on other, inferior, source material.

Further reading

The most accessible critical interpretation of Cromwell's foreign policy is in R. Hutton, *The British Republic 1649–60* (Macmillan, 1990), pages 98–113. See also M. Prestwich, 'Diplomacy and trade in the protectorate', *Journal of Modern History*, vol. 22 (1950).

A more favourable interpretation is to be found in R. Crabtree, 'The idea of a Protestant foreign policy' in I. Roots (ed.), *Cromwell: a Profile* (Macmillan, 1973) and M. Roberts, 'Cromwell and the Baltic', *English Historical Review*, vol. 76 (1961).

The best brief guide to the British context is in Hutton (above) and D. Stevenson, 'Cromwell, Scotland and Ireland' in J. Morrill (ed.), *Cromwell and the English Revolution* (Addison Wesley Longman, 1990).

20 Why was the monarchy restored in 1660?

Less than two years after Oliver Cromwell's death in September 1658 the Stuart monarchy was restored. This chapter is designed to help you tackle the question of why this came about.

One way of doing this is by taking a long-term perspective. It *could* be argued that the restoration of the monarchy was bound to happen because, from the establishment of the Republic in 1649 onwards, its government became more and more traditional in form, as the country moved slowly back towards monarchical rule. All the major constitutional changes made in the 1650s *seem* to be 'milestones on the road' to the restoration of the monarchy. This view receives support from the argument that, not only was the Republic deeply unpopular from the very beginning, but also that opposition to it grew rapidly during the 1650s. From this perspective, the explanation for the restoration of the monarchy is fairly straightforward: the events of the 1650s demonstrate that it was inevitable.

That explanation for the Restoration is perfectly reasonable. It is, however, not the one that is adopted here. For one thing, to do so would be inconsistent with the themes of previous chapters, which have suggested that the Republic under Oliver Cromwell was not a conservative regime drifting slowly back towards monarchy (see chapter 17); nor was it an unqualified failure, but one that gained fairly widespread, if unenthusiastic, acceptance (see chapters 18 and 19).

What also throws doubt on the argument that the return of monarchy was inevitable is that there is no evidence of any widespread enthusiasm for the restoration of the Stuarts until the early months of 1660. Given the armed might of the Republic under the firm leadership of Oliver Cromwell, it is perhaps not surprising that few in England were brave enough to support Royalist rebellions before 1658. More surprising is the fact that, even after Oliver Cromwell's death, it is very hard to find signs of enthusiastic commitment in England to the Stuarts. In August 1659 a planned nationwide Royalist rebellion only got off the ground in Cheshire, led by Sir George Booth, and it was easily crushed. Booth's rebellion was an even bigger flop than the one led by Penruddock in the West Country in 1655.

Once one abandons the assumption that the Restoration was inevitable, then the historical problem of explaining it becomes less straightforward and more interesting. Even Charles Stuart in exile in the Spanish Netherlands assumed that, with the collapse of Booth's rebellion, his slim chances of returning to power had been reduced even further. Until the very end of 1659 little happened to make anyone believe otherwise. Yet in May 1660 Charles returned to London amid scenes of wild Royalist enthusiasm. What is even more extraordinary is that he was restored to power unconditionally, free of any of the limitations on a monarch's power that had been proposed by his father's opponents in the 1640s.

How can one account for this extraordinary, sudden turnaround of events and the unconditional nature of the restoration of Charles II in 1660?

The failure of effective government, 1658–60

In the winter of 1659–60, as in the first years of the Republic (chapter 14) and the last months of the reign of James II in 1688–9 (chapter 23), urban and landed elites (and probably less wealthy and powerful people too) were driven by rising panic and fear into the arms of the only regime that offered them security against what they felt was an imminent descent into social and political anarchy. The reasons why they felt like this are therefore crucial to the explanation of the Restoration.

In part, the reasons are fairly straightforward. Their fears originated in the failure of all the regimes that succeeded Oliver Cromwell's Protectorate to provide effective, stable government. However, because political developments between September 1658 and May 1660 are so complicated, it can be quite difficult to understand why this happened. The first step towards overcoming this difficulty is to study the following time chart, which sets out the five main changes of regime and a few of the principal events of this period.

Time chart

The Protectorate of Richard Cromwell

1658: 3 September Richard Cromwell, Oliver's elder son, is proclaimed Lord Protector

1659: 27 January First meeting of Richard's parliament (Third Protectorate Parliament)
2 April Meetings of the General Council of Officers begin

1659: 6 April Petition of the officers to the Protector for payment of the army's wage arrears

18 April Parliament, supported by the Protector, forbids meetings of army officers

21 April Parliament's discussions of measures to control the army prompts rendezvous of soldiers in and around London, forcing the Protector to dissolve parliament on the following day

23 April–6 May Meetings of the General Council of Officers decide to recall the Rump Parliament. Richard Cromwell retires into private life

Rule by the restored Rump Parliament

1659: 12 May The Rump appoints Charles Fleetwood as C-in-C of the army and subsequently decrees that MPs should confirm the appointments of all army officers

31 July–16 August Booth's Rising in Cheshire is crushed by Lambert's army at Northwich

22/23 September Petition to parliament from Lambert's junior officers (drafted at Derby on 16 September), urging godly reform, is condemned by parliament

5 October Petition to parliament from army officers in protest

12 October Expulsion from the army by parliament of Lambert, Desborough and other officers for supporting this protest. The army is placed under a commission that included civilian republicans

13 October The army forcibly ends meetings of the Rump and establishes a Committee of Safety

Government by an army-dominated Committee of Safety

1659: 26 October Committee of Safety begins its meetings. General George Monck, the leader of the army in Scotland, refuses to support it and declares his support for the Rump

November Lambert leaves London with an army against Monck, while the Committee of Safety discusses possible new constitutions

3–13 December The Portsmouth garrison, navy and Irish army declare in favour of the Rump

23 December General Council of Officers dissolves itself and abandons power to the Rump

Rule by the Rump again

1659: 26 December Rump begins sitting again

1660: 2 January Monck and his army cross the border into England
The Rump purges the army of its enemies, including Fleetwood, Desborough and Lambert

1660: 2 February Monck's arrival in London is preceded by weeks of nationwide demonstrations and petitions in favour either of a 'free' parliament or the re-admission of MPs secluded by Pride in 1648

21 February Monck allows the re-admission of MPs secluded in 1648

16 March The Rump passes an act for new elections and declares itself dissolved

From republic to monarchy

1660: 25 April First meeting of the Convention Parliament

1 May King's Declaration of Breda is read in parliament

5 May Parliamentary resolution in favour of government by king, Lords and Commons

29 May Charles II returns to London

Two constant themes run through this history of these rapidly changing regimes, accounting for their failure:

■ The inability of different military and civilian republican factions to agree with each other for any length of time.

■ The lack of a political leader who was able (like Oliver Cromwell) to prevent these disagreements from getting out of hand.

PROFILE: *Richard Cromwell*

The career of **Richard Cromwell** is, rightly, the most famous example of the failure of political leadership in this period. However, his failure is often explained, incorrectly, in terms of the Royalist propaganda view of him as 'Tumbledown Dick'. Richard failed not because he was the weak, wimpish character portrayed by Royalists, but because he had been given little political education by his father. So anxious was Oliver Cromwell not to appear to be guilty of selfish ambition for himself and his family that he ensured that his elder son lived for most of his life well away from affairs of state. Apart from a brief spell in the army after the end of the first Civil War, Richard lived on his country estates in Hampshire. It was not until 1657 that he was appointed to the Protectorate council of state. Even then, he was not formally named as his father's successor, even though the Humble Petition and Advice allowed Oliver Cromwell to do so. After his deposition by the army he retired from public life and lived in obscurity until he died in 1712.

The short history of the third Protectorate Parliament demonstrates Richard Cromwell's failure to gain much support from the army, including his relatives, Charles Fleetwood, his brother-in-law, and John Desborough, his uncle, who (with Lambert) were now the major leaders of the army. The time chart demonstrates the mutual distrust between the army and MPs, which worked to the Protector's disadvantage, since, following the advice of civilian Cromwellians like Lord Broghill, in April 1659 he took the fatal step of supporting parliament's measures to control the army. These prompted the army to move against parliament and, then, himself.

After the dissolution of the Protectorate Parliament some members of the army, including Fleetwood, backed the continuation of the Protectorate. But pressure from junior officers and rank-and-file soldiers prevented this. As in 1647, anger over mounting wage arrears fused with demands for reform to make the army into a formidable radical political force. This pushed the army leadership (principally Lambert) into an alliance with the Commonwealthsmen, who had been working hard to persuade soldiers that they were all united on common aims, which they called 'The Good Old Cause' (a phrase used increasingly in the later 1650s). This accounts for the otherwise surprising fact that in May 1659 the army, which had expelled the Rump in 1653, and Lambert, who had incurred the Rumpers' wrath by devising the Instrument of Government, restored the Rump to power. What is not surprising is that a central theme of the Rump's brief history of power from May to October 1659 is a resurgence of military-civilian tensions, exaggerated by the fact that Lambert and Haselrige hated each other. This, once Booth's rising was over, brought about a second military expulsion of the Rump.

During the next few weeks both themes continued to shine brightly: the republican cause was still fatally weakened by civilian-military quarrels and none of the army's leaders proved capable of filling the political vacuum at the centre. The only one who might possibly have done so, Lambert, was away from the centre of events, attempting to take on the army of General Monck, who had declared for the Rump. The navy followed Monck's example, as did a key garrison at Portsmouth. Anti-army sentiments exploded into violent riots in London and elsewhere, in which apprentices took a leading role. With support ebbing away, the Committee of Safety lost its collective nerve and abandoned power to the Rump.

When it met again, the Rump (with the army's enemy, Haselrige, playing a leading role) set about purging the army of nearly half of its officer corps, continuing the civilian-military republican warfare of this period.

PROFILE: *George Monck*

Monck was a soldier who had served in the Thirty Years' War in Europe in the 1630s. During the Civil War he fought in royalist armies in Ireland and England, before he was captured in 1644. After spending 1644–6 as a prisoner of war, he changed sides and fought for parliament in Ireland in the later 1640s and with Cromwell in Scotland in 1650–51. When Cromwell returned to England in 1651 he left Monck in command there. Apart from a brief spell as a general of the fleet in the Anglo-Dutch war in 1652, Monck remained in military command of Scotland throughout the 1650s. For a few weeks after he and his army crossed the river Tweed into England on 2 January 1660 Monck, the career soldier, briefly became a major political figure. After reaching London, he allowed the MPs secluded by Pride in 1648 to return to parliament and purged republicans from his army. These decisions paved the way for the restoration of the monarchy, for which he was rewarded by Charles II with the dukedom of Albermarle. But, apart from serving as a naval commander in the Second Dutch War, his role in Restoration affairs was relatively unimportant. He died in 1670, aged 62.

Was there, though, now in the role played by **George Monck** *an exception to the theme of the failure of political leadership?*

It is possible to portray Monck as a wise soldier-politician, astutely pursuing a consistent aim of bringing about the restoration of the monarchy. This is how he later described what he had done in 1659–60. What throws doubt on this, however, is the lack of any evidence of his support for Charles's restoration until he reached London in February 1660. What seems more likely is that until then he was not clear about what should be done to resolve the crisis. Only after he returned to London, with the army leaders in disarray and with the Rump demonstrating its political bankruptcy, did he realise that there was no one in England who could provide the prospect of political stability. Like most other people in England, by February–March 1660 Monck turned to Charles Stuart as the only apparent hope for the restoration of permanent, stable government.

Fear of the Quakers

The failure of any regime after Oliver Cromwell's death to provide effective government is clearly one reason why people turned back to the monarchy. What makes it difficult to accept that this is a *complete* explanation for the mood of panic that drove many to agree to the restoration of the monarchy is that their panic seems greater than the situation warranted. Only very briefly – in the two weeks or so after the Committee of Safety abdicated power at the end of December 1659 – were there signs of a real breakdown of government and of widespread disorder. In some counties there were reports of irregular troops being raised, and not all were used as local vigilante forces. Some acted as bandits and robbers. But, as Ronald Hutton comments (see 'Further reading' section at end of chapter), order was soon restored and 'compared with the havoc of the civil wars, the disruptions of the late Interregnum were slight'. Government in the localities did not break down for long even at the end of 1659.

What, then, made people believe that it might do so? As in 1649–50, two factors were at work:

1 The first is another bout of economic depression, which raised the spectre of riots by unemployed cloth-workers, hungry agricultural labourers and small-scale farmers, and so on. In these circumstances it was felt even more important than usual that permanent, firm central government be established as quickly as possible in order to prevent a total collapse of social order.

2 The second factor is an even more important explanation for the mood that drove many people towards monarchy. This is – as in 1649–50 – the activities of groups of militant radicals. This time, however, it was not Ranters and Diggers who came to be seen as a subversive threat to the established social and political order. Now this role was filled by Quakers.

Why did the Quakers, who nowadays have a reputation for non-violence and respectability, come to be seen in the later 1650s as militant, wild fanatics?

The essence of Quakerism as it developed in the period after the end of the Civil War was the belief that men and women should follow their 'inner light' – that is, what their consciences told them was right, since this was the voice of God. This, not what church ministers or anyone else told them, should guide their lives. It was a potentially revolutionary interpretation of Protestantism, that was first preached in north-west England by charismatic and energetic evangelical preachers (of whom George Fox came to be the most well-known, because the journal of his activities survives and he lived longer than most of his colleagues) in the later 1640s and early 1650s. By the later 1650s they had had an extraordinary success in gaining converts, especially among the middling and lower sorts in society. There may have been as many as 60,000 Quakers by this time, a level of support only bettered, among new religious sects, by the Baptists. Quakers could be found all over Britain; there were 1,000 in Bristol and 10,000 in London, for example. So dynamic and successful were they that a church minister sneered (and this may be how they got their name) that they should be called Quakers, because they made people tremble at the word of God.

What made respectable society tremble about them was the fact that their activities were not confined to making spiritual conversions. Quakers became notorious among propertied people as leaders of the campaign to abolish tithes. They refused to take off their hats as a sign of deference to their social 'betters'. They refused to swear oaths. They interrupted church services when they disagreed with what was being preached. Moreover, it was common for Quakers to throw off their clothes and preach in the nude. It is a measure of Oliver Cromwell's willingness to try to understand the beliefs of all Protestants that, although he condemned their breaches of the peace, he twice had long conversations with George Fox. The attitudes of most other members of respectable society to the Quakers was much less tolerant, as can be seen by the title page of a popular pamphlet of 1655 (Figure 20.2).

The most dramatic example of the hatred and fear most people felt for the Quakers in the 1650s is the treatment meted out to **James Nayler** in 1656. The loathing of Quakers revealed in Nayler's case, if anything, grew in the later 1650s. In 1659 it reached new heights, because everywhere

---

PROFILE: *James Nayler*

Nayler (?1617–60) was one of the most charismatic and popular of the early Quaker preachers. In 1656 he was arrested on a charge of 'horrid blasphemy'. What he had done was to re-enact Christ's entry into Jerusalem by riding into Bristol on a donkey, while his supporters (mainly women) sang and paved his route with branches. So outraged were many people by this, that he was brought to London for trial and punishment by the Second Protectorate Parliament. Some MPs had constitutional qualms about whether they had the right to try Nayler, since it was not clear whether the Commons had inherited the judicial power of the abolished House of Lords. (There is not much doubt that they had not and that the constitutional irregularities of the case gave added fuel to the pressure for a new constitution in 1656–7 – see chapter 17.) Yet these reservations were swept aside and Nayler's trial went ahead. He was ordered to be branded, bored through the tongue, flogged twice, and then imprisoned for life.

Figure 20.2 *Title page of an Anti-Quaker pamphlet, 1655*

there seemed to be evidence (as in Dorothy White's Quaker pamphlet) to support the contemporary image of Quakers as fanatical revolutionaries.

God has 'come to turn the world upside down… That that, which hath ruled over may be brought down under, and that which hath been of low degree, may be raised by the power of God, to rule and have the dominion'.

Dorothy White, *A Diligent Search* (1659), quoted in B. Reay, *The Quakers and the English Revolution* (1985).

The restoration of the Rump triggered wild enthusiasm among Quakers. Some Quakers, too, had not yet embraced pacifism, and they volunteered in droves to serve as soldiers in the militias that were raised to oppose Royalist revolts in the wake of Booth's Revolt.

One consequence of this was that the restored Rump gained a contemporary reputation for radicalism, because of its association with rampant Quakerism of this kind. 'Sectaries reign, others gaze', Ralph Josselin, the vicar of Earl's Colne, noted in his diary at this time. As in the case of Barebones Parliament (see chapter 16), there was a significant gap between this image and reality. The restored Rump was full of MPs with moderate religious views. It is true that a few Quakers (including Nayler) were released from prison by the Rump, and the commission it appointed to rule Ireland patronised some Quakers and Baptists. But generally the Rump's attitude to religious radicals was hostile. However, as at other times, what people believe to be true was more important that what actually was true, and the Rump's popularity plummeted downwards as a result. There is no doubt that hostility to the Quakers made a powerful contribution to the restoration of the monarchy.

Conclusion

The explanation for the Restoration that has been put forward here is that many people were *pushed* towards it by a sense of rising panic that was made worse by the Quaker menace. One final argument needs to be put: that people were *pulled* in the same direction by the conciliatory attitude taken by the exiled king and his advisers in the declaration they issued just before the Restoration.

The Declaration of Breda was a politically astute document that included three attractive promises:

1 A free and general pardon (except for those named by parliament), which removed the fear that there would be a reign of terror against those who had collaborated with the republican regimes of the 1650s.

2 That the question of what should happen to estates confiscated during the English Revolution should be resolved by parliament. This raised royalists' hopes that their lost estates would be restored to them.

3 'Liberty to tender consciences', which was attractive to those who hoped for a continuation of religious toleration.

When the Declaration was read in parliament on 1 May 1660 the effect was to cut the ground from beneath the feet of those who hoped to impose the Treaty of Newport conditions of 1648 on the restored king. The Declaration of Breda was the final reason why this did not happen. Even before the Declaration reached Westminster, most MPs believed that the uncertainties of the times called for the establishment of a new government without a delay caused by tedious debates and conferences about the nuts and bolts of a new constitution. The Declaration removed any doubts that there might have been about this, since it made clear that the details of any restoration 'settlement' could safely be left until later.

A few days after hearing the Declaration, the Convention Parliament carried the crucial vote of 5 May. On 8 May it went even further, declaring that 'it can not be doubted that His Majesty's right and title to his Crown and Kingdom is and was every way completed by the death of his most royal father of blessed memory, without the ceremony or solemnity of a proclamation'. The contrast between that extreme Royalist statement and the abysmal support Booth's attempt to restore the king had received in August 1659 is a remarkable illustration of the rapid and dramatic change of attitudes that had taken place in England in the intervening nine months.

Tasks

Answering the following will help you pull together material on the history of the English Republic in this and previous chapters.

1 a Use material from previous chapters to make two lists: those aspects of what happened in the 1650s that might cause people at the time to have
  i become dissatisfied with republican rule,
  ii been satisfied with republican rule.
  b On balance, comparing the two lists, are there enough reasons in your lists to cause you to conclude that the collapse of republican rule and the restoration of monarchy in Britain was inevitable sooner or later?

2 Write notes, or a list of points, in answer to these questions:
  a Why did none of the republican regimes that followed Oliver Cromwell's death in 1658 last for very long?
  b Why were Quakers reviled by respectable society in the 1650s?
  c How justified were people in thinking that the country was on the brink of anarchy in the winter of 1659–60?
  d How important was the role of Monck in bringing about the Restoration?
  e Why was the Declaration of Breda so successful in persuading people to accept the return of monarchy in 1660?

Further reading

The textbooks listed at the end of previous chapters are the best initial sources of further information on this topic.

B. Reay, 'The Quakers, 1659, and the restoration of the monarchy', *History*, vol. 63 (1978) and his book *Quakers and the English Revolution* (Temple Smith, 1985) are the main sources for the importance of this radical religious group.

For a more detailed account of the period see:

R. Hutton, *The Restoration: a Political and Religious History 1658–67* (Oxford University Press, 1985).

21 The consequences of the English Revolution

You should consult this time chart when reading this and the next chapter.

Time chart

1660: Convention Parliament meets
Indemnity Act grants a general pardon, excepting only a few regicides
Charles II returns to the throne
Worcester House Conference fails to agree on a church settlement

1661: Another conference about a church settlement at Savoy House fails
First meeting of Cavalier Parliament (it then meets every year, apart from 1672 and 1676, until it is dissolved in 1679)
Militia Act; Act against tumultuous petitioning; Corporation Act preventing Dissenters from holding town offices; Act imposing press censorship; Quaker Act establishing severe punishment for Quakers
Venner's Rising in Yorkshire

1662: New Prayer Book issued by convocation
Act of Uniformity decrees that all church ministers who refuse to accept the restored Church are to leave their livings by St Bartholomew's day (24 August). About 1,909 leave the Church as a result
Hearth Tax introduced
Charles II issues the first Declaration of Indulgence

1663: The king cancels the Declaration of Indulgence

1664: Triennial Act of 1641 is replaced by a weaker Triennial Act; Conventicle Act makes illegal religious assemblies of five people and more that do not use the New Prayer Book

1665: Second Anglo-Dutch war begins
Five Mile Act prevents any preacher who does not accept the restored Church from coming within 5 miles of a town or city
Great Plague hits London

1666: France and Denmark join the war against England
Great Fire destroys large parts of London

1667: France invades and conquers the Spanish Netherlands
After Dutch naval victory in the Medway, Anglo-Dutch war is ended by the Treaty of Breda
Charles's chief minister, Clarendon, flees to France to escape parliamentary impeachment

1668: Triple Alliance between England, the United Provinces and Sweden

1670: Another Conventicle Act is passed to plug loopholes in the first Act
Charles II makes Treaty of Dover with France (there are public and private versions)

1672: Charles II issues a Second Declaration of Indulgence
Third Anglo-Dutch war begins

1673: King cancels the Declaration of Indulgence and agrees to a Test Act, forbidding non-Anglicans from holding any public office
Lord Treasurer Thomas Clifford and Lord High Admiral James, Duke of York (the king's brother and heir to the throne) resign under the terms of the Test Act

1674: Third Anglo-Dutch war is ended by Treaty of Westminster

1675–6: Charles II makes secret subsidy agreements with Louis XIV

1677: The marriage of William of Orange and Duke of York's elder daughter, Mary, is announced

1678: Allegation of a popish plot against Charles II made by Titus Oates

Did the Restoration Settlement settle anything apart from the monarchy?

Historians often identify specific points in the past at which they think major, revolutionary changes took place. Until recently it has been common to see 1660 as a major dividing line in the history of seventeenth-century England, marking the start of many permanent, major changes that transformed the country's economy, society, government and Church. Did 1660 usher in a new era in politics, government and religious attitudes? (See chapters 26 and 27 for economic and social aspects.) Did the 'settlement' made after the Restoration in 1660 in fact settle anything other than the monarchy?

The case that 1660 was a dividing line

For historians who argue that 1660 marked a major watershed in English history what happened in the 1640s and 1650s is literally the English

Revolution, an episode which shook the traditional medieval structure of the country to its roots to such an extent that in most major respects it could never be the same again. So powerful and deep-rooted were the long-term causes of the English Revolution and so violent was its course that its effects are said to have brought about the end of the Middle Ages and the beginning of modern England in two important respects:

1 *A constitutional dividing line*   It is claimed by some that, although the overthrow of the monarchy and the establishment of a republic was temporary, the effects were to weaken permanently the powers of the restored monarchy. 1660 was thus the turning-point at which the government of England diverged from the general European trend towards stronger, absolutist monarchy and began its journey towards modern constitutional, parliamentary monarchy.

2 *A religious dividing line*   1660 is seen by some as an equally decisive watershed in the role that religion played in the political and social life of the country. The Church might have been restored along with the monarchy, but religion now no longer played the important part in people's lives that it had before the English Revolution. One of the important consequences of the English Revolution is said to have been a great reaction against the religious enthusiasm which had fuelled the political and military violence of the 1640s and 1650s. The result was the growth of religious indifference, allowing the slow but inevitable rise of religious toleration. According to the most influential historian of seventeenth-century England since the Second World War, Christopher Hill, 'the 1640s and 1650s marked the end of medieval and Tudor England'.

The extent to which this view became entrenched is illustrated by the way that many English history courses in schools, colleges and universities used to begin or end in 1660. It is also reflected in the way historical writing and research has been organised. Until recently, the most important historians of Tudor and early Stuart England were a different set of people from those who worked on later seventeenth and eighteenth-century history. Consequently, the books they wrote (including many, though not all, textbooks) began or ended at the Restoration.

The case that 1660 was not a dividing line

The main aim of the rest of this chapter is to challenge the idea that 1660 was a turning-point in English political and religious history. It will be argued that the consequences of the English Revolution were not clear-cut ones that transformed the country's constitutional and ecclesiastical structure in decisive and permanent ways. On the contrary, there was much continuity of people and issues from the period before 1660 and the consequences of the English Revolution were contradictory and diverse. Issues which had motivated and divided people before 1660 (especially religion) continued to be vital ones in later Stuart England. Although most people were united in wanting the restoration of Charles II in 1660, they agreed about little else. In particular, there were major differences about what should be the shape of the restored monarchy and Church. As a result, the decisions that were made in the early 1660s about the relations between crown and parliament and between the Church and Dissent were contradictory. They do not deserve to be called 'The Restoration Settlement'. England became a monarchy again in 1660, but that is the limit of what was settled at the Restoration.

The restored monarchy

The contradictory consequences of the English Revolution can be seen, first of all, in the efforts that were made in and after 1660 to produce a constitutional settlement. Most people wanted the return of the monarchy, but there unanimity ended. What had happened during the 1640s and 1650s ensured that the powers of the restored monarchy were not conclusively settled in any clear way.

One consequence of the recent past was certainly to impose some limitations upon the powers that the crown had enjoyed before 1640. Many of the constitutional reforms passed by the Long Parliament in the early months of its meeting down to the summer of 1641 were not overturned by the Convention Parliament in 1660 or by its successor, the Cavalier Parliament, which first met in May 1661. Despite the widespread enthusiasm for the return of Charles II, most MPs were not prepared to repeal the legislation of early 1641 which had made ship-money illegal, abolished the prerogative courts of Star Chamber, the Ecclesiastical Court of High Commission and the Council of the North, along with the crown's feudal rights to wardship and knighthood fines. These measures had been passed with a large degree of agreement by both future Royalists (like Edward Hyde) and future parliamentarians in the Civil War. Consequently, their retention in the early 1660s is not remarkable.

There was, however, another consequence of the English Revolution that influenced the shape of the restored monarchy in a different way. The radical measure taken by parliament after the summer of 1641 convinced many in the early 1660s that it was the powers of parliament, not the crown, that needed curtailing. What many people remembered about the English Revolution were high taxation, centralised rule, and interference with local liberties by parliaments in and after the Civil War. For many the cause of 'parliamentary liberties' had also become tainted with a threat to turn the world upside down by Levellers, Diggers, Ranters and Quakers. MPs in Restoration parliaments were consequently even less likely than their predecessors in early Stuart parliaments to want to win the initiative in the making of government policies. On the contrary, the disturbing experiences of the recent past led to a conservative backlash, which determined many MPs to strengthen the powers of the crown rather than those of parliaments.

All the major demands made by parliaments in the 1640s – notably that parliament should control the militia and appoint all the chief officers of state – were abandoned in the 1660s. In the Militia Acts of 1661 and 1662 the Cavalier Parliament conceded sole control of the militia to the crown. Most of the other parliamentary measures that had made inroads into the royal prerogative, from the summer of 1641 onwards, were overturned. The Act of 1642 excluding bishops from the House of Lords was repealed. Severe penalties were directed against anyone who claimed that parliament had the right to legislate without the king, as parliaments had done during the Interregnum. Further Acts attacking 'tumultuous petitioning' and strengthening press censorship were aimed at preventing the kind of mass demonstrations and popular pressure used by John Pym in the early 1640s. In 1664 the Cavalier Parliament went even further in exalting the power of the crown over parliament by repealing the Triennial Act of 1641, replacing it with an emasculated Act, which did not include any means of calling parliaments if the monarch failed to do so after the maximum three-year interval between parliaments.

In short, a major consequence of the English Revolution was to strengthen the powers of the restored monarchy and to leave most of its major powers intact. English monarchs could still veto parliamentary legislation, dispense individuals from statutes, call and dissolve parliaments at will and appoint as advisers anyone they liked. The monarchy that was restored in 1660 had much in common with the personal monarchy of the early Stuarts, described in chapter 1. But it was a crown whose position, though strong, was ambiguous. The outcome of the contradictory constitutional decisions of the early 1660s was to leave the relationship between crown and parliament undefined, and consequently a source of dispute and tension in the political life of Restoration England.

What was decided at the same time about three other outstanding problems – indemnity, confiscated estates and finance – made political instability, not settlement, even more likely. It is often said that the parliaments of the early 1660s dealt well with the problems of what to do about:

- those who had opposed the king and collaborated with the regimes of the Interregnum
- lands that the crown, Church and Royalists had lost during that time
- the financial difficulties of the crown.

There is a lot of truth in this. The decision in the 1660 Act of Indemnity to pardon all but a few who had been closely involved in Charles II's execution was a wise one. Too many had collaborated with the regimes of the Interregnum to make a widespread campaign of vengeance practicable, and the situation called for a policy of 'forgive and forget'.

The restoration of estates confiscated from the crown, Church and some Royalists was about as far as parliament could go in its land settlement. A statutory return to Royalists of estates sold to help them pay fines imposed on them in the 1640s and 1650s would have meant undoing legal contracts of sale. This would have set dangerous precedents for the ownership of property.

The efforts made to solve the crown's long-standing, complicated financial problems were equally impressive. Some of the new financial measures introduced by Interregnum regimes – notably the excise first used in 1643 – were retained to compensate the crown for its loss of feudal revenue. In 1662 a new **hearth tax** was devised in an attempt to top up the crown's revenue to £1,200,000, which everyone assumed was enough with which to run the country.

KEY TERM:

Hearth tax

This new tax gained its name simply because it taxed people according to the number of fireplaces (hearths) in their houses; those with many fireplaces (and therefore big houses) naturally paying more tax than those with fewer hearths.

Unfortunately, however, all these decisions were only partially successful. To Royalists who had suffered much for the king before 1660 the pardon given to most of his enemies, together with the king's failure to order a complete restoration of their property, were sources of intense bitterness. The fact that Charles II appointed to his government men who had served the Republic did not help to make things better. It seemed, as a contemporary said, that the king was cynically rewarding 'his enemies to sweeten them, for that his friends were so by a settled principle, and that their loyalty could not be shaken'. Such sentiments were not likely to produce political harmony.

Nor was the financial settlement. It soon became clear that this was not as lavish as had been planned. The crown's actual income fell far short of the projected £1,200,000. The financial problems that had been inherited by James I in 1603 still remained, with all the potential for constitutional conflict that has been seen in previous chapters.

The restored Church

Disagreements about the kind of Church that should be restored in the 1660s were even deeper than those caused by differences over constitutional issues. Nothing could be more certain than at the Restoration religious passions continued to fuel political debate with as much fire as they had ever done. The continuation of religious controversies of the recent past ensured that the religious consequences of the English Revolution, like its constitutional impact, were diverse and contradictory.

One of the forces that shaped the restored Church in the early 1660s was a militant reaction against the religious freedom of the 1640s and 1650s that was so powerful that it dominates the scene. The panic and fear of religious sects like the Quakers, that drove the propertied classes of England into the arms of the Stuarts again, was shared by many others. In 1660 Baptists and Quakers were attacked by crowds in London and elsewhere. Maypoles – symbols of an anti-sectarian culture – were erected by popular acclamation in many English towns and villages, reflecting the popular attachment to the traditional Church that had hindered the campaign of godly reformation during the English Revolution. In January 1661 **Venner's Rising** seemed to confirm one of the other ingredients that made this religious reaction so powerful: the assumption that **Dissent** equalled Sedition.

In this climate efforts at two conferences (at the Earl of Clarendon's London lodgings, Worcester House, on 25 October 1660, and at the Bishop of Lincoln's London house between 5 April and 23 July 1661) to create a comprehensive, broad-based Church that included moderate Presbyterians had little chance of success. Both collapsed, even though they had the support of Charles II and his chief minister, Edward Hyde (Earl of Clarendon), who were anxious to honour their promise of 'liberty for tender consciences' in the Declaration of Breda. Some historians have cast doubts on the sincerity of Clarendon's commitment to 'comprehension', but the evidence of his attachment to this cause as early as 1641–2 is in his favour. In one sense, though, Clarendon's (and Charles II's) motives are irrelevant. The Church was restored, not by king and minister, but by Anglican gentry who in 1660–61 encouraged ejected ministers to return to their livings, by churchwardens who bought (or brought out of hiding) copies of the prewar Prayer Book, and by MPs in the Cavalier Parliament who between 1661 and 1665 passed the so-called **'Clarendon Code'**. This erected a narrow state Church, protected by severe penalties against all Dissenters who refused to join it.

The reaction against religious liberty that lay behind the Clarendon Code is one important consequence of the English Revolution; yet it is not the only one. There was more support for Dissenters in Restoration England than is usually recognised.

KEY TERMS:

Venner's Rising

This was a minor rising in Yorkshire of no more that 300 religious radicals, led by a Fifth Monarchist, Thomas Venner.

Dissent/Dissenters

Dissenters is the term that from now on was used to describe all those who refused to accept the Church that was restored after 1660. It was normally used to mean Protestant and not Catholic nonconformists and included a wide range of religious groups, including Baptists, Presbyterians, Independents and Congregationalists.

'Clarendon Code'

This is the phrase used to describe the following acts of parliament described in the time chart: Corporation Act, 1661; Act of Uniformity, 1662; Quaker Act, 1662; Conventicle Act, 1664; Five Mile Act, 1664; and the Second Conventicle Act, 1670. Given the fact that the Earl of Clarendon did not initiate this legislation, the label can be misleading. But it is the one most often used to describe legislation that attempted to establish a system of religious apartheid in England, restricting all public offices and access to education to Anglicans.

Not everyone sympathised with the vindictive mood that produced the Clarendon Code. Some were unwilling to recognise that the kind of comprehensive national Church that had existed before 1625 and that Cromwell had tried to revive in the 1650s had gone for ever. Studies of localities in the early years of the Restoration reveal a marked reluctance among some JPs to persecute Dissenters other than extremists like Baptists and Quakers. The preamble to a second Conventicle Act in 1670 admitted that a new one was necessary because the first one had not been enforced. Nor were all bishops willing to follow the persecuting example of the Archbishop of Canterbury, Gilbert Sheldon, but used their influence to shield Dissenters from the full force of the law, in the hope that moderate Presbyterians would drift back to the Church. Like Catholicism in Elizabethan England, Restoration Dissent survived with the protection of powerful elites. There the comparison ends, because, unlike Catholicism, Dissent not only survived but grew in popularity in later seventeenth-century England.

As will be seen in the next chapter these twin, contradictory consequences of the English Revolution – intolerance and tolerance of Dissent – were to have a major divisive effect on Restoration politics. It cannot be emphasised enough that these different attitudes to Dissent were not confined to parliamentary high politics. In most counties and towns that have been studied, politics polarised around the issue of whether or not Dissenters could be tolerated. Quite early in the 1660s these different attitudes to Dissent threatened to become a major political fault-line that might widen, re-opening the fierce conflicts of the recent past.

Conclusion

The argument of this chapter has been that in 1660 the future course of England's political and religious development – whether it would become a constitutional monarchy or a more authoritarian regime, whether religious toleration would triumph or not – was far from predetermined. The diverse consequences of the English Revolution produced, not a 'settlement', but major political and religious uncertainties and tensions. However, it would be dangerous to assume that these by themselves made inevitable major conflicts between the crown and many of its subjects, as did happen in 1679–81 and 1688–9. As has been noted, England was still governed by a personal monarchy. English monarchs still ruled as well as reigned. What the course of the country's religious and political developments might be still depended as much as ever on what they did.

Further reading

The suggestions for further reading for this chapter are listed on page 246.

22 Was the 'Exclusion Crisis' similar to that faced by Charles I?

Titus Oates, the 'Popish Plot' and the Exclusion Crisis (1678–81)

In August and September 1678 Titus Oates, who had recently been expelled from a Jesuit College at St Omer, made public allegations that implicated Jesuits, the French court and prominent people around Charles II in a plot to assassinate the king. When questioned, Oates produced a jumble of miscellaneous and inconsistent information, hinting that there were plans to coordinate the assassination with a Catholic uprising in Ireland, rebellions in Scotland and a French invasion.

All those who have submitted Oates's allegations to detailed examination have found them to be false, revealing Oates to have been an imaginative liar. Yet many at the time believed him, especially when in October 1678 Sir Edmund Berry Godfrey, the JP who had taken Oates's original deposition, was found dead in mysterious circumstances, and when shortly afterwards letters seized from Edward Coleman, a former secretary of James, Duke of York, revealed his treasonable correspondence with Jesuits and French agents. On 21 October 1678 the Cavalier Parliament unanimously passed a resolution that 'there hath been and still is a damnable and hellish plot contrived and carried on by the popish recusants for the assassinating and murdering the King and for subverting the government, and rooting out and destroying the Protestant religion'. During the subsequent judicial investigations between 1678 and 1681 35 people were tried and executed for taking part in a 'plot' that did not exist.

Also during that same period Charles II faced a powerful campaign inside and outside parliament, by people who came to be called *Whigs*, to impeach his chief minister, Thomas Osborne, and to force him to accept limitations on royal power, principally the exclusion of his Catholic brother from the succession to the throne.

The Whig campaign was resisted by people who came to be nicknamed *Tories*.

The main events of this crisis are shown in the time chart below.

Time chart

1678: December After hearing allegations that Danby had negotiated in secret with Louis XIV, the Commons impeaches him

1679: January Charles II dissolves the Cavalier Parliament (which had first been elected in 1661) in order to protect Danby
March Meeting of a newly-elected parliament (the First Exclusion Parliament): impeachment proceedings are begun against Danby; the first Exclusion Bill is read twice in the Commons

Figure 22.1 Popish Plot prints

1679: May Dissolution of the First Exclusion Parliament

1680: October Second Exclusion Parliament meets. Another Exclusion Bill passes the Commons
November The Bill is defeated in the Lords

1681: January Dissolution of the Second Exclusion Parliament
March Third Exclusion Parliament meets at Oxford. An Exclusion Bill passes both the Commons and Lords, but does not become law because the king dissolves parliament

Throughout this period popular demonstrations and petitioning campaigns take place, organised by Whigs and Tories.

Between 1678 and 1681 opposition to Charles II, which had been growing steadily in the years since the Restoration, reached new heights in what has become known as 'the Exclusion Crisis'. It has often been given this name because one of the main aims of the king's opponents was to exclude the king's brother, James, Duke of York, from the succession to the throne. An examination of the origins and the course of the crisis in the first section of this chapter will show that there are remarkable similarities between it and the great crisis faced by Charles I in 1640–41. This chapter reinforces the main theme of the last one: 1660 was not a 'dividing line' that ushered in a new era in politics and religion.

This is not to suggest, however, that nothing changed after the English Revolution. The Exclusion Crisis was not an exact replay of the earlier crisis. Unlike its origins, the outcome of the crisis of 1678–81 was very different from that of 1640–41. It was not followed by escalating attacks on the power of the crown, let alone by a civil war against the king. Quite the reverse. In 1681, unlike 1641, the opposition to the crown collapsed as dramatically and as quickly as a punctured balloon. Unlike his father, Charles II not only survived the crisis but his position became even stronger than before. Why was this? The last section of this chapter finds a major reason in changes that were brought about by the English Revolution.

Similarities between the Exclusion Crisis and the 1640–41 crisis

Three major similarities stand out. In both cases the king's opponents believed that:

■ there was a popish plot designed to subvert the Protestant Church and promote Catholicism in Britain

- there were close links between popery, absolutism, the king's chief ministers and leading bishops in the Church
- so dangerous was the threat from popery and absolutism that their campaign against it must be carried on outside as well as inside parliament.

The belief in a popish plot to subvert Protestantism

Fear of popery was central to both the crises of 1678–81 and 1640–41. In both cases this was expressed in the belief that there was a conspiracy, devised abroad (in Rome and Spain in the 1630s, in Rome and France in the 1670s) but currently being carried out at home at the highest levels of government in both Church and State, by men who were intent on subverting Protestantism and promoting Catholicism in Britain.

Moreover, the Whigs in 1678–81 and the parliamentary opponents of Charles I in 1640–41 believed that there was an active plot to promote Catholicism in Britain for three similar reasons.

1 *Religious policies and the Popish Plot* The first is that Charles II at times followed religious policies that seemed to be as favourable to Catholics as Charles I's ecclesiastical policies in the 1630s. The first 20 years of his reign after his restoration are peppered with attempts by Charles II to restrain the militant Anglican intolerance that had produced the Clarendon Code (see chapter 21). In 1662 and 1672 he issued two royal Declarations of Indulgence, suspending the penal laws of the Clarendon Code against non-Anglicans. The second declaration specifically allowed Roman Catholics to worship in private, as well as offering licences to Protestant Dissenters to hold public services.

It is impossible to be certain why Charles did this. (One of the tasks at the end of this chapter is to consider what his motives might have been.) What is certain is that Charles's indulgence policies seemed to confirm the belief that there was a popish conspiracy at court.

2 *Foreign policies and the Popish Plot (the Dutch war)* Some of Charles II's foreign policies, like those of his father, had a similar effect. The king's first major excursion into European affairs after the Restoration, the second Anglo-Dutch War (1665–7), was not unpopular (parliament granted massive taxes to finance it). But, like Charles I's wars against France and Spain in the 1620s, it was badly managed, culminating in the national humiliation of 1667, when the Dutch fleet sailed up the river Medway and towed away many of the country's finest ships that were anchored there. The impact of this disgrace was especially great, coming as it did close on the heels of the natural disasters of 1665–6 – the Great Plague and the Great Fire – which decimated life in the capital. In the later 1660s, as in the later 1620s, some of the blame for these disasters and misgovernment was deflected from the king to a minister. In 1667 Clarendon, like Buckingham earlier, was impeached by the Commons and he fled the country to become an exile again, this time for good.

More damaging to Charles II was his decision at the end of the Dutch war, while his ministers were concluding a Triple Alliance with the Dutch and Swedes, to begin negotiating a treaty with France. What made this seem foolish to some is that for the first time in the century there was evidence that France was a greater threat to English security than the Dutch, since in 1667 Louis XIV began to put his claims to neighbouring provinces into effect by invading and conquering the Spanish Netherlands. Yet Charles continued to seek an alliance with France, personally conducting the negotiations by means of correspondence with his sister, Henrietta, the wife of Louis XIV's brother, the Duke of Orleans. As was noted in chapter 1, this is a good example of 'personal monarchy' in action. As well as making a public treaty with France which committed both countries to a war against the Dutch, to be partly financed by the French, Charles II also made a private treaty with Louis XIV, which only two of his ministers knew about. This was signed in May 1670 at Dover, under cover of Charles's meeting with his sister.

'The lord king of Great Britain, being convinced of the truth of the Roman Catholic religion, and resolved to declare it and reconcile himself with the Church of Rome as soon as the welfare of his kingdom will permit, has every reason to hope and expect from the affection and loyalty of the subjects that none of the ... will ever fail ... the obedience that all peoples owe their sovereigns.'

One of the clauses of the secret Treaty of Dover, 1670, from *English Historical Documents*, vol. 8 (1953).

The reasons why Charles made this alliance with France are as clouded in mystery as his motives for issuing the Declarations of Indulgence. (At the end of the chapter you will be asked to consider what they might have been.) What is more certain is that the domestic political cost of the Dover policy (which in 1672 was implemented when war was declared again on the Dutch) was immense. Even though in March 1673 Charles revoked the Declaration of Indulgence and gave his assent to a Test Act, which excluded non-Anglicans from public office, he failed to dissociate the French alliance from its damaging Catholic and absolutist associations. Cleverly, William of Orange (who in 1672 had been appointed as Stadholder, the effective head of the United Provinces) conducted a propaganda warfare against the English crown, in pamphlets that alleged that the main aim of the Anglo-French alliance was to spread Catholicism in England.

3 *British policies and the Popish Plot* As in the 1630s, events in Ireland and Scotland also provided further evidence of dangerous Catholic trends. North of the border John Maitland (Duke of Lauderdale) exercised an authoritarian rule that some feared might be used in England. However, as in England before the Civil War, it was events in Ireland that most helped to increase mistrust of the court. After the Cromwellian conquest of Ireland, England's grip on the country was tightened by a systematic expulsion of Irish Catholic landowners from their estates. Yet when the Duke of Ormonde was replaced as Lord Lieutenant in 1669, restrictions on the Catholic Church in Ireland were relaxed and Irish Catholics were even admitted to office. It is easy to see why (as in the past) some were fearful that Ireland was being used as a testing ground for policies that might later be used in England.

The belief that there were links between Popery and absolutism

During the Exclusion Crisis the Whigs were convinced that there was a plot not only against Protestantism but against parliaments as well. Popery, they believed, was inseparable from absolutism, and those who supported both could be found at the heart of the Court and the Church.

The three reasons why the Whigs believed these things are very similar to those that caused Pym and his allies to accuse Charles I's 'evil councillors', Strafford and Laud, of a design to promote arbitrary government and Catholicism in Britain in 1640–41.

1 *Popery and absolutism* The first reason is that some of Charles II's policies seemed to be as arbitrary as those of Charles I. This is especially true of Charles II's indulgence policy. His Declarations of Indulgence of 1662 and 1672 not only aroused intense opposition because they seemed to favour Catholics but also because, in suspending parliamentary laws by royal decree, they were seen as direct a threat to parliamentary liberties as Charles I's forced loans and his arbitrary imprisonment of the Five Knights in the 1620s (see chapter 6). The Declarations of Indulgence seemed proof of a popish/absolutist design at court, especially given the presence of Catholics at Charles II's court. Here the continuity with a similar situation at the court of Charles I is a personal one, as the king's mother, Henrietta Maria, pressed her son, as she had her husband, to give favour to Catholics. The presence of prominent Catholic courtiers among Charles II's advisers – like the Earl of Bristol, Lord Arundel, Thomas Lord Clifford and Henry Bennet (Earl of Arlington) – were ominous signs of popery at court. These were amply confirmed by the conversion to Catholicism of the king's brother and heir, James, Duke of York, in 1669.

2 *Popery, absolutism and the king's minister*   Charles's chief minister between 1674 and 1678, Thomas Osborne (Earl of Danby) adopted policies that were seen as being as dangerous a threat to parliamentary liberties as had been Wentworth's in the 1630s. Like Wentworth's Irish army, it was feared that the army Danby raised might be used not against the country's enemies but against parliament. This and Danby's distribution of money and offices to MPs in the 1670s were not surprisingly seen as efforts 'to introduce an arbitrary and tyrannical way of government'. More surprising, since he followed policies of zealous Anglicanism, is another charge in the articles of impeachment against him, that he was 'popishly affected'. The only 'evidence' for this was Danby's 'arbitrary' policies. There could be no better illustration of the Whig assumption that anyone who was intent on absolutism must be a papist.

3 *Popery, absolutism and bishops*   Again mirroring what had happened in the 1630s, many leading bishops in the Restoration Church, like Laudian bishops earlier, came to be seen as promoters of popery and therefore of absolutism as well. On the face of it, the charge that Anglican bishops in the 1670s were favouring popery is as incredible as the similar accusation against Danby. What gave it credibility was the widespread assumption that popery equalled absolutism. In persecuting Protestant Dissenters some bishops laid themselves open to the charge that they were undermining Protestant unity and thereby aiding the Catholic cause. In a powerful pamphlet published in 1675, *A Letter from a Person of Quality to his Friends in the Country*, the Whig leader, the **Earl of Shaftesbury**, built on that the damning charge that there was an episcopal plot to introduce arbitrary government in Britain.

The extent of extra-parliamentary political activity

There is not sufficient space to deal with the campaign of electioneering, petitioning and mass demonstrations by Shaftesbury and the Whigs that was so well organised that many have seen the Whigs (with some validity) as the first political party in British history. The main point to make is that their activities had many parallels with the political tactics of petitioning and use of mass demonstrations employed by Pym and his

PROFILE: *Earl of Shaftesbury*

The eldest son of a wealthy Dorset gentry family, **Anthony Ashley Cooper** (1621–83) became a royalist in the First Civil War. In 1644 he changed sides and fought for the parliamentarians. During the 1650s he was a member of the Protectorate Council of State, of Barebones Parliament and all three Protectorate parliaments. But his relations with Oliver Cromwell were constantly troubled by his opposition to the political power of the army. He pressed Cromwell to take the crown in 1657 and in 1660 he cooperated with Monck in bringing about the restoration of the monarchy. (He went with the parliamentary delegation to Breda to invite Charles Stuart to return to England.) But his enthusiasm for Charles did not last. After being appointed Lord Chancellor and created **Earl of Shaftesbury** in 1672, he was dismissed in 1673, and he spent the last years of his life as a determined opponent of the king.

Shaftesbury's political career was so full of apparent U-turns that he was often accused of lack of principle by his political opponents. Yet this may be unfair. Certain consistent principles can be seen running through his career: notably a firm commitment to toleration for Protestant Dissenters and to the traditional constitution, both of which he considered to be seriously threatened by Charles II's policies of 'Absolutism and Popery'. He was acquitted of treason in 1681, but fled the country into exile, where he died shortly afterwards.

allies in the early 1640s, reinforcing the theme of continuity that has been followed in this chapter so far.

Differences between the Exclusion Crisis and 1640–41 crisis

Unlike Pym's campaign in 1640–41, that mounted by Shaftesbury and the Whigs in 1678–81 was unsuccessful. As the time chart shows, unlike Pym and the parliamentarians in 1641, the Whigs failed to secure any statutory limitations on the crown. After the dissolution of the Third Exclusion Parliament their opposition collapsed and, as will be seen in the next chapter, Charles II emerged in a stronger position than ever before.

There are many explanations why Charles II survived the Exclusion Crisis unscathed that will not be dealt with here. These include the facts that:

- Charles II's political skill was superior to that of his father
- the crown was in a stronger financial position than it had been in 1640–41
- Scotland and Ireland were now under firm English control, ensuring that there would be no second War of Three Kingdoms.

You should not ignore these explanations. However, this chapter ends by focusing on an explanation that is based on changes in English political and religious life brought about by the English Revolution. One of these (see chapter 21) was the opening up of wide divisions on the issue of whether or not Protestant Dissent could be tolerated. By and large, the Whigs drew on support from those who opposed a militant Church that was intent on persecuting Dissent. Significantly, the Tory opponents of Exclusion stressed that one of their prime concerns was to protect the Church from Dissent. This was a prime motive of many Royalists in 1642 (see page 109). The difference in 1678–81 is that the case for coming to the defence of the Church was now very much stronger, *because of what had happened during the English Revolution*.

With memories of the 1640s and 1650s still very much alive, the Tories were able to smear the Whigs as Dissenters, who, if not opposed, would put the country on a course that would again end in rebellion, regicide and republican rule. It is difficult to exaggerate the pulling power of Tory slogans in the Exclusion Crisis, like 'let not '41 come again'.

In short, the fear that there might be a second English Revolution worked to the advantage of the Tories and the crown during the Exclusion Crisis. When the Whigs proposed to interfere with the legitimate succession to the throne, it did seem as if the Tory propaganda image of them as dangerous revolutionaries was correct. Might the next stage not be to question the right of the legitimate succession to property? Would not this put the country back on the road to Ranters, Levellers and Diggers?

Finally, it is at least a possibility that the fear of putting the country back on that road not only *strengthened* the Tory cause but *weakened* the resolve of the Whigs to push theirs further. Whig magnates took armed retainers with them to the Third Exclusion Parliament. When it was dissolved they did not use them. The fear of a second English Revolution might have been as powerful in holding them back as it was in strengthening the position of the crown.

Tasks

1 In order to familiarise yourself with the detailed events of the period take two sheets of paper. Use these to make notes on the main elements (a) of continuity and (b) of change in the political and religious history of seventeenth-century Britain that are revealed by the Exclusion Crisis.

2 Divide into two groups.

Group A should consider what might have motivated Charles II to issue the Declaration of Indulgence, given the political dangers of doing so that must have been evident at the time. Some of the questions you might consider are:

a Was he a secret Catholic?

b Did he wish to gain the political support of Dissenters against the overbearing Anglican divines who criticised him for his sexual immorality?

Group B should consider why Charles II might have made the Treaty of Dover with France. Among the questions you should bear in mind are:

a Did he do it for the financial subsidies promised by Louis XIV?

b Did he want French help in a new Dutch war to get revenge for the Medway disaster?

c Did he seek 'a special relationship' with a monarch whose style of government he admired?

3 You could undertake a fairly detailed personal investigation of the Popish Plot. For example, you could begin by trying to find out more about the incidents illustrated in Figure 22.1. What some of these refer to will be evident from the information contained in this chapter. But you will need to use reference books (like those by Jones and Kenyon listed on page 246) to answer questions like:

a What is the significance of the reference to 2 September 1666 in cartoon 2?

b Who is 'Girald' in cartoon 5?

c Who are 'the Irish Ruffians' in cartoon 12?

d Who is 'Pickerin' in cartoons 13 and 24?

e Who is 'Captain Bedlow' in cartoon 15?

f Who is 'Mr Everard' in cartoon 18?

g Who are 'the 5 Jesuits' in cartoon 19?

h What is going on in cartoon 20?

i Who are the two people being taken to be executed in cartoon 21?

j Who is Sir William Waller in cartoon 23?

k Who are 'Captain Berry and Alderman Brooks' in cartoon 26?

l Who is 'Mr Dugdale' in carton 27?

m Who is 'Lord Stafford' in cartoon 29?

Do not confine your research to discovering these and other factual details of the 'Plot'. Investigate also the reasons why some believed in Titus Oates's allegations.

Further reading

Suggested further reading for chapter 21

In addition to Barry Coward, *The Stuart Age* (Addison Wesley Longman) pages 281–303, there are several useful introductory short books and pamphlets:

R. M. Bliss, *Restoration Government: Politics and Government 1660–88*, Lancaster Pamphlet (Routledge, 1985)

K. H. D. Haley, *Politics in the Reign of Charles II* (Historical Association pamphlet, 1985)

J. Miller, *Restoration England: the Reign of Charles II*, Seminar Studies in History (Addison Wesley Longman, 1985)

P. Seaward, *The Restoration* (Macmillan, 1991).

More detailed information can be found in:

J. R. Jones (ed.), *The Restored Monarchy*, Problems in Focus series (Macmillan, 1979)

R. Hutton, *The Restoration: a Political and Religious History of England and Wales, 1658–67* (Oxford University Press, 1985).

The most accessible sources for Christopher Hill's 'turning-point' view are his textbooks *The Century of Revolution* (Nelson, 1980) and *Reformation to Industrial Revolution* (Weidenfeld and Nicolson, 1969).

Suggested further reading for chapter 22

Further information can be found in Barry Coward, *The Stuart Age*, pages 314–32 and the books and pamphlets by Bliss, Haley, Miller and Seaward, listed above.

If you want more detailed information, see J. R. Jones, *The First Whigs: the Politics of the Exclusion Crisis 1678–83* (Oxford University Press, 1961) and John Kenyon, *The Popish Plot* (Penguin, 1972).

The most important recent approaches to the topic are set out in the introduction and in the essay by J. Scott in T. Harris, *et al* (eds), *The Politics of Religion in Restoration England* (Oxford University Press 1991).

23 The causes of the Glorious Revolution of 1688–9

Time chart

1681: Shaftesbury, the Whig leader, is tried on a charge of treason and acquitted. Whig supporters Edward Fitzharris and Stephen College are executed
Purges expelling Whigs from county and municipal government continue for the next 3–4 years

1682: Shaftesbury flees into exile in Holland

1683: Whig leaders Lord Russell and Algernon Sidney are executed for their alleged part in the Rye House Plot against the king

1684: No parliament is called despite the Triennial Act of 1664
Danby released from the Tower and James, Duke of York restored to the Privy Council

1685: Charles II dies and James II's accession is generally welcomed
Rebellions by Earl of Argyll (in Scotland) and by Charles II's son, the Duke of Monmouth (in south-west England), easily crushed
Executions and transportation of Monmouth's supporters by Lord Chief Justice Jeffreys ('The Bloody Assizes') cause no opposition
Louis XIV revokes the Edict of Nantes, which had given toleration to Huguenots in France

1686: James's Direction to Preachers forbids anti-Catholic sermons and Bishop Compton of London refuses to suspend a London preacher who has disobeyed it
A legal decision (*Godden v. Hales*) allows James to dispense (*i.e.* exempt) individuals from the Test and Corporation Acts
Court of Ecclesiastical Commission, established by the king to pursue Catholic policies, suspends the Bishop of London from office
A royal licensing office is established to sell certificates to Dissenters, exempting them from the Clarendon Code legislation
James begins to purge opponents from local government and replace them with Catholics. He also begins a campaign (called at the time 'closeting') to try to convert important people to Catholicism

1687: Two major Anglican Tories, the earls of Clarendon and Rochester (sons of Charles I and Charles II's minister), are dismissed

1687: James tries to force Madgalen College Oxford to accept a Catholic president

James issues his first Declaration of Indulgence

The king begins a campaign (with the Earl of Sunderland and Lord Chief Justice Jeffreys) to ensure that at the next election there will be a majority in favour of repealing the Test and Corporation Acts

Three questions are put to JPs to assess whether they will support the repeal of the Test and Corporation Acts

1688: James issues a second Declaration of Indulgence, which William Sancroft (Archbishop of Canterbury) and six bishops refuse to publish

Birth of a baby son (James) to James's wife, Mary of Modena

Sancroft and the six bishops are acquitted for petitioning against the Declaration of Indulgence

Seven leading Protestants (Edward Russell, Henry Sidney, Lord Lumley, Bishop Compton and the earls of Shrewsbury, Devonshire and Danby) send a letter inviting William of Orange to invade England. William of Orange's invasion force lands at Torbay and occupies Exeter

After a few provincial risings in William's favour, James abandons his army at Salisbury and retreats to London

Tory peers at the London Guildhall issue a declaration in James's favour, but James flees abroad

'What were the causes of the Glorious Revolution of 1688–9?' is not as controversial a question as 'What were the origins of the mid-century English Revolution?' Few, if any, topics in any period of history are! Nevertheless, historical explanations of the outbreak of the Glorious Revolution have changed greatly over the years, resulting in a major reinterpretation of the importance of the Glorious Revolution in British history (which is the subject of the next chapter).

This chapter looks at the criticisms that have been made of the idea that the Glorious Revolution was the inevitable result of long-term causes (the so-called 'Whig interpretation'). This interpretation, like the Whig explanation for the outbreak of the English Civil War (see chapter 9), looks unconvincing in the light of much recent writing on this subject, and the bulk of this chapter explains why.

However, the chapter ends with a warning not to carry revisionism too far.

The Whig interpretation of the causes of the Glorious Revolution

Two historians, above all, are associated with the Whig interpretation of the Glorious Revolution, Thomas Babington Macaulay and George Macaulay Trevelyan. Both were extremely popular historians in their own days and their influence lasted a long time after their deaths. Macaulay's unfinished, multivolumed *History of England*, published in the late 1840s and 1850s, was an instant bestseller and has never been out of print. The books of Macaulay's great-nephew, Trevelyan, principally his *England under the Stuarts* (1904) and *The English Revolution 1688–9* (1938), have been equally popular and influential.

Their interpretations of the origins of the Glorious Revolution are based on three main assumptions about the history of Britain before James II's downfall in December 1688:

- Royal absolutism in late seventeenth-century Britain was bound to fail, because the long struggle for constitutional supremacy between crown and parliament, that they believed had been in progress for much of the sixteenth and seventeenth centuries, had been settled in parliament's favour in 1660. The English Revolution rendered hopeless the attempts by Charles II and James II to revive royal absolutism.

- James II followed absolutist and Catholic policies that provoked most of his subjects to rebel against him and force him from the throne.

- William of Orange invaded England in November 1688 as 'the Great Deliverer' in order to rescue the country from royal absolutism and Catholicism and to restore English constitutional and religious liberties.

Criticisms of the Whig interpretation

Each of these three assumptions is questionable.

Was royal absolutism in later Stuart Britain bound to fail?

One cannot now be as certain as were Whig historians like Macaulay and Trevelyan that it was. Two reasons have already been seen. Firstly, there was no long struggle for constitutional supremacy in England in the sixteenth and seventeenth centuries between a 'rising', progressive parliament and a conservative, reactionary crown (see chapters 1 and 9). Secondly, there are also strong grounds for doubting that the mid-century English Revolution permanently weakened the power of the crown (see chapter 21).

A third reason is that the strong position in which the monarchy emerged from the Exclusion Crisis in 1681 became even stronger during the 1680s. Like many other European countries – including France, the German states, Sweden and Denmark – Britain seemed to be moving rapidly towards a more powerful, centralised and authoritarian system of government. It would be wrong to argue that Britain was on 'the road to absolutism'. As was explained in chapter 1, given the crown's lack of a salaried bureaucracy and a large standing army and the long tradition in England of monarchs ruling in cooperation with their leading subjects, it is highly unlikely that Britain could have developed as an 'absolutist' state in which kings and queens were able to exercise unlimited power.

Yet during the 1680s the power exercised by Charles II (until he died in 1685) and thereafter by James II increased dramatically. There are four reasons for this.

1 In the aftermath of the Exclusion Crisis Charles II very skilfully smeared his Whig opponents with the charge that they were aiming to copy the violence and republicanism of the English Revolution. His declaration dissolving parliament in 1681, which was read in all church pulpits, included a vivid reminder of the 1640s and 1650s, when 'religion, liberty and property were all lost and gone, when the monarchy was shaken off, and could never be revived till that was restored'.

2 Charles II used royal control of the judiciary to remove leading Whigs from power. Two – Russell and Sidney – were executed for their alleged part in the Rye House Plot to assassinate the king, and lesser figures (including Fitzharris and College – see the time chart) were got rid of. Shaftesbury's acquittal was an exception. He only escaped the fate of fellow Whigs because the grand jury that considered the charges against him was nominated by two London Whig sheriffs. But he was forced to flee abroad.

3 The crown strengthened its control of local government. Not only were there extensive purges of JPs in the early 1680s, ejecting those who had supported the cause of exclusion and replacing them with Tory gentlemen, but the crown conducted a successful campaign to undermine the kind of municipal independence that had secured Shaftesbury's acquittal in London. This was done by issuing *quo warranto* writs against the charters of many towns.

4 The most important reason for the growth in royal power in the 1680s was an improvement in the crown's financial position that promised to solve one of the most serious problems that had limited the effectiveness of government in Britain since at least the fifteenth century

KEY TERM:

Quo warranto

Quo warranto means literally 'by what warrant' or 'by what right'. *Quo warranto* writs were formal legal orders, demanding to know by what right towns exercised self-government. Since royal lawyers could easily find technical flaws in the answers received from most towns, and since the crown's control over leading judges was so strong, it was simple to secure judicial decisions that existing town charters were illegal. New charters were then issued, which enabled the crown to ensure that its supporters were appointed to municipal offices. From 1681 to 1685 Charles II issued 51 new charters and in 1685 James II issued 47 more.

1669–70	£990,323
1674–75	£1,430,183
1678–79	£1,325,894
1684–85	£1,370,750

Figure 23.1 *The Crown's annual revenue*

(see chapter 1). This was partly due to new taxes, like the hearth tax and excise (see chapter 21), and to the greater administrative efficiency of Danby and other financial ministers, who made the Treasury – rather than the medieval exchequer – the main financial department of government. But it was mainly due to a massive increase in the crown's revenue from customs dues that resulted from the 'commercial revolution' in England's overseas trade in the later seventeenth century (see chapter 26). By the 1680s the crown's annual revenue regularly rose above the figure of £1,200,000 which it was thought was enough to run the country effectively (see Figure 23.1).

By the mid 1680s two of the great problems that it was seen in chapter 1 threatened the stability of the state – 'the Financial Problem' and 'the British Problem' – seemed much less serious than they had ever been before in the seventeenth century. Not only was there a financial base for the establishment of strong authoritarian government in Britain, but the crown's control of Ireland and Scotland was more secure than ever before. Its grip on England is shown by the lack of any complaints when Charles II failed to call a parliament in 1684 despite the Triennial Act. When Charles II died in February 1685, his brother's accession, the source of much opposition only a few years earlier, was met by a welcoming flood of loyal addresses from the provinces. James II's first parliament, when it met in 1685, granted him a very generous financial settlement. Britain hardly seemed to be set on a road that led inevitably to limited constitutional monarchy.

Did James II's policies push most of his subjects into rebellion?

At first sight it seems as if there is no doubt that they did. The time chart at the head of this chapter reflects the growth of opposition from both Whigs and Tories to the new king's policies. So, too, does the contrast between the opposition from powerful English gentlemen to Monmouth's rebellion in 1685 in the West Country and their failure to oppose William of Orange's invasion in the same part of the country just over three years later.

The reasons for this are very similar to those that drove many to oppose Charles I in the later 1630s and Charles II in the later 1670s: fear of absolutism and Catholicism *within* England, confirmed by events *elsewhere* in Britain and in Europe.

Whether or not James II intended to establish royal absolutism in England is not known. (The task at the end of the chapter is on this interesting historical problem.) What is certain – and of more importance in explaining the course of events in his reign – is that most of his subjects came to *believe* that he did.

As in the 1630s and 1670s, the belief was strengthened by events elsewhere in Britain and in Europe. In Ireland James accelerated policies of Catholicisation by allowing Richard Talbot (Earl of Tyrconnel) to purge the army and administration of Ireland of Protestants. In 1687 Tyrconnel replaced the Protestant Earl of Clarendon as Lord Lieutenant of Ireland. In Scotland, too, James II promoted Catholicism under the guise of toleration and underlined the widespread belief that Catholicism brought absolutism by justifying his Declaration of Indulgence in Scotland by his 'Absolute power, which all our subjects are to obey without reserve'. The close identification of popery and absolutism was confirmed by events in France, where after 1685 Louis XIV began a cruel campaign against Huguenots. Many fled to settle in England bringing with them horror stories that fitted well with what many English people already believed about Catholicism: that it was inevitably accompanied by policies that would destroy parliamentary liberties and the rule of law.

As James II's reign unfolded, that was what seemed to many to be happening, not only outside the country, but inside it as well. In promoting Catholicism in England James seemed to be using the royal prerogative in an arbitrary way. The following are some of the things that James did that led people to believe that he was not only promoting Catholicism but absolutism as well (others may be found in the time chart):

■ The king's intention to repeal the Test and Corporation Acts.

■ His decision to maintain and increase in size the army used to suppress Monmouth's rebellion.

■ The promotion of Catholics in the army and in local government despite the Test and Corporation Acts.

■ The decision in the case of *Godden v. Hales* that declared that it was lawful for the king to dispense (*i.e.* exempt) individuals from these parliamentary statutes.

■ The claim in two Declarations of Indulgence in 1687 and 1688 that the king had the right to suspend parliamentary statutes.

■ His campaign in 1687 to manipulate parliamentary elections to secure a parliament that would support the repeal of the Test and Corporation Acts.

By 1688 policies like these had alienated James II from the majority of his powerful subjects to an extent that can be compared with Charles I's isolated position in 1640. The birth of a son to James and his wife, Mary of

Modena, on 10 June 1688, opening up the possibility of unlimited Catholic rule in the country, cemented the alliance of Whigs and Tories, Anglican and Dissenters against him. The seven signatories of the letter of 30 June (see time chart), asking for William of Orange's help against James II, included both Whigs and Tories.

Had the king's policies, though, brought the country to the verge of *rebellion* against James II? The bulk of the evidence that reflects opinion in England in the latter part of 1688 suggests that they had not. A detailed analysis of the answers to the three questions James II had put to JPs in October 1687 shows no evidence of widespread opposition to the king. Nor did the letter inviting William to invade England mention an intention to overthrow James. It asked merely for help in persuading James to reverse his policies.

More conclusive (since it could be argued that it would have been unreasonable to expect anyone to declare rebellious intentions at this stage) is the evidence of many Tory loyalists, like the Earl of Nottingham, who were horrified at going as far as the signatories of the June letter, which Nottingham considered 'high treason'. Few were willing to do much to help James, but most were too deeply attached to the idea that resistance to a divinely-appointed king was a sin, and too fearful of a repetition of the events after 1640, to abandon him completely. There is little sign of a Glorious Revolution in the summer of 1688.

Was William of Orange 'the Great Deliverer'?

It would be foolish of anyone to claim that they knew what **William of Orange** intended when he invaded England in 1688. The declarations he published explaining his actions are very vague. Moreover, simply because they did not mention his wife's claims to the throne (he was married to James II's elder daughter) or his own intentions to take the throne, does not mean that such ideas never passed through his mind. Yet it is likely that neither of these were his prime motives.

Why, then, did James II lose his throne?

The logical conclusion of the arguments that have been put so far in this chapter is that the answer to this question is the personality of James II. If the monarchy was intrinsically strong, if the country was not on the verge of rebellion and if William of Orange had no intention of overthrowing the king but of forcing him to enter the European war and merely to reverse his policies, then James was himself the author of his own downfall.

> **PROFILE:** *William of Orange*
>
> **W**illiam (1650–1702) was a European prince and his actions were influenced principally by events in Europe. He was the only child of William II, Prince of Orange, and Mary, eldest daughter of Charles I. In 1677 he married Mary, elder daughter of James, Duke of York (the future James II). His public life was dominated by two aims. The first was to restore his family's dominant position as *stadholder* (*i.e.* chief ruler) of the United Provinces against the competing claims of the various provinces, especially the biggest, Holland. This he largely achieved in 1672, when his rival, the grand pensionary of Holland, Johann de Witt was murdered. The second, which lasted for the rest of his life, was to protect his homeland against Louis XIV's expansionist policies. Even after the European Peace of Nijmegen in 1678 French troops annexed territories beyond the northern and eastern frontiers of France. To combat this, William sought to organise a pan-European coalition against France. Until the mid 1680s he was frustrated in this aim by opposition from pacific republicans at home and by different national interests abroad. From that point onwards, however, the European situation changed. This is the key to William's prime motive in 1688. Only at that point had he succeeded in welding together an anti-French coalition of European states. The one power he needed to complete it was England. The timing of his decision to invade (probably in April 1688) suggests strongly that his prime motive was to bring England into his European war against the French. There is little evidence that William was any more anxious than James's English opponents to lead a revolution to overthrow the king.

This is, to a large extent, plausible. Like Charles I in the early seventeenth century, it was *his* unwise policies that had destroyed the strong position he had inherited on his accession. Moreover, it was *his* decision to flee the country that ensured that he lost his throne. What would have happened if he had stayed to fight William of Orange is, of course, uncertain. But it is at least likely that, if he had continued to reverse his policies as he frantically did in his last few weeks in power, he would have gained enough loyalist support to provide serious opposition to William's army and to the few provincial risings in the Midlands and the North. Another civil war could have ensued.

Returning from the realms of speculation to more solid historical ground, James's defection gave most propertied people in England, as well as William of Orange, no alternative but to look elsewhere for a solution to the crisis. The problems involved in that will be seen in the next chapter.

Here the essential point is that the crisis came about because of James's decision to flee the country. United though many of James's subject were in wanting William of Orange's help in forcing him to reverse his policies, few wanted to secure his deposition. They were, as the historian W. A. Speck has called them, 'reluctant revolutionaries'.

Yet, it would be wrong to carry that revisionist argument too far and to portray James's opponents simply as conservatives forced to consider changes in the government by circumstances and the fear of what might happen if they did not restore political order quickly. While admitting that they were 'reluctant revolutionaries', W. A. Speck does not do that. 'They might have been reluctant actually to resist him,' he writes, 'but they were not prepared to acquiesce any longer in his rule.' One of the favourite slogans used by many of James's opponents to express their aims in 1688 was 'Liberty and Property'. Alongside their undoubted desire to preserve their property were demands for the protection of Protestantism and the rule of law from the arbitrary use of the royal prerogative. By the end of 1688 these demands had come most commonly to be expressed in the demand for 'a free parliament', as they were in one provincial declaration of December 1688.

> *'We being hearty and zealously concerned for the Protestant Religion, the Laws of the Land, and the Liberties and Properties of the subject cannot (without being wanting in our duty) be silent under those calamities wherein late prevailing Popish councils have miserably involved these Kingdoms: And we do therefore unanimously resolve to apply ourselves to his Highness the Prince of Orange who with so great kindness to these realms, so vast expense and such hazard to his person, hath undertaken by the endeavouring to procure a free Parliament to rescue us with as little effusion as possible of Christian blood from the eminent [i.e. imminent] dangers of Popery and Slavery.'*

The Declaration of the lord lieutenant, sheriff, deputy lieutenants, militia officers and 'other Protestant gentlemen' of Lancashire, 23 December 1688, quoted in W. A. Speck, *Reluctant Revolutionaries: Englishmen and the Revolution of 1688* (1988).

The Glorious Revolution was not simply the product of a pragmatic desire to preserve order but also a principled belief in Protestantism and the rule of law. Like the English Civil War nearly 50 years before, such beliefs did not make a political crisis inevitable. But they are an integral part of what happened in 1688. There were ideological, as well as 'functional', causes of the Glorious Revolution.

Task

Did James II have absolutist aims?

As noted above, historians disagree on this. Read the contrasting arguments of J. Miller and W. A. Speck, two of the major historians of this period. Which do you consider to be the more convincing?

'James's English subjects (and many later historians) equated "Popery" with "arbitrary government" and assumed that James aimed to establish absolutism as well as Catholicism. James was certainly authoritarian by nature and, after twenty-five years' waiting, revelled a little in his power as King. But that did not mean that he wished to overthrow the laws and constitution and establish an absolutism like that of Louis XIV. While he told Barillon [the French ambassador in London] with monotonous regularity that he wished to promote Catholicism, he never said that he wished to make English government like that of France. He assumed that William [of Orange] would succeed him and saw no reason to strengthen the monarchy for William's benefit ... If James stretched his powers beyond conventional limits, he did so because he could not achieve his objectives without doing so. In accusing him of trying to establish absolutism, his contemporaries and later historians confused means with ends.'

J. Miller, *James II: a Study in Kingship* (1978).

'He [James II] was determined to make the Crown appear in a more dignified light [than in the days of Charles II], one which borrowed the rays of the Sun King, Louis XIV. He sought to emulate the king of France in other ways too. The French model of absolute kingship appealed to him. The notion that all he really sought was religious toleration for Catholics, and that he only resorted to the increase of royal authority as a means to that end, and not as an end in itself, is ultimately unconvincing. He told the French ambassador at the outset of his reign that, if parliament did not grant him sufficient funds, he would cashier it and resort to raising revenue by force. Of course, one must be sceptical about what he told Barillon, and it could be that he was boasting about his intention to emulate Louis XIV. But he was deadly serious when he tried to repeal the Habeas Corpus Amendment Act of 1679 as well as the Test and penal laws. This Act [The Habeas Corpus Amendment Act which guaranteed the right of everyone to be brought to trial and not to remain indefinitely imprisoned] passed by the first Exclusion Parliament, was subtitled, "For the better securing the liberty of the subject" ... James was determined to repeal it, since he considered it to be destructive of royal authority.'

W. A. Speck, *Reluctant Revolutionaries: Englishmen and the Revolution of 1688* (1989).

Now answer the following questions:

1 a What side is Miller on?
   b What does he say about James's unconstitutional actions?
   c What does he say about his intentions?

2 a What side is Speck on?

b What evidence does he cite to support his case?

c What does he say about Miller's view?

3 Much of the argument seems to hinge on James's intentions: what is your view about these?

4 a What evidence would you use to support Miller?

b What evidence would you use to support Speck?

5 What is your final conclusion?

Further reading

The relevant pages in Barry Coward, *The Stuart Age* (Addison Wesley Longman) are pages 333–344.

The best brief books on the topic are:

J. Miller, *The Glorious Revolution*, Seminar Studies in History (Addison Wesley Longman, 1983)

M. Mullett, *James II and English Politics 1678–88*, Lancaster Pamphlets (Routledge, 1994).

There are two longer, excellent books:

W. A. Speck, *Reluctant Revolutionaries: Englishmen and the Revolution of 1688* (Oxford University Press, 1989)

J. R. Jones, *The Revolution of 1688 in England* (Weidenfeld and Nicolson, 1972).

The best biography of James II is:

J. Miller, *James II: a Study in Kingship* (Wayland, 1978).

24 What was changed by the Glorious Revolution?

Time chart

1689: January English Convention Parliament meets (until January 1690) and votes that the throne is to be offered jointly to William and Mary

February Declaration of Rights read to William and Mary in the Banqueting Hall in London. Later in the month William III and Mary II are crowned (subsequently about 400 non-jurors refuse to swear an oath of allegiance to them)

March James II lands in Ireland
Scottish Convention Parliament meets and makes radical demands in the Claim of Right and Articles of Grievances

May–June Grand Alliance (England, United Provinces, Emperor, Spain, Savoy and German states) is formed against France

May Toleration Act is passed by the English Convention
Irish 'Patriot Parliament' passes anti-English legislation (subsequently repealed by English parliaments in 1690–91 and the Dublin parliament in 1692)

July Jacobite Scots win a victory at Killiecrankie
Scottish Convention Parliament abolishes bishops

August Jacobite Scots are defeated at Dunkeld

November Convocation meets and demands anti-Dissenter measures

December Bill of Rights passed by the English Convention Parliament

1690: March William III's first parliament meets and grants the crown excise for life but customs for only four years

May Scottish Convention Parliament abolishes the Lords of Articles

June Scottish Convention Parliament restores full Presbyterian government

July William III's victory at Battle of the Boyne

October Treaty of Limerick ends the war in Ireland

Whig historians following Macaulay and Trevelyan (see the last chapter) had no doubt that the Glorious Revolution had a major, decisive impact on the country. According to them, it put it firmly on the road towards parliamentary constitutional monarchy, political stability and religious toleration, that were all characteristics of Britain from the eighteenth century onwards. The Glorious Revolution marked a sharp break from authoritarian personal monarchy, political upheavals and religious intolerance that had been the hallmarks of Britain before 1688.

The criticisms of the Whig interpretation of the causes of the Glorious Revolution that were surveyed in the last chapter, however, have cast doubts on the idea that 1688–9 was a major dividing line in the country's history. To some historians, the prime aim of the opponents of James II were conservative. Before James's flight abroad, it is said, they merely wanted to put a stop to the king's innovations. Once James had gone, they were full of zeal, not for change, but to restore political order as soon as possible. The result has been that some have suggested that, far from being a major dividing line in British history, 1688–9 merely brought about a change of monarchs.

These contrasting interpretations of the Glorious Revolution, therefore, make it very important to determine what the events of 1688–9 changed and what they did not.

What the Glorious Revolution changed

The impact of the Glorious Revolution was most marked in Scotland and Ireland. But even in England, though less sweeping decisions were taken, they ensured that the country would never be the same again.

Scotland

The Glorious Revolution brought about major changes in Scotland. Of all the three British kingdoms, what happened there most merits being described as a 'revolution'. The decisions made by the Scottish Convention Parliament that met in March 1689 were much more radical than those that were included in the English Declaration of Rights. The key demands of the Scottish Parliament that were sent to William and Mary in the Claim of Right and the Articles of Grievances were:

■ repeal of the 1669 Act of Supremacy which had brought the Kirk under English control

■ abolition of bishops

■ abolition of the **Lords of Articles**.

KEY TERM:

Lords of Articles

The **Lords of Articles** were ministers appointed by the crown to control political (and especially parliamentary) affairs in Scotland.

Not surprisingly, William's first reaction was to block these demands. But within months, as can be seen from the time chart, he had accepted them all. There are two reasons why. The first is that Scottish Presbyterian opinion was highly organised in the Scottish Parliament. The second, more important, reason is that events in 1689–90 brought home to William how reliant he was in Scotland on the support of Presbyterians in Lowland Scotland. In the summer of 1689 rebel supporters of James II in the Scottish Highlands won a major victory at Killiecrankie, and the rebellion was only defeated with the help of Scottish Presbyterians from the Lowlands. This had to be paid for by William, who agreed to legislation in the Scottish Parliament in 1690 that ensured that the Scottish Kirk and parliament were more independent of England than ever before.

Ireland

The impact on Ireland represented less of a break with the past, but it nonetheless brought about major and permanent changes in the history of the country. The immediate impact was to raise the hopes of Irish Catholics of relief from persecution. James's invasion of Ireland ignited an explosion of Catholic militancy, seen in the Dublin 'Patriot Parliament' that met in May 1689 and passed legislation, proclaiming Irish independence of England. That alone did not prompt William III's military campaign in Ireland (which included his victory at the Battle of the Boyne on 1 July 1690, that is still celebrated by Ulster Orangemen). Security considerations – the need to make a pre-emptive strike against a threatened Jacobite invasion of England – were as important in William's thinking about Ireland as they were about Scotland. When that threat was over, peace was made with the Irish rebels on fairly generous terms by the Treaty of Limerick. But these were quickly overthrown. The legislation of the 'Patriot Parliament' was repealed in English parliaments in 1690 and 1691 and in the Dublin parliament in 1692.

The result was to confirm the ascendancy in Ireland of a narrow Anglo-Irish landed class and an episcopal Church that had little support in the country. The main impact of the Glorious Revolution in Ireland was to complete the English Protestant ascendancy of the country that had been held back by James II.

England

In comparison with Ireland and Scotland the changes brought about in England as a result of what happened after James's flight in December 1688 were less clear-cut. They are nevertheless important. Three major ones deserve special emphasis.

1 *The Glorious Revolution changed the succession to the English throne not only in 1689 but in the future*. James's flight in December 1688 posed everyone major problems about what to do about the succession to the throne. The Tories faced the most difficult dilemma. Their attachment to the

KEY TERM:

Non-jurors

Non-jurors were those, mainly clergymen, who refused to swear oaths of allegiance to William and Mary and resigned their public offices after the Glorious Revolution.

belief in the divine right of kings and the legitimate succession to property (including the throne) ought to have led them to refuse to recognise any other monarch than James II. In fact, only a tiny minority of **non-jurors** took that course. For the majority of Anglican Tories, such a course was difficult to take: although James II might be the lawful monarch, he was a Catholic and he was not present in England, thus threatening the imminent breakdown of public order.

In the period immediately after James's flight, many Tories attempted to reconcile their conscientious attachment to the principle of divine right and their yearning for the protection of property by two ingenious schemes that would allow them to support monarchs other than James II:

▪ *A regency*? By this scheme William would exercise regal power in Britain but as the regent of James II who, though absent, would retain the title of king.

▪ *Queen Mary*? By this scheme Mary, William's wife and James's elder daughter, would be sole monarch and William would merely be her consort. This scheme relied on two assumptions: that James had 'deserted' his throne and that the baby born in June 1688 was not the son of James II and his wife, Mary of Modena, but an impostor smuggled into Mary's bedroom in a warming pan!

The attitude of the Whigs to the succession required less convoluted solutions, but some got into difficulties by suggesting that William should rule alone on the radical (and inaccurate) grounds that James II had been deposed in December 1688 for breaking an ancient contract made between monarchs and the people.

Events forced both Whigs and Tories to change these attitudes to the succession in 1689. Tory proposals were doomed to failure, not only by the difficulty of the task of proving the truth of the warming-pan story, but by the fact that William made it very clear that he would not rule as a regent or in a subordinate position to his wife. 'I will not be my wife's gentleman usher' was the blunt but effective way he made that point. As a result, most Tories were forced to accept a view that was impossible to reconcile to their belief in the legitimate succession of the crown: that the throne was 'vacant' and must be filled by someone other than James II *or* William ruling as regent for James *or* Mary ruling alone. Similarly, in order to secure a speedy settlement, the Whigs were forced to abandon their insistence that James had been deposed in 1688 and to accept that he had 'abdicated' the throne.

KEY TERM:

Convention Parliament

The **Convention Parliament** of 1689 was not strictly a proper parliament, because, like the Convention Parliament of 1660 that restored the monarchy, it was not called by the king.

> 'That King James the Second, having endeavoured to subvert the constitution of the kingdom by breaking the original contract between king and people, and by the advice of Jesuits and other wicked persons having violated the fundamental laws and having withdrawn himself out of this kingdom, has abdicated the government and that the throne is thereby become vacant.'

The resolution adopted by the **Convention Parliament** on 28 January 1689.

This resolution of the Convention Parliament is the outcome of these compromises and is the basis of the decision that was taken in February to offer the throne jointly to William and Mary.

One other crucial decision about the succession to the throne was taken early in 1689 that had long-term consequences. Parliament voted that it was 'inconsistent with the safety and welfare of a Protestant kingdom to be governed by a popish prince'. This went even further than the Exclusion Bills of the 1679–81 crisis, which had merely attempted to exclude from the succession one Catholic, James Duke of York (see chapter 22). In the Bill of Rights of December 1689 a more radical proposal was confirmed, when the succession after the heirs of William and Mary was said to be in the heirs of Mary's sister, Anne, excluding all Catholics or anyone married to a Catholic – a provision that has remained in force to the present day.

2 *The Glorious Revolution limited the new monarchs' powers in England.* As will be seen, these limitations were not as sweeping either as many historians have thought or as some contemporaries wanted. Yet three things happened in 1689–90 that ensured that William and Mary had less freedom to exercise royal power than either they would have liked or than other British monarchs before them had enjoyed:

- The first was that they had (unlike any previous British monarch) to swear an oath at their coronation that they were bound to rule 'according to the statutes in Parliament agreed on'. There was, of course, no guarantee that they would keep this promise, but the significance of the fact that it was made should not be underestimated.

- The second was that shortly before William and Mary were offered the throne a document known as the Declaration of Rights was read to them in the Banqueting Hall in Whitehall, London. This was later, in December 1689, enacted by parliament as a statute, the Bill of Rights. This reflected a fairly widespread feeling among both Whig and Tory MPs that the chance should not be missed, as it had been in 1660, to

put conditions on the monarch's power. 'All the world will laugh at us, if we make a half-settlement,' said the Whig, William Sacheverell. 'Will you establish the crown and not secure yourselves?' asked the Tory, Sir Edward Seymour. William later disclaimed that he had accepted the crown on condition that he approved the Declaration of Rights. There is, in fact, no evidence that he (or Mary) gave their assent to it before they were crowned. Yet the Declaration (later Bill) of Rights does contain a few new limitations on the power of English monarchs. These were not as sweeping as some that had been planned, but, of the rights the crown had exercised during the reigns of Charles II and James II, the following were declared illegal in 1689:
- the power to suspend parliamentary statutes
- the power to dispense [*i.e.* exempt] individuals from parliamentary statutes
- the right to maintain standing armies in peacetime
- the right to establish commissions for ecclesiastical causes.

In 1690 William and Mary were granted an inadequate financial settlement: the excise for life and customs for only four years. There is no doubt that this was a deliberate attempt to prevent the crown from becoming financially independent of parliament, reflected in the view of Colonel John Birch during the financial debates: 'Our greatest misery was, our giving it [an adequate financial grant] to King James for life, and not from three years to three years, and so you may have often kissed his hands there.' The intention in 1690 was to make William, unlike his predecessors since 1681, call parliaments regularly.

3 *The Glorious Revolution gave legal freedom of worship to Protestant Dissenters.* As will be seen, the Toleration Act of 1689 did not, by any means, pave the way for widespread religious toleration in England. Yet the Act did give legal freedom of worship to all Protestants who were not willing to be members of the Church of England, except **Unitarians**. The philosopher, John Locke, mentioned the Act's limitations, but welcomed it as decisive break with the past.

KEY TERM:

Unitarians

Unitarians (who were sometimes known as Socinians) were those who denied the doctrine of the Trinity. This is one of the central doctrines accepted by most of the major Christian Churches: that God is Father, Son and Holy Ghost (*i.e.* that Jesus was both God and man). By rejecting this doctrine Unitarians denied the divinity of Jesus.

'*Toleration has now at last been established by law in our country. Not perhaps as wide in scope as might be wished by you and those like you, who are true Christians and free from ambition or envy. Still, it is something to have progressed so far. I hope that, with these beginnings, the foundations have been laid of that liberty and peace, in which the church of Christ is one day to be established.*'

Locke's letter to a friend in the United Provinces, quoted in O. Grell *et al* (eds), *From Persecution to Toleration* (1991).

What the Glorious Revolution did not change

It did not end Whig–Tory divisions

The Glorious Revolution had brought a temporary end to Whig–Tory wrangling that had grown in the 1670s and 1680s. William III, by appointing both Whigs and Tories to key offices in England, demonstrated that he aimed to act as an even-handed monarch standing above faction, as had James I (see chapter 5), no doubt intending to maintain the political peace.

The rapid reappearance of political quarrels between Whigs and Tories over issues of principle (mainly their attitudes to Dissenters) and office-holding indicated William III's failure. As will be seen in the next chapter, these divisions were to be widened greatly under the pressure of the country's involvement in a major European war.

It did not bring about the end of religious intolerance

The Toleration Act of 1689 gave most Protestants legal freedom to worship, but it did not bring about the end of religious intolerance. Why?

This is largely explained by the fact that what many in England wanted in 1688–9 was not religious toleration, but the creation of a more comprehensive Church of England than had been erected in the 1660s (see chapter 21). The main efforts of some churchmen and politicians immediately after William's accession, therefore, were to try to provide means by which most Protestants, hitherto excluded from the Church of England, would feel able to become members of it. To that end the leading advocate of 'comprehension', Daniel Finch (second Earl of Nottingham), introduced a Comprehension Bill in parliament early in March 1689. He was hoping that it would tempt the majority of Protestant Dissenters to join the Church of England. At the same time, he introduced a Toleration Bill that was intended to grant limited freedom of worship to the minority who remained outside the Church.

During the course of 1689 the Comprehension Bill failed to become law. Not all Anglicans were willing to cooperate with Protestant Dissenters, fearing that any concessions would mean the end of the Anglican monopoly in Church and State. Such fears were not helped by events in Scotland. The triumph of Scottish Presbyterianism and the abolition of episcopacy made it increasingly difficult for William and the Earl of

Nottingham to keep the Comprehension Bill alive in the Commons. What killed it was the open display of opposition to it from rank-and-file clergy when Convocation met in November 1689. This was as fierce as anything seen since the anti-Dissenter furore in the early days of the Cavalier Parliament in the early 1660s (see chapter 21).

As a result, only the Toleration Bill was passed by parliament. In these circumstances its limited scope is unsurprising. Many Dissenters could now legally worship in freedom, but only at the expense of humiliating conditions – the doors of their meeting houses had to remain open during their religious services, for example. More seriously, the Test Acts, restricting all public offices to those who had a certificate of attendance at services held in parish churches of the Church of England, remained unrepealed. Protestant Dissenters were still second-class citizens despite the Glorious Revolution.

Moreover, as will be seen in the next chapter, Anglican intolerance of Protestant Dissent that lay behind this situation, and which had been temporarily suspended in the face of the common Catholic enemy in the reign of James II, grew rapidly in intensity in the 1690s and early 1700s.

It did not bring about the end of personal monarchy

Important as were the limitations put on the powers of the new monarchs by the coronation oath, the Declaration (and Bill) of Rights and the financial settlement of 1690, they were much smaller than had been intended by some in the Convention Parliament in 1690. The best illustration of this is a comparison of the programme of sweeping constitutional changes proposed by a parliamentary committee in its report in February 1689 and the shortened list of limits put on royal power in the Bill of Rights.

Why was the Bill of Rights emasculated in this way? One reason is that William's hostility to constitutional limitations being imposed on him was well known, and ambitious politicians at the start of the new reign took the hint. Above all, however, the major reason was that, as in 1660 (see chapter 20), most MPs were driven to a speedy settlement by panic at the thought of what might happen if the lack of a settled government were prolonged. The men of 1689 were no less fearful of the collapse of order than were the men of 1659–60. In this climate the demands of those, like radical Whig zealots ('the true Whigs' as they were called), for major constitutional and ecclesiastical changes were swept aside. In the view of many, the pressing need for the re-establishment of monarchical authority took precedence over the luxury of lengthy debates that a programme

Parliamentary demands, February 1689

The demands ('heads of grievances') that a parliamentary committee in February 1689 wanted William and Mary to agree to before their coronation. Only the ones marked with an asterisk (*) were included in the Bill of Rights.

The new monarchs should recognise that:

* The royal power of dispensing or suspending laws was illegal.
* The commission for ecclesiastical causes was illegal.
* Levying money by royal prerogative without parliamentary approval was illegal.
* Prosecuting people for exercising their right to petition the king was illegal.
* Raising and maintaining a standing army in peacetime was illegal.
* Protestants may keep arms for their common defence.
* Elections to parliaments ought to be free.
* There ought to be freedom of speech in parliament.
* There ought to be no excessive bail, excessive fines or cruel and unjust punishments.
* Jurors ought to be openly appointed and jurors in treason trials ought to be freeholders.
* All grants of fines and forfeitures before conviction were illegal.
* Parliaments should be held frequently.

In addition, Acts should be passed:

– to reorganise the militia
– to secure the rights and freedom of electing MPs and the rights and privileges of parliaments
– to secure frequent parliaments
– to prevent parliaments from sitting too long
– to prevent cities, towns etc. from *quo warranto* writs
– to prevent a member of the royal family from marrying a Catholic
– to force monarchs on their accession to maintain the Protestant religion and laws and liberties of the country
– to enable Protestants to exercise their religion freely and to unite Protestants in the matter of public worship as far as may be to regulate procedure in treason trials
– to ensure that judges are appointed 'during good behaviour' with fixed salaries and not 'during the king's pleasure' and therefore under royal control
– to secure subjects against excessive bail and fines and cruel and unusual punishments
– to reform abuses in the appointment of sheriffs and the execution of their offices
– to reform the appointment of jurors to prevent corrupt and false verdicts
– to reform the Court of King's Bench
– to reform the Court of Chancery and other law courts
– to prevent the buying and selling of offices
– to grant the right of *habeas corpus* to prisoners *i.e.* the right to be brought to trial and not to be kept in prison at the king's pleasure
– to prevent the grants and promises of fines and forfeiture before conviction
– to redress grievances in levying the hearth tax
– to redress abuses in levying and collecting the excise.

of major constitutional changes would require. Like the Toleration Act, the Bill of Rights was the outcome of pressing needs and not careful thought and planning. It was, as a result, a limited document.

Conclusion

The main aim of this chapter has been to establish that, although the events of 1688–90 had important effects on the Church and constitution in Scotland, Ireland and England, by 1690 the nature of government in Britain (and especially in England) had not changed *fundamentally* from the pattern described in earlier chapters of this book.

However, it will be seen in chapters 28 and 29 that by the time the last Stuart monarch died in 1714 such a fundamental change had taken place. The powers of the monarch were now much more limited than ever before. Personal monarchy had been transformed into limited parliamentary monarchy. There had also been a transformation in the effectiveness and strength of government in Britain. By the end of the Stuart Age the country was not only Great Britain *in name* (after the union of England and Scotland in 1707) but also great *in fact*.

After 1689 there emerged a more powerful British state than ever before. The Glorious Revolution contributed to that process but only directly in a limited way. However, its indirect contribution to it was more important. One consequence of the Glorious Revolution that has not yet been mentioned in this chapter was the involvement of Britain in a long period of European warfare. It was this (see chapter 29) that was the major agent of constitutional change that transformed Britain in fundamental ways in the later seventeenth and early eighteenth centuries.

Task: turning-points?

This task refers to this chapter and to chapter 21 and focuses on the idea of *turning-points* in history.

Reading both chapters will have shown you that this is an idea that is not without difficulties. As we have seen, some historians refuse to use the concept of turning-point at all for either 1660 or 1688–9. We have also seen that even historians who use the concept disagree about whether 1660 or 1688–9 was the more important turning-point.

1 The first thing you should consider is whether it is useful to identify turning-points in history. Are there dates in the past that mark the appearance of permanent, decisive changes from what had gone on before?

Everyone in the class should write a short paragraph, explaining their view on this question. Some of these should then be read out as the basis for a class discussion on this issue. This will be useful preparation for the following task which should be done individually.

2 On two sheets of paper, headed 1660 and 1688–9, make lists of reasons why both dates can (a) be regarded and (b) not regarded as turning-points.

3 Now draw your own conclusions.
  a Do you think that it is valid to regard one or both of these dates as turning-points?
  b Which has the stronger claim to be regarded as a major turning-point?

Further reading

See Barry Coward, *Stuart Age*, pages 355–68 (for England), 368–70 (for Ireland) and 414–15 (for Scotland).

J. Miller, *The Glorious Revolution* Seminar Studies in History (Addison Wesley Longman, 1983).

W. A. Speck, *Reluctant Revolutionaries: Englishmen and the Revolution of 1688* (Oxford University Press, 1988).

J. Carter, 'The revolution and the constitution' in G. Holmes (ed.), *Britain after the Glorious Revolution* (Macmillan, 1969) is a good statement of the anti-Whig view of the Glorious Revolution.

25 Why was there a 'Rage of Party', 1689–1714?

Time chart

1689: England joins the Grand Alliance in a war against France

1690: General election is followed by first session of William's first parliament (March–May) – MPs make limited financial settlement
Second session (Oct. 1690–Jan. 1691) establishes Commission of Public Accounts
War news: allied defeat at sea off Beachy Head; William's victory at the Battle of the Boyne

1691: Third session of parliament (Oct. 1691–Feb. 1692) sees attacks on royal control of judges
War news: French capture Mons; General Ginkel defeats Irish at Limerick

1692: Fourth session of William's first parliament (Nov. 1692–March 1693) – Tories demand a 'blue water' war but MPs approve a land tax to pay for a land war in Europe
War news: French navy defeated in Bay of La Hogue; French army take Namur; drawn battle at Steenkirk

1693: Fifth session of parliament (Nov. 1693–April 1694) sees resignation of Tory Secretary of State Nottingham
War news: French army takes Nuy; drawn battle at Neerwinden

1694: Whig Junto leaders appointed to royal offices and pilot through a financial revolution (including foundation of the Bank of England)
Sixth session of William's first parliament (Nov. 1694–May 1695) – Tories attack Whig finance and the land war
Triennial Act passed
Queen Mary dies

1695: Licensing Act lapses allowing more press freedom
General election results in William's second parliament
First session of new parliament (Nov. 1695–April 1696) – more attacks on Whig finance and establishment of a Tory Land Bank, which quickly collapses
War news: William III recaptures Namur

1696: Fenwick Plot to assassinate William is revealed (about 90 Tory MPs refuse to swear oath of loyalty to the king)
Second session of parliament (Oct. 1696–April 1697)

1697: Third session of William's second parliament (Dec. 1697–July 1698) sees attacks on the standing army
War ends with Treaty of Ryswyck

1698: General election results in William's third parliament
William III makes secret Partition Treaty to prevent France gaining Spanish throne on death of Carlos II

1699: Second session of William's third parliament (Nov. 1699–August 1700) – more Tory attacks on the Whig Junto

1700: William's Second Partition Treaty
Death of last surviving son of heir to throne, Princess Anne, brings first succession crisis for a century
Death of Carlos II of Spain brings prospect of renewed European war

1701: First of two general elections this year results in William's fourth parliament (Feb.–June), which passes Act of Settlement settling succession of English throne on heirs of James I, Sophia (Electress of Hanover) and her son, George
James II dies and his son (the Young Pretender) is recognised by Louis XIV as James III
Second general election produces William's fifth parliament (Dec. 1701–May 1702), which passes Abjuration Act forcing MPs to take oath against the succession of the Young Pretender

1702: William III dies and is succeeded by Queen Anne
Britain, United Provinces and Austria declare war on France
General election results in Anne's first parliament (Oct. 1702–Feb. 1703) – Tories demand an Occasional Conformity Bill

1703: Second session of Anne's first parliament (Nov. 1703–April 1704) – Tory attacks on Dissenters continue
Scottish Parliament passes anti-English measures (Act Anent Peace and War; Wine Act; Wool Act; Security Act – see key terms, page 305)
War news: Methuen Treaty with Portugal commits Britain to war in Spain as well as in Netherlands and Germany

1704: Third session of Anne's first parliament (Oct. 1704–March 1705) – Tory attacks on the cost of the war
War news: Gibraltar captured by British forces; English naval victory off Malaga; Marlborough's victory at Blenheim

1705: English Parliament passes Aliens Act by which Scots will be treated as aliens unless they agree to the Hanoverian Succession
Scottish parliament appoints commissioners to begin talks on Anglo-Scots union
General election is followed by meeting of Anne's second parliament (Oct. 1705–March 1706)

1706: English parliament passes Regency Act
Anglo-Scots talks on union continue
Second session of Anne's second parliament (Dec. 1706–April 1707)
War news: Marlborough wins another major victory at Ramilles

1707: Act of Union between England and Scotland creates Great Britain
Third session of Anne's second parliament (Oct. 1707–April 1708) sees Tory attacks on the policy of 'no peace without Spain'

1708: Whig victory in general election is followed by Whig Junto appointments as queen's ministers and first session of Anne's third parliament (Nov. 1708–April 1709)
War news: Marlborough defeats the French at Oudenarde

1709: British parliament passes Naturalisation of Protestants Act
Whig Junto impeaches Henry Sacheverell
Second session of Anne's third parliament (Nov. 1709–April 1710)
War news: Marlborough defeats the French at Malplaquet

1710: Sacheverell's trial prompts riots in London. He is found guilty but receives a light sentence
General election produces massive Tory majority in first session of Anne's fourth parliament (Nov. 1710–June 1711)
War news: peace talks begin; British forces defeated in Spain

1711: British parliament passes Land Property Qualification Act
Second session of Anne's fourth parliament meets (Dec. 1711–June 1712)

1712: British parliament passes Occasional Conformity Act and repeals Protestant Naturalisation Act
War news: peace talks resume at Utrecht

1713: Third session of Anne's fourth parliament (April–July)
General election produces another massive Tory majority
War is ended by Treaty of Utrecht

1714: Anne's fifth parliament meets (Feb.–July); passes Schism Act, preventing establishment of Dissenter schools
Anne dies; the Elector of Hanover is crowned George I

As was noted in the last chapter, the Glorious Revolution of 1689 did not herald a period of political calm. On the contrary, the last 25 years of the period covered by this book saw an eruption of political rivalry between Whigs and Tories that was more intense and lasted far longer than that which had divided the country during the Exclusion Crisis of 1679–81. Britain became what has been rightly called 'a divided society', since the 'rage of party' between Whigs and Tories spread beyond the narrow world of Westminster politics to affect the country as a whole.

This long period of prolonged political instability is an extremely confusing one. Although the time chart is designed to help you to cope with this, its length reflects the complexity of the politics of the reigns of William III and Queen Anne.

The aim of this chapter is to help you to make sense of this turbulent period by raising three central questions:

■ Why was there a 'rage of party' between 1689 and 1714?

■ What did Whigs and Tories in this period stand for?

■ How serious a threat to political stability was the 'rage of party'?

Why was there a 'rage of party' between 1689 and 1714?

Historians have not always agreed that the political instability of the period can be explained in terms of party political rivalry. For a period after the end of the Second World War, following the very influential work of Lewis Namier on mid-eighteenth-century politics, it became fashionable to argue that the political rivalries of the period were caused by competing *family and personal interests* and not by *party political principles*.

Those who have studied earlier chapters of this book, however, will not be surprised to learn that historical interpretations are subject to dramatic change. This one is no exception. In the 1960s the Namierite analysis of late seventeenth and early eighteenth-century politics was abandoned as a result of severe criticism from two historians, J. H. Plumb and G. Holmes, whose reputations still tower over the history of this period. They, and other historians, found evidence in **division lists** that the vast majority of MPs voted consistently on Whig and Tory party lines during most of the reigns of William III and Queen Anne. Studies of London during the same period have shown that party political rivalries were even reflected in the establishment of rival Whig and Tory dining and drinking clubs, and fashionable coffee and chocolate houses. In provincial England, too, evidence of many of the signs of modern party politics is abundant: especially local Whig and Tory party constituency organisations, party agents, campaigning literature, canvassing and so on.

Three general reasons help to account for this 'rage of party':

1 The first is that it was a period which saw parliaments meeting much more frequently than they had ever done before. Indeed after 1689 parliaments met every year (and have continued to do so ever since). The

KEY TERM:

Division lists

Division lists are records of the votes of MPS in the Commons and of peers in the Lords.

KEY TERMS:

Franchise

The **franchise** is the right to vote. In comparison with the present day few people had the franchise, which was restricted to men with considerable wealth. But during the seventeenth century more people gained the franchise. One effect of inflation was to increase the numbers of people entitled to vote in county elections, *i.e.* freeholders who received more than 40 shillings (£2) a year, a figure set in the fourteenth century. Despite efforts by the crown to restrict the franchise in borough elections by its *quo warranto* campaign (see page 250), the electorate in many towns was quite large. [To enfranchise means to give the vote to someone.]

Newspapers

The first recognisably modern **newspapers** were published during the English Revolution. After the Restoration, however, the only newspapers that were published were heavily censored official gazettes. With the lapse of the Licensing Act in 1695 press censorship ended, producing a publication explosion of newspapers and political magazines. The first daily newspaper, *The Daily Courant*, appeared in 1702.

constitutional significance of, as well as the reasons for, this will be looked at in chapter 29. Here the essential point to make is that frequent parliamentary sessions made it possible for MPs to make closer alliances than hitherto with like-minded colleagues and for divisions on political issues to continue and develop, uninterrupted by long gaps between parliamentary sessions.

2 An even more potent cause of growing political rivalries was the frequency of general elections in the quarter-century after 1689. There were more than twice as many general elections between 1689 and 1715 (11) than between 1660 and 1688 (5). The principal cause of this was the Triennial Act of 1694, which limited the life of individual parliaments to three years. A major consequence was rightly pointed out in the preamble to the Septennial Act in 1716, which blamed the 1694 Act for 'occasioning … more violent and lasting heats and animosities among the subjects of the realm, than were ever known before'. Frequent general elections helped to maintain political rivalries at a fever pitch. They also prevented the crown from building up a 'court party' of MPs on whom it could rely, thus making parliaments less open to royal influence and management than after the passage of the 1716 Act which enacted a minimum gap of seven years between general elections.

3 Also vital in explaining the eruption and maintenance of the political controversies which divided the nation after 1689 is the emergence of a larger, more independent and better informed electorate than ever before. The electorate had been growing throughout the seventeenth century, as more people gained the **franchise**. By the 1690s the total electorate was 4.3 per cent of the total population, only just short of the percentage enfranchised by the Great Reform Act of 1832 (4.7 per cent). In the days before secret ballots and laws against bribing electors the independence of this fairly large electorate is, of course, questionable. It is not insignificant that sustained attempts were made to influence the electorate by arguments, as well as by free beer at election times. Moreover, increasingly, these arguments were put in print, in **newspapers**.

These general conditions making for political controversies did not make the great 'rage of party' of this period inevitable. What did was the existence of four interrelated issues, which prompted very different reactions from Whigs and Tories:

- the country's involvement in a full-scale European war
- the significance of the Glorious Revolution and the succession to the throne
- the union of England and Scotland
- the Church.

What did Whigs and Tories stand for?

Whigs in this period stood for:

1 The country's full-scale involvement in the wars against France, 1689–97 and 1701–13 on land and at sea.

2 Greater toleration of Protestant Dissenters than had been granted by the Toleration Act of 1689.

3 The belief that there had been resistance in 1689 ('the Revolution Principles') and a commitment to the Protestant succession to the throne.

4 The Union of England and Scotland into one country, Great Britain.

Tories, on the other hand, stood for:

1 A limited naval war against France and, later on, withdrawal from the war altogether.

2 Defence of the Church of England and loathing of Dissenters.

3 The belief that there had been no resistance in 1689, and uncertainty about the legality of what had been done at the Glorious Revolution.

4 England and Scotland remaining as two separate countries, even though they shared the same monarch.

Between 1690 and 1694 these different party political positions temporarily disappeared, largely because both Whigs and Tories appear to have undergone a major transformation. This was a period which saw the establishment of the Commission of Public Accounts (see chapter 29), on which both Whigs and Tories collaborated on a programme to control the crown's expenditure. For a few years this anti-court campaign makes the politics of the period more explicable on 'court–country' than 'Whig–Tory' lines. Increasingly, however, from about 1694 onwards the 'country' criticism of the court became identified with the Tory Party, signalling a major transformation in the positions of both Whigs and Tories of pre-1689 days. For it was the Whigs, not Tories, who now emerged as the champions of a strong executive. Increasingly, the crown was forced to appoint to key offices of state a new generation of Whigs, who in one crucial respect were 'new' Whigs: **Junto Whigs**.

Yet the significance of this transformation should not be exaggerated. In their attitudes to the four divisive issues of this period, and especially on the key issue of the Church, there are many elements of continuity between the Whig–Tory divisions of the Exclusion Crisis and politics after the Glorious Revolution.

KEY TERM:

Junto Whigs

The leading **Junto Whigs** were Sir John Somers, Charles Montague (later Lord Halifax), Thomas Wharton (later Lord, Earl and Marquis Wharton), Edward Russell (later Earl of Orford), who were all strongly in favour of the war and much less vociferous than their Whig predecessors – like Shaftesbury in the later 1670s and early 1680s – in proclaiming 'parliamentary liberties'. As Bishop Gilbert Burnet rightly commented at the time: 'By an odd reverse the Whigs, who were now employed, argued for the prerogative, while the Tories seemed zealous for public liberty.'

Different Whig and Tory views about the wars against France

The wars against France in this period had fundamental effects on the British constitution and on Britain's status and role as an international power (see chapter 29). They were also important in fuelling the controversies of post Glorious Revolution politics. The key features that made the wars so important are that they were long, extensive and expensive.

The first period of war lasted from 1689 to 1697. It took place on sea and land, largely in Flanders and northern Europe. The main aim of the allies was to prevent Louis XIV from breaking up the League of Augsburg of German states and to maintain allied unity against French attempts to secure the succession to the Spanish throne if the ailing Carlos II should die. When the war began again in 1702 it lasted even longer, until 1713. It spread to southern Europe and Spain, as well as northern Europe, in order to prevent Louis XIV from uniting the Bourbon and Habsburg thrones in the person of his grandson, Philip of Anjou. Warfare on such a scale involved colossal expense. It has been estimated that military spending on the war of 1689–97 amounted to over £36 million and on the war of 1702–13 nearly £65 million.

At the start of both wars the nation was united behind the war effort. Tories as well as Whigs appreciated the threat posed by French aggression to English security, which was made obvious in 1690 by James II's invasion of Ireland, and in 1701, on James II's death, by Louis XIV's recognition of James's son as 'James III'. But in both cases the initial national unity in favour of the war quickly crumbled and distinct Whig and Tory attitudes to the war emerged.

The *Whig attitude to the wars* is simpler and easier to deal with. Its first main characteristic is consistent and enthusiastic support for the war effort, on land as well as on sea. The Whigs even maintained support for war in Spain in the early 1700s when the war there was marked by major disasters (one of the Whig party political slogans was 'No Peace without Spain'). Secondly, they worked energetically to provide new means of financing the expensive wars. In this they were very successful. The Million Loan Act (1693), establishing a national lottery, the foundation of the Bank of England in 1694, which tapped huge City of London loans, and the reformation of the coinage in 1696 were the keystones of a Whig financial revolution, which saw the most extensive changes in public finance since the 1640s (see chapter 29). These made a major contribution to the French defeat in Europe.

The *Tories' attitude to the war effort*, in contrast, was typified by rapid

KEY TERMS:

'Monied interest'

'Monied interest' was a sneering phrase used by Tories to describe merchants, bankers, investors or anyone connected with the financial institutions that developed during the wars with France in the 1690s and 1700s. Like most political slogans it was not used in a precise way, but was meant to conjure up images of wealthy war profiteers, who kept the war going in order to line their own pockets.

'The Church in Danger'

Like 'the monied interest' this phrase was commonly used by Tories in their political battles with Whigs. It meant more than that Protestant Dissenters were threatening the Church of England. The slogan implied that Dissenters were also subversive republicans who were undermining the whole fabric of the social and political order.

disillusionment with it. Why? Some of the reasons are similar to those that led to parliamentary criticism of the way Charles I and Buckingham had managed the wars against France and Spain in the 1620s. Not only were there attacks on military and naval incompetence, but (as in the 1620s) some MPs were deeply opposed to a land war. The arguments of High Tory leaders like Rochester in both the 1690s and 1700s in favour of a cheap naval war ('a blue water war') are similar to those used by MPs who condemned England's involvement in a land war in Europe in the 1620s (see chapter 6).

There the comparison ends. As the war against France developed, Tory disillusionment with it was fuelled by something that was completely absent in the early seventeenth century: the belief that the war was being continued unnecessarily. After major allied victories at Blenheim (1704) and elsewhere, many Tories began to wonder why the war was being prolonged. Many found the answer in the assumption that the war was being fought merely for the vested interests of Whigs – 'the **monied interest**' – and foreigners. For these reasons, from 1708 onwards Tory demands for the conclusion of a speedy peace settlement grew in intensity.

Different Whig and Tory views about the Church and Dissent

Among those blamed by the Tories for prolonging the war were Dissenters. This points to another (and arguably *the*) major cause of party political conflict in this period, the issue of Dissent.

The *Tories' hatred of Dissent* immediately after the Glorious Revolution grew even more during the next 20 years. **'The Church in Danger'** became one of the most potent Tory political slogans of this period. When Convocation met in 1701, there were violent attacks on the leaders of the Church, including Archbishop of Canterbury Tenison, for their complacency in the face of this threat. Why were the Tories so hostile to Dissent at this time?

The main reason is their belief that the threat of Dissent to the Anglican monopoly of Church and State was growing rapidly. Limited though the Toleration Act was (see last chapter), it did allow licensed religious services to take place other than in parish churches. Between 1689 and 1715, 3,614 Dissenting meeting houses were licensed, in addition to the foundation of many Dissenting schools. What made this seem worse was that it was accompanied by the appearance of novel theological doctrines that seemed to be dangerously heretical, like the views of Unitarians (see key term, page 263). Even more shocking was the publication of books like John Toland's *Christianity not Mysterious* (1696), which demanded that

KEY TERM:

Occasional conformity

This was the practice that enabled Dissenters to evade the Test and Corporation Acts, which restricted public offices to members of the Church of England. To get round this some Dissenters attended parish church services very occasionally in order to receive certificates of attendance from a magistrate and so qualify for public office. Tory efforts to plug this loophole in the law throughout the reign of Queen Anne by passing an Occasional Conformity Act were eventually successful in 1711. Another temporary Tory legislative success against Dissenters was the Schism Act of 1714, which made illegal the establishment of Dissenting academies.

PROFILE: *Dr Henry Sacheverell*

Sacheverell (1674–1724) was a High Anglican Fellow of Magdalen College, Oxford, who conducted a long-running campaign against Dissenters in fiery sermons and provocative pamphlets. 'Presbytery and republicanism go hand in hand', he thundered in a sermon in 1702.

On 5 November 1709 he delivered another controversial sermon against Dissenters, *In Peril Against False Brethren*, that was widely distributed in print. As a result the Whigs decided to impeach him, alleging that his sermon was a 'malicious, scandalous and seditious libel'. His trial took place amid tremendous contemporary popular controversy, which exploded on the night of 1–2 March 1710 into mob violence in London. It was directed against Sacheverell's enemies, Dissenters, whose chapels and meeting houses were systematically destroyed by pro-Church, pro-Sacheverell rioters. Although Sacheverell was found guilty at his trial in the House of Lords, it was by a narrow majority of 69 to 52 and he was only given the mild punishment of three years' suspension from preaching.

all aspects of Christianity that could not be explained rationally should be rejected (see chapter 29). What, above all, caused Tory anger at Dissent was what became known as '**occasional conformity**'.

The Whigs were much more tolerant of Dissent. The Whigs' repeal of both the Occasional Conformity and Schism Acts after 1714 is in line with their attitude to Dissent during the Exclusion Crisis (see chapter 22). They consistently opposed Tory High Anglicanism, following what was known as 'Low Church' policies, aimed at allowing toleration of Protestant Dissent not only in Britain but also elsewhere. In 1709 a Whig Act allowed Protestants from the Palatinate to become English citizens, a measure that was repealed shortly afterwards by a Tory-dominated House of Commons.

The case of Dr Sacheverell

The trial of **Dr Sacheverell** in 1710 is a remarkable illustration of the contrasting Whig and Tory attitudes to Dissent. It also illustrates important differences between the parties about the Glorious Revolution and the Protestant succession.

What made Sacheverell especially objectionable to the Whigs is that not only was he a prominent exponent of Anglican religious intolerance, he also challenged the Whig interpretation of what had happened in 1689.

Although the Whigs made compromises in 1689 (see chapter 24), they maintained later that James II's downfall had been brought about by resistance to a tyrannical monarch. Sacheverell attacked this basic Whig 'Revolution Principle' by asserting that James had abdicated and therefore the Tory principles of passive obedience and Divine Right of Kings had not been compromised.

These differences were closely linked with different attitudes to the Protestant succession. The significance of these can be exaggerated. Most Tories, like most Whigs, supported the Protestant succession. Few Tories were committed **Jacobites**. But Tories were much less certain than Whigs about the legality of accepting the Protestant succession after 1689.

Two incidents illustrate this uncertainty. In 1702 the Abjuration Act required all office-holders, MPs, clergymen, teachers and lawyers to take an oath repudiating the claims of the Pretender to the throne. The Tory leader, the Earl of Nottingham, only complied after being reassured by the Archbishop of York that 'you are left as much at liberty after you have taken this oath'. Rank-and-file Tory MPs were similarly uneasy about the oath and tried to push through a parliamentary bill extending by a year the time limit for taking the oath. Three years later this same Tory ambiguity to the Protestant succession was again displayed in the fierce opposition to the Regency Bill, which established the form of the interim government which would rule on Queen Anne's death but before the arrival of her Protestant Hanoverian successors. Most Tories might not have been Jacobites but, as a contemporary said in 1705, it *seemed* as if they were aiming 'to destroy the succession'.

Different attitudes to the Union of England and Scotland

The Whigs' support for, and the Tories' opposition to, the Union of England and Scotland in 1707 (see chapter 28) raises one final point about the issues that underlay the 'rage of party' in this period. This is that, although they have been listed and discussed separately here, they were closely interconnected.

The *conversion of the Whigs to the cause of union* is inseparable from their enthusiastic prosecution of the wars against France. They worked for the union largely to prevent Scotland from being drawn into the wars as France's ally. Their tolerant attitude towards Dissent, too, ensured that they were less opposed than the Tories to uniting with a nation with a Presbyterian-dominated Kirk.

The *Tories' opposition to the union*, on the other hand, reflected their growing lack of enthusiasm for the war effort. It was also closely connected with their fears that the English Church was in danger from Dissent. Presbyterianism north of the border was seen as a clear sign that the danger came, not only from within England, but from outside as well.

How serious a threat to political stability was 'the rage of party'?

This chapter ends on a cautionary note, advising you to consider carefully claims that the country's political stability was seriously endangered by the 'rage of party'. To do this you will need to define what you mean by 'political stability'. J. H. Plumb's definition in his book *The Growth of Political Stability* (1967) was 'the acceptance by society of its political institutions and of those classes of men or officials who control them'.

Fierce though the political controversies of this period were, there is little evidence that they led anyone to question the country's political institutions or the men who controlled them, as had happened in the 1640s and 1650s.

Two reasons why the 'rage of party' in the 1690s and early 1700s did not threaten the stability of the state in this way can be suggested.

1 The memories of the conflicts of the mid seventeenth century were still very strong at this time. The determination of many never to allow that kind of thing to happen ever again was a powerful restraint against allowing political controversies to get out of hand.

2 Economic progress and rising standards of living in the later seventeenth and early eighteenth centuries provided fertile ground for political stability, not instability. These are the subject matter of the next two chapters.

Task

It is uncertain whether 'the rage of party' in this period seriously threatened the stability of the state. What is not in doubt is that people at the time got very angry with each other when they talked about the country's involvement in war, the Church and Dissent, the union of England and Scotland and the succession. If you are sceptical about that, just look at the violent loathing of Dissenters that drove some people to tear down chapels and meeting houses in London in the Sacheverell riots of 1710. Another illustration is Figure 25.1.

Figure 25.1 Frontispiece of a Whig pamphlet published in 1710 called 'A Dialogue Betwixt Whig and Tory'. The figure in the middle (Britain?) is faced with the choice between Whig **liberty** (symbolised by images of English commerce, justice and freedom) and Tory **slavery** (represented by symbols of foreign oppression, poverty and an expensive standing army i.e. a slave-galley, a whip, a wooden shoe and a heavily burdened horse).

This task is designed to help you understand why people at that time felt so deeply about issues that might seem to be fairly unimportant now. You can do the task either individually or as a group discussion.

Individually   Take four sheets of paper. Head them 'the war'; 'the Church and Dissent'; 'the union of England and Scotland'; and 'the succession'. Divide each sheet in two and head each section 'the Whig case' and 'the Tory case'. Then list the arguments that you think Whigs and Tories would have used to justify the respective party political positions on these four issues.

Group discussion   Divide into two groups. Members of group A are Whigs in 1710. Members of group B are Tories in 1710. Everyone in the group should be briefed on what is the 'party line' on each issue. Each group could select four members to be its principal spokesperson on the four controversial issues.

Your debate may need firm handling by the person in the chair. If this proves to be the case, you might well be on the way to understanding why there was a 'rage of party' between 1689 and 1714!

Further reading

B. Coward, *The Stuart Age* (Addison Wesley Longman, 1991) pages 365–445.

G. Holmes, *The Making of a Great Power: Britain 1660–1722* (Addison Wesley Longman, 1993).

W. A. Speck, *Tory and Whig: the Struggle for the Constituencies 1701–15* (Macmillan, 1972).

W. A. Speck, 'Conflict in society' in G. Holmes (ed.), *Britain after the Glorious Revolution* (Macmillan, 1969).

The best detailed books on this period are:

J. H. Plumb, *The Growth of Political Stability 1675–1725* (Macmillan, 1967)

G. Holmes, *British Politics in the Reign of Queen Anne* (Macmillan 1967, revised ed. 1987).

Part Three

Conclusion: Change and continuity – later Stuart Britain

This book began with four chapters on the economy, social structure, government and major religious beliefs in England in 1603. The main aim of the last four chapters of the book is to assess the extent to which each of these had changed during the 'long' seventeenth century, that is by the death of the last Stuart monarch, Queen Anne, in 1714.

As in previous chapters which have tackled the question of historical change, *continuity* – the fact that some things did not change – will not be forgotten. This is especially important because some things that remained the same throughout the seventeenth century have not always been given sufficient emphasis by historians. Of these, the continuing importance of religion has sometimes been ignored.

As well as focusing on historical continuity, these last chapters will also bring out major historical *changes* that occurred in the seventeenth century. In addition to witnessing the union of England and Scotland as Great Britain, the Stuart 'century' was a decisive one in the emergence of a British State that was new in many other important ways.

Were these changes part of an inevitable progress towards the establishment of 'modern Britain'? The theme that runs through these last chapters is that they were not. Instead it will be argued that what emerged by 1714 was a country that was not 'modern'; nor was it 'medieval'. The *distinctive* character of Britain by the early eighteenth century was a blend of change and continuity that is best described as 'early modern'.

26 How much had the country's economy changed?

Economic continuity

There is no doubt that by 1714 the economy of the country was much more prosperous than it had been in 1603. As will be seen in this chapter, major changes occurred that made the British economy one of the most advanced in Europe by the early eighteenth century. But was Britain now set on the road to the later eighteenth-century **Industrial Revolution**, as is sometimes assumed?

What makes this doubtful is that the idea that there was an 'Industrial Revolution' at all in Britain in the later eighteenth century is a questionable one. During the last 20 years economic and social historians have shown that as late as the first accurate census in 1851 most people in Britain worked in agricultural occupations and/or were employed in small-scale handicraft occupations. 'The Industrial Revolution' probably did not take place until the later *nineteenth* century.

It is therefore not surprising that at the end of the Stuart age few signs can be found of a later, 'modern' industrial economy. There were no factories and what large-scale manufacturing there was occurred not in the production of goods that later were made in factories, like woollen cloth and nails, but ships and coal. Moreover, even shipyards and coalmines usually employed hundreds rather than thousands of workers.

Many features of the British economy in the early eighteenth century had remained unchanged during the preceding century.

■ Most manufactured goods were still produced by the domestic system (see chapter 2). As in the early seventeenth century, this did not preclude extensive manufacturing operations, organised by wealthy capitalist entrepreneurs. But there had been no shift away from small-scale handicraft manufacture during the seventeenth century. Entrepreneurs (clothiers, iron masters etc.) still distributed raw materials to workers (often part-time farmers) in their own homes and workshops.

■ It was still predominantly an agrarian economy, in that the vast majority of Britons made their living on, or from, the land.

KEY TERM:

Industrial Revolution

Until the early 1970s historians generally assumed that in Britain from about the second half of the eighteenth century onwards there occurred 'the Industrial Revolution'. By this they meant a fairly rapid economic and social transformation confined mainly to the late 1700s–early 1800s, which saw the spread of factories and steam-driven machinery as the main means of producing manufactured goods, the growth of large industrial towns and the emergence of a mass industrial workforce.

1656	5.181
1661	5.141
1671	4.982
1681	4.930
1691	4.931
1701	5.085
1711	5.230

Figure 26.1 The population of England and Wales, 1656–1711 (in millions)

■ It was still an economy that could be easily upset by harvest failures, especially when this happened in successive years (*e.g.* 1657–61 and 1691–8).

■ Nor did the later seventeenth and early eighteenth centuries mark the end of severe trade depressions. Those of 1696–7 and 1709 had as devastating an effect on the economy as did the trade crisis of the early 1620s.

Economic change: an improving economy

What makes this slightly surprising is that the middle of the seventeenth century marked the end of the rise in population and prices that had been forces making for economic progress in the later sixteenth and early seventeenth centuries (see chapter 2).

The change to population and price stability

From the 1650s the population estimates of the Cambridge Group for the Population and Social Structure of England show a marked change from the situation described in chapter 2 (see Figure 26.1). The size of the country's population, which had risen steadily during the previous 150 years, fell for a time in the later seventeenth century. Even in 1741 it had only recovered to a figure slightly higher (5.576 millions) than its high point in the 1650s.

KEY TERM:

Great Plague

The **Great Plague** was the last major outbreak of bubonic plague in England. It swept through the country in 1665 but had most disastrous effects in London, where an estimated 70,000 died. It is now known that bubonic plague is carried by a flea that lives on black rats. These were at home in the insanitary conditions of the capital. Bubonic plague had been endemic in western Europe since the Black Death epidemic of 1348–9. Its disappearance in England after 1665 could have been caused by the rebuilding of a cleaner London after the Great Fire of 1666 and the imposition of stricter regulations at Britain's ports. But these reasons are not totally convincing. Along with the reasons why more people decided to marry later or not marry at all in this period, it is one of many things about which historians of Stuart England are uncertain.

Why did the long period of population expansion end? The answer lies partly in the fact that later seventeenth-century England was hit unusually hard by devastating outbreaks of epidemic diseases. The '**Great Plague**' of 1665 is the last national outbreak of the deadly bubonic plague that had been the scourge of Europe throughout the Middle Ages. There were still many other killer diseases (mainly influenza, typhus and smallpox) against which there was no effective medical protection and which periodically (as in 1657–8, 1665–6 and 1680–81) became of epidemic proportions.

Emigration to the new American colonies also accounts for the declining population. But more important are changes in the level of fertility. Among all social classes the birth rate fell, caused by couples marrying later than they had done in later Tudor and early Stuart England, combined with a rise in the numbers of those who never married.

The fact that the Price Revolution of sixteenth and early seventeenth centuries ended at the same time as the demographic expansion is not coincidental. Since the Price Revolution had largely been caused by a rapidly rising population pressing on scarce resources (see chapter 2), it is not surprising that when that pressure eased prices no longer rose. For about a century after 1660, apart from the 1690s (coinciding with a run of bad harvests), agricultural prices generally fell (although at a gentle rate).

What were the economic consequences of this new situation? Did the end of rising population and prices remove the main pressures for economic enterprise and innovation? It would be wrong to assume that they did. Falling or stagnant demand and prices can be powerful incentives to farmers and manufacturers to produce and sell more in order to offset falling profits.

Agricultural change

This is supported by the sharp rise in the productivity of agriculture in later Stuart England, as farmers adopted more generally new farming methods that had only been experimented with on a small scale in the early seventeenth century. There were other reasons for this. Landlords, as well as farmers, were no doubt influenced by a new intellectual climate that favoured innovation and 'improvement', which became a popular buzz-word of the period. Even the Royal Society, which received a charter from Charles II in 1661, conducted a national survey of new farming practices, and information about them was spread by a rapidly growing number of agricultural newsletters and textbooks (see Figure 26.2).

One is driven to the conclusion that the fact that falling food prices meant that some tenants were finding it difficult to pay their rents is the main reason for an upsurge of interest in new crops and farming methods. Of these, easily the most important was the solution that was found to the major problem that was facing agriculture in England in the seventeenth century: the shortage of fertilisers, especially animal manure, caused by the inability to maintain large permanent flocks of sheep and herds of cattle (see chapter 2). During the later seventeenth century the problem was overcome by the widespread use of fodder crops, principally **turnips** and new breeds of grass, like clover, that could be stored for winter animal feed. When adopted in the light-soil areas of East Anglia and western England, for example, they helped to transform (using the dung of large sheep flocks) barren heathland and chalkland into rich grain lands.

The new crops could not be grown everywhere, especially in the heavy soil, clay vales of midland counties like Leicestershire and Northamptonshire, that gradually shifted from grain to cattle and dairy production. But there is no reason to doubt that, nationally, agricultural

KEY TERM:

Turnips

Turnips were one of the roots of England's economic progress, increasing wealth and rise to international greatness by the early eighteenth century. To most urban dwellers turnips are fairly mundane and insipid roots that rate low in popularity in any list of vegetables for domestic consumption. It may come as a surprise, therefore, to learn that in the history of English agriculture its introduction was a major innovation, rivalling in importance the application of chemical fertilisers in the later nineteenth century. The reason was that it provided a means for farmers to improve the fertility of their soil and thus increase agricultural productivity. Viscount Townshend, a Whig politician in the early eighteenth century, got the nickname 'Turnip Townshend' for his interest in turnips, but they were being grown well before his day. In the 1670s farmers on the Norfolk estates of the Walpole family regularly used the 'Norfolk' crop rotation (turnips, barley, clover and wheat).

Figure 26.2 *Title page of one of the most popular textbooks on farming in later Stuart England, John Worlidge's* Systema Agriculturae, *first published in 1669. It went through many later additions.*

Systema
Agriculturæ.
Being
The Mystery Of Husbandry
Discovered and
layd Open
by
J W

output increased fairly sharply in the later Stuart period. The best evidence for this is that from the 1670s onwards England for the first time in its history regularly exported grain and continued to do so for about the next century. As output increased, grain prices fell.

All this did not amount to 'an Agricultural Revolution' because the pace of change in farming was inevitably too slow and piecemeal to be called 'revolutionary'. But the seventeenth century nevertheless saw important advances that ensured that agricultural production normally met the nation's demand for food more than adequately.

Manufacturing change

There are at least three major changes that occurred in the manufacturing sector of the economy of England after the middle of the seventeenth century:

1 The textile industry became more diversified. The manufacture of woollen broadcloths continued to diminish in contrast with the production of New Draperies – like light, coloured fabrics from East Anglia and heavy serges from Devon. Now there was also a rapid development of non-woollen textiles, like silk, produced by French Huguenot refugees in Spitalfields in London, and linen, made in Lancashire.

2 The textile industry lost its overall dominance as other industries expanded. These are difficult to categorise briefly, but they included:

■ primary industries like coalmining (marked by the opening up of new coalfields in north-west England and Wales, as well as the older coalfields in the north-east), the smelting of lead, copper and tin (using coal-powered reverbatory furnaces), and iron production (that continued to expand, still mainly using charcoal-powered blast furnaces, despite the fact that Abraham Darby had discovered in 1709 a method of using coal as a fuel);

■ secondary industries, producing a wide range of consumer goods: older industries (like brewing, pottery manufacture and small metal wares), as well as new ones (like tobacco and sugar refining and the manufacture of fine quality glass, paper and silk, using improved technologies brought to England by French religious refugees).

3 There was an improvement in the means of internal trade. These have not received as much attention as the famous turnpike and canal revolutions of the later eighteenth century, probably because they were individually apparently insignificant: local river and harbour improvements, the introduction of stagecoach and carrier services and newspaper advertising. Collectively, they are an important reflection of the developing economy of later Stuart England.

Commercial change

Like the early seventeenth century, developments in overseas trade in this later period have received a lot of attention from historians. But, unlike the earlier period, this attention is justified. Historians are quite rightly wary of using the word 'revolution', but in the case of overseas trade in the later seventeenth and early eighteenth centuries there is ample justification for describing what happened as 'a Commercial Revolution'. The changes that occurred were rapid and major:

1 Before 1650 English exports were dominated by one commodity, woollen cloth. By the early eighteenth century exports were diverse. They included many different manufactured goods as well as the re-export of foreign goods (mainly sugar from the Caribbean, tobacco from the American colonies, and Indian calico and tea).

2 Before 1650 most of English trade had been with Europe. By the early eighteenth century the volume of this trade had not diminished but it was now rivalled in value by new trades further afield: in sugar and tobacco with the Caribbean and American colonies, in colonial slave labour and chocolate with Africa, and in tea and calico (and later rice) with the Far East.

3 Before 1650 most of English overseas trade was channelled through London. After 1650 London's _relative_ importance declined and provincial ports grew in importance, notably west-coast ports like Glasgow, Whitehaven, Liverpool, Bristol and Exeter, and east-coast ports like Newcastle and Hull.

4 Before 1650 English merchants had largely been out-traded in world markets by the Dutch. After 1650 this situation was gradually reversed, so that by the early eighteenth century British (English and Scottish) merchants had secured a major share in the colonial slave trade, the European carrying trade and the trade in Far Eastern goods. Britain's commercial dominance of international markets, which was now only threatened by the French, was reflected in the emergence in London of marine insurance and credit facilities. By the early eighteenth century London, not Amsterdam, was the centre of the commercial world.

5 These contrasts are emphasised by the rapid rise in the value of total imports (by nearly 50 per cent) and total exports (nearly 100 per cent) between the 1660s and the 1720s.

Conclusion

Why are these economic changes of major historical importance?

A more useful way of answering this question than attempting to link these economic changes to an 'Industrial Revolution' *in the future* is to assess their impact in the later seventeenth and early eighteenth centuries. They had major consequences *at the time*.

One important effect deserves special emphasis. The economic changes meant (as will be seen in the next chapter) that most people in Britain in the later seventeenth and early eighteenth centuries were better off than their predecessors had been in the previous century. This increase in national wealth, *if it could be tapped by the government*, represented the potential for an enormous expansion in the power of the State. It was not, of course, inevitable that the government would be able to do that. Yet by 1714 means had been found of doing this (see chapter 29). The consequences were dramatic. The significance of Britain's economic progress in the later Stuart period is that it laid the foundation, not for a future Industrial Revolution, but for Britain's emergence much earlier as a major international power.

Further reading

The best general textbook on this later period (as on the earlier period) is D. C. Coleman, *The Economy of England 1450–1750* (Oxford University Press, 1979).

Most of the books and pamphlets listed at the end of chapter 2 are also relevant here. See also:

C. Wilson, *England's Apprenticeship 1603–1763* (2nd edn, Addison Wesley Longman, 1984)

R. R. Davis, *A Commercial Revolution: English Overseas Trade in the Seventeenth and Eighteenth Centuries* (Historical Association pamphlet, 1969).

For a critical look at the idea of 'an Industrial revolution', see M. Fores, 'The myth of a British Industrial Revolution', *History*, vol. 66 (1981).

27 How much had English society changed?

'The emergence of a consumer society'?

KEY TERM:

Baroque

Baroque is a term used to describe the style of architecture (also painting, sculpture and music) that had evolved in sixteenth-century Europe, principally in Italy. It only reached England in this period. In the case of architecture baroque denotes ornamented buildings on the grand scale, characterised by massive, complex designs and incorporating splendid sculptures. In the hands of gifted architects – like Sir Christopher Wren, Sir John Vanbrugh and Nicholas Hawkesmoor – the Baroque style was used to produce magnificent buildings, including St Paul's Cathedral, the Sheldonian Theatre in Oxford, Greenwich Hospital, Blenheim Palace and Castle Howard (see Figure 27.1).

If someone in 1603 had been transported through time to 1714 he or she would have found much that was familiar in the social life of the country. He or she would have seen many signs of the hierarchical society of their own day (see chapter 3), especially enormous inequality in the distribution of wealth. The time traveller would have seen side by side familiar displays of fabulous wealth and abject poverty.

The traveller might have found rather strange the architectural styles in which some of the great new mansions of the rich were being built. By the later seventeenth and early eighteenth centuries the fashion was to design houses in a continental **Baroque** style that had not been seen in early Stuart England. By the later Stuart period it was widely used by fashionable architects, like Wren, Vanbrugh and Hawkesmoor, as well as by many others, including great landowners who designed their own houses. The time traveller would not have been surprised by the magnificence of these buildings, especially if he or she had seen Jacobean mansions, like the Earl of Salisbury's house at Hatfield in Hertfordshire, the Howard family's great house at Audley End in Essex or the Earl of Dorset's at Knole in Kent.

Castle Howard in Yorkshire (Figure 27.1) is one of the grandest houses built in the later period, but there were many others built around the same time. The wealth of their owners was displayed not only in the extravagant buildings and grand parks that surrounded them (sometimes villages being demolished to accommodate them), but also in their interiors that were stuffed with expensive furniture, porcelain, pictures and sculptures.

As in his or her own day, elsewhere the time traveller would have seen signs of widespread poverty. Many of these, like the insubstantial hovels of the poor in villages and towns, have now disappeared. Some of the almshouses built to house the poor have survived, as has the evidence of the increasing amounts of money that was being poured into poor relief in the later seventeenth and early eighteenth centuries. The annual

Figure 27.1 *Castle Howard, Yorkshire, designed by Vanbrugh for the Earl of Carlisle in 1720*

amount collected in compulsory poor rates alone rose from about £250,000 in the 1650s to £700,000 by 1700. Private charity, too, still played a part in alleviating poverty, as can be seen in Figure 27.2.

In 1695 Gregory King gave a dramatic (if exaggerated) illustration of the poverty problem in later Stuart England, when he calculated that over half of the people in his own day were dependent on charity for survival at some time in their lives. They were, as he wrote, 'decreasing the wealth of the kingdom'.

Nor would the time traveller from 1603 probably have been surprised by the signs of the insecurity of life at the end of the Stuart age. He or she would have found people at that time still as concerned as those in his or her own time about the dire effects that harvest failures had on people's lives. Epidemic killer diseases (though not now bubonic plague) still struck rich and poor alike (Queen Mary died in 1694 from smallpox) in what seemed random ways that many people could only explain as the mysterious working of divine providence. The time traveller would still have found that infant mortality was very high, also affecting all social classes (all Queen Anne's 18 babies, that were born annually from the time of her marriage when she was 18, had died by 1702, when she became queen of England). It may be that life had become, if anything, even more insecure since 1603. The calculations done by the Cambridge Group for the History of Population and Social Structure show that the

Figure 27.2 *'The Tichborne Dole' by Gillis Van Tilborg, painted in 1670*

average expectation of life of English people may have been lower at the end of the seventeenth century than at the beginning.

Social change

Yet, if recent work on the social history of the later Stuart period is correct, then our time traveller might have noticed four significant social changes:

1 The emergence of a tripartite rural society

As the time traveller passed through the countryside he or she would have seen that, as well as the familiar large houses of wealthy land-owners, there were now fewer small-scale farmers. He or she would have been struck by the greater number of large farms that employed a size-able workforce of landless labourers.

Why had large landowners managed to maintain their social dominance?

What makes this question interesting is that landowners faced more difficulties after 1640 than before. In the century before 1640 there had been a substantial growth in the numbers and wealth of large land-owners, who had been the main beneficiaries of the expanding popula-tion of that period, which enabled them to increase their rent-roll incomes at least in line with the Price Revolution. Those favourable con-ditions changed in the middle of the seventeenth century. Although very few lost their estates, as was once thought, some landowners suffered quite severe short-term damage from the Civil War, as their tenants were conscripted for military service or their estates were plundered by armies of both sides (see chapter 11). Moreover, for many landowners life did not get any easier from an economic point of view after 1660. As the pop-ulation rise ended and food prices fell (see chapter 26), new tenants were not easy to find and existing tenants found it increasingly difficult to pay their rents. Landlords began to complain more and more about 'the decay of rents', especially when taxation continued to rise and did not fall back to its very low pre-1640 levels.

How, then, did landowners survive these difficulties? Not all did survive and some were forced to sell land to pay off their escalating debts. Those who did survive were large landowners, partly because they used a new legal device – **strict settlements** – but, more importantly, because they had the resources to do so. Large landowners could borrow money to tide them over difficult times more easily than smaller landowners. They could also marry their sons to wealthy heiresses. The consequence is that

Strict settlements

Strict settlements were agreements made between a landowner and his heir (usually his eldest son when he married), which gave the heir an adequate income from the family estates for life. In return the heir abandoned his right to sell or grant away the bulk of the family estates and property. Instead he promised to keep them intact to pass on to his heir. Strict settlements were used increasingly by great landed families from about the mid seventeenth century.

the later seventeenth and early eighteenth centuries saw a drift of property into fewer and fewer hands. In contrast to the century before 1640 which had seen a growth in the numbers and wealth of a landed elite of landowning nobility and gentry, the next century was one in which they consolidated their wealth and maintained their powerful position. In 1690, it has been calculated, 50 per cent of the cultivated land of the country was in their hands.

Why had some small-scale farmers disappeared and why were there now more landless labourers?

A more marked change in landed society took place in the later seventeenth and early eighteenth centuries among those who were not landowning gentlemen. Like all social changes this one was a long and slow process, but during the later Stuart period there took place an acceleration in the decline of smaller-scale farmers and in the growth of a new pattern of large farms worked by a mass of landless farm labourers.

This was less marked in 'forest-pasture' regions (see chapter 3), where small-scale farmers were largely engaged in animal husbandry (pig rearing, cattle fattening, dairying, etc.). These farmers were able to supplement their incomes in difficult times by part-time employment in manufacturing. They were also cushioned against the worst effects of falling agricultural prices because it was grain (not meat and dairy) prices that fell most sharply in this period. Forest communities – like those in the New Forest in Hampshire and the Forest of Arden in Warwickshire, and smallholders in the south Lancashire Pennines, south Yorkshire around Sheffield, and the west Midlands – survived unchanged by combining pastoral farming with wood crafts, textile weaving, or the manufacture of cutlery, hammers, axes and nails.

The trend towards large farms was most apparent in 'fielden' or 'champion' regions (see chapter 3), which were largely sheep and corn economies. Here small-scale farmers were highly vulnerable to the sharp drop in grain prices after 1650. In most of the areas that have been studied – the chalk areas of Wiltshire, the sheep–corn areas of East Anglia and the Cotswolds, for example – small-scale farmers were gradually forced to sell up, farms were amalgamated ('engrossed' is the contemporary word for it) and a new tripartite landholding pattern emerged: landlords, prosperous farmers, landless labourers.

2 The growth of the professions and 'the middling sort'

As the time traveller travelled around the country, the visitor from 1603 might also have met more people than in his or her own time who lived and worked away from the land. The towns the traveller passed through would have had fairly grand houses owned by professional people (mainly lawyers and doctors) as well as merchants. Like Celia Fiennes on her visit to Nottingham in 1697 (see quote), the time traveller might have seen more evidence than in his or her own day of craftsmen who worked full-time in producing manufactured goods.

> '[At Nottingham] they make brick and tile by the town; the manufacture of the town mostly consists of the weaving of Stockings, which is a very ingenious art; there was a man that spunn Glass and made severall things in Glass birds and beasts. I spunn some of the glass and saw him make a Swan presently, with divers coloured glass he makes Buttons which are very strong and will not breake; Nottingham is very famous for good ale ...'
>
> C. Morris (ed.), *The Illustrated Journeys of Celia Fiennes 1685–c.1712* (1982).

Why did this period see the growth of the professions?

Professor Holmes, who has done most work on this topic, calculated that between 1680 and the 1730s there was a 70 per cent increase in the number of professional people. The main explanations for this are to be found in two other changes that occurred in later Stuart England:

- a general rise in standards of living (see below)
- the expansion of government (see chapter 29).

The effect of the first change was to increase the demand for the services of people like lawyers, doctors, architects and schoolteachers. The professional organisations of doctors and lawyers had begun before this time. Both had developed internal hierarchies: doctors with the establishment of the Royal College of Physicians in 1518, the College of Barber Surgeons in 1540 and the Society of Apothecaries in 1617; and lawyers when they attempted to make distinctions between barristers, who practised in the central law courts, attorneys, who were only to represent litigants in courts, and solicitors, who were only to represent clients outside courts. It was not until the expansion in numbers of lawyers and doctors by the end of the seventeenth century that both experienced a rise in

Scriveners and notaries

These were people who specialised in drawing up legal documents of all kinds. Sometimes they combined this with moneylending.

status and the development of a professional identity similar to that of a much older profession, the clergy.

Architects and schoolteachers (and others that provided services, like landscape gardeners, surveyors, land agents, estate stewards, **scriveners** and **notaries**) were not in the same league as clergymen, lawyers and doctors, but all grew in numbers to meet the demands of a more wealthy society by 1714.

The effects of the second change was to bring about an expansion of the royal bureaucracy, especially as William III's and Anne's wars against France during the 1690s and early 1700s prompted the expansion of financial, military and diplomatic departments. These mark the beginning of 'a civil service' (see chapter 29). Civil servants like Samuel Pepys and William Blathwayt can therefore be added to the expanding professional group in English society by the early eighteenth century.

Did this period see the emergence of 'the middling sort'?

Most professional people thought of themselves as gentlemen. Many were the sons of gentlemen or later bought landed estates and became landed gentlemen. During the course of the seventeenth century a new phrase, 'the middling sort', was increasingly used to describe other social groups which were growing in importance but could not be as easily fitted into the traditional landed social hierarchy.

'The middling sort' were merchants and tradesmen, who increased in numbers and wealth with the Commercial Revolution (see chapter 26), and craftsmen and retailers, who emerged to meet the growing demand for consumer goods (see below). They are social groups on whom little serious historical work has been done and about whom, consequently, major historical problems remain unanswered. One question – were the 'middling sort' the forerunners of the 'middle classes' of later British society? – is particularly important. The present evidence suggests that they did not have the group cohesion – class consciousness – to support that idea. The most that can be said in the present state of knowledge is that the 'middling sort' label reflects one of the many changes in a society that was becoming more diverse and pluralistic than ever before.

3 Urbanisation

Our time traveller would be particularly unobservant if he or she did not also comment, not only on the way that London had continued to grow since the early seventeenth century, but that in 1714 towns in provincial England were much more numerous and much larger in size.

Was there an 'urban renaissance' in later Stuart England?

The historian Peter Borsay has invented the phrase 'urban renaissance' to describe this social change. By the early eighteenth century there were many more and bigger towns in the country than in 1603. It was a change that was not purely quantitative; it involved also a change in attitude. There emerged, writes Borsay, 'a far more acute urban culture and consciousness, sharply defined from that of rural society'.

Hard statistics, though, clearly demonstrate the increasing importance of towns and townspeople between 1603 and 1714. During that time London became the largest city in western Europe (the only one that was bigger in Europe was Constantinople) as its population grew from about 200,000 to 575,000. It was still easily the largest city in the country and something like two-thirds of townspeople lived there. But there had also been marked growth in provincial towns by 1714. In 1603 there were only two provincial towns with over 10,000 inhabitants (Norwich and Bristol) and only five towns with 5,000–10,000 inhabitants (York, Exeter, Newcastle, Salisbury and Oxford); in 1714 at least six towns had over 10,000 inhabitants and 18 had 5,000–10,000. The percentage of the population living in towns roughly doubled during the seventeenth century (from 8 to 16 per cent). During the same period, whereas the national population only increased by 23 per cent, the urban population grew by 100 per cent.

'From about the 1670s (or perhaps earlier),' writes P. Corfield in her survey of urban development in the sixteenth and seventeenth centuries, 'something of the configuration of modern urban England began to merge at least in outline'. This is certainly true when one looks at the rapid increases in the populations of later Stuart ports like Liverpool and Glasgow and industrial towns like Manchester, Nottingham, Leicester, Birmingham and Leeds.

A more significant development than this, though, in this period is the growth of provincial towns that provided the same kind of social and cultural facilities as London. Spa towns, like Bath and Tunbridge Wells, and county towns, like Durham, York, Norwich, Chester, Preston, Shrewsbury and countless others, developed as 'Little Londons'. They became more attractive places in which to live. Like London, which was rebuilt after the Great Fire, they had wider streets and squares, and coffee and chocolate houses that were social centres, where (for example) newspapers were available to be read. Their inhabitants developed a civic pride, reflected in imposing public buildings like the new town hall at Abingdon (Figure 27.3).

Figure 27.3 *Abingdon Town Hall, built in 1682*

This new urban culture also resulted in the building, even in modest-sized towns, of assembly rooms, where concerts and art exhibitions, for example, could be put on. London was, of course, the major national centre of the theatre for Restoration plays by major figures from John Dryden to William Congreve. But the later Stuart period saw the beginnings of provincial commercial theatres. Towns became places also where other leisure activities, including sports like horseracing, cricket and prize-fighting were commercialised and made more widely available to more people than ever before.

These developments relate to a final major social change that surely would have been apparent to our time traveller: that people in 1714 generally enjoyed a much better standard of living than they did in 1603.

4 The emergence of 'a consumer society'

What might have been the biggest shock of all to the visitor from 1603 was the fact that many ordinary people were able to afford goods, services and entertainment that had been restricted to a privileged few in his or her own time. Some of the goods being sold – like coffee, chocolate and tobacco – would have been new to him or her. Others – like sugar, meat and bread made from wheat, that people were buying in great quantities – would probably have astonished. When the traveller went into the houses of people who were not gentry, he or she would also surely have been taken aback by the greater luxury and comfort in which people lived by 1714.

Had a consumer society emerged by 1714?

There is good case for arguing that it had. As D. C. Coleman pointed out: there was now 'a more substantial and more widely distributed reserve of disposable income [in England] than anywhere else in Europe'. The reasons why this was so have already been mentioned. Rapidly rising agricultural productivity, combined with falling food prices, meant that many people had more money to spend on things other than the basic necessities of life. Demand for the good things of life came now, not only from the landed and mercantile elites as always, but also from a growing non-landed sector of society (professional people, 'the middling sort') that began to want to acquire them and had the wealth to do so. Moreover, the falling prices of the period opened up the possibility of better conditions of life to an even wider number of people than that, since as inflation ended *real* wages rose. Not everyone by any means escaped from a life of poverty and hardship, but many people, other than the nobility and gentry, now had the opportunity to choose and buy more varied clothes and food and drink and to live in better houses than ever before.

One illustration of the changes in clothes and diet is the way in which many of the new products from America, the Caribbean and the Far East – exotic eastern textiles, sugar, tobacco and so on – that in the 1660s were re-exported in large quantities, were by the early eighteenth century retained for sale in Britain. Another is the development of cattle-rearing in the Surrey and Kent Wealds and the Midland counties, and the development of a major brewing industry. In 1603 the staple items of the diet of ordinary people were cheese and a little bacon, various types of beans, bread made from rye or barley, and weak, home-produced beer; by 1714 they regularly ate meat, together with white bread made from wheat and sweet puddings; they also drank chocolate, coffee and strong beer.

KEY TERM:

Probate inventories

Probate inventories were lists of the possessions of someone who had just died. They were attached to the will of the deceased in order to ensure that his or her wishes, expressed in the will, were carried out. Since some probate inventories are full descriptions, room by room, of a person's house, they are a marvellous primary source for social historians.

The evidence of better housing conditions is to be found in **probate inventories**. Even the houses of rural and urban labourers now usually had two floors, separate parlours, living rooms and bedrooms, which had fireplaces and glass windows, furnished with high-quality linen, pottery plates and dishes.

Conclusion: a 'modern' or 'early modern' society?

Were, then, the outlines of modern British society emerging during the later Stuart period? Certainly, a time traveller from Victorian Britain transported back to 1714 would have been less surprised than the visitor from 1603 by the features that have been commented on above. Britain in 1714 in those respects was more recognisably modern than England in 1603.

However, it can be as misleading to search for the origins of modern society in late seventeenth and early eighteenth-century Britain as it is to look for the origins of the Industrial Revolution. Society had changed in several striking ways during the Stuart 'century', but some major ele ments remained unchanged. The most convincing conclusion is t¹ British society by 1714 was neither 'medieval' nor 'modern'. It was, ¹ a phrase that captures the *distinctiveness* of the social scene at tha᾿ 'early modern'.

Task

Look at the painting of the Tichborne Dole of 1670 (Fiꞔ a wealthy landowner from Hampshire, Sir Henry Tichᵏ surrounded by his family, relations, household offiс᾿ his gentry neighbours, his tenants and other men children who lived near his large and impressive occasion is the annual dole (*i.e.* charitable distᵎ

Answer the following questions about the ᵖ this chapter and in previous chapters, partᵎ

1 In what ways do you think that it reflᵎ
English society at this time? Look pᵎ
different social status (reflected iᵣ
wearing) are standing in relatiᴼ
Tichborne himself.

2 What can you tell from his r
on the right of the paintiᵣ *300*

3 How important was hospitality and expenditure on charity generally in maintaining social cohesion in the seventeenth century?

4 Can you think of reasons why landed gentlemen might not feel as secure as Sir Henry Tichborne is portrayed as being in this painting?

5 Can you think of any reasons why this painted image of a tightly-knit and harmonious society might not reflect reality?

Further reading

The textbooks by Coward, Wrightson and Sharpe, listed at the end of chapter 3, also cover this later period.

On the important urban developments of this period, see:

P. Corfield, 'Urban developments in England and Wales in the 16th and 17th centuries' in J. Barry (ed.), *The Tudor and Stuart Town: a Reader in English Urban History 1530–1688* (Addison Wesley Longman, 1990)

P. Borsay, 'Culture, status and the English urban landscape' in P. Borsay (ed.), *The Eighteenth-Century Town: a Reader in English Urban History* (Addison Wesley Longman, 1990).

On the development of a 'consumer society', see the articles by J. Plumb and N. McKendrick in N. McKendrick (ed.), *The Birth of a Consumer Society* (Europa, 1982).

On the growth of the professions, see:

G. Holmes, 'The professions and social change' in G. Holmes (ed.), *Politics, Religion and Society in England 1679–1742* (Hambledon Press, 1986)

G. Holmes, *Augustan England: Professions, State and Society 1680–1730* (Allen and Unwin, 1982).

28 The emergence of Great Britain

Time chart

1604–6: James I's plans for a 'perfect union' of England and Scotland collapse

1654: Cromwell and Council issue an ordinance uniting England and Scotland

1659: Cromwellian Union ordinance declared null and void by the restored Rump

1689–90: Glorious Revolution in Scotland establishes Scottish independence from England

1692: Glencoe Massacre

1700: Darien colony abandoned amid Scottish allegations of English treachery

1702: William III proposes union of England and Scotland and commissioners begin preliminary negotiations

1703: Union negotiations collapse
Scottish parliament passes anti-English measures

1705: English parliament passes anti-Scots Aliens Act
English and Scottish commissioners resume negotiations on a union

1706: Treaty of Union creating Great Britain agreed by the commissioners

1707: Treaty of Union ratified by the parliaments in Scotland (110 votes to 67) and in England; receives the royal assent as the Act of Union

1708: British parliament passes Treason Act, establishing a common law of treason in Britain, thus undermining Scottish legal independence

1712: British parliamentary Toleration Act giving freedom to supporters of an **episcopalian** Church in Scotland seen as an attack on the independence of the Scottish Kirk

1711–13: New duties and taxes on linen, salt and malt hit Scottish traders

KEY TERM:

Episcopalian

An **episcopalian** church is one that has bishops. (*Episcopus* is Latin for bishop.)

The Union of England and Scotland

This chapter encourages you to think about why England and Scotland overcame their mutual hostility in 1707 and united as one country, Great Britain. Since it is a question that has been (and still is) the subject of historical controversy, you can make up your mind about it.

What is not in any doubt is that what was created by the Union was a new British state. It did not, of course, create a new British *nation*. It would be a long time before some English and Scots men and women began to think of themselves as 'Britons', and not all of them ever did accept (or indeed have accepted) that they were (or are) anything other than English or Scottish. But Great Britain, as the new state was called, was new in two major respects:

1 It was a political union of two countries which hitherto had had separate governments and parliaments and which, since 1603, had merely had the same monarch. In 1707 Scotland surrendered its legislative independence and in future was to be subject to the laws of the British parliament at Westminster. There were to be 16 Scottish peers (elected by their fellow peers) in the House of Lords and 45 MPs representing Scottish constituencies in the House of Commons. The symbol of this new political union was the adoption of a new flag, the 'union jack'.

2 It was also an economic union of two hitherto independent countries. By virtue of the Act of Union of 1707 all subjects of the new state of Great Britain were to enjoy freedom of trade within Britain and in the British colonies. The symbol of this new united British free-trade area was the adoption of a common currency and standardised weights and measures.

It was *not* a legal or religious union. The Act of Union specifically maintained the separate systems of law in Scotland and England. It also declared that the Scottish Presbyterian Kirk was to be independent of the control of bishops in the English Church. But the important nature of what *was* changed by the Union should not be underestimated.

Why was Great Britain created in 1707?

One of the reasons why this question is not straightforward to answer is that the dominant themes of Anglo-Scottish relations before 1707 are hostility and suspicion. Any answer will need to take account of this, especially because relations between the two countries, if anything, worsened throughout the seventeenth century and by the early 1700s were very strained and tense. From this perspective, the Union in 1707 was a most unexpected outcome.

This is easily seen by an examination of the political situations in both England and Scotland in the early 1700s. Only a few years before the Treaty of Union was made, hostility to it in both countries was intense.

Hostility to the Union in England in the early 1700s

The situation in England regarding the Union in the early 1700s was very similar to that a century earlier (see chapter 5). As in the early 1600s, the proposal for a legislative union of England and Scotland came from the crown. Like James I at the start of the Stuart age, William III near its end initiated discussion on 'an incorporating union' of his two kingdoms in parliament in the last years of his reign. Queen Anne's accession saw no change in royal policy; with royal blessing, English and Scottish commissioners met for preliminary discussions on a union in November 1702.

The reaction of many English MPs to these royal initiatives was remarkably similar to that of their predecessors a century earlier – as you can see by comparing Sir Edward Seymour's reason for opposing union with Scotland in 1700 (below) with the speech made in parliament in 1607 by Nicholas Fuller (source H in chapter 5).

> *Seymour said he opposed the union 'for this reason: that a woman being proposed to a neighbour of his in ye country for a wife, he said he would never marry her, for she was a beggar, and whoever married a beggar cou'd only expect a louse for a portion'.*
>
> E. M. Thompson (ed.), *Correspondence of the Family of Hatton* (Camden Society, 1898).

In addition to economic arguments like this against Union, many Englishmen (especially Tories) had strong religious reasons for not wanting close association with Presbyterian Scots. Recent developments had done much to strengthen them. The re-establishment of Scottish Presbyterianism after the Glorious Revolution and the expulsion of bishops north of the border (see chapter 24) was seen with horror by English Tories who believed that their Church was 'in danger' from Protestant Dissent (see chapter 25). In the face of this kind of reaction the Union negotiations of 1702–3 quickly broke up.

Glencoe Massacre

On 13 February 1692 the head of the Highland MacDonald clan and 37 clansmen, women and children were slaughtered by troops commanded by a clan member of the MacDonald's enemies, the Campbells. The massacre was authorised by the king's principal adviser on Scottish affairs with William III's approval, as punishment for MacDonald's failure to take an oath of allegiance to the king that all Highland chiefs had been ordered to take by 1 January 1692. MacDonald had, in fact, taken the oath of allegiance, even though a few days after the deadline.

Darien Scheme

This was a proposal by a newly-established trading Company of Scotland to establish a colony at Darien on the Isthmus of Panama in Central America, that would develop as an important staging post in the transport of valuable spices from the Far East to Europe. Many Scottish merchants hoped that it would be a remedy for the country's severe economic depression. Unfortunately, these hopes were dashed and the scheme had to be abandoned. William III forbade both English merchants from investing in the Scottish Company and English colonists from supplying the Darien colony. The Scottish Company's collapse was widely seen north of the border as another example of English treachery.

Act Anent Peace and War

This declared that, after Queen Anne's death, the Scottish Parliament, not the crown, would have the right to make peace and declare war. [NB 'Anent' is an archaic word meaning 'concerning'.]

Hostility to Union in Scotland in the early 1700s

The situation in Scotland was even more hostile to the cause of Union. Why?

The recent past was, if anything, even more influential in Scotland than in England in embittering relations between the two countries. The Cromwellian conquest and James II's and Lauderdale's later attempt to impose autocratic English rule on Scotland had hardly endeared the Scots to the English. The Scottish Glorious Revolution was, in part at least, a ringing assertion of Scottish independence against that kind of treatment (see chapter 24).

Some of William III's policies in Scotland after 1689 inflamed Scottish nationalism and hostility to its southern neighbour even more. Two episodes stand out in this respect: the **Glencoe Massacre** and the **Darien Scheme**.

The serious disruption of Anglo-Scottish relations in the wake of the Darien Scheme is clearly evident in the Scottish Parliament of 1703–4, which seemed set, not on union, but on a course of further separation from England. Despite the efforts of the Queen's commissioner, James Douglas (Earl of Queensbury), Scots MPs from all parts of the political spectrum – republicans, like Andrew Fletcher of Saltoun, and Jacobites, like James Douglas (Duke of Hamilton) – united in passing a series of measures that were a direct challenge to English authority, the **Act Anent Peace and War**, the **Wine and Wool Acts** and the **Act for the Security of the Kingdom**.

Nor did anti-English feelings subside in the following months. Even when the Union proposals were being discussed in the Scottish Parliament in the autumn of 1706 angry crowds demonstrated against the Union on the streets of Glasgow, Edinburgh and other towns.

Why was the Union achieved despite the opposition to it?

This is obviously one of the central questions you will have to address. The purpose of the next section is not to answer that question for you, but to suggest some possible reasons why the Act of Union might have been passed in 1707.

KEY TERMS:

Wine and Wool Acts

These allowed merchants to trade between Scotland and France, despite an English ban on trading with the French.

Act for the Security of the Kingdom

This threatened that the Scottish Parliament would not choose the Hanoverians as monarchs on Anne's death unless 'there be such conditions for government settled and enacted as may secure the honour and sovereignty of this crown and kingdom, the frequency and power of Parliaments, the religion, liberty and trade of the nation from English or any foreign influence'.

The use of bribery

Some Scots politicians were converted to the cause of Union by bribery. So marked is the contrast between the violent opposition to England in the Scottish parliamentary session of 1703–4 and the acceptance of Union in 1706–7 that this has been seen as a strong possibility. Professor W. Ferguson published an article in 1964 which claimed that Scottish politicians were persuaded to vote for Union by grants of offices and cash and promises to be released from debts that they owed. An important example is John Campbell (Earl of Argyll), who, when he was asked by the queen's ministers to return to Scotland from military service with Marlborough in Europe to support the political cause of Union, demanded rewards in return. He was promoted to major-general and given an English dukedom and his relatives and friends were also showered with titles and other rewards.

> '*My Lord, it is surprising to me that my Lord Treasurer [Sidney Lord Godolphin], who is a man of sense, should think of sending me up and down like a footman from one country to another without ever offering me any reward. Thier is indeed a sairtain service due from every subject to his Prince, and I shall pay the Queen as fathfully as any body can doe; but if her ministers thinks it for her service to imploy me any forder I doe think the proposall should be attended with an offer of a reward.*'
>
> Argyll to the Earl of Mar, 18 July 1706, quoted in W. Ferguson, 'The making of the treaty of union of 1707', *Scottish Historical Review* (1964).

Although such rewards were not distributed on a large scale by the English government, there is no doubt that the Campbells were not the only Scottish politicians to receive money, offices and titles in 1706–7.

Change in political circumstances

The political circumstances in both countries changed between 1703–4 and 1706–7. In Scotland in 1703–4 the anti-English legislation had been supported by politicians, not all of whom were in favour of political separation from England. Those in favour of the Hanoverian Succession (often called at the time 'Countrymen') had lined up with Jacobites in voting for these measures in the wake of the hostility to England aroused by the Glencoe Massacre and the Darien Scheme. In 1705 some of the 'Countrymen', organised in a political group nicknamed 'The Squadron', realised the dangers of playing into the hands of the Jacobites and so endangering the Hanoverian Succession. In 1706–7, consequently, they changed their political tactics and began to work for Union.

In England, too, the Union was passed in 1706–7 in different political circumstances from those at the start of Anne's reign in 1702, when Tory opposition had succeeded in killing preliminary Union negotiations between English and Scottish commissioners. By 1705–6 the political fortunes of the Whigs had revived, especially after the general election of the autumn of 1705, which resulted in Whig majorities in the Commons as well as in the Lords. The Whig Junto (see chapter 25), a pro-Union faction like the Squadron in Scotland, were now in a powerful position. They proposed to Godolphin that he support an Aliens Bill to force the Scots to give serious consideration to Union negotiations. The Aliens Act, passed by the English Parliament in March 1705, recommended that the queen appoint commissioners to negotiate a union. It also threatened that, unless the Scots accepted the Hanoverian Succession by the end of the year, imports of all Scottish staple products into England would be banned, all Scots would be treated as aliens and therefore all Scottish property in England would be endangered.

The war with France

From the English point of view there would have been no Union with Scotland but for the war in which the country was engaged with France. It is no coincidence that the warmest supporters of Union in England were those who were the most enthusiastic backers of the crown's commitment to the war in Europe, the Whigs. For the crown and the Whigs deteriorating relations between England and Scotland were a serious threat to the war effort. For one thing, Scotland was a major source of recruits for the allied armies in Europe against Louis XIV. Even more serious was the prospect of a Jacobite invasion from Scotland with the support of French troops. These security considerations were powerful ones in converting the crown, its ministers and the Whigs to the idea of a closer union between England and Scotland. This is an argument that receives support from the willingness of the crown and Whigs to grant legal, religious and economic concessions as bait for the Scots to enter a political Union.

Fear of Jacobitism

There was a political argument for Union that appealed to anti-Jacobites in Scotland, who feared that an independent Scotland would only benefit the Pretender. Even if there was not a Jacobite restoration in Scotland, a civil war between the Presbyterian Lowlands and Jacobite Highlands was a distinct possibility. So too was a recurrence of what had happened in the middle of the seventeenth century, when Scotland had tied its fortunes to other Stuart pretenders to the English throne. Only ardent Jacobites could have looked forward to a recurrence of the political chaos that this had entailed.

Economic considerations

Some Scots were converted to Union by economic considerations. Like other reasons pushing the Scots towards Union, this one has not been accepted by everyone. Not only W. Ferguson has seen the Union as the product of unprincipled political manoeuvres, as can be seen by this more recent assessment by P. J. Riley.

> 'The union was made by men of limited vision for very short-term and comparatively petty, if not squalid, aims. In intention it had little to do with the needs of England and even less with those of Scotland, but a great deal to do with private political ambitions ... Contrary to an apparently reasonable hypothesis, trade considerations seem to have exerted no influence worth speaking of.'
>
> P. J. Riley, *The Union of England and Scotland* (1978).

Yet there were strong economic arguments for the Scots to unite with England, most of which were put at the time by pro-unionist pamphleteers, including Daniel Defoe.

According to these people, union with England would benefit those Scottish landowners and merchants whose economic fortunes had become increasingly tied to England during the seventeenth century. This especially applied to those involved in the trans-border trade in cattle, coal and grain, which was currently hindered by hostile import tariffs. The removal of these and the opening up of the growing English trade to north America would be of enormous benefit, it was said, to merchants like those in Glasgow who were hit by the Navigation Acts passed by English Parliaments in the 1650s and 1660s. On a more general level Sir Edward Seymour's argument opposing Union from the English point of view (see page 303) could be used by propagandists like Defoe to persuade the Scots of the economic advantages of entering a union with a country that everyone knew was more prosperous and economically advanced than theirs.

Concessions to Scottish nationalism

The Scots were persuaded to accept Union by three major concessions to Scottish nationalism made by the English negotiators.

1 Scotland was to retain its own legal system, thus silencing the opposition of what might have been a very vocal interest group, the lawyers.

2 This applies even more forcefully to the English concession that the Scottish Kirk should remain independent, since it is difficult to imagine a more militant group of people at any time than Scottish Presbyterian ministers. Even though it was known that Union would not mean a British uniformity of religion (as James I and Charles I had wanted in the early seventeenth century), Presbyterian ministers did not discourage mob demonstrations against hated bishops in a number of towns on the eve of Union. It is difficult to believe, however, that the removal of the threat to the Scottish Kirk did not reduce the opposition of its ministers and supporters to the Union.

3 Not only did the Scots secure an economic union, they were also granted what was known as 'the Equivalent'. This was a cash payment of nearly £400,000 by the English to discharge the debts on the Scottish Treasury (including salary arrears) and to provide compensation for those who had lost money in the Darien Scheme.

Conclusion

Not surprisingly, given the conditions in which it was passed, the survival of the Act of Union for nearly three centuries would have been difficult to forecast in 1707.

What happened in the first few years of the Union made its survival seem even more unlikely. Between 1708 and 1713 the new British Parliament passed a series of measures that seemed designed to undermine many of the advantages Scotland had gained. The time chart at the head of this chapter lists major parliamentary attacks after 1707 on Scottish legal and religious independence, and economic measures that worked to Scotland's disadvantage. It is not surprising that in 1713 Scottish MPs at Westminster tried to push through the repeal of the Act of Union.

Why the Union survived is, then, no easier to explain than why the Union was made. The likelihood that the answers to both historical problems are not unconnected is one of the things you might bear in mind as you begin to work on this topic yourself.

Further reading

G. Holmes, *The Making of a Great Power: Late Stuart and Georgian Britain 1660–1722* (Addison Wesley Longman, 1993), chapter 20.

T. C. Smout, 'The road to union' in G. Holmes (ed.), *Britain after the Glorious Revolution* (Macmillan, 1969).

29 The formation of the British State

Professor G. Holmes's words provide the theme for this final chapter.

*'No one who studies British history before and after the year 1688–9
should fail to be aware that in passing from one period to the other we are
crossing one of the great divides on the entire landscape of "early modern"
and modern times.'*

Continuity

Before assessing the important ways in which the government of the
country had changed by 1714, it is essential to emphasise what had *not*
changed. Four major similarities between government in 1603 and 1714
can be identified:

- Monarchs still held immense personal political power.
- The royal court was still a major political forum.
- Local government remained in the hands of powerful local men.
- The government of the country was still potentially unstable.

Monarchs' personal political power

Neither of the last two Stuart monarchs were people who were likely to
relinquish royal prerogatives readily. This might seem more true of
William III than his successor. William's autocratic temperament and
determination not to concede any royal powers are as well known to historians as they were to contemporaries. Queen Anne, however, has
sometimes been portrayed as a weak ruler, who had not the mental
or physical toughness to protect the monarch's personal powers.
Certainly, during her reign Anne was continually ill, suffering from gout
and other circulatory complaints, brought on by her terrible maternal
history. But it would be unwise to build on that fact the assumption that
Anne was a pawn in a male political world. None of her ministers –
including powerful characters like Sidney Godolphin and Robert Harley –
ever made the mistake of underestimating, as some historians have done,
Anne's attention to public affairs and her independence. She was as

Managers

This was the word used at the time to describe those close advisers of William III and Queen Anne who, like them, were anxious not to allow either Whigs or Tories to dominate the royal government. The three principal 'managers' in Anne's reign were Sidney Godolphin (Earl of Godolphin), John Churchill (Duke of Marlborough) and Robert Harley (Earl of Oxford). All three were closer to the Tories than the Whigs, but nevertheless they tried to ensure that royal ministers and officials were not chosen solely from one party.

Placemen

Placemen were office-holders. Because they were appointed by the crown, it was thought – by those who wanted to limit the powers of the crown – that placemen would not be as independent as MPs but would slavishly follow the wishes of their royal masters.

determined as any of her predecessors to maintain the monarch's political power.

Nor was she totally unsuccessful. Using royal **managers**, Queen Anne at times resisted the power of political parties. Moreover, she followed William in successfully resisting some attempts to put statutory limitations on royal power. The most important attempt to do that was the Act of Settlement of 1701, one of the aims of which (see chapter 25) was to settle the succession after Anne's death on the Protestant Hanoverians. It also had another purpose, revealed in its full title: 'An Act for the further limitation of the Crown and better securing the Rights and Liberties of the Subject'. But none of its provisions limited the Stuarts' power, since the Act did not come into effect until after Anne's death. Moreover, by then two of the most serious limitations on royal power in the Act had been repealed: in 1706 **placemen** were allowed to sit in parliament after being re-elected and the demand that all royal business be transacted publicly in the privy council was dropped.

The royal court

The court still had just as important a function as 'a point of contact' and fount of honour as it had had in the early seventeenth century. Not only were ambitious politicians well aware that successful political careers depended, as ever, on retaining the favour of the monarch, but it is clear that the political system still would not function effectively without the distribution of royal patronage. Sir Robert Cecil's comment in 1610 that 'for a king not to bountiful were a fault' was still as true in the early eighteenth century as it had been in the reign of James I. Moreover, royal patronage continued to have this vital function throughout the eighteenth century.

Local government

If anything, the control of local government by wealthy local men was more secure after 1660 than it had ever been. At the Restoration there was a violent reaction against what had happened during the English Revolution, when some men from outside the landed elite had been appointed to sit on parliamentary county committees. From the 1660s onwards great efforts were made to ensure that local government should be in the 'safe' hands of the propertied, who sat as JPs on the commissions of the peace.

Potentially unstable government

This point needs no elaboration, since it forms the theme of chapters 21–25. Nor does one of the causes of political instability need much emphasis, since the continuity of religion as a divisive political issue throughout the Stuart age has also been underlined already. Of the three threats to the stability of government identified in chapter 1, the Religious Problem was still as powerful as it had been in 1603.

It is true that the nature of the Religious Problem had changed in three major ways:

1 Religious uniformity had ended. In 1603 people had differed about what kind of Church there should be, but almost no one challenged the idea that there should be just one national Church to which everyone was forced to belong (see chapter 4). By 1714 it was widely recognised that this idea was dead. All attempts to restore a comprehensive national Church, from the republican regimes of the 1650s onwards, had failed. Limited though it was, the Toleration Act had given legal recognition to most Protestants who chose not to attend the Church of England. By the end of the Stuart age Protestant Dissenters (or as they were later called, Nonconformists) had become an important and distinct group in British society. Religious diversity had replaced religious uniformity.

2 People began to argue the case for religious toleration. Religious persecution had not disappeared by 1714. Far from it! But some people – like the philosopher John Locke in his *Essay Concerning Toleration* (1667) and *Letter Concerning Toleration* (1685) – argued that religious persecution should be abandoned because it did not work. They had a point. As later authoritarian regimes have found, dissent was not crushed by persecution; on the contrary (as in the case of John Bunyan who wrote a classic account of his faith, *Pilgrim's Progress*, in gaol in the reign of Charles II), persecution could deepen, not shake, commitment to nonconformist views the penal laws were designed to eradicate. The logical conclusion was that religious persecution should end.

3 Irreligion and scepticism grew. Complaints that this was happening were exaggerated. They reflected the fears of churchmen and orthodox opinion rather than the reality. Yet they were not completely without substance. In a book published in 1696, *Christianity Not Mysterious*, John Toland argued that anything in Christianity that could not be explained by reason (even a central Christian doctrine like that of the Resurrection) should be rejected. Toland's ideas (often known as Deism) were those of a minority. But it would have been unthinkable for anyone to have published them in 1603.

These changes ought not lead you to assume that religion had lost its central pace in people's lives or in politics. If you have any doubts about this, then take another look at chapters 21–25. There you will see that anti-

Catholicism and different attitudes to Protestant Dissent were major reasons for violent political controversies between Whigs and Tories. Events like the Sacheverell riots of 1710 also illustrate that religion was still a major disruptive force in British political life.

Had a revolution in government taken place by 1714?

There are enough major differences between the nature of government in 1603 and 1714 to justify claiming that a revolution in government had taken place. Not only, as was seen in the last chapter, did English government became British government, but government was transformed in two other major respects:

■ From personal monarchy to parliamentary constitutional monarchy, ensuring that British government departed permanently from a general European trend towards authoritarian government.

■ From a government that was administratively and financially weak and able to exercise only limited influence in European affairs to one with a powerful state bureaucracy and wealth that enabled it to become a major European power for the first time.

The rest of this chapter addresses the question of why and how these changes came about. The key lies in the Financial Revolution of the period after 1689, which enabled the government to tap the growing wealth of the country (seen in chapter 26), so bringing about a solution to the long-standing Financial Problem (described in chapter 1).

Why was there a financial revolution after 1689?

The answer lies primarily in the nature of the wars against France between 1689 and 1713 (see time chart for chapter 25 on pages 269–271). These wars were extraordinary in several respects. Not only were they the first long military campaigns on the continent of Europe that British troops had been committed to since the mid fifteenth century, but the scale of British involvement had no parallel in the past. In the 1690s and early 1700s British troops fought at various times in the Low Countries, parts of Germany and in Spain. The numbers of troops involved were also unprecedented. The army rose from 10,000 soldiers in 1689 to an annual average size of 76,404 in the war of 1689–97 and 92,708 in the war of 1702–13. (The latter figure was probably over 7 per cent of the adult male population of England.)

As well as a land war, this was a war at sea. The British navy fought in campaigns in the Channel, the North and Irish Seas, and later in the Mediterranean, North Atlantic and Caribbean. By Anne's reign the navy employed about 40,000 sailors. In the size and sophistication of its ships and armaments it was the largest and most powerful force in Europe.

These statistics point to another important novel feature of the wars against France: they cost much more than any previous war in which the country had been involved. The average annual expenditure on the war of 1689–97 was nearly £5.5 million; the figure rose to an average of £7 million a year on the war of 1702–13. Both wars probably cost a grand total of £40 million.

In comparison with the amounts spent by present-day governments on defence, such figures seem ludicrously small. What puts them into perspective is a comparison with wartime expenditure in the recent past: the £7 million per annum spent on the war of 1702–13 was roughly five times more than the annual cost of the Second Dutch War of 1665–7.

So unprecedented were the huge costs of the French war that the king's ministers (principally the Whig Junto – see chapter 25) desperately devised new money-raising schemes, including a state lottery. It rapidly became apparent, however, that more comprehensive means were needed than these. The result was a series of measures that were first put into effect in the 1690s and which marked such a permanent and fundamental change in the financial system of the government that they merit the label 'the Financial Revolution'.

What was the Financial Revolution?

As has been seen, efforts to find solutions to the financial problem facing monarchical government is a recurring theme of seventeenth-century English history. Until the 1690s these efforts had met with only limited success. The Great Contract scheme collapsed dramatically in 1610 (see chapter 5). The parliamentary regimes of the 1640s had more success (see chapter 11). But, apart from the excise, most of the wartime financial innovations of the 1640s were abandoned at the Restoration.

It would be misleading to give the impression that what was done in the 1690s was totally new. During the Restoration period finance ministers, principally Sir George Downing, began to devise new methods of public credit that were built on after 1689. Yet it was not until the demands for money to fight the war against France became pressing that there was a fundamental change from the system of public finance in the country that the Stuarts had inherited in 1603.

KEY TERMS:

Land Tax

The **Land Tax** began as a one-off tax levied in 1692–3 at the rate of four shillings (20p) in the £ on incomes from land. It soon became a regular, annual tax, marking the beginning of permanent, high-yield direct taxation in England. (The assessments of the 1640s and 1650s [see chapter 11] were only collected irregularly after 1660.) The landed classes grumbled at the Land Tax, as you might expect, but they paid it. This is to be explained in part because it was not always collected at the high 20 per cent rate, but sometimes at the lower rates of two shillings (10p) and three shillings (15p) in the £. It was also (unlike the excise) administered by local landowners.

Stop of the Exchequer

This describes what Charles II did in 1672, when he refused to repay a debt of about £1 million to London merchants and bankers that was now due. Although he continued to pay his creditors 6 per cent per annum interest, the Stop was hardly likely to make royal borrowing easier in the future.

The Financial Revolution consisted of two types of change:

1 The first was a *revolution in taxation*. For much of the seventeenth century (apart from the 1640s and 1650s) taxation in England was generally very low. Restoration governments raised new taxes (see chapter 21 for the hearth tax from the 1660s, for example), but it was not until the 1690s that taxation increased greatly and became a major part of the crown's revenue. The crown's annual income from taxes was roughly stable between the 1660s and 1680s (just over £1 million per annum); by 1690 it was £3 million and by 1710 it had risen to £5.3 million.

These large sums were raised principally by three types of taxation. Customs dues and excise taxes were both extended to more commodities than ever before and duties were raised to unheard-of levels. Excises were especially lucrative and were now raised on basic items like leather, malt and salt, as well as beer and other liquors. Between 1688 and 1702, 23.2 per cent of the crown's income came from this source.

However, by this time the government had devised an even more productive tax, the **Land Tax**, which was now providing 32.5 per cent of its income. By 1714 taxation, which in 1603 had been an extraordinary source of income, was now a normal part of the crown's revenue. From being the lightest taxed country in Europe in 1603 Britain had become by 1714 the most heavily taxed. Its inhabitants were paying on average roughly twice as much per head as their contemporaries across the Channel in France.

2 The second feature of the Financial Revolution was *a revolution in government borrowing*. Before the Financial Revolution monarchs filled the gap between government expenditure and income by borrowing money using their own private assets as security. Not surprisingly, investors were not always eager to take on such a risk and incidents like the **Stop of the Exchequer** in 1672 undoubtedly did nothing to increase public confidence in making loans to the crown.

The big change that was made during the Financial Revolution is that government loans were raised by promising repayment, not from the monarch's private purse, but from parliamentary taxes. This was a principle that had only been used once previously, when in 1665 Sir George Downing devised a scheme for raising money to fight the Second Dutch War. In order to encourage investors to lend the government money, creditors were promised repayment in rotation out of a fund guaranteed by parliament.

From 1693–4 onwards this principle was used extensively in government borrowing. It can be see in:

- The Million Loan Act of 1693, which allowed the king to borrow £1 million, promising that the creditors would be repaid by new parliamentary excise duties.

- The foundation in 1694 of the Bank of England, which began primarily as an institution to raise loans for the crown. In return for a loan of £1,200,000, the interest on which (like the Million Loan) was to be paid from parliamentary taxes, the creditors were given the right to establish a national bank to provide banking services. But the Bank of England's main function in its early years was to borrow money for the government on the security of parliamentary taxation.

What had happened is that government debts were not now simply the king's debts. They had become (as they still are) the National Debt.

The consequences of the Financial Revolution

1 *From personal monarchy to parliamentary constitutional monarchy* The first, which is the more famous of the two main consequences, is that the solution to the crown's long-standing Financial Problem had a political cost: monarchs were increasingly forced to concede that parliaments should have a more important place in the constitution than ever before.

To a certain extent this is reflected in parliamentary statutes, of which the most important are:

- An Act of 1690 that established a parliamentary Commission of Public Accounts. As the price for massive grants of parliamentary war taxation, William III was forced to agree to the establishment of this commission, whose members were appointed by parliament and which was given wide powers to examine the state of the public finances. From now on royal officials were regularly summoned by the commission to account for the way they spent public money. The commission is a major illustration of parliament's new, important role in the government of the country.

- The Triennial Act, 1694. Monarchs previously had always had the power to dissolve parliaments when it suited them. This was a very effective way of enabling them to get rid of troublesome parliaments (as had Charles I in the later 1620s) or to keep parliaments in being for a long time and to control them by patronage (as Charles II's minister, Danby, had tried to do with the Cavalier Parliament). By declaring that there must be a general election at least once every three years this Act took away one of the crown's major constitutional powers.

The main changes which limited the crown's constitutional powers after 1689 were not brought about by legislation, but by direct effects of the Financial Revolution. Three such changes are particularly important:

■ Before 1689 parliaments met irregularly; but ever since 1689 there have been annual sessions of parliament. These have been necessary, not simply to provide taxation in time of war, but also to provide regular taxation in order to allow the government to continue to borrow money in peacetime as well.

■ Before 1689 monarchs had had complete freedom in their choice of ministers; after 1689 they were increasingly forced to concede that sometimes they had to choose ministers whom they did not necessarily like but whom they knew could get parliamentary approval for essential matters like grants of money.

■ Before 1689 monarchs had been able to make their own foreign policy; after 1689 they were increasingly forced to consult parliaments. When William III's secret treaties with foreign powers (the Partition Treaties in the late 1690s, which attempted to carve up the Spanish kingdom and empire on the death of Carlos II) became public, there was a parliamentary storm, which proved to be a turning-point in the making of British foreign policy. From that point onwards no international treaty has ever been made by a British monarch or government without parliament's consent.

2 *From personal monarchy to a British State* The emergence of these limitations on royal power by parliaments brought major changes to the way the country was governed by 1714. They were accompanied by another change that has not generally received as much attention but is at least as important; the growth of a central government that was now much bigger, wealthier and potentially more powerful than ever before.

The Financial Revolution, which solved the Financial Problem that had faced all governments in the sixteenth and seventeenth centuries, gave the royal government access to money on a scale that had not been available to any previous government. It was accompanied by development of a new, powerful state bureaucracy in Britain. Like the Financial Revolution, this was something that did not suddenly emerge in 1689. During the Anglo-Dutch wars of the reign of Charles II financial institutions, especially the Treasury, had grown in size and professionalism. But the most rapid steps towards the creation of a massive state bureaucracy in Britain took place as a direct result of the wars against France in the 1690s and early 1700s. The numbers of officials employed in financial departments, like the customs, excise, treasury and exchequer, more than doubled in this period. By the 1720s, according to Professor Holmes, there were over 12,000 permanent bureaucrats employed in government service: about a tenfold increase since the days of Charles I.

Even more important than the increase in its size was the emergence of new attitudes among some of these officials. They began to see themselves less as 'the king's servants' and more as 'the state's servants' with a developing tradition of public service. It is possible to see the outlines of a non-political civil service in Britain by 1714. The government of the country began to take on some of the characteristics of an impersonal state and to appear less like a personal monarchy.

The effect was the creation of a much more formidable government than ever before. In 1603 the machinery of the state was very limited. Early Stuart monarchs, like their Tudor predecessors, were unable to take a leading role in Europe. This was true of English governments (with the exception of Cromwellian government in the 1650s) for much of the seventeenth century.

By 1714 this was no longer true. England had become Great Britain in fact as well as in name and had well and truly emerged as a great power in Europe.

Tasks

At the start of this book four main threats to the political stability of the country in 1603 were identified: the Financial Problem, the Religious Problem, the British Problem and the Personality Problem.

To what extent did any of these still threaten to disrupt the government of the country in 1714?

1 a Use your notes on previous chapters in this book (and the index to the book to find relevant passages in previous chapters).
  b Deal with each of these 'Problems' in turn.

2 a Define the problem as it existed in 1603.
  b Describe how far the problem still existed in 1714.
  c Suggest reasons for your answer to **2 b**.

3 You could now build up an overview of the period using a multiple timeline. Completing it would help you to see the period as a whole; once completed, it would act as a useful revision aid.

Use a large sheet of paper. Put a dateline from 1603 to 1714 down the side. Divide the sheet into four columns next to the dateline for the four problems above. Note key events or trends in each column that are relevant to each problem.

Index